THE RISE OF MANAGERIAL COMPUTING:

THE BEST OF
THE CENTER FOR
INFORMATION SYSTEMS RESEARCH
SLOAN SCHOOL OF MANAGEMENT
MASSACHUSETTS INSTITUTE
OF TECHNOLOGY

THE RISE OF MANAGERIAL COMPUTING:

THE BEST OF
THE CENTER FOR
INFORMATION SYSTEMS RESEARCH
SLOAN SCHOOL OF MANAGEMENT
MASSACHUSETTS INSTITUTE
OF TECHNOLOGY

Edited by
John F. Rockart and Christine V. Bullen

DOW JONES-IRWIN
Homewood, Illinois 60430

This publication is designed to provide accurate and authoritative information in regard to the subject matter covered. It is sold with the understanding that the publisher is not engaged in rendering legal, accounting, or other professional service. If legal advice or other expert assistance is required, the services of a competent professional person should be sought.

From a Declaration of Principles jointly adopted by a Committee of the American Bar Association and a Committee of Publishers.

ISBN 0-87094-757-5

Library of Congress Catalog Card No. 85–73006

Printed in the United States of America

4 5 6 7 8 9 0 DO 3 2 1 0 9 8

Preface

In the first half of the 1980s it has become increasingly evident that clerical staff and managerial personnel in organizations of all types will eventually interact with the organization's available information, and with each other, through a computer. Today's "end user computing" era is leading to what management authority Peter Drucker terms the "Information-Based Organization."

Managerial use of computer-based information has been a major research theme at the Sloan School of Management at MIT for the past 15 years. Several of the classic articles in the fields of decision support systems, executive support systems, critical success factors, end user computing, and now, expert systems have been written by the faculty and research staff of the Sloan School's Center for Information Systems Research (CISR). The 19 articles in this book have been selected from the Center's Working Papers and present, in one volume, a significant portion of the seminal thinking in the field of managerial interaction with computers.

The Center for Information Systems Research was established at the Sloan School of Management, Massachusetts Institute of Technology, in 1974 to define, research, and report on significant managerial issues in the utilization of computer-based information systems. The CISR Working Paper series is the Center's major vehicle for publishing its research findings. Today, the series contains over 125 working papers, many of which have appeared in leading academic and business journals.

Over the years, research on fundamental issues has been performed in areas such as decision support systems, the information needs of managers, and end user computing. This research has been funded by a select group of sponsoring organizations from a wide range of industries. Our sponsors also provide invaluable assistance in defining and investigating significant research areas, ensuring that our efforts are relevant to managers in both the public and private sectors.

CISR is dedicated to disseminating significant research findings to the information systems user community through teaching programs, conferences, working papers, and publications. This book is an expression of our commitment to the continuing communication of ideas in the rapidly evolving field of managerial interaction with computers.

This book would not have been possible without the efforts of the outstanding faculty, dedicated research staff, and enthusiastic administrative staff, who have made CISR a successful and ongoing research group. Their commitment to CISR, and the strong support of the School's deans and our sponsors, is gratefully acknowledged. In addition, special thanks go to Research Associate David De Long for his help in organizing the book, to Associate Director Judith Quillard for her editorial comments, and to Grace Brennan and John Mahoney for their administrative and secretarial support.

John F. Rockart
Christine V. Bullen

Introduction

Less than two decades ago, the term "end user" could not be found in the information systems literature. The role of the computer in major organizations was restricted to the environment of the "glass house"—a somewhat isolated place where the paperwork necessary for the corporation's day-to-day functioning was spewed out by large computers in long runs on well-designed forms. Only computer professionals inhabited this place. Their primary purpose was to automate an increasing number of paperwork processing applications previously performed entirely by clerical personnel.

The function responsible for the production of this paperwork (the paychecks, payroll registers, invoices, bills of lading, accounts receivable listings, and so forth) was called the data processing department. Its world was COBOL-oriented and carefully controlled to ensure efficient, accurate processing of the organization's vital data. At the same time, it was also a hectic environment, constantly pressurized by an ever-increasing backlog of applications to be put on the computer and continual, unending changes in the operating environment caused by changes in the hardware and software systems supplied by vendors.

Fit into the tight schedule of this centralized computer shop was the periodic production of a stack of management reports on their highly recognizable, light green and white striped paper. Sometimes weighing many pounds, but very often providing little useful information, these reports were rolled out on a daily, weekly, or monthly schedule. Changing report formats to make them more useful to individual managers often took weeks, months, or even years.

Only in the parts of the corporation where scientists or engineers could be found working with third-generation languages such as FORTRAN did anyone other than a few computer professionals have direct access to the computer. Only these technically oriented people, most often working on their own large time-sharing computers, were able to devise their own programs and to run them when they pleased.

For those involved in the day-to-day operations of the firm (e.g., sales and marketing people, financial staff, manufacturing managers), the thought of being able to directly access and manipulate the increasing amount of data being stored in computer files was nothing more than an idle wish. The computer was viewed as a "data processing" (read *paperwork* processing) machine. The computer center was operated and managed with this purpose clearly in mind. And both hardware and software from "mainframe" manufacturers were built primarily for this purpose.

Not until the early 1970s did this vision of the computer's role in organizations begin to change. The long journey began—the journey to the point at which all information users in an organization will have workstations on their desks and easy access to the data and text they need to carry out their jobs as effectively as possible. One and a half decades later, the journey is still incomplete, and there is a long road yet to travel. As this book is published, less than 20 percent of the information workers in developed countries have terminal-based access to information that would better enable them to carry out their jobs.

There is, however, an undeniable movement toward this end. Five years ago there were 4.2 million computer terminals in use. Today there are almost 15 million. In the same period personal computer sales have grown rapidly—from 285,000 to 2.1 million. Many of these personal computers are already linked to mainframe computers as terminals. Others are providing stand-alone computing for the smaller but still substantial number of end users who do not need access to the corporate data banks stored on large computers.

Problems in supporting end user computing abound today. Hardware and software incompatibilities exist in most organizations. And we are just beginning to understand the largest problem of all—the data problem. The networks and the systems software, which are needed to allow access to distributed data no matter where it is located, are not yet in place. Data today are often incompatible from one part of the organization to another. Words like inconsistent, redundant, undefined, inaccurate, and uncataloged apply to most corporate data. The poor business analyst who wishes to find, access, and manipulate all the information applicable to a newly defined problem often has a long and tedious job merely assembling the data. Then, he or she is apt to find that there is little that can be done with the somewhat inaccurate, incompatible data sets that have been accumulated.

Yet there is little doubt that the tide is flowing toward the day when all those needing access to the corporation's information will be able to attain it in a timely manner. Many computer resources have already been put in place toward this end. And, increasingly, competitive business conditions, which demand more, better, and more timely information, are ensuring a change in the computer's role—shifting it from an isolated paperwork-producer to an easily accessible, combined information warehouse and communications highway for everyone in the organization.

THE INFORMATION-BASED ORGANIZATION

How will this transformation in the computer's role ultimately affect the organization? Clearly no one knows. But a somewhat different organization appears to be evolving already—an organization in which all information users will have access to the data and text they need and will be able to communicate both data and text quickly with others. The elements of a new "information-based" organization are taking shape. Management guru Peter Drucker has provided his insights into this new organizational structure. In an article entitled, "Playing in the Information-based 'Orchestra,'" in *The Wall Street Journal* (June 4, 1985), Drucker writes that the organization of the future is rapidly becoming a reality. He defines this organization as "a structure in which information serves as the axis and as the central structural support." Drucker notes that a number of businesses are today already restructuring management and redesigning the organization as an "information-based organization." Among those he cites are Citibank, Massey-Ferguson, some of the large Japanese trading companies, and a division of General Electric.

Thus Drucker and others, who speculate about organizations in which information is fully accessible, believe that many of today's jobs will be among the missing, while levels of management that remain "will find themselves with far bigger, far more demanding, and far more responsible jobs." A new class of worker will emerge—the "soloist." These soloists are specialists in particular areas—from technical research personnel to service professional taking care of special groups of customers. They will work from increasingly accessible data sources and will fill roles that are unusual but ever more vital.

In an organization with many of these "soloists," some managerial processes are clearly changing. For example, traditional beliefs concerning managerial "span of control" are becoming suspect. Like Drucker, we have seen spans of control increase in companies that have state-of-the-art information access and communication systems. For example, at one large midwestern insurance company, which has a firm-wide electronic mail system, a senior vice president saw his number of direct reports jump from 2 to 7, while the CEO now has 14 direct reports and no executive assistant.

Meetings, too, are different. In some organizations, unusual aggregations of people "meet" in computer-based synchronous or asynchronous "conferences" to solve problems and to plan for the future. This new way of work leads to a decidedly nonhierarchical approach in organizational structure. And it requires an increasing sense of responsibility on the part of each individual in the organization—leading to a greater sense of involvement in and responsibility for the ultimate success of the organization on the part of more people than ever before.

The information-based organization requires effective use of information technology. Even more important, it requires getting the right information to the right person at the right time. As Drucker notes, the information-based organization must be willing to ask "Who requires what information, when and where?" These questions obviously should be asked in all organizations even today. But, as Drucker also notes, "When a company builds its organization around modern information technology, it *must* ask these questions."

FIFTEEN YEARS OF EVOLUTION

During the past 15 years, questions concerning the information needed by each managerial or staff information user have become increasingly important. Equally significant, however, have been questions concerning the types of uses (applications) that can most effectively be supported by the computer, the types of hardware best for each person's applications, the types of software necessary, and the telecommunications technology (both hardware and software) most appropriate. In each of these areas, there has been a need for descriptive research to report on and categorize the ways that forward-looking managers are employing the available technologies. Secondly, there has been a need for conceptual frameworks to help managers understand the issues involved and to assist their thinking with regard to the choices that have to be made. There has also been a need for "normative" statements of what "should be" to spark new ideas with regard to managerial use of computers. Finally, there has been a need for pragmatic implementation guidelines so that managers can make use of available technology most effectively.

Since the early 1970s, the faculty, research staff, and graduate students associated with the Center for Information Systems Research (CISR) at the Sloan School of Management at MIT have had the good fortune to be heavily involved in all phases of this research. A primary, if not *the* primary, focus of the center has been to identify new directions with regard to managerial use of computer-based information. A number of the groundbreaking studies and significant concepts in the field of managerial use of information have emerged from papers written by the faculty and staff associated with CISR at the Sloan School.

This book brings together several of those papers. In all, 19 different articles chronicle significant aspects of the history of the managerial use of computing. We trace this history from the early 1970s and the first conceptualization of "decision support systems"—systems that focused on supporting one or more persons in the execution of a repetitive decision-making process—to a time in the mid-1980s when managers routinely use computer-based workstations for multiple functions. In almost any firm today, some managers access computer-based stock market quotations, receive "electronic mail," query databases for all the articles written on a certain subject, perform data analysis, and run large-scale optimization models. In short, most of the functions for which a computer would be useful to support the day-to-day information and communication needs of line managers, staff, and clerical personnel are being performed in some company today. True, all managers do not yet have these capabilities. But a solid base has been built, and computer use is expanding.

THE BEGINNINGS

It was not always so. When Michael S. Scott Morton began conceptualizing the idea of decision support systems in the late 1960s and early 1970s, the world of computer usage he saw on the commercial side of organizations was entirely one of transaction processing. Each organization was then in the throes of either the first or second eras of computer usage, and both involved paperwork processing.

The first of the two paperwork-processing eras began in the early 1950s and was devoted to *accounting*-oriented applications, such as payroll, accounts payable, and general ledger. Usually performed on large, centralized mainframes, these applications were run in large "batches." In this, they mirrored the way the accountant worked in the precomputer world. Groups of transactions were assembled, and the payroll was done in a batch once a week. In like manner, batches of accounts payable were done every few days. Then, with all the transactions assembled, the general ledger was posted and printed out on either a monthly or quarterly basis.

The second, or *operational*, era's efforts focused not on accounting with its "historical" perspective but on the day-to-day needs of the firm's logistics functions. A new set of "clients" began using the computer. For the most part, they were first-line supervisors and clerical personnel involved in processing orders or manufacturing the firm's products. On-line connection with the files of data stored in the computer allowed order entry personnel and manufacturing managers to know the exact status of inventories, customer credit limits, and/or particular jobs in the plant so that they could effectively fill customer orders or state expected delivery dates of products being manufactured to order. However, the primary purpose of the second era applications was again only to speed the flow of paper. In general, reports still were turned out in strict formats on a periodic basis.

Because the software was cumbersome and the hardware expensive, few managers used the computer as an analytic tool for expanding their understanding of the competitive environment or for supporting their decision-making processes.

It was to this world, that Michael S. Scott Morton brought the concept of decision support systems. Ralph Sprague and Eric Carlson, in their well-received 1982 book *Building Effective Decision Support Systems,* noted that "the concepts involved in DSS were first articulated in the early 1970s by Michael S. Scott Morton under the term 'management decision systems.' A few firms and a few scholars began to develop and research DSS, which became characterized as *interactive* computer-based systems that *help* decision makers utilize *data* and *models* to solve *unstructured* problems."

The firms and scholars to whom Sprague and Carlson referred were reacting, either explicitly or implicitly, to the challenge Scott Morton laid down in his seminal 1971 book *Management Decision Systems*. He wrote, "Computer technology has advanced at a rapid rate but thus far has had little if any direct impact on managerial action. This new technology offers the possibility of coupling the manager, at any level and in any environment, with information and decision-making support from the computer. These technological advances, then, call for a shift in thinking by managers and systems designers at least as radical as that required when computers were first introduced at the functional level in the late 1950s."

A decade later that shift in thinking is still in progress. But whether it is called *management decision systems, decision support systems* (as it has been called through most of the decade), or *management support systems,* the field that resulted from that shift in thinking is no longer the sole property of a "few firms and a few scholars."

Scott Morton's original concept of what initially might have been called "interactive computer systems" was rapidly expanded in the early 1970s by a host of his students and colleagues working to understand multiple aspects of this new field. Thomas P. Gerrity and David A. Ness provided much of the momentum for the technical work in the field. Both Gerrity and Ness were involved in the development of decision support systems to be utilized by practicing managers. Each wrote about various aspects of managing data, developing the processing routines (sometimes called models), and utilizing the hardware involved.

At the same time, several researchers focused on the behavioral and organizational aspects of implementing decision support systems in organizations. Michael Ginzberg, for example, clearly showed that no particular small set of factors (such as top management support) could be clearly isolated as the key to DSS implementation. Rather, he noted that implementation is a *process*, and he focused on the benefits of using the well known change-process models from organizational behavior to guide successful implementation of decision support systems. Steven Alter, in a study of more than 50 decision support systems, also focused on implementation. He identified eight risk factors, which, if present, increased the probability of DSS failure. He noted three "integration processes" that can help to minimize these risks.

In these early days, some researchers focused on the attributes of managers, in particular their problem-solving approaches, as a clue to DSS use or nonuse. One of the first to link managerial cognitive processes and DSS was Charles Stabell. The topic of managerial thought processes was, and remains, a difficult field to explore. What goes on in a manager's mind may be important to DSS use but is obviously more difficult to access than attributes of the technology, the organization, or the process used to implement the DSS. In an in-depth study of a major decision support system, Stabell found that the DSS had done little to change the ways in which managers made decisions. But his work pointed out the need to better understand the object of decision support systems—the decision-making process itself.

A major contributor to the research in the area of decision support systems over the last decade has been Peter G. W. Keen. Keen's multiple writings in the field, several of which are included in this volume, have played an important role in defining the field itself. His work has spanned the continuum from technical aspects of DSS to aspects of implementing systems in real organizations, to cognitive processes, to the controversial justification process for DSS systems. In particular, in a seminal paper on justification included in this volume, Keen pointed out that support systems of all types are justified in a different manner than traditional first and second era data processing systems. Keen suggests a justification technique he terms "value analysis." Noting that value analysis is similar to cost/benefit analysis, he points out, however, that managers who justify decision support systems primarily emphasize the managerial benefits first and the cost second. Moreover, many of the "benefits" are based on sound managerial estimates of future "soft" savings or increases in revenue that cannot be stated with certainty. Thus, Keen played a major role in the evolution of decision support systems by differentiating them from traditional paper processing systems on yet another important dimension.

Both early and more recent work on decision support systems has focused on the process of *design and implementation* of the DSS. Keen and others have focused on an iterative design process known as "prototyping" as the only really viable approach to the effective installation of these systems. Sprague and Carlson in their 1982 book point out the several reasons for this approach. "First a prototype usually gets the DSS into use as early as possible. Early use can provide assistance to the decision maker to feedback to the builders. Second, prototyping is considerably cheaper than a 'full-build' approach, which delays installation until the DSS is complete. Third, prototyping is a convenient way of keeping the DSS simple, which is valuable to both builders and users. Finally, prototyping lowers risks and expectations." If the prototype is not useful it can be "thrown away" without major expenditure.

The mantle of leadership in the decision support field at CISR, originally taken by Scott Morton and then passed on to Keen, is increasingly being assumed by a number of able younger faculty members. Two of these are John Henderson and Michael Treacy, whose insights into the current state of decision support systems are also presented in the first section of this book.

All of this DSS research, along with that of many others, has played a significant role in helping information systems professionals and line managers realize that computers can be effectively used on-line and interactively by managers and staff to analyze data and assist the decision-making process.

ON TO "SUPPORT SYSTEMS"

In the late 1970s, it became clear that not all decision support systems were actually being used to assist managers in making decisions. Among those who noticed this was Keen, who wrote that the field ought to be called "support systems," since managerial interaction with computers was clearly being used for purposes other than direct assistance to decision making. Recognizing that the semistructured, repetitive decision processes for which decision support systems were designed occurred only at certain levels and in certain parts of the organization, Keen noted that there was an evolving set of organizational support systems to which were soon added the fields of office automation and executive support.

Executive Support Systems

In particular, CISR's researchers have been interested in the field of "executive" support systems. Because they affect the most significant people in an organization, executive support systems are of interest to both observers of the managerial scene and to practicing information systems managers who have to implement them.

A common conception about executives, based heavily on the work of Henry Mintzberg and John Kotter, is that they have little time to spend on analysis. Executives most certainly are not computer users. Mintzberg saw the executives he studied as hurried, harried, multi-tasking people who spent most of their time working through others, sitting in meetings, and acting as the figurehead for their organizations. They had little time to think about the information they needed much less the time or energy to analyze data. Rather, they worked through their staffs and subordinate line managers.

Kotter has conceptualized the senior executive role as having two major functions. First, the executive is heavily involved in building a "network" of people he can draw on for information and turn to for action in particular areas. This network consists of managers internal to the executive's firm and people external to that firm (e.g., suppliers, public figures, and others). The second major task of the senior executive is to build an "agenda" to guide how he allocates his own time to particular projects and to serve as a springboard for his interactions with those in his network. Kotter, like Mintzberg, found no senior executive with a computer terminal on his desk.

It appears, however, that computers can be used effectively in carrying out executive responsibilities. A small but rapidly growing number of senior executives are now accessing both text and data through workstations on their desks, in their homes, and sometimes in their attache cases while they travel.

Today, the field of executive support is in its infancy. Research concerning several of the "early adopters" is presented in the third section of this book. As the book goes to print, we are in the process of completing a major study of 25 other organizations whose senior executives are routinely accessing information through the computer. Perhaps the most interesting conclusion from the current study is that the fundamental planning and control processes of the organizations are being changed as senior executives increasingly understand the computer's ability to access and assemble information concerning the ongoing operations of their firms.

BUT WHAT INFORMATION IS NECESSARY?

In particular at the senior executive level, but also at all other levels in the firm, it is not enough to emphasize the technical tools and the implementation processes of support systems. Since the process of gathering, storing, and making accessible various types of data is both difficult and expensive, it is very important for potential users of management support systems to determine the exact information that will be most useful to them.

A number of methods have been suggested to help users in this identification process. One of the most successful techniques, currently being used by more than two dozen consulting firms and hundreds of companies, is the "critical success factors" (CSF) method. This simple and straightforward method is based on one of the oldest managerial concepts—the need for managers to *focus* on the few most significant aspects of their job responsibilities.

The conceptual underpinnings of the CSF method go back at least as far as 1808. At that time, Baron von Clausewitz, writing on the "principles of war" for the German General Staff, identified the principle of "concentration of forces." Von Clausewitz wrote that less able generals scattered their forces throughout the entire battle area whereas more capable generals concentrated their forces on the few significant battles. More recently, Peter Drucker and other managerial gurus have picked up the same theme. Drucker, writing in his book *The Effective Executive,* notes that a major characteristic of effective executives is that they concentrate their efforts on the few most important aspects of their responsibilities.

The CSF method is now being used in two major ways in the information systems field. First, it is being used in some organizations to help individual managers think through their information needs. Second, it is being used by some information systems planners to help senior management determine development priorities for particular decision support systems and traditional data processing systems. In this latter guise, the CSF method is, in effect, a methodology for information systems planning. Part 3 of this book and the Appendix provide articles concerning both uses.

FROM DSS TO EUC

The early decision support systems were isolated systems developed by a handful of pioneers. They ran on relatively slow, relatively expensive computers whose terminals had limited capabilities to provide good graphical output. Software capabilities were limited and the design process uncertain. It took a foresighted manager to authorize the construction of a DSS.

Times have changed. Computers today, for equivalent power, cost less than a tenth of those in 1975. New hardware, in the forms of personal computers and high resolution graphic terminals, provide not only significant economies in processing but also improved interaction capabilities and crisper, more understandable output. Software packages such as Lotus 1-2-3 make it far easier for the nonprogramming end user to utilize the computer's capabilities. More computerized data is available both from sources within the firm and from thousands of external data bases that provide information on customers, competitors, industries, and the economy as a whole. Systems to facilitate the interchange of electronic mail or enable computer conferencing can be bought, installed, and utilized by an organization with relatively little effort. Finally, much is now known concerning the design and implementation of systems to be used directly by managers. The prototyping approach, rather than being a novelty, is now well understood.

These improved capabilities in technology have led, in the early 1980s, to a veritable explosion of what is now termed "end-user computing." In Part 4 of this book, two articles explore this emerging end user environment. They discuss the various types of end users who exist, how they are using the computer, and managerial guidelines for the management of the end user explosion in the use of both mainframe and personal computers.

Clearly, the rapid growth of end user computing is setting the stage for the information-based organization.

AND NOW?

Drucker's vision of an information-based organization is still far from a reality. The research outlined in this book provides a history of major parts of the movement toward the information-based organization. Today, however, as Michael S. Scott Morton points out in his article "The State of the Art of Research in Management Support Systems" (Part 4), we still have much to learn about the broad field he now terms "management support systems." In fact, Drucker's insight is just that—an insight. Understanding the impact of information technologies, both computer and communication, on the management of firms will come from extensive research to be performed over the next several years.

It is clear, as another article in the final section points out, that new systems (such as expert support systems, which have been derived from the field of artificial intelligence) will continue to emerge and add new dimensions and new capabilities to the field of managerial interaction with computers. At this writing, it is not clear what ultimate impact artificial intelligence, or the particular branch known as expert systems, will have on management and organizations. Much research must be devoted to understand these potential impacts.

Finally, it is also apparent that line management will play an increasingly significant role in the conception, design, and management of computer-based systems within their organizations. Although the final article in the book focuses on the need for the very senior executives in the firm to do so, it is necessary for line managers at all levels to become involved in the management of information technology within their organizations.

Today, line managers have several major responsibilities. They manage the operations of their organization (whether it is a division, a product line, or a department). In addition, line managers have the acknowledged responsibility for the management of finances, personnel, and the planning process. In each of these areas, they are assisted by staff organizations (the controller's staff, the personnel staff, and the strategic planning staff). Yet the ultimate responsibility for managing each of these organizational resources lies in the province of the line manager. Now it is clear that line managers have a new responsibility. This is the management of information technology. Here, too, the relevant staff experts (the information systems department) can provide aid and assistance to the line manager.

The ultimate responsibility for effective use of the technology is now increasingly devolving squarely on the shoulders of line management. As we move toward the information-based organization, with its ubiquitous presence of information technology, the information systems staff cannot possibly have the organizational reach or knowledge to understand each different functional use of the computer. Line management must increasingly take responsibility for the many decisions that must be made concerning the use of information technology in their departments. This issue of line management responsibility is a significant new factor in the field of managerial use of computers. The book appropriately closes on this note.

REFERENCES

Alter, Steven L. "A Study of Computer-Aided Decision Making in Organizations." Ph.D. dissertation, MIT, 1975.

Drucker, Peter F. *The Effective Executive.* New York: Harper & Row, 1957.

———— "Playing in the Information-Based 'Orchestra.' " *The Wall Street Journal,* June 4, 1985.

Gerrity, Thomas P. "The Design of Man-Machine Decision Systems." Ph.D. dissertation, MIT, 1970.

Ginzberg, Michael J. "A Process Approach to Management Science Implementation." Ph.D. dissertation, MIT, 1975.

Gupta, Amar, and Hoo-min D. Toong. *Insights Into Personal Computers.* New York: IEEE Press, 1985.

Kotter, John P. *The General Managers.* New York: The Free Press, 1982.

Mintzberg, Henry. *The Nature of Managerial Work.* New York: Harper & Row, 1973.

———— "The Manager's Job: Folklore and Fact." *Harvard Business Review,* 53, no. 4 (1975), pp. 49–61.

Ness, David N. "Decision Support Systems: Theories of Design." Paper presented at the Wharton Office of Naval Research Conference on Decision Support Systems, University of Pennsylvania, Philadelphia, 1975.

Scott Morton, Michael S. *Management Decision Systems: Computer Based Support for Decision Making.* Cambridge, Mass.: Division of Research, Harvard University, 1971.

Sprague, Ralph H., and Eric D. Carlson. *Building Effective Decision Support Systems.* Englewood Cliffs, N.J.: Prentice-Hall, 1982.

Stabell, Charles B. "Individual Differences in Managerial Decision Making Processes: A Study of Conversational Computer Usage." Ph.D. dissertation, MIT, 1974.

Contents

PART 1
DECISION
SUPPORT SYSTEMS

The opening article in this section is the classic by Gorry and Scott Morton, "A Framework for Management Information Systems," which appeared in 1971. In this article, the authors stress the importance of focusing on the key decisions which are made in an organization in order to understand the information systems which should be developed. Their well-known framework is used to characterize organizational activity in terms of the types of decisions required. It combines Robert Anthony's classic categories of managerial activity with Herbert Simon's concept of the "structuredness" of decisions. The result is a framework that can be used as a planning tool to help managers understand the types of information systems that best support various managerial activities.

As could be expected with an article that first appeared in 1971, the technology review section is out of date. However, the concern expressed for a better understanding of how people solve problems is still manifest in current research. This article remains pertinent because of the way it brings order to the difficult task of analyzing the managerial decision process and then matches information systems tools to the high priority problems.

An undisputed pioneer in the decision support systems (DSS) field, Peter G. W. Keen is the author of the next three of the six papers in this section. The first paper, "Decision Support Systems: A Research Perspective," provides an excellent review of the field, with clear definitions and an introduction to the concept of "adaptive design" as integral to the definition of DSS. Through the process of case-based research, Keen surfaces three additional issues critical to the successful design of DSS: the need for proper data management, an understanding of task representation, and an understanding of the organizational forces at work. Although this article also references "old" technology in the software product discussed, the issues discussed are still as real and critical to decision support systems design today as they were at that time, and they will continue to be so in the future.

The second paper, "Decision Support Systems and Personal Computing," (written with Richard D. Hackathorn) is particularly intriguing as it introduced the term *personal support* just as personal computers were emerging. The application cited, "an information processing activity in which the end user has direct personal control over all stages of the activity," well describes the area of personal support. Of equal interest, the personal support type of DSS is sharply contrasted with organizational support and group support. The authors point out that the latter two forms of DSS are more complex because of the interdependencies introduced by the increased number of individuals involved in the decision. This concept of interdependencies is used to extend the Gorry and Scott Morton framework and adds an important dimension for analyzing information systems applications. The article also points out that a DSS can serve as an important communication and coordination vehicle when used in the group or organizational support mode.

In the third paper, Keen addresses the key question: How should decision support systems be justified? He points out that traditional cost/benefit analyses fail when applied to DSS because the benefits resulting from the use of a DSS are usually qualitative and therefore difficult to value. In addition, since a DSS evolves and changes, neither the costs nor the benefits are static. Keen proposes an approach he calls value analysis, where the question asked is not "What are the quantifiable benefits?" but rather, "What level of benefits is needed to justify the cost?" The approach is patterned after that used in analyzing the decision to proceed on an R&D project, which he argues is more similar to the development of a DSS than is a traditional MIS project. In a time when justification of systems projects has gained renewed importance (e.g., personal computer acquisition, office systems development) and benefits remain difficult to quantify, this article provides an intriguing and useful approach.

In a slight shift of gears, the fifth paper, by Henderson and Schilling, examines the implementation of a DSS in a community mental health organization. Although the example is a public sector one, it provides a clear description of the development and use of a DSS, and is therefore of value to private sector readers. The role of the DSS as a process support aid and communication vehicle is described, and the resulting impacts of its use are significant. The concluding section of the paper highlights six DSS design and implementation issues of significant importance. This is a more traditionally academic paper than most of those appearing in this volume. However, its findings are eminently practical.

The final paper in this section, "Future Directions in DSS Technology," looks at the potential impact of the rapid innovation and evolution of DSS hardware and software. Among the topics Treacy explores are the increasingly comprehensive DSS software capabilities, the emergence of expert systems, the shift in focus on DSS hardware from minis and mainframes to microcomputers, and, finally, problems of integrating diverse DSS applications at the data and interface levels.

Chapter One
A Framework for Management Information Systems

G. ANTHONY GORRY
MICHAEL S. SCOTT MORTON

INTRODUCTION

A framework for viewing management information systems (MIS) is essential if an organization is to plan effectively and make sensible allocations of resources to information systems tasks. The use of computers in organizations has grown tremendously in the 1955 to 1971 period, but very few of the resulting systems have had a significant impact on the way in which management makes decisions. A framework which allows an organization to gain perspective on the field of information systems can be a powerful means of providing focus and improving the effectiveness of the systems efforts.

In many groups doing MIS work, this lack of perspective prevents a full appreciation of the variety of organizational uses for computers. Without a framework to guide management and systems planners, the system tends to serve the strongest manager or react to the greatest crisis. As a result, systems activities too often move from crisis to crisis, following no clear path and receiving only *ex post facto* justification. This tendency inflicts an unnecessary expense on the organization. Not only are costly computer resources wasted, but even more costly human resources are mismanaged. The cost of systems and programming personnel is generally twice that of the hardware involved in a typical project, and the ratio is growing larger as the cost of hardware drops and salaries rise.[1] Competent people are expensive. More importantly, they exist only in limited numbers. This limitation actively constrains the amount of systems development work that can be undertaken in a given organization, and so good resource allocation is critical.

Developments in two distinct areas within the last five years offer us the potential to develop altogether new ways of supporting decision processes. First, there has been considerable technological progress. The evolution of remote access to computers with short turnaround time and flexible user interfaces has been rapid. Powerful minicomputers are available at low cost and users can be linked to computer resources through inexpensive typewriter and graphical display devices. The second development has been a conceptual one. There is emerging an understanding of the potential role of information systems within organizations. We are adding to our knowledge of how human beings solve problems and of how to build models that capture aspects of the human decision-making processes.[2]

The progress in these areas has been dramatic. Entirely new kinds of planning and control systems can now be built—ones that dynamically involve the manager's judgments and support him with analysis, models, and flexible access to relevant information. But to realize this potential fully, given an organization's limited resources, there must be an appropriate framework within which to view management decision making and the required systems support. The purpose of this paper is to present a framework that helps us to understand the evolution of MIS activities within organizations and to recognize some of the potential problems and benefits resulting from our new technology. Thus, this framework is designed to be useful in planning for information systems activities within an organization and for distinguishing between the various model-building activities, models, computer systems, and so forth which are used for supporting different kinds of decisions. It is, by definition, a static picture, and is not designed to say anything about how information systems are built.

In the next section we shall consider some of the general advantages of developing a framework for information systems work. We shall then propose a specific framework which we have found to be useful in the analysis of MIS activities. We believe that this framework offers us a new way to characterize the progress made to date and offers us insight into the problems that have been encountered. Finally, we shall use this framework to analyze the types of resources that are required in the different decision areas and the ways in which these resources should be used.

FRAMEWORK DEVELOPMENT

The framework we develop here is one for managerial activities, not for information systems. It is a way of looking at decisions made in an organization. Information systems should exist only to support decisions, and hence we are looking for a characterization of organizational activity in terms of the type of decisions involved. For reasons which we make clear later, we believe that an understanding of managerial activity is a prerequisite for effective systems design and implementation. Most MIS groups become involved in system development and implementation without a prior analysis of the variety of managerial activities. This has, in our opinion, prevented them from developing a sufficiently broad definition of their purpose and has resulted in a generally inefficient allocation of resources.

In attempting to understand the evolution and problems of management information systems, we have found the work of Robert Anthony and Herbert Simon particularly useful. In *Planning and Control Systems: A Framework for Analysis*,[3] Anthony addresses the problem of developing a classification scheme that will allow management some perspective when dealing with planning and control systems. He develops a taxonomy for managerial activity consisting of three categories and argues that these categories represent activities sufficiently different in kind to require the development of different systems.

The first of Anthony's categories of managerial activity is *strategic planning:* "Strategic planning is the process of deciding on objectives of the organization, on changes in these objectives, on the resources used to attain these objectives, and on the policies that are to govern the acquisition, use, and disposition of these resources."[4] Certain things can be said about strategic planning generally. First, it focuses on the choice of objectives for the organization and on the activities and means required to achieve these objectives. As a result, a major problem in this area is predicting the future of the organization and its environment. Second, the strategic planning process typically involves a small number of high-level people who operate in a nonrepetitive and often very creative way. The complexity of the problems that arise and the nonroutine manner in which they are handled make it quite difficult to appraise the quality of this planning process.

The second category defined by Anthony is *management control:* "the process by which managers assure that resources are obtained and used effectively and efficiently in the accomplishment of the organization's objectives."[5] He stresses three key aspects of this area. First, the activity involves interpersonal interaction. Second, it takes place within the context of the policies and objectives developed in the strategic planning process. Third, the paramount goal of management control is the assurance of effective and efficient performance.

Anthony's third category is *operational control,* by which he means "the process of assuring that specific tasks are carried out effectively and efficiently."[6] The basic distinction between management control and operational control is that operational control is concerned with tasks (such as manufacturing a specific part) whereas management control is most often concerned with people. There is much less judgment to be exercised in the operational control area because the tasks, goals, and resources have been carefully delineated through the management control activity.

We recognize, as does Anthony, that the boundaries between these three categories are often not clear. In spite of their limitations and uncertainties, however, we have found the categories useful in the analysis of information system activities. For example, if we consider the information requirements of these three activities, we can see that they are very different from one another. Further, this difference is not simply a matter of aggregation, but one of fundamental character of the information needed by managers in these areas.

Strategic planning is concerned with setting broad policies and goals for the organization. As a result, the relationship of the organization to its environment is a central matter of concern. Also, the nature of the activity is such that predictions about the future are particularly important. In general, then, we can say that the information needed by strategic planners is aggregate information, and obtained mainly from sources external to the organization itself. Both the scope and variety of the information are quite large, but the requirements for accuracy are not particularly stringent. Finally, the nonroutine nature of the strategic planning process means that the demands for this information occur infrequently.

The information needs for the operational control area stand in sharp contrast to those of strategic planning. The task orientation of operational control requires information of a well-defined and narrow scope. This information is quite detailed and arises largely from sources within the organization. Very frequent use is made of this information, and it must therefore be accurate.

The information requirements for management control fall between the extremes for operational control and strategic planning. In addition, it is important to recognize that much of the information relevant to management control is obtained through the process of interpersonal interaction.

In Table 1 we have summarized these general observations about the categories of management activity. This summary is subject to the same limitations and uncertainties which are exhibited by the concepts of management control, strategic planning, and operational control. Nonetheless, it does underscore our contention that because the activities themselves are different, the information requirements to support them are also different.

This summary of information requirements suggests the reason why many organizations have found it increasingly difficult to realize some of their long-range plans for information systems. Many of these plans are based on the "total systems approach." Some of the proponents of this approach advocate that systems throughout the organization be tightly linked, with the output of one becoming the direct input of another, and that the whole structure be built on the detailed data used for controlling operations.[7] In doing so, they are suggesting an approach to systems design that is at best uneconomic and at worst based on a serious misconception. The first major problem with this view is that it does not recognize the ongoing nature of systems development in the operational control area. There is little reason to believe that the systems work in any major organization will be complete within the foreseeable future. To say that management information systems activity must wait "until we get our operational control systems in hand" is to say that efforts to assist

TABLE 1   Information Requirements by Decision Category

Characteristics of Information	Operational Control	Management Control	Strategic Planning
Source	Largely internal ─────────────▶		External
Scope	Well defined, narrow ─────────▶		Very wide
Level of aggregation	Detailed ─────────────────▶		Aggregate
Time horizon	Historical ────────────────▶		Future
Currency	Highly current ─────────────▶		Quite old
Required accuracy	High ──────────────────────▶		Low
Frequency of use	Very frequent ──────────────▶		Infrequent

management with systems support will be deferred indefinitely.

The second and perhaps most serious problem with this total systems view is that it fails to represent properly the information needs of the management control and strategic planning activities. Neither of these areas *necessarily* needs information that is a mere aggregation of data from the operational control data base. In many cases, if such a link is needed, it is more cost effective to use sampling from this data base and other statistical techniques to develop the required information. In our opinion, it rarely makes sense to couple managers in the management control and strategic planning areas directly with the masses of detailed data required for operational control. Not only is direct coupling unnecessary, but it also can be an expensive and difficult technical problem.

For these reasons it is easy to understand why so many companies have had the following experience. Original plans for operational control systems were met with more or less difficulty, but as time passed it became increasingly apparent that the planned systems for higher management were not being developed on schedule, if at all. To make matters worse, the systems which were developed for senior management had relatively little impact on the way in which the managers made decisions. This last problem is a direct result of the failure to understand the basic information needs of the different activities.

We have tried to show in the above discussion how Anthony's classification of *managerial* activities is a useful one for people working in information systems design and implementation; we shall return later to consider in more detail some of the implications of his ideas.

In *The New Science of Management Decision,* Simon is concerned with the manner in which human beings solve problems regardless of their position within an organization. His distinction between "programmed" and "nonprogrammed" decisions is a useful one:

> Decisions are programmed to the extent that they are repetitive and routine, to the extent that a definite procedure has been worked out for handling them so that they don't have to be treated *de novo* each time they occur. . . . Decisions are nonprogrammed to the extent that they are novel, unstructured, and consequential. There is no cut-and-dried method of handling the problem because it hasn't arisen before, or because its precise nature and structure are elusive or complex, or because it is so important that it deserves a custom-tailored treatment. . . . By nonprogrammed I mean a response where the system has no specific procedure to deal with situations like the one at hand, but must fall back on whatever *general* capacity it has for intelligent, adaptive, problem-oriented action.[8]

We shall use the terms *structured* and *unstructured* for programmed and nonprogrammed because they imply less dependence on the computer and more dependence on the basic character of the problem-solving activity in question. The procedures, the kinds of computation, and the types of information vary, depending on the extent to which the problem in question is unstructured. The basis for these differences is that in the unstructured case the human decision maker must provide judgment and evaluation as well as insights into problem definition. In a very structured situation, much if not all of the decision-making process can be automated. Later in this paper we shall argue that systems built to support structured decision making will be significantly different from those designed to assist managers in dealing with unstructured problems. Further, we shall show that these differences can be traced to the character of the models which are relevant to each of these problems and the way in which these models are developed.

This focus on decisions requires an understanding of the human decision-making process. Research on human problem solving supports Simon's claim that all problem solving can be broken down into three categories:

The first phase of the decision-making process—searching the environment for conditions calling for decision—I shall call *intelligence* activity (borrowing the military meaning of intelligence). The second phase—inventing, developing, and analyzing possible courses of action—I shall call *design* activity. The third phase—selecting a course of action from those available—I shall call *choice* activity. . . . Generally speaking, intelligence activity precedes design, and design activity precedes choice. The cycle of phases is, however, far more complex than the sequence suggests. Each phase in making a particular decision is itself a complex decision-making process. The design phase, for example, may call for new intelligence activities; problems at any given level generate subproblems that in turn have their intelligence, design, and choice phases, and so on. There are wheels within wheels. . . . Nevertheless, the three large phases are often clearly discernible as the organizational decision process unfolds. They are closely related to the stages in problem solving first described by John Dewey: "What is the problem? What are the alternatives? Which alternative is best?"[9]

A fully structured problem is one in which all three phases—intelligence, design, and choice—are structured. That is, we can specify algorithms, or decision rules, that will allow us to find the problem, design alternative solutions, and select the best solution. An example here might be the use of the classical economic order quantity (EOQ) formula on a straightforward inventory control problem. An unstructured problem is one in which none of the three phases is structured. Many job-shop scheduling problems are of this type.

In the ideas of Simon and Anthony, then, we have two different ways of looking at managerial activity within organizations. Anthony's categorization is based on the purpose of the management activity, whereas Simon's classification is based on the way in which the manager deals with the problems which confront him. The combination of these two views provides a useful framework within which to examine the purposes and problems of information systems activity. The essence of this combination is shown in Figure 1. The figure contains a class of decisions we have called semistructured—decisions with one or two of the intelligence, design, and choice phases unstructured.

Decisions above the dividing line in Figure 1 are largely structured, and we shall call the information systems that support them "structured decision systems" (SDS). Decisions below the line are largely unstructured, and their supporting information systems are "decision support systems" (DSS). The SDS area encompasses almost all of what *has* been called management in-

FIGURE 1 Information Systems: A Framework

	Operational Control	Management Control	Strategic Planning
Structured	Accounts receivable	Budget analysis— Engineered costs	Tanker fleet mix
	Order entry	Short-term forecasting	Warehouse and factory location
	Inventory control		
Semistructured	Production scheduling	Variance Analysis— Overall budget	Mergers and acquisitions
	Cash management	Budget preparation	New product planning
Unstructured	PERT/COST systems	Sales and production	R&D planning

formation systems (MIS) in the literature—an area that has had almost nothing to do with real managers or information but has been largely routine data processing. We exclude from consideration here all of the *information handling* activities in an organization. A large percentage of computer time in many organizations is spent on straightforward data handling with no decisions, however structured, involved. The payroll application, for example, is a data handling operation.

In Figure 1 we have listed some examples in each of the six cells. It should be stressed, however, that these cells are not well-defined categories. Although this may sometimes cause problems, the majority of important decisions can be classified into their appropriate cell without difficulty.

DECISION MAKING WITHIN THE FRAMEWORK

Planning and Resource Allocation Decisions. An immediate observation can be made about the framework we have presented. Almost all the so-called MIS activity has been directed at decisions in the structured half of the matrix (see Figure 1), specifically in the "operational control" cell. On the other hand, most of the areas of greatest concern to managers, areas where decisions have a significant effect on the company, are in the lower half of the matrix. That is, managers deal for the most part with unstructured decisions. This implies, of course, that computers and related systems which have so far been largely applied to the structured operational control area have not yet had any real impact on management decision making. The areas of high potential do not lie in bigger and better systems of the kind most companies now use. To have all the effort concentrated in only one of the six cells suggests at the very least a severe imbalance.

A second point to be noted on the planning question is the evolutionary nature of the line separating structured from unstructured decisions. This line is moving down over time. As we improve our understanding of a particular decision, we can move it above the line and allow the system to take care of it, freeing the manager for other tasks. For example, in previous years the inventory reordering decision in most organizations was made by a well-paid member of middle management. It was a decision that involved a high degree of skill and could have a significant effect on the profits of the organization. Today this decision has moved from the unstructured operational control area to the structured. We have a set of decision rules (the EOQ formula) which on average does a better job for the standard items than do most human decision makers. This movement of the line does not imply any replacement of managers, since we are dealing with an almost infinite set of problems. For every one we solve, there are 10 more demanding our attention.

It is worth noting that the approach taken in building systems in the unstructured area hastens this movement of the line because it focuses our analytical attention on decisions and decision rules. We would therefore expect a continuing flow of decisions across the line, or at least into the "grey" semistructured decision area.

Through the development of a model of a given problem-solving process for a decision in one of the cells, we can establish the character of each of the three phases. To the extent that any of these phases can be structured, we can design direct systems support. For those aspects of the process which are unstructured (given our current understanding of the situation), we would call on the manager to provide the necessary analysis. Thus a problem might be broken down into a set of related subproblems, some of which are "solved" automatically by the system and the remainder by the user alone or with varying degrees of computational and display support. Regardless of the resulting division of labor, however, it is essential that a model of the decision process be constructed *prior* to the system design. It is only in this way that a good perspective on the potential application of systems support can be ascertained.

Structured/Unstructured Decisions. Information systems ought to be centered around the important decisions of the organization, many of which are relatively unstructured. It is therefore essential that models be built of the decision process involved. Model development is fundamental because it is a prerequisite for the analysis of the value of information, and because it is the key to understanding which portions of the decision process can be supported or automated. Both the successes and failures in the current use of computers can be understood largely in terms of the difficulty of this model development.

Our discussion of Structured Decision Systems showed that the vast majority of the effort (and success) has been in the area of structured operational control where there is relatively little ambiguity as to the goals sought. For example, the typical inventory control problem can be precisely stated, and it is clear what the criterion is by which solutions are to be judged. Hence we have an easily understood optimization problem. This type of problem lends itself to the development of formal "scientific" models, such as those typical of operations research.

Another important characteristic of problems of this type is that they are to a large extent "organization independent." By this we mean that the essential aspects of the problem tend to be the same in many organizations, although the details may differ. This generality has two important effects. First, it encourages widespread interest and effort in the development of solutions to the problem. Second, it makes the adaptation of general models to the situation in a particular organizational setting relatively easy.

The situation with regard to areas of management decision making is quite different. To the extent that a given problem is semistructured or unstructured, there is an absence of a routine procedure for dealing with it. There is also a tendency toward ambiguity in the problem definition because of the lack of formalization of any or all of the intelligence, design, or choice phases. Confusion may exist as to the appropriate criterion for evaluating solutions, or as to the means for generating trial solutions to the problem. In many cases, this uncertainty contributes to the perception of problems of this type as being unique to a given organization.

In general, then, we can say that the information systems problem in the structured operational control area is basically that of implementing a given general model in a certain organizational context. On the other hand, work in the unstructured areas is much more involved with model development and formalization. Furthermore, the source of the models in the former case is apt to be the operations research or management science literature. In the latter case, the relevant models are most often the unverbalized models used by the managers of the organization. This suggests that the procedure for the development of systems, the types of systems, and the skills of the analysts involved may be quite different in the two areas.

Although the evolution of information systems activities in most organizations has led to the accumulation of a variety of technical skills, the impact of computers on the way in which top managers make decisions has been minimal. One major reason for this is that the support of these decision makers is not principally a technical problem. If it were, it would have been solved. Certainly there are technical problems associated with work in these problem areas, but the technology and the technological skills in most large organizations are more than sufficient. The missing ingredient, apart from the basic awareness of the problem, is the skill to elicit from management its view of the organization and its environment, and to formalize models of this view.

To improve the quality of decisions, a systems designer can seek to improve the quality of the information inputs or to change the decision process, or both. Because of the existence of a variety of optimization models for operational control problems, there is a tendency to emphasize improvement of the information inputs at the expense of improvement in the decision-making process. Although this emphasis is appropriate for structured operational control problems, it can retard progress in developing support for unstructured problem solving. The difficulty with this view is that it tends to attribute low quality in management decision making to low quality information inputs. Hence, systems are designed to supply more current, more accurate, or more detailed information.

While improving the quality of information available to managers may improve the quality of their decisions, we do not believe that major advances will be realized in this way.[10] Most managers do not have great informational needs. Rather, they have need of new methods to understand and process the information already available to them. Generally speaking, the models that they employ in dealing with this information are very primitive, and as a result, the range of responses that they can generate is very limited. For example, many managers employ simple historical models in their attempts to anticipate the future.[11] Further, these models are static in nature, although the processes they purport to represent are highly dynamic. In such a situation, there is much more to be gained by improving the information processing ability of managers in order that they may deal effectively with the information that they already have, than by adding to the reams of data confronting them, or by improving the quality of those data.[12]

If this view is correct, it suggests that the Decision Support Systems area is important and that these systems may best be built by people other than those currently involved in the operational control systems area. The requisite skills are those of the model builder based on close interaction with management, structuring and formalizing the procedures employed by managers, and segregating those aspects of the decision process which can be automated. In addition, systems in this area must be able to assist the evolution of the manager's decision-making ability through increasing his understanding of the environment. Hence, one important role of a DSS is educative. Even in areas in which we cannot structure the decision process, we can provide models of the environment from which the manager can develop insights into the relationship of his decisions to the goals he wishes to achieve.

In discussing models and their importance to systems in the DSS area, we should place special emphasis on the role which the manager assumes in the process of model building. To a large extent, he is the source upon which the analyst draws. That is, although a repertoire of "operations research" models may be very valuable for the analyst, his task is not simply to impose a model on the situation. These models may be the building blocks. The analyst and the manager in concert develop the final structure. This implies that the analyst must possess a certain empathy for the manager, and *vice versa*. Whether the current systems designers in a given organization possess this quality is a question worthy of consideration by management.

This approach in no way precludes normative statements about decision procedures. The emphasis on the development of descriptive models of managerial problem solving is only to ensure that the existing situation is well understood by both the analyst and the manager. Once this understanding has been attained, various approaches to improving the process can be explored. In fact, a major benefit of developing descriptive models of this type is the exposure of the decision-making process to objective analysis.

In summary, then, we have asserted that there are two sets of implications which flow from our use of this framework. The first set centers on an organization's planning and resource allocation decision in relation to information systems. The second set flows from the distinction we have drawn between structured and unstructured types of decisions. The focus of our attention should be on the critical *decisions* in an organization and on explicit modeling of these decisions prior to the design of information systems support.

The second major point in relation to the structured/unstructured dimension that we have raised is that the kinds of implementation problems, the skills required by the managers and analysts, and the characteristics of the design process are different above and below the dashed line in Figure 1. In discussing these differences, we have tried to stress the fundamental shift in approach that is required if decision support systems are to be built in a way that makes them effective in an organization. The approach and technology that have been used over the last 15 years to build information systems in the structured operational control area are often inappropriate in the case of decision support systems.

IMPLICATIONS OF THE FRAMEWORK

Systems Design Differences. The decision categories we have borrowed from Anthony have a set of implications distinct from those discussed in connection with the structured and unstructured areas. The first of these has to do with the systems design differences that follow from supporting decisions in the three areas.

As was seen earlier, information requirements differ sharply among the three areas. There are few occasions in which it makes sense to connect systems directly across boundaries. Aggregating the detailed accounting records (used in operational control) to provide a base for a five-year sales forecast (required for a strategic planning decision) is an expensive and unnecessary process. We can often sample, estimate, or otherwise obtain data for use in strategic planning without resorting to the operational control database. This does not imply that we should *never* use such a database, but merely that it is not necessarily the best way of obtaining the information.

This point is also relevant in the collection and maintenance of data. Techniques appropriate for operational control, such as the use of on-line data collection terminals, are rarely justified for strategic planning systems. Similarly, elaborate environmental sampling methods may be critical for an operational control decision. In looking at each of the information characteristics in Table 1, it is apparent that quite different databases will be required to support decisions in the three areas. Therefore, the first implication of the decision classification in our framework is that the "totally-integrated-management-information-systems" ideas so popular in the literature are a poor design concept. More particularly, the "integrated" or "company-wide" database is a misleading notion and even if it could be achieved would be exorbitantly expensive.

Information differences among the three decision areas also imply related differences in hardware and software requirements. On the one hand, strategic planning decisions require access to a database which is used infrequently and may involve an interface with a variety of complex models. Operational control decisions, on the other hand, often require a larger database with continuous updating and frequent access to current information.

Differences in Organizational Structure. A second distinction is in the organizational structure and the managerial and analyst skills which will be involved across the three areas. The managerial talents required, as well as the numbers and training of the managers involved, differ sharply for these categories. The process of deciding on key problems that might be worth supporting with a formal system is a much smaller, tighter process in the strategic planning area than in the operational control area. The decision to be supported is probably not a recurring one and will normally not involve changes in the procedures and structure employed by the remainder of the firm. Because it is a relatively isolated decision in both time and scope, it need not involve as many people. However, the process of defining the problem must be dominated by the managers involved if the right problem and hence the best model formulation are to be selected. Similarly, the implementation process must be tightly focused on the immediate problem. The skills required of the managers involved are analytical and reflective, rather than communicative and procedural. In the strategic planning case, the manager must supply both the problem definition and the key relationships that make up the model. This requires an ability to think logically and a familiarity with models and computation. In the case of operational control, the particular solution and the models involved are much more the concern of the technical specialist. This is not to say that in unstructured operational control the manager's judgment will not be involved in the process of solving problems. However, his role in *building* that model can be much more passive than in the strategic area.

The decision process, the implementation process, and the level of analytical sophistication of the managers (as opposed to that of the staff) in strategic planning all differ quite markedly from their counterparts in operational control. The decision makers in operational control have a more constrained problem. They have often had several years in which to define the general nature of the problem and to consider solutions. In addition, to the extent that these managers have a technical background, they are more likely to be familiar with the analysis involved in solving structured and unstructured problems. In any event, the nature of the operational control problem, its size, and the frequency of the decision all combine to produce design and implementation problems of a different variety. The managers involved in any given problem tend to be from the decision area in question, be it strategic planning, management control, or operational control. As a result, their training, background, and style of decision making are often different. This means that the types of models to be used, the method of elucidating these from the managers, and the skills of the analysts will differ across these three areas.

As the types of skills possessed by the managers differ, so will the kinds of systems analysts who can operate effectively. We have already distinguished between analysts who can handle structured as opposed to unstructured model building. There is a similar distinction to be made between the kind of person who can work well with a small group of senior managers (on either a structured or unstructured problem) and the person who is able to communicate with the various production personnel on an unstructured job-shop scheduling problem, for example.

In problems in the strategic area, the analyst has to be able to communicate effectively with the few managers who have the basic knowledge required to define the problem and its major variables. The skills required to do this include background and experience which are wide enough to match those of the line executives involved. Good communication depends on a common understanding of the basic variables involved, and few analysts involved in current MIS activity have this skill.

A breadth of background implies a wide repertoire of models with which the analyst is familiar. In the operational control area, an analyst can usefully specialize to great depth in a particular, narrow problem area. The depth, and the resulting improvement in the final system, often pays off because of the frequency with which the decision is made. In the strategic area the coverage of potential problems is enormous and the frequency of a particular decision relatively low. The range of models with which the analyst is familiar may be of greater benefit than depth in any one type.

In addition to the managerial and analyst issues raised above, there is a further difference in the way the information systems group is organized. A group dealing only with operational control problems would be structured differently and perhaps report to a different organizational position than a group working in all three areas. It is not our purpose here to go into detail on the organizational issues, but the material above suggests that on strategic problems, a task force reporting to the user and virtually independent of the computer group may make sense. The important issues are problem definition and problem structure; the implementation and computer issues are relatively simple by comparison. In management control, the single user, although still dominant in his application, has problems of interfacing with other users. An organizational design that encourages cross functional (marketing, production, distribution, etc.) cooperation is probably desirable. In operational control, the organizational design should include the user as a major influence, but he will have to be balanced with operational systems experts, and the whole group can quite possibly stay within functional boundaries. These examples are merely illustrative of the kind of organizational differences involved. Each organization has to examine its current status and needs and make structural changes in light of them.

Model Differences. The third distinction flowing from the framework is among the types of models involved. Again looking at Table 1 and the information differences, it is clear that model requirements depend, for example, on the frequency of decisions in each area and their relative magnitude. A strategic decision to change the whole distribution system occurs rarely. It is significant in cost, perhaps hundreds of millions of dollars, and it therefore can support a complex model, but the model need not be efficient in any sense. An operational control decision, however, may be made frequently, perhaps daily. The impact of each decision is small but the cumulative impact can involve large sums of money. Models for the decision may have to be efficient in running time, have ready access to current data, and be structured so as to be easily changed. Emphasis has to be on simplicity of building, careful attention to modularity, and so forth.

The sources of models for operational control are numerous. There is a history of activity, the problems are often similar across organizations, and the literature is extensive. In strategic planning, and to a lesser extent management control, we are still in the early stages of development. Our models tend to be individual and have to come from the managers involved. It is a model creation process as opposed to the application of a model.

In summary then, we have outlined implications for the organization which follow from the three major decision categories in the framework. We have posed the issues in terms of operational control and strategic planning, and with every point we assume that management control lies somewhere in between the two. The three major implications we have discussed are the advisability of following the integrated database path; the differences in managerial and analyst skills as well as the appropriate forms of organizational structure for building systems in the three areas; and differences in the types of models involved. Distinguishing among decision areas is clearly important if an organization is going to be successful in its use of information systems.

SUMMARY

The information systems field absorbs a significant percentage of the resources of many organizations. Despite these expenditures, there is very little perspective on the field and the issues within it. As a result, there has been a tendency to make incremental improvements to existing systems. The framework we suggest for looking at decisions within an organization provides one perspective on the information systems issues. From this perspective, it becomes clear that our planning for information systems has resulted in a heavy concentration in the operational control area. In addition, there is a series of implications for the organization which flows from the distinction between the decision areas. Model structure and the implementation process differ sharply between the structured and unstructured areas. Database concepts, types of analysts and managers, and organizational structure all differ along the Strategic Planning to Operational Control axis.

We believe that each organization must share *some* common framework among its members if it is to plan and make resource allocation decisions which result in effective use of information systems. We suggest that the framework that has been presented here is an appropriate place to start.

FOOTNOTES

1. See Taylor and Dean (9).
2. See Scott Morton (6) and Soelberg (8).
3. Anthony (2).
4. Anthony (2), p. 24.
5. Anthony (2), p. 27.
6. Anthony (2), p. 69.
7. See, for example, Becker (3).
8. Simon (7), pp. 5–6.
9. Simon (7), pp. 2–3.
10. See Ackoff (1).
11. See Pounds (5).
12. See Gorry (4).

REFERENCES

1. Ackoff, R. "Management Misinformation Systems." *Management Science* 11, no. 4 (December 1967), pp. B147–B156.
2. Anthony, R. N. *Planning and Control Systems: A Framework for Analysis.* Boston: Division of Research, Harvard Business School, 1965.
3. Becker, J. L. "Planning the Total Information System." In *Total Systems,* ed. A. D. Meacham and V. B. Thompson. New York: American Data Processing, 1962, pp. 66–73.

4. Gorry, G. A. "The Development of Managerial Models." *Sloan Management Review* 12, no. 2 (Winter 1971), pp. 1–16.

5. Pounds, W. F. "The Process of Problem Finding." *Industrial Management Review* 11, no. 1 (Fall 1969), pp. 1–20.

6. Scott Morton, M. S. *Management Decision Systems.* Boston: Division of Research, Harvard Business School, 1971.

7. Simon, H. A. *The New Science of Management Decision.* New York: Harper & Row, 1960.

8. Soelberg, P. O. "Unprogrammed Decision Making." *Industrial Management Review* 8, no. 2 (Spring 1967), pp. 19–30.

9. Taylor, J. W., and N. J. Dean. "Managing to Manage the Computer." *Harvard Business Review* 44, no. 5 (September–October 1966), pp. 98–110.

Chapter Two
Decision Support Systems:
A Research Perspective

PETER G. W. KEEN

1. INTRODUCTION

Decision Support Systems (DSS) represent a concept of the role of computers within the decision-making process. The term has become a rallying cry for researchers, practitioners, and managers concerned that Management Science and the Management Information Systems fields have become unnecessarily narrow in focus. As with many rallying cries, the term is not well defined. For some writers, DSS simply mean interactive systems for use by managers. For others, the key issue is support, rather than system. They focus on understanding and improving the decision process; a DSS is then designed using any available and suitable technology. Some researchers view DSS as a subfield of MIS, while others regard it as an extension of management science techniques. The former define decision support as providing managers with access to data, and the latter as giving them access to analytic models.

Research on DSS gained momentum around 1974. Only in the late 70s did it reach a critical mass and expand beyond a fairly

Center for Information Systems Research Working Paper No. 54, Sloan School of Management, MIT, Cambridge, Mass., March 1980.

Many of the ideas expressed in this paper belong as much to my colleagues at The Wharton School, University of Pennsylvania, Philadelphia, 1978–79, as to myself. In particular, the concepts of task representation were developed by Gerry Hurst, Dick Hackathorn, and myself, and extended through discussions with John Henderson and Tom Gambino. The research framework owes much to a seminar on DSS run by Dick Hackathorn.

narrow circle. By 1979, almost 30 fairly detailed case studies of DSS had been published. As the concept has become fashionable it has been used in looser and looser ways. Last year's article on "interactive marketing models" is cut-and-pasted and resubmitted with "decision support systems" sno-paked in instead. It may well be that DSS are more important as a liberating rallying cry than as a theoretical concept. However, the published case studies and conceptual proposals imply a coherent framework that makes DSS a meaningful discipline for both research and practice.

This paper presents a formal definition of DSS. It aims at answering two key questions:

1. Is the term really necessary?
2. If so, what are the research issues it implies?

The key argument is that the term *DSS* is relevant to situations where a "final" system can be developed only through an adaptive process of learning and evolution. The design strategy must then focus on getting finished; this is very different from the management science and data processing approaches. The research issues for DSS center around adaptation and evolution; they include managerial learning, representation of tasks and user behavior, design architecture, and strategies for getting started.

2. DEFINITIONS OF DSS

Most work on DSS adopts one of the following conceptions, even if only implicitly:

1. A DSS is defined in terms of the *structure of the task* it addresses.
2. DSS require a distinctive *design strategy* based on evolution and "middle-out" techniques.
3. DSS support the cognitive processes of individual decision makers; *decision research* provides descriptive insights into management problem solving and normative theories for defining how to improve its effectiveness.
4. DSS reflect an *implementation strategy* for making computers useful to managers; this strategy is based on the use of skilled intermediates, responsive service, and "humanized" software interfaces.

None of these conceptions necessarily implies interactive computer systems; a DSS is defined in terms of context and use.

There is no *technical* conception for which one cannot readily generate counterexamples. For instance, the design architecture, mode of use, and available functions of an airline reservation system are virtually the same as those in many databased DSS. If a given DSS is identical to, say, a standard interactive model, there seems no value whatsoever in using a new label. DSS become a meaningful research topic only if the term can be shown to be a *necessary* concept. In the pragmatic conte: of information systems development and analytic techniques, calling a system a DSS must lead to some actions, by the designers or users, that would not have occurred otherwise; the actions should contribute to the effective development of the system or its effective use.

A potential strength of the DSS movement has been that it has at least tried to link theory and practice. It describes real systems used in real organizations by real problem-solvers, not experiments involving captive students. At the same time, since it explicitly argues that DSS are different from traditional systems, the better empirical work addresses conceptual issues, if only assertively. The available studies of DSS thus often provide illustrations, extensions, or counterexamples that can be used to test and extend their authors' conceptual assumptions.

3. CASE-BASED STUDIES OF DSS

This is not a survey paper, but many of the ideas expressed in it come from a detailed analysis of 30 articles or chapters in books that describe particular DSS in detail.[1] (Appendix 2–1 provides the necessary references.) Some clear and general conclusions can be drawn from the studies:

1. The actual uses of the DSS are almost invariably different from the intended ones; indeed, *many of the most valued and innovative uses could not have been predicted when the system was designed.*
2. Usage is personalized; whether a system is recently operational or has been in place for some time, there are wide variations among individuals in how they use its functions.
3. DSS evolve; case studies frequently state that key factors explaining successful development are a flexible design architecture that permits fast modification and extension and a phased approach to implementation.
4. The functions DSS provide are generally not elaborate; complex systems are evolved from simple components.

5. While the orthodox (academic) faith views DSS as tools for individual decision makers,[2] users regard the concept as more relevant to systems that support organizational processes. They also feel they do not really use DSS for *decision making*.
6. Major benefits identified by users are flexibility, improved communications (of, for example, the logic of an analysis), insight, and learning.
7. DSS are frequently used by managers through intermediaries and chauffeurs; while an interactive computer system is essential for ease of access, there is little interactive problem solving.

Examples of all these points are shown in Appendix 2–2. They add up to a fairly clear picture of DSS development that differs from the orthodox faith in important details. In the first place, they suggest that the term *decision support system* is too broad and the cognitive focus of much of the research too narrow. Keen and Hackathorn argue that a distinction should be made between:

a. Personal Support Systems (PSS), for use by individuals in tasks which involve no interdependencies, so that the user can indeed make a decision.
b. Group Support Systems (GSS), for tasks with "pooled" interdependencies which thus require substantial face-to-face discussion and communication.
c. Organizational Support Systems (OSS), for tasks involving "sequential" interdependencies.

A PSS may thus support a manager's own budget *decision*, a GSS support the budget *negotiation*, and an OSS support the organizational budget *process*.

Several writers have been uneasy with the D in DSS. It largely reflects the cognitive focus—even bias—in the early DSS research, which draws on Simon's theories of individual decision making and concepts of cognitive style and cognitive complexity. Organizational Support Systems far outnumber PSS in the published case studies and require a very different theoretical base, which is so far lacking.

4. MIDDLE-OUT DESIGN

The studies strongly support the concept of middle-out design for DSS.[3] Almost all the descriptions of DSS implementation highlight careful use of prototypes, continued incremental development, and response to users' changing demands. Writers such as Ness, Courbon, Grajew, and Tolovi, and Berger and Edelman make a strong implicit case for viewing X Support Systems (where X may stand for Decision, Management, Personal, Organizational, Interactive, or whatever) as an adaptive design strategy.

The obvious question is: Is the strategy a general one for interactive systems or needed only for particular situations? Middle-out design differs most from traditional techniques in that it explicitly proceeds without functional specification. Data processing (DP) has learned, through vicarious trial-and-error learning and occasional reflection, that systems development requires planning before programming. Brooks' brilliant and somewhat rueful review of software engineering, *The Mythical Man-Month*, established that coding is only 10 percent of the total effort in the system's development life cycle. Standard textbooks generally recommend that around 40 percent of the effort go to analysis and specifications, 10 percent to coding, 30 percent to testing, and 20 percent to installation (and another 100–300 percent to maintenance). The vocabulary of DP is full of terms like *signing-off*, *functional specifications*, and making a system *operational*.

The DSS case studies, including those in which the design strategy was not based on middle-out, contradict the recommendations underlying the systems development life cycle. This clearly implies that defining a system as a DSS, rather than, say, as an interactive information retrieval system, *does* make a difference. It shifts the development process from a focus on delaying coding to getting going on it as fast as possible, from aiming toward a clearly defined "final" system to implementing an initial one that can then be firmed up, modified, and evolved. The systems development life cycle is a strategy for getting finished; *adaptive design* (this term captures all the middle-out, incremental, and evolutionary techniques scattered throughout the case studies) is a method for getting started.

5. "SEMISTRUCTURED" TASKS

Viewing DSS in terms of the design process is not enough to integrate all the conclusions from the case studies. It also sidesteps key conceptual issues raised by the decision research and task-centered conceptions of DSS. Gorry and Scott Morton's *A Framework for Management Information Systems* (1971) was a seminal paper for DSS. It built on Simon's concept of programmed and nonprogrammed tasks and identified semistructured tasks as those requiring special treatment. Structured tasks can be automated or routinized, thus replacing judgment, while unstructured ones entirely involve judgment and defy computerization. Semistructured tasks permit a synthesis of human judgment and the computer's capabilities.

There are several problems with this argument. The terms *structured* and *unstructured* point to a spectrum of tasks, but there is no real operationalization of *semistructured*. More importantly, it is unclear if structure is perceptual or intrinsic to the task. Stabell also points out that organizations often *decide* to treat an unstructured task as if it were structured; the degree of structure is then socially defined, as well as perceptual.

The Gorry–Scott Morton framework is not a complete or convincing theoretical statement. The range of applications, technologies, and mode of use of the DSS described in the case studies are too broad to fit into it. (This applies also to Gorry and Scott Morton's use of Anthony's distinction between strategic planning, management control, and operational control. Scott Morton (1971) suggests that DSS apply to the first two areas, but Berger and Edelman give striking examples of a DSS for operational control.)

Despite the looseness of its definition and the lack of comprehensive supporting evidence in the case studies, Gorry and Scott Morton's notion of semistructured tasks is intuitively convincing. Keen and Scott Morton rely on it in explaining the concept of support, rather than replacement, of managerial judgment. Any effort to define how a DSS helps improve effectiveness in decision making, and not just efficiency, has to introduce some similar notion of the relationship between task structure and process (Stabell, and Carlson and Sutton).

6. DSS REDEFINED

A central argument of this paper is that what Gorry and Scott Morton present, and Gerrity, Scott Morton, Stabell, and Keen and Scott Morton later extend, is not the general case but a special one. The following definition of support systems meshes the task-centered perspective into that of adaptive design and also picks up on the most interesting finding from the case studies, the unpredictability of DSS usage:

The label "support system" is meaningful only in situations where the "final" system must emerge through an adaptive process of design and usage.

This process may be needed for a variety of reasons:

1. The designer or user cannot provide functional specifications or is unwilling to do so. *A "semistructured" task is such an instance:* we either lack the necessary knowledge to lay out procedures and requirements (i.e., the degree of structure is perceptual) or feel that such a statement can never be made (i.e., the lack of structure is intrinsic to the task).
2. Users do not know what they want and the designers do not understand what they need or can accept; an initial system must be built to give users something concrete to react to (this is the assumption underlying middle-out).
3. Users' concepts of the task or decision situation will be *shaped* by the DSS. The system stimulates learning and new insights, which in turn stimulate new uses and the need for new functions in the system. The unpredictability of DSS usage surely reflects this learning, which can be exploited only if the DSS evolves in response to it.
4. Intended users of the system have sufficient autonomy to handle the task in a variety of ways, or differ in the way they think to a degree that prevents standardization. In this situation, any computer support must allow personalized usage and be flexible.

While (3) states that the DSS shapes the user, (4) equally suggests that the user shapes the DSS.

This conception makes DSS a necessary concept. For any given system development effort, it makes a great deal of difference whether or not the implementers view it as requiring a DSS as opposed to a marketing model, retrieval system, report generator, etc. It would be a severe mistake to rely on traditional development techniques if the final system will evolve only through the ongoing interaction of designer and user, learning, personalized use, or the evolution of new functions. Learning, adaptation, and evolution are made feasible by building a "DSS" and not a "model." If these are not needed for effective development and use of a system, then one should build it as a "model" in the traditional way and the new label is not relevant.

This definition of DSS in terms of adaptive design and use provides a base for a research framework that is consistent with

FIGURE 1   An Adaptive Framework for DSS

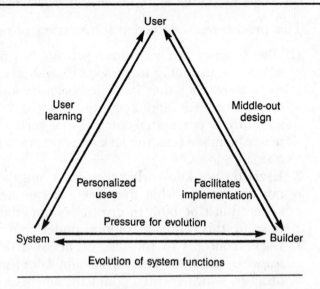

the empirical findings of the case studies and that integrates the conceptual issues they raise or reflect. There seems to be three overall issues for a theory of DSS:

1. Understanding the dynamics of the adaptive relationship between user, designer, and technical system.
2. Analyzing tasks in relation to users' processes and criteria for system design.
3. Developing an organizational focus to complement the cognitive perspective and thus include Organizational as well as Personal Support Systems.

7. ADAPTIVE DEVELOPMENT AND USE

Figure 1 shows the adaptive links between the major actors involved in any DSS development and the technical system. The arrows represent a direction of influence. For example, System→User indicates that learning is stimulated by the DSS while User→System refers to the personalized, differentiated mode of use that evolves. The two adaptive processes work together: an effective DSS encourages the user to explore new alternatives and approaches to the task (S→U). This in itself stimulates new uses of the system, often unanticipated and idiosyncratic (U→S).

The arrows are not merely a convenient schematic. They help clarify whether a particular system should be called a DSS. For example, an airline reservation system is technically similar to many retrieval-based DSS. However, it is not intended to stimulate learning (S$\nrightarrow$U), nor are there personalized modes of usage; there is a "right" way to operate the system and the user must adjust to it, not vice versa (U$\nrightarrow$S). Similarly, an interactive planning model that is used to assess a predetermined range of alternatives is a system for solutions, not for learning. It need not be flexible and adapt to the user (U$\nrightarrow$S).

The arrows also represent requirements for successful DSS development and use. For example, if the system forces users to follow a fixed set of procedures, learning cannot be exploited:

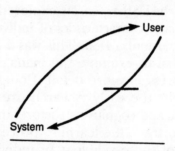

In effect the DSS contains its own obsolescence. It stimulates new approaches which it in turn inhibits.

The definition of DSS as applicable in situations where the final system must evolve from adaptive development and use thus implies:

1. A system is a DSS only if each of the arrows is relevant to the situation.
2. Where they are relevant, the design process must ensure they are not blocked by inflexible design structures, failure to allocate resources for implementing new functions, or lack of a direct relationship between user and designer.
3. Each arrow represents a distinctive aspect of research and practice.

Figure 1 ignores the context of the DSS development process, especially the task to be supported and the wider organization. Before expanding it, however, it seems useful to discuss each adaptive link in relation to DSS research. There are three loops:

$$S \supset U, \ U \supset B, \text{ and } S \supset B.$$

7.1 The System-User Link

$S \supset U$: this, in the context of Personal Support Systems, may be termed the *cognitive loop*. (The issue of organizational support will be discussed separately.) The link $S \frown U$ concerns managerial learning and $U \frown S$ the individuals' exploitation of the DSS capabilities and/or their own learning. The cognitive loop helps explain the consistent finding in the case studies that individuals use a given DSS in very different ways and that uses are so often unintended and unpredicted. This seems a natural outcome of the sequence $S \frown U \frown S \frown U \ldots$

Much early DSS research explored aspects of the cognitive loop, particularly characteristics of individual problem solving that influence the use of a DSS. This was a fairly static analysis and it seems essential to examine the managerial (and organizational) learning process in more detail. Doing so requires richer theoretical models; the early research drew on limited concepts of cognitive style and cognitive structure, that were at too high a level of analysis to track the learning process. They focused on general aspects of the psychology of individual differences (Stabell, Carlisle, Grochow).

7.2 The User-Builder Link

The link $U \supset B$ is the *implementation loop*.

a. $U \frown B$ highlights a key aspect of adaptive design, discussed by Ness and Courbon, et al. Ackoff long ago pointed out that users do not know what they need. The middle-out approach relies on the quick delivery of an initial system to which users can respond and thus clarify what they really want. Middle-out design is the means by which the *designer* learns from the *user;* it also ensures that the user drives the design process.

b. $B \frown U$: this link has been explored in studies of DSS implementation that examine the role of the "integrating agent" (Bennett), intermediary (Keen), chauffeur (Grace), and change agent (Ginzberg). DSS are a service rather than a product and require that the designer understand the users' perspective and processes, build credibility, and be responsive to their evolving needs.

The implementation loop is both well researched and well understood. The empirical work of Courbon, Grajew, and Tolovi is an exhaustive and precise test of the concepts of adaptive design. The more diffuse discussions of implementation are less operational (Bennett, Keen, Ginzberg, and Scott Morton).

7.3 The System-Builder Link

This *evolution loop* (S⊂B) is less easy to label than the others. While the case studies show again and again that DSS evolve, and much of the conceptual work relevant to DSS recommends evolutionary development (Little, 1975), there are few detailed, longitudinal studies or theoretical models. It is perhaps easiest to view the links in relation to the other loops. Managerial learning (S⌒U) and personalized uses (U⌒S) put strain on the existing system. This builds pressure for evolution (S⌒B). New functions are then provided (B⌒S). The case studies imply that this is not a continued, evenly paced process, but occurs in discrete phases (see also Andreoli and Steadman). Users explore the initial system for a while and gradually become confident with it. At a certain point, it becomes apparent that a new function needs to be added to the system. Quite often, usage does not really take off until this extension is provided; the "new" system leads to very different volumes and modes of use than the earlier one (Andreoli and Steadman).

The S⌒B link needs research. Keen and Gambino have employed the common device of a data trap to track individuals' use of a DSS (see also Stabell, and Andreoli and Steadman), in terms of emerging patterns and "command sequences." The argument is that users initially use the commands of the DSS as single words (e.g., "LIST", "REGRESS"), but later develop, largely via the adaptive processes of the cognitive loop, what are effectively sentences; they use consistent sequences of commands and build up their own analytic routines. This process is easy to identify; the hypothesis is that it triggers demand for, or readiness to use, new commands.

The other link, B⌒S, is easier to explain. It simply involves the designer adding new capabilities to the DSS. This obviously is feasible only *a.* If the design architecture is modular, flexible, and easily modified.

  b. The programmer can implement new functions cheaply and quickly.

  c. The designer maintains ongoing contact with the users.

The advocates of APL as "the" language for DSS (Contreras, Keen), of end user languages (Keen and Wagner), and "command-driven" interfaces all emphasize the need for program structures and programming methods to facilitate evolution. The case studies indicate that the success of a DSS often depends on its evolution rather than its initial use, and on fast, responsive implementation.

  Discussions of DSS evolution focus on new functions and commands. There is relatively little exploration of the evolution of data and data structures.[4] Model-based DSS seem easier to both build and evolve than do databased ones. DSS research currently lacks a focus on handling data management issues.

7.4 Summary

There is not room here to discuss each adaptive link in Figure 1 in any detail. The preceding summary covers only a few issues relevant to research. It is hoped that Figure 1 constitutes a definition of DSS development that clarifies what a DSS is and is not, and what actions and processes it involves. Each arrow represents a clear research area relevant to DSS practice.

8. THE TASK CONTEXT

Figure 1 ignores the task to be supported. Obviously, a DSS can be built only if the designer understands the task at a level of detail sufficient to:

  a. Relate the task to the users' processes.

  b. Design the functions of the DSS.

  c. By extension, relate the users' processes to the DSS functions.

  At present, methodologies for describing tasks, user processes, and system functions are at too high a level to integrate the three components.[5] For example, one may classify an individual in terms of cognitive style (e.g., intuitive versus systematic), classify the task as semistructured, and the system as an interactive retrieval system. This provides no link between task characteristics and detailed design criteria and user behavior. DSS research needs to find a level and method of representing tasks that permit this link. Such a method does not yet exist. Hackathorn's and Meldman's use of network models comes closest, but is not intended as a general methodology for DSS.

The ideas presented below require a major research effort[6] before they can be validated and made operational. In a way, they pick up on Gorry and Scott Morton's discussion of "semistructured" tasks, at a more molecular level:

1. The tasks a DSS addresses involve some degree of discretion, inference, and selection of information; if this is not so, there are no adaptive links between user and system (U⊃S). A whole task is composed of subtasks. The whole task may be the university admissions decision, portfolio management, media selection, etc., etc. The subtasks are discrete intellectual operations, such as:

    Calculating a sum.
    Searching for a value.
    Comparing two variables on a graph.
2. The subtasks identify the potential functions for the DSS, e.g., CALC, FIND, COMPARE.
3. User behavior and user learning can be described in terms of the sequence of and change in subtasks.
4. Use of the DSS can be tracked in relation to the functions.

This level of representation has several practical and conceptual merits. It also suggests that DSS should be command-driven. Keen and Alter argue that the commands correspond to the users' verbs (e.g., "LIST", "GRAPH"). Keen adds that if a function in a system does not relate directly to some concept in the users' mind, it really cannot be used. Carrying out a task involves a sequence of verb-related subtasks (Do this . . . then this . . .). Using a DSS involves invoking a sequence of verb-based commands. Evolving it means adding new commands. Learning is identifiable only in terms of use of new commands or redefinition of existing ones, and personalized use is apparent from the choice of commands.

In a structured task the subtasks can be clearly specified and the sequence in which they are invoked predicted. A "semistructured" task is thus one where either not all the subtasks can be represented and hence translated into DSS commands or they can be represented but the sequence not predicted. Focusing on subtasks, rather than whole tasks, retains the intuitive appeal of the Gorry–Scott Morton framework but eliminates its problems of definition. In addition, doing so addresses Stabell's point, that a whole task is often socially defined; two universities may handle the admissions process—the whole task—very differently, but it will have common subtasks.

Keen and Scott Morton, building on Gerrity and Stabell, discuss DSS design as a balance between descriptive and prescriptive understanding of the decision process. Supporting users implies providing commands that correspond to their existing (or at least desired) verbs. Improving the effectiveness of their decision making means identifying new commands and stimulating their use through the adaptive processes described by Figure 1.

A number of DSS researchers share this focus on subtasks. Blanning outlines the equivalent of a generative grammar for DSS that goes beyond verbs. Keen and Gambino suggest that most whole tasks require a common set of verbs; almost any DSS needs such functions as "GRAPH", "LIST", "SELECT", and "DESCRIBE" (provide descriptive statistics). Henderson et al have designed a set of experiments on DSS use which track user behavior at the command and subtask level.[6]

The ideas presented above are tentative and a proposal for research rather than a conclusion from it. The central postulate is that adaptive design and use of DSS, DSS evolution, managerial learning, etc., require a decision research process where the level of analysis is at the subtask level. Much of the vagueness of DSS concepts disappears when this is provided. Of course, the research issue is how to represent the subtasks. Contreras, following on Berry, argues that they are linguistically at the level of APL functions, which can be further broken down into primitives. Blanning adopts a similar perspective.

Figure 2 adds the task dimension to the adaptive loops. Whatever methodology or theoretical model of task structure and performance is used, it is obvious that the representation can only be at the subtask level if it is to translate an understanding of how the users think, and an assessment of how their performance can be made more effective into specific functions in a DSS.

FIGURE 2   Task Context

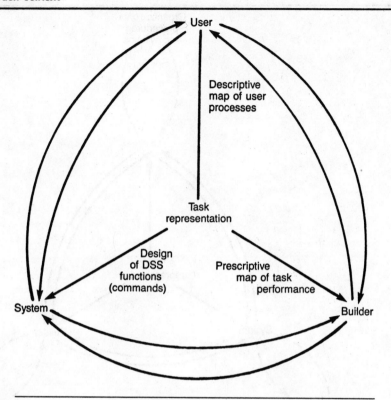

9. CONTEXTUAL ISSUES IN DSS DEVELOPMENT

Figure 3 expands Figure 2 to include contextual forces. The additional links are not so much adaptive influences as limiting ones. For example, organizational procedures may constrain user discretion and behavior (O⌒U). In several of the case studies, DSS were not effectively used because the organization's control, communication, and reward systems provided no incentive. Clearly, the extent to which organizational procedures affect individuals in a given task determines whether the situation requires a Personal, Group, or Organizational Support System. In turn, the extent to which the user(s) can influence the procedures (U⌒O) limits the organizational learning a DSS can stimulate.

In a similar fashion, the DSS itself is constrained by the or-

---

FIGURE 3 *Organizational Issues*

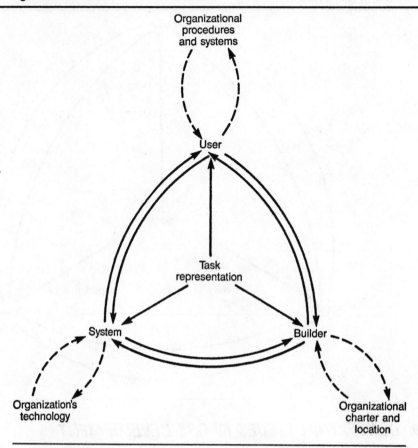

---

ganization's available technology (T⌒S). This includes data as well as computer power, and the base of reliable operational systems and technical expertise on which a DSS capability is built. The case studies mainly describe successful systems but there are several suggestions that DSS will not take root in an organization that has not yet provided managers with standard data processing and reporting systems. In such situations, DSS are seen as a luxury or as irrelevant.

The link S T is a reminder that learning and evolution can be blocked by the inability to obtain additional technology. Keen and Clark found that use of their DSS for state government policy and analysis was strongly constrained by states' existing technology and procedures for operating it. In addition, managerial learning and evolution of the DSS may require new data and structures or lead to an overloading of the organization's time-sharing computer. The whole adaptive process in Figure 3 breaks down when any influence is absent or blocked.

The final contextual issue addressed by Figure 3 is the charter for the builder. The implementation loop relies on facilitation and middle-out design. This requires a close relationship between the user and builder, which may not be feasible if:

1. The two groups are geographically or psychologically isolated.
2. The designers are part of a unit, such as Data Processing, with no mandate for innovation.
3. The organization's charge-out policies and procedures for project justification discourage exploration and require "hard" benefits. Keen points out that DSS often provide mainly qualitative benefits. They "improve" a decision process and it is unlikely that one can point in advance to a "bottom-line" payoff, especially if the value of the system is in the end determined by an adaptive, evolutionary process.

Many DSS builders are either consultants or academics, who can be brought into an organization by the user and who thus have relative freedom to define their role. A major constraint on developing a DSS capability may be the lack of a suitable organizational charter.

10. CONCLUSION

The additions to the earlier schema made in Figure 3 address the question of Organizational Support Systems raised earlier and left hanging. Figure 1 provides a complete research framework for Personal Support Systems. Figure 3 is far more tentative. Substantial research on organizational issues for DSS is needed, and no effort will be made here to justify or elaborate on this preliminary identification of organizational forces constraining DSS. The more important point is that Figure 1, and the definition of DSS it reflects, seem to provide a robust and adequately precise framework for DSS research. The representation of sub-tasks indicates a theoretical, if not yet practical, methodology for studying and building DSS.

If the framework presented here is valid, then decision support is a meaningful and independent discipline. The existing research base is fairly strong in certain areas, especially the implementation loop. There are more than enough case studies available to point up issues, such as the nature of managerial learning and DSS evolution, that should be explored at a more precise level, often through laboratory experiments. The major conceptual problems concern subtask representation, and a theoretical base for Organizational Support Systems. The term *decision support systems* is an excellent rallying cry. Decision support can be an equally outstanding field of study.

APPENDIX 2–1
Case Studies of DSS

Until definitions of DSS are firmly established, it will be difficult to keep track of the literature on the topic. Three references contain most of the case-based descriptions used for the review in this paper:

1. Keen and Scott Morton, *Decision Support Systems: An Organizational Perspective* (1978). This represents the orthodox faith. It includes fairly detailed descriptions of seven DSS. It excludes (largely because it filters the world through MIT-colored glasses, but also due to the long lead time between writing and publishing) the work of Courbon, Grajew, and Tolovi and most of that done at Wharton by Ness and Hurst. It has a comprehensive bibliography.

2. Carlson, Morgan, and Scott Morton, eds., *Proceedings of a Conference on Decision Support Systems* (1977). This contains very little conceptual material and emphasizes real-world applications. It has a strong show-and-tell flavor. Whereas Keen and Scott Morton use case descriptions to illustrate the concepts of a DSS, in this volume practitioners demonstrate their view of what aspects of the concept have practical value. It seems clear that on the whole they do not share Keen and Scott Morton's emphasis on the cognitive characteristics of the individual decision maker but focus instead on organizational processes.

3. Alter, *Decision Support Systems: Current Practices and Future Challenges* (1980). This book is based on case studies of 56 systems, only a few of which are DSS. There are 7 detailed cases, some of which overlap with Keen and Scott Morton, and Carlson and Scott Morton. Alter is partly concerned with sharpening the practical definitions of DSS by looking at innovative systems in general. He uses the term *decision support system* fairly loosely, mainly since his is an exploratory study which specifically asks if it is useful to identify a system as a DSS.

A fourth study, by Courbon, Grajew, and Tolovi, describes three experimental DSS projects. Le Moigne criticizes Keen and Scott Morton's book as *"partial et partiel"*—incomplete and limited to the U.S. experience. He feels that French researchers are more advanced than the Americans. Certainly the work of Courbon, Grajew, and Tolovi builds on earlier research imaginatively and effectively.

The best bibliographies on DSS are in Keen and Scott Morton and in Courbon, Grajew, and Tolovi. In the list below, the major sources of reference are identified as Keen and Scott Morton (K–M), Carlson and Scott Morton (C), and Alter (A). The major cases are:

AAIMS: An Analytic Information Management System (C and A)

BIS: Budget Information System (A)

BRANDAID: Marketing Brand Management (K–M)

CAUSE: Computer Assisted Underwriting System at Equitable (A)

CIS: Capacity Information System (K–M)

EIS: Executive Information System (C)

GADS: Geodata Analysis Display System (K–M)

GMIS: Generalized Management Information System (K–M)

GPLAN: Generalized Planning (C)

IMS: Interactive Marketing System (A)

IRIS: Industrial Relations Information System (C)

ISSPA: Interactive Support System for Policy Analysts (Keen and Gambino)

MAPP: Managerial Analysis for Profit Planning (C)

PDSS: Procurement Decision Support System (International Harvester, private paper)
PMS: Portfolio Management System (K–M and A)
PROJECTOR: Strategic Financial Planning (K–M)
REGIS: Relational Generalized Information System (C)

APPENDIX 2–2

1. Unanticipated Uses
   PMS—Intended use, investment decisions tool; actual use, marketing tool and customer relations.
   MAPP—Intended use, financial planning; actual use, revealed branch bank irregularities.
   PROJECTOR—Intended use, analyzing financial data to answer preplanned questions; actual use, alerted users to new issues and unplanned questions.
2. Personalized Uses
   GADS—Public officials (police and school system users) could imagine solutions then use GADS to test hypotheses; individual users' values placed on variables led to entirely different conclusions.
   REGIS—Encouraged data browsing, discerning new relationships and questions.
   PMS—Wide variance in fuction combinations used by individual managers.
3. Evolution
   BIS—Initial system modular in structure; database separate from applications programs; new programs added incrementally without upsetting database.
   PMS—Initial prototype followed by full implementation, doubled number of programs in six months.
   CAUSE—Four evolutionary versions; deliberate emphasis on phased development to build credibility and capability; routines increased from 26 to 200 during the evolutionary period.
4. Simple Functions

> AAIMS—60 verblike commands used, "DISPLAY", "PLOT", "QUARTERLY", "CHANGE", . . .
>
> ISSPA—"DESCRIBE", "EQUITY", "REGRESS", "HISTO", "RANK", "NTILES", . . .
>
> PMS—"SCATTER", "SCAN", "STATUS", "TABLE", "GRAPH", "SUMMARY", "GROUP", . . .

5. Organizational Support System
   CAUSE—Supports underwriting process, including data definition and collection.
   PDSS—Stabilized purchasing agents' ordering system.
   IRIS—Supports operations control in industrial relations applications

6. Benefits
   CAUSE—Reduced need for employer specialization; increased possibilities of internal reorganization; gave opportunity to newer employees.
   PROJECTOR—Time effectiveness improved "by a factor of 20"; forced consideration of related issues; "confidence-inspiring" analysis.
   MAPP—Better product definitions and costing allocation; promoted internal learning.

7. Intermediaries
   GADS—Chauffeur used as teacher and translator; used to save time to get as many possible solutions as quickly as possible.
   IMS—50 percent of use by junior researcher with no decision-making authority; intermediary used only to push buttons, not make decisions.
   PMS—Secretaries operate; managers specify desired output.

FOOTNOTES

1. The analysis is contained in a report by Keen, "A Review of DSS Case Studies" (draft).

2. Keen and Scott Morton's book on DSS is mistakenly subtitled "An Organizational Perspective." The authors herewith recant.

3. The term was created by Ness, who built many of the early DSS and trained, at MIT and Wharton, many DSS designers. His working papers and case studies in Alter and in Keen and Scott Morton show the development of the middle-out concept. Courbon, Grajew, and

Tolovi have extended it in some brilliant empirical studies; they use the term *l'approche evolutive.*

4. LeMoigne has drawn attention to this and points out that Keen and Scott Morton entirely ignore data management issues.

5. Stabell has developed a range of techniques for decision research at several levels of analysis. However, they focus on task and on the individual, and do not as yet include DSS design criteria.

6. John C. Henderson, Thomas Gambino, and J. Ghani, private communication.

REFERENCES

Ackoff, R. L. "Unsuccessful Case Studies and Why." *Operations Research* 8, no. 4 (March–April 1960), pp. 259–63.

Alter, S. L. *Decision Support Systems: Current Practices and Continuing Challenges.* Reading, Mass.: Addison-Wesley, 1980.

Andreoli, P., and J. Steadman. "Management Decision Support Systems: Impact on the Decision Process." Master's thesis, Sloan School of Management, MIT, 1975.

Anthony, R. N. *Planning and Control Systems: A Framework for Analysis.* Cambridge, Mass.: Harvard University Graduate School of Business Administration, Studies in Management Control, 1965.

Bennett, J. "Integrating Users and Decision Support Systems." In *Proceedings of the Sixth and Seventh Annual Conferences of the Society for Management Information Systems,* ed. J. D. White, Ann Arbor: University of Michigan, July 1976, pp. 77–86.

Berger, P., and F. Edelman. "IRIS: A Transaction-Based Decision Support System for Human Resources Management." *Database* 8, no. 3 (Winter 1977).

Berry, P. "The Democratization of Computing." Paper presented at II Symposium Nacional de Systemas Computacionales, Monterrey, Mexico, March 15–18, 1977.

Blanning, R. "The Decision to Adopt Strategic Planning Models." Working papers, The Wharton School, University of Pennsylvania, Philadelphia, 1979.

Brooks, F. P. *The Mythical Man-Month.* Reading, Mass.: Addison-Wesley, 1975.

Carlisle, J. "Cognitive Factors in Interactive Decision Systems." Ph.D. dissertation, Yale University, New Haven, Conn., 1974.

Carlson, E. D., and M. S. Scott Morton, "Proceedings of a Conference on Decision Support Systems," *Database* 8, no. 3 (Winter 1977).

Carlson, E. D., and J. A. Sutton. *A Case Study of Non-Programmer Inter-*

active Problem-Solving. IBM Research Report RJ1382, San Jose, Calif.: 1974.

Contreras, L. "Decision Support Systems and Corporate Planning." Private communication, 1978.

Courbon, J. C.; J. Grajew; and J. Tolovi. "Design and Implementation of Interactive Decision Support Systems: A Evolutionary Approach."

Gerrity, T. P., Jr. "The Design of Man–Machine Decision Systems." Ph.D. dissertation, Sloan School of Management, MIT, 1970.

Ginzberg, M. J. "A Process Approach to Management Science Implementation." Ph.D. dissertation, Sloan School of Management, MIT, 1975.

Gorry, G. A., and M. S. Scott Morton. "A Framework for Management Information Systems." *Sloan Management Review* 13, no. 1 (Fall 1971), pp. 55–70.

Grace, B. F. *Training Users of Decision Support Systems.* San Jose, Calif.: IBM Research Report RJ1790, May 1976.

Grochow, J. M. "Cognitive Style as a Factor in the Use of Interactive Computer Systems for Decision Support." Ph.D. dissertation, Sloan School of Management, MIT, 1974.

Hackathorn, R. D. "Research Issues in Personal Computing." Proceedings of the National ACM Conference, Washington, D.C., December 1978.

Keen, P. G. W. "Computer Systems for Top Managers: A Modest Proposal." *Sloan Management Review* 18, no. 1 (Fall 1976), pp. 1–17.

Keen, P. G. W., and David Clark. "Simulations for School Finance, a Survey and Assessment." Research report to Ford Foundation, November 1979.

Keen, P. G. W., and T. Gambino. "Mythical Man-Month Revisited." CISR working paper No. 57, May 1980.

Keen, P. G. W., and M. S. Scott Morton. *Decision Support Systems: An Organizational Perspective.* Reading, Mass.: Addison-Wesley, 1978.

Keen, P. G. W., and G. Wagner. "Implementing Decision Support Systems Philosophy." *Datamation,* November 1979.

Little, J. D. C. "Brandaid." *Operations Research* 23, no. 4 (May 1975).

Meldman, J. "Decision Support Systems for Legal Research." Paper presented at the II Symposium Nacional de Systemas Computacionales, Monterrey, Mexico, March 15–18, 1977.

Ness, D. N. "Decision Support Systems: Theories of Design." Paper presented at the Wharton Office of Naval Research Conference on Decision Support Systems, University of Pennsylvania, Philadelphia, November 4–7, 1975.

Scott Morton, M. S. *Management Decision Systems: Computer-Based Support for Decision Making.* Cambridge, Mass.: Division of Research, Harvard Business School, 1971.

Simon, H. A. "A Behavioral Model of Rational Choice." In *Models of Man,* ed. H. A. Simon. New York: Wiley, 1957, pp. 241–60.

Stabell, C. "Decision Research: Description and Diagnosis of Decision Making in Organizations." In *Decision-Making Research: Some Developments,* ed. D. Heradstreit and O. Narvesen. Oslo, Norway: Norsk Utenriks politisck Institute, 1977.

Chapter Three
Decision Support Systems and Personal Computing

PETER G. W. KEEN

RICHARD D. HACKATHORN

1.0 MOTIVATION FOR DECISION SUPPORT

Decision Support Systems (DSS) are interactive computer aids designed to assist managers in complex tasks requiring human judgment. The aim of such systems is to support and possibly to improve a decision process. *Personal Computing* (PC) is a more recent term that describes the direct use of small-scale systems by an individual for any information processing task. The user has complete control over all aspects of the technology: access, usage, program development, and data management.

This paper explores the relationship between DSS and PC. The aim is to clarify key issues relevant to helping managers make effective use of computer technology in their own jobs. The paper provides an overview of DSS and suggests a distinction between Personal Support and Organizational Support that in itself seems critical to effective application of the concept of Decision Support. The paper then discusses design and development of systems for personal support and concludes with an assessment of key research issues. The overall objective is: (1) to define where

Center for Information Systems Research Working Paper No. 47, Sloan School of Management, MIT, Cambridge, Mass., October 1979.

The authors wish to acknowledge the valuable discussions with faculty and students of the BA508A graduate seminar, "Personal Support Systems," during the spring of 1979 at The Wharton School, University of Pennsylvania, Philadelphia.

personal computing fits into decision support; and (2) to exploit the opportunities that personal computing provides.

1.1 Decision Support Systems

The DSS movement began about 10 years ago. It was largely stimulated by MIT's Project MAC, which both provided access to computing power for the individual user for the first time and pointed toward a human-machine symbiosis that promised vast increases in our ability to handle complex problems (Licklider, 1965). There have been several studies of DSS usage in organizations (Alter, 1980; Keen and Scott Morton, 1978). A coherent conceptual framework for Decision Support is emerging, and practitioners are extending the academic work of DSS by building innovative systems to support a range of managerial tasks.

Decision Support requires a detailed understanding of the manager's habits, needs, and concepts. Unlike OR/MS and much of traditional MIS, Decision Support is based on descriptive paradigms of decision making rather than prescriptive and rationalistic perspectives. A central theme in Decision Support is that one cannot improve something one does not understand. The act of "supporting" a manager implies a meshing of analytic tools into his or her existing activities.

The term *decision support systems* is partly a rallying cry. There is no formal theory of decision support as yet; theory largely emerges from practice in this applied field. Now that many systems have been built and a number of conceptual studies completed, we can begin to generalize from experience and thus adequately define the field. It is becoming apparent that the key word is "support" and that the term *decision* may be context-free, misleading, or even inaccurate.

Most of the conceptual literature on DSS has emphasized the individual manager. Its theoretical base comes from cognitive psychology; the focus is on human problem solving, rather than organizational decision making. It is clear, however, that practitioners are far more concerned with organizational issues. The systems that they need are built around activities that involve planning and coordination. While the priesthood of the DSS faith prescribes a system to support a manager's budget *decision*, the lay missionaries build a system to support the organization's budget *process*.

1.2 Personal Computing

The term *personal computing* is also a new rallying cry. Born out of the hectic enthusiasm of computer hobbyists, the PC area has emerged from minor applications of microprocessors to having broad impacts on many segments of society (Isaacson et al., 1978). Admittedly pushed along by new technology, PC is taking on more substantive meaning and brings new insights to the fundamental issue of linking computing technology and the individual. Hackathorn (1978) defines personal computing as an information-processing activity in which the end user has direct personal control over all stages of the activity. This definition implies a personal relationship to the technology that complements the Personal Support side of DSS. PC shares many of the same aims as DSS, while emphasizing small-scale technology and localized systems. The experience and ambitions of those who march under the PC banner have much to offer true believers in DSS. The hardware and software tools developed by PC can similarly extend the applications of DSS, and decision support provides an experience base and design criteria for PC.

1.3 Conclusions from Previous Research

The personal computing field is very new and lacks research to build upon (Niles, 1978). However, there have been several detailed descriptions of DSS usage, and sufficient experience has been gained to permit at least the following conclusions:

1. "Easy" applications of DSS (i.e., ones in which the likelihood of success is high) are those which involve such functional areas as finance, where it is simple to find aspects of the problem-solving process that can be better handled by the machine than by the manager. In general, it is most practicable to build a DSS around a micro decision (e.g., the selection of a product price or setting an advertising budget) or convenient retrieval of data (e.g., an automated file drawer).
2. "Hard" applications by contrast are those where there are many interdependencies, as in strategic planning, and where a manager's problem solving or decision is only part of a more complex process. Macro decisions, such as

FIGURE 1   DSS Structure

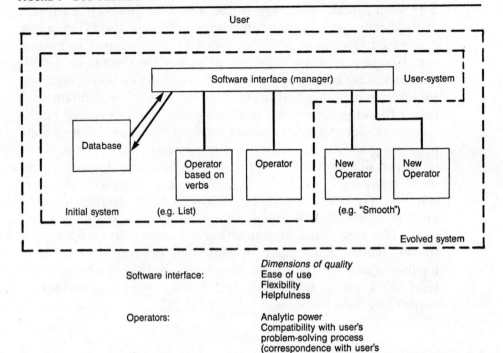

Software interface:
Operators:

Dimensions of quality
Ease of use
Flexibility
Helpfulness

Analytic power
Compatibility with user's
problem-solving process
(correspondence with user's
verbs)

creating a divisional plan with interdepartmental activities and multicriteria problems, pose substantial difficulties in implementation. It should be noted that easy applications generally involve Personal Support and the hard ones involve Organizational Support. Practitioners want to tackle the hard problems and may not gain much insight from experience with PS.

3. DSS evolve. The final system is very different from the original one. New tools shape new uses, and vice versa. Managers learn from a DSS and often evolve imaginative new applications. This means that the initial design is partly an experiment; a good DSS contains mechanisms for its own obsolescence (or evolution, depending on one's perspective).

4. The evolutionary nature of DSS has led to a design strategy that emphasizes getting started through a flexible system that can be easily and quickly changed and extended. A common structure has emerged: a DSS consists of a

software interface that manages the User–System dialog and a set of modular routines that correspond to verbs or operators (e.g., "DISPLAY," "COMPARE," "EXTRAPO-LATE," "FIND," or "SMOOTH"). Evolving a DSS largely means adding new operators, as shown in Figure 1.

5. DSS are hard to evaluate since they provide mainly quali-tative benefits and take a long time to institutionalize. Fur-thermore, 'improved' decision making is not necessarily the same as better decision outcomes. A DSS can not be sim-ply plugged into the organization but requires a complex process of adjustment and adaptation.

6. Support involves a very detailed understanding of the de-cision process, task, user, and organizational setting in which the system is to be embedded.

It seems clear that a standardized design structure has emerged from independent efforts to build DSS and that it is the notion of support and its corollaries—evolution and learning—that makes a DSS different from interactive models or on-line information systems.

2.0 DEFINITION OF SUPPORT SYSTEMS

One major problem in defining Support Systems is that this area has been principally characterized by computer technology; how-ever, the concept of decision support does not necessarily imply a computer-based system. It may be more meaningful to empha-size decision support, and then to evade the issue by stating that a DSS should be based on any available and suitable technology. Decision support involves finding criteria for defining "suitable." On the other hand, "available" technology has meant time-shar-ing or minicomputers until recently. The technology is now changing very rapidly to include computer networks and micro-computers. The basic objective of applying the technology to support decision processes remains the same.

2.1 Utilizing Computer Technology

The concept of support has been contrasted with that of "re-placement" in the DSS literature (Keen and Scott Morton, 1978). Models, graphics, analytic techniques, software, and hardware are all potential tools that need to be matched to their context. Simply building a system in no way guarantees its use. For the manager, there are ways of applying quantitative methods and computer technology:

1. Ignore them and do nothing. There have been so many examples of insensitive, unrealistic, and incorrect application of technology to management tasks that it is arguable that in many situations the managers' own experience and judgment is preferable and more effective than any computer system (Hoos, 1972).
2. Replace decision making. This is the traditional aim of Operations Research, Management Science, and data processing. The technology is used to rationalize, automate, and establish rules and procedures for particular tasks. Thus, a credit-scoring model can replace the loan officer's analysis and judgment (although usually the officer can override the model).
3. Support the decision process. This clearly falls between the extremes of doing nothing and replacing human involvement. Support means augmentation of existing processes, improvement, education, and provision of ad hoc tools that can be integrated into problem solving, communication, and analysis.

A key difference between replacement and support, that in itself implies a different design approach, is that the former aims at solving a problem or getting an answer while the latter focuses on helping a person. For replacement the area of emphasis is the task or decision itself. A complete system is needed that allows the whole task to be performed through the system. There can be no concept of learning and adaptation, since the design is centered around the task structure. By contrast, support suggests ongoing development so that the main aim is to begin and facilitate the process of augmentation and improvement.

The "best" system for replacement is one that improves efficiency and/or generates a better solution. For support, a "good" system improves procedures and processes. It may be hard to link these to outcomes and to "hard" benefits. Because of this, there can rarely be a reliable prediction of system uses and hence of costs and benefits. Obviously, a proposal to support a task must be justified in much the same way as one to replace decision making. But, in this situation, the estimates of costs and benefits and outlines for design are essentially a research and development activity. It is foolish to plan this activity as if it were a predictable and final venture. Instead, one uses a phased strategy and assumes that some preliminary experiment is needed that can be carefully evaluated and that provides direct guidelines for further development. In general, this initial phase will be small-scale and based on prototypes. The replacement strategy is one of creating products; these may be complex and innovative but are not exploratory and evolutionary. The R&D nature of decision support implies distinctive techniques for system building:

1. The main problem is to get started, to build a complete "first" system that can then evolve.
2. There must be continual learning, in a literal sense. For Personal Support (PS) the area of study is the users' problem-solving processes; for Organizational Support (OS), information flows and needs for coordination.

2.2 Levels of Support Systems

A frequently cited framework for discussing DSS has been Gorry and Scott Morton's (1971), which combines Simon's dichotomy of task structuredness (i.e., structured versus unstructured) with Anthony's classification of managerial activities (i.e., operational control, management control, and strategic planning). This framework seems to apply equally well to both extremes of PS and OS. The main proposal of this paper is that a third dimension—task interdependency—should be added, as shown in Figure 2.

The most obvious characteristic of situations in which DSS has been successfully implemented to assist managers (i.e., the "easy" applications discussed in Section 1.3) is that the user can make a complete decision with the aid of the system. There are no interdependencies with other actors or units. By contrast, several DSS recently developed to support planning activities in large organizations involve tasks that are highly dependent on other organizational units. This type of interdependency is called "sequential" by Thompson (1967) and involves a sequence of decisions, each of which cannot be carried out until the preceding one passes on some output. Between sequential and independent lies "pooled" interdependency, which is more complex and fluid. Activity A

FIGURE 2

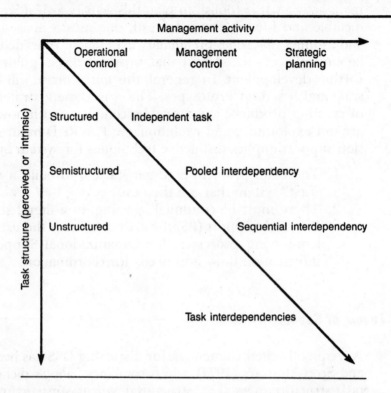

requires inputs from Activity B but also passes data back to A. A process with pooled dependency is highly interactive among the activities.

Examples of sequential, pooled, and independent tasks in relation to the Anthony framework are shown in Figure 3.

Where the task does not involve any interdependencies, the manager can reach a decision through his or her own private analysis, though when the choice has been made, it must obviously be communicated to others. The point is that the problem-solving activities do not involve interdependencies. In this situation, Personal Support may be of great value and the quality of the decision improved by the provision of a system designed for direct and individual use by the manager.

Where the task involves sequential interdependencies, each individual's activities must mesh closely with those of others. Any computer-based aid will be as much a vehicle for communication and coordination as for problem solving. For example, Organizational Support for budgeting will need to provide facilities for

FIGURE 3 Expanded Gorry–Scott Morton Framework

		Independent	Pooled	Sequential
Operational Control	*Structured*	Order filling	Scheduling room assignments	Order entry
	Unstructured	Notice writing	Scheduling management meetings	Shipping and receiving
Management Control	*Structured*	Task scheduling	Task assignment	Project costing
	Unstructured	Promotion decision	Personnel matters	Budget formulation
Strategic Planning	*Structured*	Office arrangement	Factory location	Factory building
	Unstructured	Time scheduling	Top management hiring	Merger

storing disaggregated, detailed budgets at the department level, and allow these to be integrated first by division and then for the company as a whole.

Pooled interdependency requires face-to-face negotiations and discussions. No single unit can carry out its work without interaction with others. This suggests an additional type of support—Group Support (GS). This allows users to develop joint plans through a system that provides fast response and that is designed to permit easy exploration of alternatives and explanation of analysis.

The three types of support—Personal (PS), Group (GS), and Organizational (OS)—all share a common aim. However, it is essential to distinguish among these types of support as distinct, but related, components of a support system:

1. PS focuses on a user or class of users in a discrete task or decision (e.g., setting a price, selecting a stock) that is relatively independent of other tasks.
2. GS focuses on a group of individuals, each of whom are engaged in separate, but highly interrelated tasks (e.g., office activities).
3. OS focuses on an organizational task or activity involving a sequence of operations and actors (e.g., building a divisional marketing plan, capital budgeting).

A PS system may be used within an OS system. For example, each manager may use a small-scale system to help set his own marketing budget, and the divisional staff then coordinates and integrates these budgets using an OS system. In both cases the aim of the system is to support the user's decision making; the key difference is that PS focuses on a person, while OS is on an organizational process.

While the conceptual literature on DSS emphasizes personal support, several of the most successful applications of decision support involve group support and, more recently, organizational support. For example, the DSS built by Scott Morton (1971) which facilitated marketing and production planning provides group support. It allowed managers from two departments to come together and use the system as a means of making trade-offs, sharing ideas, and reaching a consensus.

There are at least a few DSS, designed for Personal Support, that have been difficult to institutionalize because the broader task really involved sequential interdependency. For example, BRANDAID is a system that in one company substantially facilitated the development of marketing plans by individual brand managers (Keen and Scott Morton, 1978). Their plans were integrated at the next level of the organization. This required a very different process of analysis. In particular, the problem of "cannibalization" (i.e., the plan for an individual brand might result in sales being gained at the expense of another of the company's products) had to be addressed. In addition, the managers responsible for integrating the plans required brand decisions to be presented in a format that was not directly compatible with the outputs from BRANDAID. This whole process needed organizational support in addition to or in place of this personal support.

This concept of levels of support seems important not only

in relation to DSS. For instance, Office Automation (OA) is a packaging of some differentiated technical building blocks very much like DSS. The conceptual literature on OA emphasizes personal support, such as text editing, document preparation, and electronic mail. These are tools that assist and appeal to professional "knowledge workers." Practitioners are far more concerned with Organizational Support. They wish to use OA to streamline order entry operations, coordinate decentralized activities, and improve the efficiency of large-scale administrative functions. The literature on OA does not seem to acknowledge the differences in priority and focus; hence, differences in the design criteria for personal and organizational support are also not acknowledged.

3.0 FOCUS ON PERSONAL SUPPORT

The discussion above provides a more differentiated definition of support systems and clarifies where Personal Computing and DSS can be meshed. The rest of this paper focuses on Personal Support, which has been only dealt with peripherally in the DSS literature. The empirical studies published so far provide very little insight into PS. Of the six systems described by Keen and Scott Morton (1978), only one, PROJECTOR, was really used for Personal Support. On the whole, only large organizations have been able and willing to undertake the risky effort of implementing experimental systems. In addition, the emergence of small-scale microcomputers, which has created the personal computing field, is very recent. We now have a technology for PS but need to shape the concepts necessary for building personal support systems. Decision Support provides some guidelines but few examples.

3.1 Components of a System for Personal Support

A system for Personal Support can be viewed as analogous to a staff assistant to whom a manager issues commands—"Do this!" (Keen, 1976). A major research issue is how to identify the user's verbs and build an interface that provides the same quality, flexibility, and ease of communication expected with a staff assistant. For OS, the research questions are more complex, and there has been less empirical or conceptual work to build upon. How can a range of users be supported? Should the interface be more structured and standardized? How can a DSS be meshed into the organizational context of communications, control systems, and demand for coordination?

From the perspective of a staff assistant, the components for Personal Support divide into three main parts:

1. The interface: Is the manager able to talk with the PS system as with a staff assistant? How much does he or she have to learn to structure the dialogue?

2. The operators: Do they correspond to the manager's command: "Do this!"? Obviously, the comparison is not a literal one, but it provides some useful criteria for design. For example, if the interface does not facilitate a simple dialogue in which the PS system can explain its responses if necessary (through a "help" command), or is not built around the manager's vocabulary, it cannot support him or her in the way an assistant does. Similarly, if the operator cannot be directly related to a verb, it is unlikely that it will be used since: (1) it cannot easily be integrated into the user's concepts and activities; and (2) it is not clear what it supports. For Organizational Support, the corresponding analogy is with a staff coordinator. In both cases, the distinguishing feature of the human is flexibility and adaptivity. The quality and usefulness of the support system similarly depends on these attributes.

3. The database: The database is equivalent to the assistant's file cabinet or a library. Clearly, the contents, indexing, and access method determine the range, flexibility, cost, and adaptability of uses.

3.2 Building, Using, and Evolving

Personal support implies no "final" or predefined system. Whereas one may be able to identify the necessary steps and modes of use for an organizational process (i.e., in building OS system), it seems clear that the necessary focus is on the person when developing a PS system. This implies the need to:

1. Design a dialogue first.
2. Provide a preliminary set of operators.
3. Permit the manager to learn from the system.
4. To evolve the PS system by extending its operators.

Learning and flexibility seem to be central aspects of support. They suggest a design sequence similar to Ness's definition of "middle-out." On the basis of observation of the uses and discussions which aim at identifying key verbs, the designer builds an interface, which is complete enough to permit a meaningful user–system dialogue but which will certainly need later alteration or extension. A preliminary set of operators is implemented. The user now has a concrete system with which to react, and the designer has a vehicle by which to verify his design.

The natural sequence of development of a system for PS is:

1. Using existing operators: The initial system is a complete one, not a prototype. The operators reflect the verbs that the user relied on prior to the development of the PS system or ones that are easy to use but that also provide new capabilities.

2. Constructing sequences of operators: If the tool is of any value, it is likely the user will soon develop sequences of analysis, will in effect build up higher-level routines (e.g., in analyzing a customer account: first use "STATUS", then "REPORT", "PROFIT"; or when reviewing monthly results: use "TREND", "SUMMARIZE", "PLOT"). These sequences will tend to be user-specific.

3. Developing new operators: A key assumption here is that as the user gains experience and confidence in the system, he or she will be ready for (or even specify) new operators. Learning leads to new verbs.

4. Changing existing operators: Fine-tuning a PS system may mean modifying operators, or occur as a result of the user's learning (e.g., adverbs qualify a verb and introduce differentiated subfunctions within existing operators).

5. Adding data about objects: In general, items in the database are nouns. The phrase "graph profits versus sales expenses" translates into an operator "GRAPH" with the two nouns "PROFIT" and "SALES EXPENSES" being its arguments.

6. Changing data structures relating to objects: The database is a retrievable set of objects which may need a particular organization or set of definitions for the interface to identify them and associate them with the operators that act on them.

These six aspects of use and evolution provide a link between the behavioral concept of support and the technical realization of that concept—a support system. Support begins by identifying verbs and nouns. Learning, and hence the evolution of the support system, similarly involves new verbs. An operator must be defined in terms of a verb and vice versa for the system to evolve.

It needs to be acknowledged that the first four items on the above list are easy to handle with existing software. An interface can be redesigned without affecting the operators; the system seems entirely different to the user even though it performs the same functions. Operators can be added and altered, especially if a flexible development language, like APL, is used. However, it is far more difficult to manage and change data structures. There is little discussion in the DSS literature on database design and the tools for data storage in PC are at present very limited.

3.3 The Dynamics of Interaction

The discussion above implies both interactive use of a PS system and interactive development. The design process relies on evolution. Clearly, the key first step is to identify "good" verbs. Berry (1977), whose discussion of "levels of language" in the use of APL parallels that in Section 3.2 above, gives the example of an economist whose job involves forecasting commodity prices. His explanation of his work is elaborate, and he stresses its complexity, and difficulty. Berry points out that carefully listening reduces the task to "smooth prices," which requires an APL function for exponential smoothing.

Some verbs are obvious; most PS systems will require retrieval and display routines such as "PLOT", "LIST", "FIND", or "TABLE". In some cases the verb reflects a complex analytic routine, such as "PROJECT". This routine invokes a dynamic programming model that involves complex assumptions and techniques. The key point made here is the direct relationships between managerial learning and extension of the PS system, and between evolutionary use and evolutionary design. Obviously, the interface must be built so that new operators can be added easily and quickly.

A central difference between traditional approaches to the design of computer tools and those needed for support systems is that the former assume completeness of specification and a "final" system. For PS, the issue is getting started, building a system that the user can relate to and that can encourage learning and evolution. The most effective approach for this seems to be to put most effort into the development of a "humanized" interface and a few key operators.

4.0 RESEARCH ISSUES RELATED TO PERSONAL SUPPORT

One test of the validity of the PS framework is whether a set of research issues can be formulated that will produce a deeper understanding of the issues. The research issues will be presented in two categories: (1) those issues that we need to know about before proceeding further with PS; and (2) gaps that become apparent in existing DSS research when viewed from a PS perspective.

4.1 Identifying Important Verbs

For PS we need to know a great deal about the user and must develop effective methodologies for studying decision processes (Stabell terms this "decision research"). In particular, designers must be able to identify important verbs and define criteria for designing the software interface. In both cases the outputs from the process must be couched in a form that allows direct translation into software (and occasionally hardware) design (Berry, 1977; Contreras, 1978). Some key research questions in this respect are:

1. How many important verbs do most decision makers use? Clearly, if the average is five it will be far easier to get started with a PS system than if it is 20 or 200.
2. What verbs do decision makers in different tasks have in common? Does there exist a set of primitive verbs that can form the initial personal support and be evolved into a useful support system for a manager? It seems likely that there are some general verbs used for search and display of data ("FIND", "PLOT", "LIST", etc.).
3. What is a "good interface"? What are the users' measures of usability and quality? (Sterling, 1975; Little, 1975) At present "humanizing" or "customizing" the interface is a haphazard task with few validated rules.

These questions all focus on better ways of applying existing skills and technology for PS system development. They are primarily empirical in nature. There are other more elusive conceptual issues to be resolved. Most obviously, if the distinction between PS and OS is valid, we need to revise the existing loose definitions of Decision Support. The cognitive focus of most DSS research (Keen and Scott Morton, 1978; Stabell, 1974) seems fully applicable for PS, but there is relatively little work relevant to OS. The propositions of Galbraith (1973; 1977) about organizational information processing seem of practical value here.

4.2 Lack of Good Research Methodology

Many of the gaps in our current knowledge are methodological and empirical. There is a complete absence of comparative research and effective use of case studies to validate or illustrate key concepts. Keen and Scott Morton (1978) provide some detailed descriptions of DSS. These suffer, however, from the lack of distinction between PS and OS; several of the systems are discussed as PS system but are clearly OS systems (especially the Portfolio Management System which is the main example in the book). One conclusion to be drawn from the arguments presented here is that we need more descriptions of DSS usage; if the issue is getting started and then evolving the system, we must get a detailed understanding of how managers learn the general patterns of evolution. One key question is the extent and speed of change:

1. Do managers tend to rely on operators that support their existing verbs and not accept ones that require new concepts and modes of analysis?
2. What type of operators—data-based, model-based, heuristic, analytic, conceptual, etc.—seem most beneficial or acceptable to the user? Are they based on individual differences, cognitive style, etc.?

Many of the questions above involve measurement. The tools for studying decision processes are primitive, at best. Protocol analysis, structured interviews, and questionnaires are the most widely used (and least validated) approaches. The problem is probably more complex for PS than OS. Organizational flows can be reliably identified (Hackathorn, 1977a), but cognitive processes are elliptic and often not observable. Stabell's argument, that the key issue for Decision Support is the development of methodologies for studying individual decision processes, seems of central relevance for PS. Regardless of available technologies, this rests on a comprehensive understanding of the individual user.

5.0 CONCLUSIONS

Most applications of Personal Computing have been simply extensions of programmable calculators, video games, and simple data retrieval. The PC journals provide few examples of practical uses that go much beyond checkbook balancing. At the same time the microprocessor-based hardware underlying PC has pushed toward small business systems with canned software packages for the typical clerical functions. The scope and direction of these developments have been determined largely by "technology push," rather than being pulled by the information processing needs of individuals.

PC requires a conceptual base for exploiting the potential of small-scale computer technology. Our argument here is that Personal Support provides such a framework. By definition, it involves discrete tasks that do not require complex linkages with other systems and procedures. The aim of PC is essentially that of Decision Support: to provide individuals with tools under their own control so that they can adopt and adapt them to become extensions of their own problem-solving processes.

Current concepts of PC focus very narrowly on the technology. As with Decision Support, the technology should be seen only as a means to an end. Unless PC defines that end, it has no systematic base for identifying applications and developing design strategies. The meshing of PS and PC constitutes that base. It seems clear that the technology of PC, software as much as hardware, can be used to provide cheap personal tools for managers. The cost factor is important mainly in reducing risk. That is, it is far easier to justify a Personal Support System whose initial hardware costs under $1,000 than one involving a larger investment and relatively high usage cost. Since PC relies on evolving larger systems from small prototypes, the tools of PC seem highly suited to the R&D process of building the initial version that is tailored to the needs and decision processes of a particular individual.

Personal Computing extends Decision Support. The challenge now is to carry out the decision research that can clarify where to apply the new technology. Just as Decision Support has moved from a somewhat vague rallying cry to an emergent discipline for research and practice, so too can Personal Computing build its distinctive technical base and provide decision makers with effective tools that they now lack.

REFERENCES

Alter, S. L. "A Study of Computer-Aided Decision Making in Organizations." Ph.D. dissertation, Sloan School of Management, MIT., Cambridge, Mass., 1975.

————. "How Effective Managers Use Information Systems." *Harvard Business Review*, 1976.

————. *Decision Support Systems: Current Practices and Future Challenges.* Reading, Mass.: Addison-Wesley, 1980.

Berry, P. "The Democratization of Computing." Paper presented at II Symposium Nacional de Systemas Computacionales, Monterrey, Mexico, March 15–18, 1977.

Carlisle, J. "Cognitive Factors in Interactive Decision Systems." Ph.D. dissertation, Yale University, New Haven, Conn., 1974.

Carlson, E. D., ed. "Proceedings of a Conference on Decision Support Systems." *Database* 8, no. 3 (Winter 1977).

Contreras, L. E. "Decision Support Systems and Corporate Planning." Private communication, 1978.

Galbraith, J. R. *Designing Complex Organizations.* Reading, Mass.: Addison-Wesley, 1973.

————. *Organizational Design,* Reading, Mass.: Addison-Wesley, 1977.

Gerrity, T. P. "The Design of Man-Machine Decision Systems: An Application to Portfolio Management." *Sloan Management Review* 12, no. 2 (Winter 1971), pp. 59–75.

Gorry, G. A., and M. S. Scott Morton. "A Framework for Management Information Systems." *Sloan Management Review* 13, no. 1 (Fall 1971), pp. 55–77.

Hackathorn, R. D. "Design Criteria for Decision Support Systems." Proceedings of the 9th Annual Conference on the American Institute of Decision Science, Chicago, October 1977 (b), pp. 150–52.

————. "Modeling Unstructured Decision Making." Proceedings of a Conference on Decision Support Systems. *Database* 8, no. 3 (Winter 1977 (a), pp. 41–42.

————. "Research Issues in Personal Computing." Proceedings of the National ACM Conference, Washington, D.C., December 1978, pp. 547–51.

Hoos, I. R. *Systems Analysis in Public Policy.* Berkeley: University of California Press, 1972.

Isaacson, P., et al. "The Oregon Report: Personal Computing." *IEEE Computer* 11, no. 9 (September 1978), pp. 86–97.

Keen, P. G. W. "Computer Systems for Top Managers: A Modest Proposal." *Sloan Management Review* 18, no. 1 (1976), pp. 1–17.

————. "The Intelligence Cycle: A Differentiated Perspective on Infomation Processing." In *American Federation of Information Processing Societies Proceedings, 1977 National Computer Conference* 46 (1977), pp. 317–20.

————. "Information Access for the Policy Analyst: A Portable Technology." Presented to the American Educational Finance Association, January 1979.

————. "Decision Support Systems and the Marginal Economics of Effort." Working Paper No. 79-03-16, Department of Decision Sciences, The Wharton School, University of Pennsylvania, Philadelphia, 1979.

Keen, P. G. W., and E. M. Gerson. "The Politics of Software Engineering." *Datamation,* November 1977, pp. 80–86.

Keen, P. G. W., and R. D. Hackathorn. "Studies of Decision Support Systems: A Review and Critique." Working Paper No. 79-03-17, Department of Decision Sciences, The Wharton School, University of Pennsylvania, Philadelphia, 1979.

Keen, P. G. W., and Scott Morton, M. S. *Decision Support Systems: An Organizational Perspective.* Reading, Mass.: Addison-Wesley, 1978.

Kling, R. "The Organizational Context of User-Centered Computer Program Designs." Working paper, Department of Information and Computer Science, University of California, Irvine.

Licklider, J. C. R. *Libraries of the Future,* Cambridge, Mass.: MIT Press,1965.

Little, J. D. C. "Brandaid." *Operations Research* 23, no. 4 (May 1975), pp. 628–73.

Ness, D. N. "Decision Support Systems: Theories of Design," Paper presented at Office of Naval Research Conference on Decision Support Systems, University of Pennsylvania, Philadelphia, November 4–7, 1975.

Ness, D. N., and G. E. Hurst. "Type P and Type S Systems." Working Paper No. 78-03-01, Department of Decision Sciences, The Wharton School, University of Pennsylvania, Philadelphia, 1978.

Niles, J. M.; P. Gray; F. R. Carlson; and J. Hayes. "The Personal Computer and Society: A Technology Assessment." Presented at the National Computer Conference, Anaheim, Calif., June 1978.

Scott Morton, M. S. *Management Decision Systems: Computer-Based Support for Decision Making.* Cambridge, Mass.: Division of Research, Harvard Business School, 1971.

Stabell, C. B. "On the Development of the Decision Support Systems as a Marketing Problem." Paper presented at the International Federation for Information Processing Congress, Stockholm, Sweden, August 1974.

————. "Decision Research: Description and Diagnosis of Decision Making in Organizations." In *Decision-Making Research: Some Developments*, eds. D. Heradstreit and O. Narvesen. Oslo, Norway: Norsk Utenriks politisck Institute, 1977.

Sterling, T. D. "Humanizing Computerized Information Systems." *Science* 190, (December 19, 1975), pp. 1168–72.

Thompson, J. D. *Organizations in Action.* New York: McGraw-Hill, 1967.

Chapter Four
Value Analysis: Justifying Decision Support Systems

PETER G. W. KEEN

INTRODUCTION

Decision Support Systems (DSS) are designed to help improve the effectiveness and productivity of managers and professionals. They are interactive systems frequently used by individuals with little experience in computers and analytic methods. They support, rather than replace, judgment in that they do not automate the decision process nor impose a sequence of analysis on the user. A DSS is in effect a staff assistant to whom the manager delegates activities involving retrieval, computation, and reporting. The manager evaluates the results and selects the next step in the process. Table 1 lists typical DSS applications.[1]

Traditional cost/benefit analysis is not well suited to DSS. The benefits they provide are often qualitative; examples cited by users of DSS include the ability to examine more alternatives, stimulation of new ideas, and improved communication of analysis. It is extraordinarily difficult to place a value on these. In addition, most DSS evolve. There is no "final" system; an initial version is built and new facilities are added in response to the users' ex-

Reprinted by special permission of the *MIS Quarterly* 5, no. 1, 1981. Copyright 1981 by the Society for Information Management and the Management Information Systems Research Center

TABLE 1   Examples of DSS Applications

DSS	Applications	Benefits
GADS Geodata Analysis Display System	Geographical resource allocation and analysis; applications include sales force territories, police beat redesign, designating school boundaries	Ability to look at more alternatives, improved teamwork, can use the screen to get ideas across, improved confidence in the decision
PMS Portfolio Management System	Portfolio investment management	Better customer relations, ability to convey logic of a decision, value of graphics for identifying problem areas
IRIS Industrial Relations Information System	*Ad hoc* access to employee data for analysis of productivity and resource allocation	*Ad hoc* analysis, better use of "neglected and wasted" existing data resource, ability to handle unexpected short-term problems
PROJECTOR	Strategic financial planning	Insight into the dynamics of the business, broader understanding of key variables
IFPS Interactive Financial Planning System	Financial modeling, including mergers and acquisitions, new-product analysis, facilities planning, and pricing analysis	Better and faster decisions, saving analysts' time, better understanding of business factors, leveraging managing skills
ISSPA - Interactive Support System for Policy Analysts	Policy analysis in state government; simulations, reporting, and *ad hoc* modeling	*Ad hoc* analysis, broader scope, communication to/with legislators, fast reaction to new situations
BRANDAID	Marketing planning, setting prices, and budgets for advertising, sales force, promotion, *etc.*	Answering "What if?" questions, fine-tuning plans, problem finding
IMS Interactive Marketing System	Media analysis of large consumer data base, plan strategies for advertising	Helps build and explain to clients the rationale for media campaigns, *ad hoc* and easy access to information

perience and learning. Because of this, the costs of the DSS are not easy to identify.

The decision to build a DSS seems to be based on value, rather than cost. The system represents an investment for future effectiveness. A useful analogue is management education. A company will sponsor a five-day course on strategic planning, organizational development, or management control systems on the basis of perceived need or long-term value. There is no attempt to look at payback period or ROI, nor does management expect a direct improvement in earnings per share.

This article examines how DSS are justified and recommends Value Analysis (VA), an overall methodology for planning and evaluating DSS proposals. The next section illustrates applications of DSS. Key points are:

1. A reliance on prototypes.
2. The absence of cost/benefit analysis.
3. The evolutionary nature of DSS development.
4. The nature of the perceived benefits.

The section on the Dynamics of Innovation relates DSS to other types of innovation. It seems clear that innovation in general is driven by "demand–pull"—response to visible, concrete needs"—and not "technology push."

The Methodologies for Evaluating Proposals section briefly examines alternative approaches to evaluation: cost/benefit analysis, scoring techniques, and feasibility studies. They all require fairly precise estimates of, and tradeoffs between costs and benefits and often do not handle the qualitative issues central to DSS development and innovation in general. The final part of the article defines Value Analysis.

The overall issue this article addresses is a managerial one:

1. What does one need to know to decide if it is worthwhile to build a DSS?
2. How can an executive encourage innovation while making sure money is well spent?
3. How can one put some sort of figure on the value of effectiveness, learning, or creativity?

It would be foolish to sell a strategic planning course for executives on the basis of cost displacement and ROI. Similarly, any effort to exploit the substantial opportunity DSS provide to help managers do a better job must be couched in terms meaningful to them. This requires a focus on value and a recognition that qualitative benefits are of central relevance. At the same time, systematic assessment is essential. The initial expense of a DSS may be only in the $10,000 range, but this still represents a significant commitment of funds and scarce programming resources. The methodology proposed here is based on a detailed analysis of the implementation of over 20 DSS. It is consistent with the less formal approaches most managers seem to use in assessing technical innovations. Value analysis involves a two-stage process:

1. Version 0: This is an initial, small-scale system which is complete in itself, but may include limited functional capability. The decision to build Version 0 is based on:
   a. An assessment of benefits, not necessarily quantified.
   b. A cost threshold—is it worth risking this amount of money to get these benefits?

   In general, only a few benefits will be assessed. The cost threshold must be kept low, so that this decision can be viewed as a low-risk R&D venture, and not a capital investment.

2. Base System: This is the full system, which will be assessed if the trial Version 0 has successfully established the value of the proposed concept. The decision to develop it is based on:
   a. Cost analysis: What are the costs of building this larger system?
   b. Value threshold: What level of benefits is needed to justify the cost? What is the likelihood of this level being attained?

A major practical advantage of this two-stage strategy is that it reduces the risks involved in development. More importantly, it simplifies the tradeoff between costs and benefits, without making the analysis simplistic. It is also a more natural approach than traditional cost/benefit analysis; until value is established, *any* cost is disproportionate.

DECISION SUPPORT SYSTEMS

The DSS applications shown in Table 1 cover a range of functional areas and types of task. They have many features in common:

1. They are *nonroutine* and involve frequent ad hoc analysis, fast access to data, and generation of nonstandard reports.
2. They often address "what if?" questions; for example, "What if the interest rate is X percent?" or "What if sales are 10 percent below the forecast?"
3. They have no obvious correct answers; the manager has to make qualitative trade-offs and take into account situational factors.

The following examples illustrate the above points:

1. GADS. In designing school boundaries, parents and school officials worked together to resolve a highly charged political problem. A proposal might be rejected because it meant closing a particular school, having children cross a busy highway, or breaking up neighborhood groups. In a previous effort involving redistricting, only one solution has been generated, as opposed to six with GADS over a four-day period. The interactive problem solving brought out a large number of previously unrecognized constraints such as transportation patterns and walking times, and parent's feelings.
2. BRANDAID. A brand manager heard a rumor that his advertising budget would be cut in half. By 5:00 P.M. he had a complete analysis of what he felt the effect would be on this year's and next year's sales.
3. IFPS. A model had been built to assess a potential aquisition. A decision was needed by 9:00 A.M. The results of the model suggested the acquisition be made. The senior executive involved felt uneasy. Within one hour, the model had been modified and "what if" issues assessed that led to rejection of the proposal.
4. ISSPA AND IRIS. Data which had always been available, but not accessible, were used to answer ad hoc, simple questions. Previously, no one bothered to ask them.

These characteristics of problems for which DSS are best suited impose design criteria. The system must be:

1. *Flexible* to handle varied situations.
2. *Easy to use* so it can be meshed into the manager's decision process simply and quickly.
3. *Responsive* because it must not impose a structure on the user and must give speedy service.

4. *Communicative* because the quality of the user-DSS dialogue and of the system outputs are key determinants of effective uses, especially in tasks involving communication or negotiation. Managers will use computer systems that mesh with their natural mode of operation. The analogy of the DSS as a staff assistant is a useful one.

Many DSS rely on prototypes. Since the task the system supports is by definition nonroutine, it is hard for the user to articulate the criteria for the DSS and for the designer to build functional specifications. An increasingly popular strategy is thus to use a flexible DSS "tool" such as APL, or a DSS "Generator" (15). These allow an initial version of a "Specific DSS" to be delivered quickly and cheaply. It provides a concrete example that the user can react to and learn from. It can be easily expanded or modified. The initial system, Version 0, clarifies the design criteria and specifications for the full DSS. Examples of this two-phase strategy include:

1. ISSPA—built in APL. Version 0 took 70 hours to build and contained 19 commands. The design process began by sketching out the user-system dialogue. New user commands were added as APL functions. Ten of the 48 commands were requested by users, and several of the most complex ones were entirely defined by users.

2. AAIMS—an APL-based "personal information system" for analysis of 150,000 time series. The development was not based on a survey or user requirements, nor on any formal plan. New routines are tested and "proven" by a small user group.

3. IRIS—a prototype was built in five months and evolved over a one-year period. An "executive language" interface was defined as the base for the DSS and a philosophy was adopted of "build and evaluate as you go."

4. CAUSE—There were four evolutionary versions. A phased development was used to build credibility. The number of routines was expanded from 26 to 200.

There have been several detailed studies of the time and the cost needed to build a DSS in APL. A usable prototype takes about 3 weeks to deliver. A full system requires another 12 to 16 weeks.[2]

End user languages similarly allow fast development. One such DSS "generator" is Execucom's IFPS (Interactive Financial Planning System), a simple, English-like language for building stra-

TABLE 2 IFPS Development Process

	Data Processing	Staff Analyst	Middle Management	Top Management
Who requested the application	0	4	30	66
Who built it	3	53	22	22
Who uses the terminal	0	70	21	9
Who uses the output	0	6	42	52

tegic planning models. The discussion below is based on a survey of 300 IFPS applications in 42 companies.[3] The models included long-range planning, budgeting, project analysis, evolution of mergers, and acquisitions.

The average IFPS model took five days to build and contained 360 lines (the median was 200). Documented specifications were developed for only 16 percent. In 66 percent of the cases, an analyst simply responded to a manager's request and got something up and running quickly. Cost benefit analysis was done for 13 percent, and only 30 percent have any objective evidence of "hard" benefits. 74 percent of the applications replace manual procedures. Given that most of the responding companies are in the Fortune 100, this indicates the limited degree to which managers in the planning functions make direct use of computers.

Most DSS are built outside data processing, generally by individuals who are knowledgeable about the application area. Table 2 gives figures on where requests for IFPS applications come from and how they are built.

The IFPS users were asked to identify the features of the language that contributed most to the success of the DSS. In order of importance, these are:

1. Speed of response.
2. Ease of use.
3. Package features (curve-fitting, risk analysis, what if?).
4. Sensitivity analysis.
5. Time savings.

The evolutionary nature of DSS development follows from the reliance on prototypes and fast development. There is no "fi-

TABLE 3 **Relative Use of DSS Operators (PMS)**

Operator	Percentage of Use by Each Manager						Percentage of Use by All Users
	A	B	C	D	E	F	
Table	22	22	38	22	76	57	47
Summary	40	10	30	8	0	38	17
Scan	0	26	5	24	0	0	4
Graph	14	4	13	30	5	0	8
Directory	2	0	0	0	1	4	1
Others	22	38	14	16	18	1	23

nal" system. In most instances, the system evolves in response to user learning. A major difficulty in designing DSS is that many of the most effective uses are unanticipated and even unpredictable. Examples are:

1. PMS—the intended use was to facilitate a portfolio-based, rather than a security-based, approach to investment. This did not occur, but the DSS was invaluable in communicating with customers.
2. GPLAN—the DSS forced the users (engineers) to change their roles from analysts to decision makers.
3. PROJECTOR—the intended use was to analyze financial data in order to answer preplanned questions and the actual use was as an educational vehicle to alert managers to new issues.

Usage is also very personalized, since the managers differ in their modes of analysis and the DSS is under their own control. For example, six users of PMS studied over a six-month period differed strongly in their choice of operators (see Table 3).[4]

The benefits of DSS vary; this is to be expected, given the complex situational nature of the tasks they support and their personalized uses. The following list shows those frequently cited in DSS case studies, together with representative examples.[5] (Table 4 summarizes the list.)

1. Increase in the Number of Alternatives Examined
   • Sensitivity analysis takes 10 percent of the time needed previously.
   • Eight detailed solutions generated versus one in previous study.

TABLE 4   DSS Benefits

	Easy to Measure?	Benefit Can Be Quantified in a "Bottom Line" Figure?
1. Increase in number of alternatives examined	Y	N
2. Better understanding of the business	N	N
3. Fast response to unexpected situations	Y	N
4. Ability to carry out ad hoc analysis	Y	N
5. New insights and learning	N	N
6. Improved communication	N	N
7. Control	N	N
8. Cost savings	Y	Y
9. Better decisions	N	N
10. More effective teamwork	N	N
11. Time savings	Y	Y
12. Making better use of data resource	Y	N

- Previously took weeks to evaluate a plan; now takes minutes; therefore much broader analysis.
- Users could imagine solutions and use DSS to test out hypotheses.
- "No one had bothered to try price/profit options before."

2. Better Understanding of the Business

- President made major changes in company's overall plan, after using DSS to analyze single acquisition proposal.
- DSS alerted managers that an apparently successful marketing venture would be in trouble in six month's time.
- DSS is used to train managers; gives them a clear overall picture.
- "Now able to see relationships among variables."

3. Fast Response to Unexpected Situations
   - A marketing manager faced with unexpected budget cut used the DSS to show that this would have a severe impact later.
   - Helped develop legal case to remove tariff on petroleum in New England states.
   - Model revised in 20 minutes, adding risk analysis; led to reversal of major decision made one hour earlier.

4. Ability to Carry Out Ad Hoc Analysis
   - 50 percent increase in planning group's throughput in three years.
   - The governor's bill was published at noon "and by 5 PM I had it fully costed out."
   - "I can now do QAD's—quick-and-dirties."
   - System successfully used to challenge legislator's statements within a few hours.

5. New Insights and Learning
   - Quickened management's awareness of branch bank problems.
   - Gives a much better sense of true costs.
   - Identified underutilized resources already at analysts' disposal.
   - Allows a more elegant breakdown of data into categories heretofore impractical.
   - Stimulated new approaches to evaluating investment proposals.

6. Improved Communication
   - Used in "switch presentations" by advertising agencies to reveal shortcomings in customer's present agency.
   - Can explain rationale for decision to investment clients.
   - Improved customer relations.
   - "Analysis was easier to understand and explain. Management had confidence in the results."
   - "It makes it a lot easier to sell (customers) on an idea."

7. Control
   - Permits better tracking of cases.
   - Plans are more consistent and management can spot discrepancies.
   - Can "get a fix on the overall expense picture."

- Standardized calculation procedures.
- Improved frequency and quality of annual account reviews.
- Better monitoring of trends in airline's fuel consumption.

8. Cost Savings
   - Reduced clerical work.
   - Eliminated overtime.
   - Stay of patients shortened.
   - Reduced turnover of underwriters.

9. Better Decisions
   - "He was forced to think about issues he would not have considered otherwise."
   - Analysis of personnel data allowed management to identify for the first time where productivity gains could be obtained by investing in office automation.
   - Increased depth and sophistication of analysis.
   - Analysts became decision makers instead of form preparers.

10. More Effective Teamwork
    - Allowed parents and school administrators to work together exploring ideas.
    - Reduced conflict—managers could quickly look at proposal without prior argument.

11. Time Savings
    - Planning cycle reduced from 6 man-days spread over 20 elapsed days to a half day spread over 2 days.
    - "Substantial reduction in manhours" for planning studies.
    - "[My] time-effectiveness improved by a factor of 20."

12. Make Better Use of Data Resource
    - Experimental engineers more ready to collect data since they knew it would be entered into a usable system.
    - "More cost-effective than any other system (we) implemented in capitalizing on the neglected and wasted resource of data."
    - Allows quick browsing.
    - "Puts a tremendous amount of data at manager's dis-

posal in form and combinations never before possible at this speed."

Table 4 adds up to a definition of managerial productivity. All the benefits are valuable but few of them are quantifiable in ROI or payback terms.

In few of the DSS case studies is there any evidence of formal cost/benefit analysis. In most instances, the system was built in response to a concern about timeliness or scope of analysis, the need to upgrade management skills, or the potential opportunity a computer data resource or modeling capability provides. Since there is little *a priori* definition of costs and benefits, there is little *a posteriori* assessment of gains. A number of DSS failed in their aims, but where they are successful, there is rarely any formal analysis of the returns. Many of the benefits are not proven. In managerial tasks there is rarely a clear link between decisions and outcomes, and a DSS can be expected to *contribute* to better financial performance, but not directly cause it. In general, managers describe a successful DSS as "indispensable" without trying to place an economic value on it.

THE DYNAMICS OF INNOVATION

DSS are a form of innovation. They represent:

1. A relatively new concept of the role of computers in the decision process.
2. An explicit effort to make computers helpful to managers who on the whole have not found them relevant to their own job, even if they are useful to the organization as a whole.
3. A decentralization of systems development and operation, and often a bypassing of the data processing department.
4. The use of computers for "value added" applications rather than cost displacement.

There is much literature on the dynamics of technical innovations in organizations.[6] Its conclusions are fairly uniform and heavily backed by empirical data. Surveys of the use of computer planning models support these conclusions. In nine cases studied[7] the decision to adopt planning models was based on:

1. Comparison with an ongoing system which involves examining either a manual or partially computerized system and deciding that some change is desirable.
2. Comparison with a related system, such as a successful planning model in another functional area.
3. Initiation of a low-cost project.
4. Comparison with competitors' behavior resulting in the use of a "reference model" which reduces the need to estimate the impact of a model not yet constructed on improved decisions and performance.

Even in traditional data processing applications, the emphasis on value rather than cost is common. A survey of all the proposals for new systems accepted for development in a large multinational company found that even though cost/benefit analysis was formally required, it was used infrequently.[8] The two main reasons for implementing systems were:

1. Mandated requirements, such as regulatory reports.
2. Identification of one or two benefits, rarely quantified.

Traditional cost/benefit analysis is effective for many computer-based systems. It seems clear, however, that it is not used in innovation. This may partly be because innovations involve R&D; they cannot be predefined and clear specifications provided. There is some evidence that there is a conflict in organizations between groups concerned with performance and those focused on cost. In several DSS case studies, the initiators of the system stress to their superiors that the project is an investment in R&D, not in a predefined product.

Surveys of product innovations consistently find that they come from customers and users rather than centralized technical or research staff. Well over three quarters of new products are initiated by someone with a clear problem looking for a solution.[9] Industrial salesmen play a key role as "gatekeepers" bringing these needs to the attention of technical specialists. Even in the microprocessor industry, the majority of products are stimulated in this way by "demand pull," not by "technology push."[10]

Case studies indicate that DSS development reflects the same dynamics of innovation as in other technical fields. Table 5 states the same dynamics of innovation as in other technical fields.

TABLE 5   Dynamics of DSS Innovation

Innovations are value-driven.	Main motivation for DSS is "better" planning, timely information, ad hoc capability, *etc.*
Early adopters differ from late adopters.	DSS are often initiated by line managers in their own budgets; once the system is proven other departments may pick it up.
Informal processes are central.	DSS development usually involves a small team; key role of intermediaries knowledgeable about the users and the technology for the DSS; data processing rarely involved; frequently DSS are "bootleg" projects.
Cost is a secondary issue.	Costs are rarely tracked in detail; DSS budget is often based on staff rather than dollars; little charge-out of systems (this may reflect item below).
Uncertainty reduced by "trialability," ease of understanding, clear performance value.	Use of prototypes; emphasis on ease of use.

METHODOLOGIES FOR EVALUATING PROPOSALS

There are three basic techniques used to evaluate proposals for computer systems in most organizations:

1. Cost/benefit analysis and related ROI approaches—this views the decision as a *capital investment.*
2. Scoring evaluation—this views it in terms of *weighted scores.*
3. Feasibility study—this views it as *engineering.*

Each of these is well suited to situations that involve hard costs and benefits, and that permit clear performance criteria. They do not seem to be useful—or at least used—for evaluating innovations or DSS.

Cost/benefit analysis is highly sensitive to assumptions such as discount rates and residual value. It needs artificial and often arbitrary modifications to handle qualitative factors such as the value of improved communication and improved job satisfaction. Managers seem to be more comfortable thinking in terms of perceived value and then asking if the cost is reasonable. For example, expensive investments on training are made with no effort at quantification. The major benefits of DSS listed in Table 4 are mainly qualitative and uncertain. It is difficult to see how cost/benefit analysis of them can be reliable and convincing in this context.

Scoring methods are a popular technique for evaluating large-scale technical projects, such as the choice of a telecommunications package, especially when there are multiple proposals with varying prices and capabilities. Scoring techniques focus on a list of desired performance characteristics. Weights are assigned to them and each alternative rated. For example:

Characteristic	Weight	Alternative	Weighted Score
Response time	.30	15	4.5
Ease of use	.20	20	4.0
User manual	.10	17	1.7

Composite scores may be generated in several ways: mean rating, pass–fail, or elimination of any alternative that does not meet a mandatory performance requirement. Cost is considered only after all alternatives are scored. There is no obvious way of deciding if alternative A, with a cost of $80,000 and a composite score of 67, is better than B, with a cost of $95,000 and a score of 79.

Feasibility studies involve an investment to identify likely costs and benefits. They tend to be expensive and to focus on defining specifications for a complete system. They rarely give much insight into *how* to build it, and assume that the details of the system can be laid out in advance. DSS prototypes are a form of feasibility study in themselves. They are a first cut at a system. Some designers of DSS point out that Version 0 can be literally thrown away. Its major value is to clarify design criteria and establish feasibility, usefulness, and usability. The differences between a prototype and a feasibility study are important:

1. The prototype moves the project forward, in that a basic system is available for use and the logic and structure of the DSS already implemented.
2. The prototype is often cheaper, if the application is suited to APL or an end user language.
3. The feasibility study is an abstraction and the prototype is concrete. Since DSS uses are often personalized and un-

anticipated, direct use of the DSS may be essential to establishing design criteria.

There is no evidence that any of these methods are used in evaluating DSS, except occasionally as a rationale or a ritual. More importantly, almost every survey of the dynamics of innovation indicates that they do not facilitate innovation and often impede it.

VALUE ANALYSIS

The dilemma managers face in assessing DSS proposals is that the issue of qualitative benefits is central, but they must find some way of deciding if the cost is justified. What is needed is a systematic methodology that focuses on:

1. Value first, cost second.
2. Simplicity and robustness. Decision makers cannot, and should not have to, provide precise estimates of uncertain, qualitative future variables.
3. Reducing uncertainty and risk.
4. Innovation, rather than routinization.

The methodology recommended here addresses all these issues. It relies on prototyping which:

1. Factors risk, by reducing the initial investment, and the delay between approval of the project and the delivery of a tangible product.
2. Separates cost and benefit, by keeping the initial investment within a relatively small, predictable range.

If an innovation involves a large investment, the risk is high. Since estimates of costs and benefits are at best approximate, the decision maker has no way of making a sensible judgment. Risk if factored by reducing scope. An initial system is built at a cost below the capital investment level; the project is then an R&D effort. It can be written off if it fails. By using the DSS one identifies benefits and establishes value. The designer is also likely to learn something new about how to design the full system. The prototype accomplishes the same things as a feasibility study, but goes further in that a real system is built.

The benefit of a DSS is the incentive for going ahead. The complex calculations of cost/benefit analysis are replaced in value analysis by simple questions that most managers naturally ask and handle with ease:

1. What exactly will I get from the system?
   - It solves a business problem.
   - It can help improve planning, communication, and control.
   - It saves time.

2. If the prototype costs $X, do I feel that the cost is acceptable?

Obviously the manager can try out several alternatives—"If the prototype only accomplishes two of my three operational objectives, at a lower cost of $Y, would I prefer that?" The key point is that value and cost are kept separate and not equated. This is sensible only if the cost is kept fairly low. From case studies of DSS, it appears that the cost must be below $20,000 in most organizations for value analysis to be applicable.

This first stage of value analysis is similar to the way in which effective decisions to adopt innovations are made. It corresponds to most managers' implicit strategy. The second stage is a recommendation; there is no evidence in the literature that it is widely used, but it seems a robust and simple extension of Version 0. Once the nature and value of the concept has been established the next step is to build the full DSS. The assessment of cost and value now needs to be reversed:

1. How much will the full system cost?
2. What threshold of values must be obtained to justify the cost? What is the likelihood they will occur?

If the expected values exceed the threshold, no further quantification is required. If they do not, then there must either be a scaling down of the system and a reduction in cost, or a more detailed exploration of benefits.

Value analysis follows a general principle of effective decision making—simplify the problem to make it manageable. A general weakness of the cost/benefit approach is that it requires knowledge, accuracy, and confidence about issues which for innovations are unknown, ill-defined, and uncertain. It therefore is more feasible to:

1. Establish value first, then test if the expected cost is acceptable.

2. For the full system, establish cost first, then test if the expected benefits are acceptable.

Instead of comparing benefits against cost, value analysis merely identifies relevant benefits and tests them against what is in effect a market price: "Would I be willing to pay $X to get this capability?" It is essential that the benefits be accurately identified and made operational. The key question is how would one know that better planning has occurred? The prototype is in effect an experiment in identifying and assessing it.

Figure 1 illustrates the logic and sequence of value analysis. The specific details of the method are less important than the overall assumptions, which have important implications for anyone trying to justify a DSS, whether as a designer or user. Marketing a DSS requires building a convincing case. Figure 1 can be restated in these terms:

1. Establish value—the selling point for a DSS is the specific benefits it provides for busy managers in complex jobs.
2. Establish cost threshold—"trialability" is possible only if the DSS is relatively cheap and installed quickly. If it costs, say, $200,000, it is a capital investment, and must be evaluated as such. This removes the project from the realm of R&D and its benefits since the focus of attention moves to ROI and tangible costs and therefore inhibits innovation.
3. Build Version 0—from a marketing perspective this is equivalent to "strike while the iron is hot." Doing so is possible only with tools that allow speedy development, modification, and extension.
4. Assess the prototype—for the marketer this means working closely with the user and providing responsive service.

Two analogies for DSS have been mentioned in this article: the staff assistant and management education. The strategy, used to justify DSS depends upon the extent to which one views such systems as service innovations and investments in future effectiveness, as opposed to products, routinization, and investment in cost displacement and efficiency. The evidence seems clear—DSS are a potentially important innovation. Value is the issue, and any exploitation of the DSS approach rests on a systematic strategy for identifying benefits, however qualitative, and encouraging R&D and experimentation.

FIGURE 1 *Value Analysis*

Establish Value:

Define operational list of benefits:

E.g., solves urgent business problem, provides a flexible tool for recurrent analysis, makes planning data quickly accessible, saves time in recurrent ad hoc reporting.

Determine Cost Threshold:

Define maximum that one would be ready to pay to gain the benefits.
Determine if a prototype can be built that delivers the necessary capabilities.

Build Version 0:

Define an architecture that permits the full system to be evolved from the initial Version 0.
Define routines for prototype.

Assess Prototype:

Review benefits; revise and extend list.
Review desired and obtainable capabilities.
Define functional capabilities of full system.

Establish Cost of Version 1:

How much will the full system cost?

Determine Benefit Threshold:

What levels of benefits must be obtained to justify the investment in the full system?
What is the likelihood these can be obtained?

Build Version 1

Evolve Version N

Review usage, evaluate new capabilities desired or obtainable.
Establish cost.
Determine benefit threshold.

Stage 1

Stage 2

FOOTNOTES

1. Detailed descriptions of each DSS shown in Table 1 can be found in the following references:

   GADS: Keen and Scott Morton (12). Carlson and Sutton (6)
   PMS: Keen and Scott Morton (12). Andreoli and Steadman (2)
   IRIS: Berger and Edelman (3)
   PROJECTOR: Keen and Scott Morton (12)
   IFPS: Wagner (19)
   ISSPA: Keen and Gambino (11)
   BRANDAID: Keen and Scott Morton (12), Little (14)
   IMS: Alter (1)

   Other DSS referred to in this article are:
   AAIMS: Klaas (13), Alter (1)
   CAUSE: Alter (1)
   GPLAN: Haseman (9)

2. See Grajew and Tolovi (8) for a substantiation of these figures. They built a number of DSS in a manufacturing firm to test the "evolutive approach" to development.

3. IFPS is a proprietary product of Execucom, Inc., in Austin, Texas. The survey of IFPS users is described in Wagner (19).

4. See Andreoli and Steadman (2) for a detailed analysis of PMS usage.

5. This list is taken verbatim from Keen, "Decision Support Systems and Managerial Productivity Analysis" (10).

6. See Tornatzky et al. (16).

7. See Blanning (4).

8. See Ginzberg (7).

9. See Utterback (17).

10. See von Hippel (18).

REFERENCES

1. Alter, S. *Decision Support Systems: Current Practice and Continuing Challenges.* Reading, Mass.: Addison-Wesley, 1980.

2. Andreoli, P., and J. Steadman. "Management Decision Support Systems: Impact on the Decision Process." Master's thesis, Sloan School of Management, MIT, Cambridge, Mass., 1975.

3. Berger, P., and F. Edelman. "IRIS: A Transaction-Based DSS for

Human Resources Management." In "Proceedings of a Conference on Decision Support Systems," ed. E. D. Carlson, *Database* 8, no. 3 (Winter 1977), pp. 22–29.

4. Blanning, R. "How Managers Decide to Use Planning Models." *Long Range Planning* 13 (April 1980).

5. Carlson, E. D., ed. "Proceedings of a Conference on Decision Support Systems." *Database* 8, no. 3 (Winter 1977).

6. Carlson, E. D., and J. A. Sutton. "A Case Study of Non-Programmer Interactive Problem Solving." IBM Research Report, RJ1382, San Jose, Calif., 1974.

7. Ginzberg, M. J. "A Process Approach to Management Science Implementation." Ph.D. dissertation, Sloan School of Management, MIT, Cambridge, Mass., 1975.

8. Grajew, J. and J. Tolovi, Jr. "Conception et Mise en Oeuvre des Systems Interactifs d'aide a la Decision: l'approche Evolutive." Doctorial dissertation, Université des Sciences Sociales de Grenoble, Institut d'Administration des Entreprises, France, 1978.

9. Haseman, W. D. "GPLAN: An Operational DSS." In "Proceedings of a Conference on Decision Support Systems," ed. E. D. Carlson, *Database* 8, no. 3 (Winter 1977), pp. 73–78.

10. Keen, P. G. W. "Decision Support Systems and Managerial Productivity Analysis." Paper presented at the American Productivity Council Conference on Productivity Research, Houston, Tex., April 1980.

11. Keen, P. G. W., and T. Gambino. "The Mythical Man-Month Revisited: Building A Decision Support System in APL." Paper presented in the APL Users Meeting, Toronto, Canada, September 1980.

12. Keen, P. G. W., and M. S. Scott Morton. *Decision Support Systems: An Organizational Perspective.* Reading, Mass.: Addison-Wesley, 1978.

13. Klaas, R. L. "A DSS for Airline Management." In "Proceedings of a Conference on Decision Support Systems," ed. E. D. Carlson, *Database* 8, no. 3 (Winter 1977), pp. 3–8.

14. Little, J. D. C. "BRANDAID." *Operations Research* 23, no. 4 (May 1975), pp. 628–73.

15. Sprague, R. H., Jr. "A Framework for the Development of Decision Support Systems." *MIS Quarterly* 4, no. 4 (December 1980), pp. 1–26.

16. Tornatzky, L. G. et al. "Innovation Processes and Their Management: A Conceptual, Empirical, and Policy Review of Innovation Process Research." National Science Foundation working draft, October 19, 1979.

17. Utterback, J. M. "Innovation in Industry and the Diffusion of Technology." *Science* 183 (February 1974).

18. von Hippel, E. "The Dominant Role of Users in the Scientific Instrument Innovation Process." *Research Policy,* July 1976.

19. Wagner, G. R. "Realizing DSS Benefits with the IFPS Planning Language." Paper presented at the Hawaii International Conference on System Sciences, Honolulu, Hawaii, January 1980.

Chapter Five
Design and Implementation of Decision Support Systems in the Public Sector

JOHN C. HENDERSON
DAVID A. SCHILLING

INTRODUCTION

Developing and implementing decision aids in the public sector is a challenging task. As Lamm (14) points out, the political process tends to promote those that survive or win, not those seeking truth. Often, the essential benefit of a decision aid—a valid model—is the very element that most threatens the survival of the public decision maker. It is not surprising that Brill (3) notes, "Designing a solution to a public sector problem is largely an art."

Hammond (8) suggests that it may not be sufficient to provide decision aids unless explicit attention is given to how these aids support effective learning. Without effective learning support dysfunctional consequences are likely to result from policy-making processes. Although Hammond argues a quasi-experimental approach is a necessary condition for learning, he notes that the strong quasi-rational model or inquiry represented by the application of management science techniques has had positive impact on public sector decision making. For example, management science models can help to externalize multiple objectives and, when combined with the results of quasi-experiments, provide an enhanced learning environment.

The need to facilitate access to decision aids as well as to support individual and organizational learning is explicitly addressed in the decision support systems literature (1). The basic design strategy for DSS begins with an analysis of the decision process and adaptively developing a tool for the user to learn about and cope with semistructured decisions.

Experience in DSS design has also indicated the importance of flexibility, ease of use (at least by an intermediary), and adaptability. Design methodologies such as middle-out (16) or prototyping (12) are explicitly directed toward achieving these characteristics. These design approaches assume there will be significant user and analyst learning in terms of both the technology and the decision process. This learning is enhanced (perhaps even made possible) by developing an initial system with the characteristics described above. As both the user and analyst move along a learning curve, the system is adapted to support their evolving information and learning needs.

The trend in public sector applications of management science techniques seems consistent with this perspective. Public sector planning models have evolved from those that focus on efficiency to those that attempt to describe and account for conflicting objectives (18). The application of multi-objective models in areas such as fire station location (22), police patrol scheduling (20), and water resource management (15) are some recent illustrations. Recursive frameworks (4, 11) have been proposed that use a multi-objective planning model to establish system parameters and then disaggregate these solutions using heuristic and simulation models in order to evaluate their impact on system operations. This iterative approach is quite consistent with the adaptive design concepts proposed by DSS researchers.

Research on the application of decision support systems in the public sector has emphasized the need to address both the problems of conflicting objectives and the need to better support the traditional data analysis efforts of the policy analyst. Hammond notes that both forms of decision aids are necessary. Providing these types of decision aids in a user-friendly, adaptive mode is the objective of many current research efforts.

DECISION SETTING

This research will focus on a decision support system designed and implemented for the Franklin County (Ohio) Mental Health and Retardation Board. The board oversees 40 contract agencies which provide required community-wide mental health services. The nature of the decision process for allocation decisions is critical in this environment. There must be opportunities for various constituencies, representing diverse interests, to have an influence on complex programmatic and financial decisions. Unfortunately, within this realm of complexity the decision makers are often untrained. They are chosen based on the constituencies and values they represent, rather than on their knowledge of the problem area or their expertise as planners or decision makers. They serve in a voluntary mode, meeting infrequently and typically under severe time constraints. It is little wonder that decisions often reflect the relative power of a special interest group rather than some overall set of community goals and priorities.

The Franklin County MHR Board, faced with increasing demand and an eroding resource base,[1] began an effort to improve the quality of their budget planning and allocation process. They identified a need to clarify and link community goals to a comprehensive model for mental health delivery. They sought a budget process that would provide board members with a better understanding of how specific allocations affected program level and overall community mental health system goals.

As a starting point they chose the Balanced Service System (BSS) model as the fundamental conceptualization of a mental health service system. The BSS is a model of mental dysfunctioning used by the Joint Commission on Accreditation of Hospitals (JCAH) to generate standards for community mental health programs. In its basic form the BSS model consists of two primary service dimensions: the service *function* (crisis stabilization, growth, and sustenance) and the service *environment* (protective, supportive, and natural). The function indicates the nature of the service while the environment describes where the service is provided. Each of 200 possible service types are assigned to one of the cells of this two-dimensional matrix. Figure 1 depicts this matrix and includes examples of the types of services in each cell. This model satisfies requirements for a comprehensive mental health framework and also provides the basis for externalizing

FIGURE 1 The Balanced Service System Categories

		FUNCTION		
		Crisis Stabilization	Growth	Sustenance
ENVIRONMENT	Protective	Psychiatric ward of a state hospital	Private psychiatric hospital	Long-term care in a state institution
	Supportive	Twenty-four-hour community emergency center	Outpatient service at a community mental health center	Chronic patient deinstitutional- ization
	Natural	Court-appointed probate screening	Direct group counseling at the workplace	Chronic patient living with foster family

board goals. As will be discussed, the goal structure addresses both specific program areas (e.g., a particular cell in the service delivery matrix) and systemwide goals (e.g., the need to balance service delivery across a range of service environments).

The board also recognized the need for an adequate decision aid. They began an effort to develop a decision support system that would: (*a*) provide a direct link between board goals (as formulated using the BSS model) and allocation decisions, (*b*) provide a means to better understand the trade-offs between goals and the impact of altering goal priorities, (*c*) provide the means to easily incorporate new restrictions, policies, or cost and service parameters into decisions, and (*d*) provide training tools for board members. Given these needs, a DSS design and implementation effort was undertaken. The following sections describe the resulting DSS and its impact.

DSS FRAMEWORK

One of the basic concepts of DSS is the need for flexibility and adaptability. As many public sector researchers note (3), successful public sector decision aids must be able to accommodate unanticipated changes both to the structure of embedded models as

FIGURE 2 Decision Support System Framework

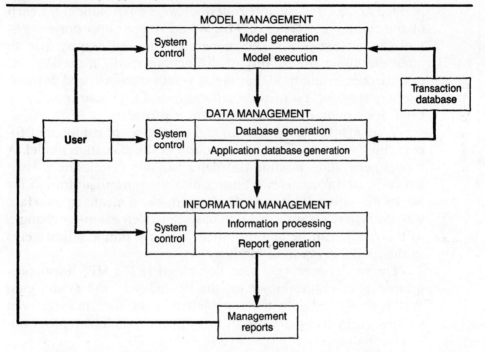

well as to the nature of the user interaction. Achieving these system characteristics is a fundamental goal of the DSS designer. This flexibility and adaptability can be provided through a modular design. The system framework employed in this study (Figure 2) is consistent with that proposed by Sprague and Carlson (24). It consists of three basic components; model management, data management, and information management, and it provides a user-friendly interface. Each component is decoupled as much as possible and consists of a set of well-defined processing modules. This modularity minimizes the number of system interdependencies, thereby allowing most changes to be relatively localized and straightforward. Further, various processing modules are written in a high-level, analysis-oriented language (SAS). This language provides many data-processing oriented macro statements and parameterized routines which substantially reduce the time required to generate or modify particular system components. In cases where this language did not meet specific needs the module was written in Fortran or a macro command language.

While initial prototyping efforts focused on the development of a mathematical model, the eventual success of the DSS depended on an effective, integrated software environment for each of the component systems. This would suggest appropriate system characteristics for DSS generators as well as give rise to questions about the validity of distinctions made in the DSS literature concerning model-oriented versus data-oriented decision support systems. To provide a background for these remarks, a brief description of each component is provided.

Model Management. The model management component focuses on the generation and execution of the allocation model. A model generation module translates variable definitions, system structure, and parameter estimates into an appropriate format for model execution. This module also provides a means to interface with the system's transaction database. Relatively extensive changes to the model can be accomplished by fairly simple adjustments to the model generation module.

The model execution module utilized IBM's MPS linear programming package. However, the flexibility of the model generator, combined with the capabilities of the data management component, permit the use of any appropriate linear programming software.

Finally, as with each component of the DSS, the model management component includes processing modules to interface with the host operating system and provides for interactive dialogue with the user. This aspect, termed system control, enables much of the operation of the model management component to be relatively transparent to the user and provides the means to integrate this component with other parts of the system.

Data Management. The purpose of the second component, data management, is to provide the foundation for a delivery system by merging the solution database with various other databases (e.g., variable labels, historical data trends, etc.) in order to create an integrated solution database. From this solution database, selected application databases are extracted for use by the application programs. The application databases create significant efficiency in the subsequent information processing modules. It is important to note that this component decouples the generation and execution of the model from the generation of management information. It is, in fact, the role of a data management component to isolate changes to application programs from changes to primary data sources (in this case, changes to the allocation model).

The data management component also provides the means to access and analyze data stored in the system's transaction database. As will be discussed later, this capability proved necessary for the successful implementation of the DSS. A high-level language (SAS) provided efficient processing of large files[2] as well as the ability to quickly adapt parameter calculations for changes in both problem structure and specific data sources.

Information Management. The information processing component creates a wide range of managerial reports. To achieve adaptability and flexibility, this component consists of a number of applications programs that operate on extracted application databases. This structure permits modifications to a particular program or report to be localized and, therefore, greatly simplifies the adaptation of the information generation process. This component uses visual representations such as value paths and bar graphs to augment traditional tabular reports. The system allows easy manipulation of both the representation form as well as the particular format via a user interface environment.

THE MODEL

The complex and political nature of the allocations decision highlighted the utility of a *model-based* decision support system. The complexity arose not only from the great variety of allocation decisions required, but also from their interrelationships. These issues were addressed by formulating a linear programming resource allocation model.

The selection of an appropriate model structure was influenced by several considerations. First, the presence of lay decision makers and other nontechnical users favored a model structure which was intuitive and, therefore, easy to understand. Second, due to the prototyping/evolutionary approach used in system development, the model had to be capable of extensive elaboration. Third, the chosen structure should address the multiple objective nature of the decision problem, namely the competing Balanced Service System categories. Finally, it was important that the model help strengthen the behavioral link between the newly adopted BSS framework and the decision maker's existing perceptions of system-wide needs.

In response to these desired characteristics a goal programming model structure was selected. Goal programming has been used and tested in a wide variety of multiple objective decision situations with sophisticated users as well as novices. Such a model structure can respond well to evolutionary development. In addition, the multiple BSS objectives could be represented in a straightforward fashion using countywide service needs as goal levels. By directing the board's attention toward balancing these services, the behavioral link between the BSS framework and a board member's current cognitive model could be improved.

The model formulation follows a class goal programming structure and is discussed in detail by Henderson and Schilling (10). While the details of this model are not germane to this article, a brief overview is provided so that the DSS and the evolving model can be discussed.

The primary decision variables reflected the amount of dollars from each funding source allocated to each service type provided by each agency. There were four different sources of funds to be accounted for, resulting in over 500 variables. Besides the budget constraints, which limited total dollars available from each funding source, restrictions were specified on the percentage increase and decrease that any agency's budget might change. Similarly, the total countywide funding level for each service was limited in the amount that it might shift. These agency and service funding restrictions were included to ensure that any allocation shifts would be politically feasible. For example, defunding an entire agency or service in a single year would be extremely difficult to implement. The board specifically chose a strategy that would spread major funding level changes over several planning periods.

Legal restrictions were incorporated which addressed the legislative and contractual stipulations of specific funding sources. For example, federal regulations require that the proportion of federal funds to public funds must be no more than three to one.

Consistent with a goal programming approach, constraints were included that measured goal deviations and created an objective function minimizing the weighted deviations from the BSS goal levels. Since none of the goal levels was attainable, given current or foreseeable funding levels, the deviations were all one-sided. The priority weightings of the deviational variables served as a tool for identifying group conflict and consensus formation as well as a mechanism by which the group could examine alternative allocation patterns.

While goal programming has seen numerous applications, it nonetheless has several potential pitfalls. Of most concern in this application was the possibility of solution manipulation, as discussed by Harrald et al. (9). In such a situation, arbitrary bounds are added to the model in an attempt to force acceptable solutions. This activity often occurs when the model is too simplistic and unrealistic. This problem can be particularly troubling in a prototyping implementation effort where both the DSS and model evolve from a simple, first-cut system. In order to inhibit arbitrary manipulation, all proposed structural changes were subjected to extensive discussion and debate with board and staff members. Changes were introduced only if a consensus opinion existed that the modification was a fundamental policy elaboration. For example, during initial development two basic model improvements were made. It became apparent that the model ignored differences in services based on client age and area of residence. To rectify this inadequacy, constraints were added to ensure that each client age group and geographic area received at least a minimum level of funding. In another instance, it was determined that some services (termed supplemental) were required when, and only when, other basic services were purchased. Constraints were then written to reflect this observation. Both of these model changes were not attempts to contrive solutions but, in fact, represented evolutionary enhancements to the model which resulted from the decision-maker learning. In support of these conclusions it is worth noting that these modifications were still present in the model three years later.

The Decision Process

In the public sector, the key word is often "process." The means by which a decision is reached can often receive more attention than the decision itself. In designing and implementing a DSS, issues of process become paramount. A common perception among users is that some of their decision-making power may be sacrificed. For example, one of the by-products of a model-based DSS is that decision criteria must be made more explicit. Attention is then directed toward the mechanism by which these criteria are established and applied. This externalization often represents a major change for public sector decision makers.

The likelihood of successful implementation is increased as the magnitude of resultant change is decreased (13). To this end, minimizing unnecessary process modifications is very desirable. In the case of Franklin County, the planning and allocation process involved group decision making throughout. There was strong commitment among board members to a planning process which utilized an interacting group to obtain a consensus. The board members felt such an approach was both politically feasible and enhanced the opportunity for debate and compromise.

To avoid the pitfalls of interacting groups an estimate-discuss-estimate procedure was used to generate goal weights (6, 7). This process calls for each committee member to review the results of a DSS analysis. Each member then assigns importance points (the sum of which equals one hundred) to the various goals.[3] The distribution and mean of the collective votes were tabulated and fed back to the group to stimulate discussion and promote conflict resolution. Following this debate, a second allocation of importance points occurred. This vote-discuss-vote sequence has been shown to be effective in estimating parameters and for facilitating group consensus (6). The average weights produced by the second voting were used as priority weights on the deviational variables in the goal programming model. The model was then solved to generate an allocation pattern and the vote-discuss-vote cycle was repeated.

This group process is the solution technique for the goal programming model. It is essentially a multi-party extension of a simple, iterative search technique for determining the appropriate weights of objectives. Its relatively unsophisticated structure is easily understood by nontechnical decision makers and it blends easily into the existing group process. This simple format provides an effective means to initiate the DSS prototyping effort.

As the implementation proceeded, the decision makers became quite comfortable with interpreting the goal weights. The DSS allowed the decision makers to directly link changes in weights with changes in allocation. At later stages in the process minority opinions (i.e., average weights based on a subset of the group members) were analyzed to further support group debate. Later, input from other constituencies (originally outside the process) was easily incorporated.

Results

This implementation represents a single data point and, hence, results are quite tentative. However, the study represents an actual DSS implementation, and its usage over a three-year period provides a significant opportunity to critique DSS concepts. Two major insights emerged from this study: (*a*) the critical relationship between DSS and the more traditional MIS functions, and (*b*) the characteristics of third generation DSS technology, particularly DSS technology applicable to the public sector.

Rockart and Flannery (19) found the desire for independence from the MIS function to be a major factor behind end user computing. This desire for independence is often associated with DSS. This research does not support the notion that DSS design will be independent of the MIS function. Specifically, a distinction between model-oriented DSS and data-oriented DSS does not appear appropriate. The DSS implemented in this study was conceived as model-oriented and initial development efforts emphasized the modeling aspects of the system. And, yet, experience demonstrated that the capability to link the model to the large transaction database was critical throughout the prototyping effort. We speculate that successful DSS applications will generate requirements to link the DSS to the basic data processing systems in the organization. The DSS implementation significantly altered both the data definitions and the data flow associated with the board's transaction data systems. This resulted in *increased* interdependencies between the DSS user and the MIS organization. The DSS implementation served as a catalyst to generate the commitment necessary to implement a data administration function. The structure of the model became the basis for redesign of the data collection activities. While this served to help institutionalize the DSS and ensure reliable input data for the allocation model, it also created the need for end users to work closely with the MIS organization. As board expectations for data quality increased, the credibility of the DSS became more sensitive to the database maintenance efforts of the MIS organization. Thus, the ongoing success of the DSS became directly linked to the effectiveness of the MIS organization.

This finding is consistent with other research on public sector decision making. Hammond (8), Keen and Gambino (12), and others have noted the traditional reliance of public sector analysts on descriptive data analysis to support the policy analysis process. The DSS experience supports the need for the public sector model-based DSS to provide for descriptive data analysis as well. Again, had the system been unable to easily respond to this data-intensive analysis, the implementation effort would have suffered.

The study suggests that DSS may provide increased opportunities for innovations in the MIS function. Much like the introduction of new products requires different management and technical practices, the design and implementation of a DSS requires approaches that differ from the more traditional MIS practices. Yet, if successful, the DSS creates an ever increasing dependence between the DSS end user and the MIS function. This seems particularly true in the public sector where the use of such systems may result in precedent-setting policies.

A second major insight relates to the characteristics of third generation DSS technology, particularly as they may apply to the public sector. Future public sector model-based DSS generators must address at least three needs: easy incorporation of an equity dimension, enhanced data analysis capabilities, and increased communication capabilities.

As the Franklin County implementation proceeded, system modifications centered around both the ability to change the model and the ability to alter information processing and basic data management modules. In many cases, changes in the model structure focused on issues of equity. As Savas (21) points out, there are a variety of conflicting ways to operationalize notions of equity. Initially, the model did not explicitly operationalize equity relationships. While some relationships indirectly created solutions which were more "equitable," they were not explicitly formulated to do so. For example, legal constraints which required minimum levels of services offered by agencies may have their origin in the equity notion of equal outputs.

However, as the DSS evolved the board sought to *explicitly* ensure equity in the allocation of funds. For example, constraints forcing distribution of funds between geographical areas were added. These efforts to ensure that small, geographically isolated providers received at least a minimum allocation represented Savas's equity concept of equal inputs per unit area.

Many discussions centered around developing constraints that would reflect the board's concern for equal access. The ability to generate model structure, to easily test, and eventually incorporate these structural changes was an important capability. This need to consider equity issues in the public sector resulted in a technological demand for at least a *three*-dimensional model. One must be able to easily accommodate program activity, time, and equity dimensions in the model. This suggests that current automated spreadsheet modeling languages, that are essentially two-dimensional, may be inadequate for end user system development in the public sector.

Previous discussions addressed the need to link the model-based DSS to the transaction system of the organization. This linkage results in the DSS user becoming an important stakeholder with regard to procedures to define, collect, and maintain elementary data. It also suggests that third generation technology must have the capability to conduct a wide range of data analysis. As previously mentioned, this type of analysis has become standard practice for most public sector policy analysts. The need is to provide a single DSS that can adequately provide both modeling and data management capabilities.

Finally, third generation DSS technology must place greater emphasis on communication capabilities. This study emphasized the need for alternative modes of presentation, i.e., graphical versus tabular. The need to incorporate a graphics capability in DSS is widely recognized. However, this study suggests that the communication needs for a public sector DSS extend beyond providing for alternative modes of presentation. Public sector analysts have significant requirements for distribution of the results of their analysis. This distribution normally takes the form of reports, memos, and/or press releases. This suggests significant benefits will be gained by linking the DSS into the automated office environment. For example, data related to the model-based DSS should be easily accessible by the word processing system within the office.

The growing research findings relating to the use of adaptive design or prototyping for DSS were strongly supported by this implementation. A prototyping design strategy similar to those discussed by Keen and Gambino (12) was used to design the DSS. While this strategy proved effective, it also created high expectations on the part of the user for easy modifications. As the DSS grew in complexity, meeting these expectations became difficult. The modular design of this system, which explicitly recognized a need for model management, proved crucial to meeting these high expectations. The implementers were able to evolve a matrix-generation language with self-contained high-level commands and flexible user interface with little or no impact on the command structure for the data or information management components. Further, each component proved necessary to the success of the implementation. These experiences suggest that while prototyping is successful as a general strategy, structured design concepts and associated design aids are quite important.

This study also provided insight into the process used by board members to validate the model and the DSS. This process appeared to have three distinct stages. The first stage was the acceptance of a conceptual structure for modeling a mental health system (the BSS model) and for utilizing a multi-criteria allocation model. This stage involved fairly abstract debates at the board level concerning (*a*) comparison of the BSS model with other models of a mental health system, (*b*) reviewing alternative processes for obtaining information about the impact of allocation strategies, and (*c*) reviewing alternatives for conducting sensitivity analyses.

The second stage involved a macro-operational verification in which inputs to the model were varied and trends in output were examined to determine if the outputs of the model made intuitive sense or could be logically accounted for. This stage resulted in structural changes to the model and helped to establish the content of several management reports.

Finally, the third stage involved validation through micro-operational sampling. This consisted of individuals selectively examining input data, model parameters, and then tracing outputs at very detailed levels. Evaluations were made based on personal experience or independent data sources. For example, a board member might ask to see the unit cost for a particular type of childrens' service at a particular agency because he/she had been a provider in that environment. At this point, the implementation became linked to the ability to trace the origins of these parameters to the actual day-to-day transaction database. If inconsistencies were found or new formulations developed, the transaction database had to be used to provide new input to the model. On several occasions, the transaction database was used to clarify demand characteristics or system demographics that were not explicitly incorporated into the model. Had this capability been lacking, concerns about data quality would have impeded the implementation process and the DSS would not have been effective. Thus, while the model-based DSS basically operated on files extracted from a large transaction database, the ability to easily interact with the transaction database still played a major role in the implementation process.

Impact on the Community Mental Health System

It is important to mention the impact of implementing this DSS on the total mental health system. As noted earlier, a DSS should serve as a learning support tool that is capable of addressing both strategic and operational issues. In this study a decision to transfer the budget for mental retardation services to another community board was arrived at and justified, in part, by examining the allocation models developed for both areas. This examination showed programmatic independence (e.g., no shared resources or facilities) and led to a conclusion that community level goals for these two areas were not in conflict.

Similarly, the system was used to illustrate the impact of alternative cost accounting approaches, to communicate the impact of federal fund-matching requirements, and to examine a wide range of operational issues. Its uses have evolved beyond providing direct support for the allocations process. For example, extensive "what if" analysis has been performed in the context of contingency planning for the success or failure of a proposed tax levy. The DSS also became a focal point to revamp data collection processes, to establish new controls over system-wide data flows, and to create or legitimize new data requirements. As a direct result of this system implementation a completely new data collection format was created and a new collection process institutionalized. This effort established new validation procedures used in acquiring data as well as produced a means to train providers on the BSS model of the mental health system.

The quantity of cost- and service-related data obtained from agencies was substantially increased (by nearly a factor of two) over previous years. The agencies were asked, for the first time, to indicate preferences on budget *reductions,* i.e., where and at what level they would place lower limits.

As might be expected, this new information management effort led to a desire for greater control over data quality and expansion of the types of data made available. Prior to the implementation of the DSS, such cooperation and involvement in the collection and quality control of data were lacking. To a large extent, the DSS created a planning process that justified the effort and cost necessary to provide such data. Since these data were also used for other financial and policy analysis tasks, the DSS produced a significant secondary impact on board functions.

Finally, the process established well-defined points within the budget process where priorities were established and decisions made. This had, and will continue to have, a fundamental impact on the mechanism by which the community can influence allocations. In essence, the board established, for the first time, direct linkages between a conceptual model of a mental health system, how such a system should function (goals), and the allocation process employed to achieve these goals.

CONCLUSIONS

Generalizations cannot be made from a single data point; however, the external validity of these experiences is high in that the system was successfully implemented and continues to be used both for allocations decisions and for "what if" planning questions. Furthermore, these experiences appear generally consistent with the growing body of research on DSS, and thus merit the following conclusions.

First, process (the way a system or organization arrives at a decision) is critical in public sector decision making. Perhaps the most fundamental conclusion of this work is the need for the management scientist to provide a process-support aid rather than a model that provides an answer. Thus, the importance of providing a range of learning and decision aids within an integrated, yet adaptive system is stressed.

Second, the emerging theory of DSS addresses a blend of design strategy, system characteristics, and required technological building blocks. This work supports most current thinking with regard to these areas. Prototyping, as a design strategy, proved effective both in terms of defining user information needs as well as providing a mechanism to support user and analyst learning. The system characteristics of adaptability, flexibility, modularity, simplified man-machine interface, and alternative modes of presentation proved necessary to successful implementation. Thus, we find empirical support for the basic principles of DSS.

Third, model selection and formulation need careful attention. The model structure must match the problem structure, but it must also support decision-maker understanding. Institutionalization of a DSS that uses a complex model is facilitated when the model serves both as an analytic tool and as a conceptual model. Care must also be taken to circumvent model usage traps.

In a prototyping/evolutionary environment, the analyst must closely scrutinize model modifications in order to avoid the temptation of solution manipulation and to ensure model integrity. Failure to do so can invalidate the entire DSS while still appearing (at least to the untrained eye) to perform correctly.

Fourth, the distinction between model-oriented DSS and data-oriented DSS, and the notion of independence for DSS users, does not appear appropriate, given these experiences. This system was conceived as a model-oriented DSS and initial efforts were directed toward the modeling aspect of the system. And yet experience demonstrated that the capability to link the model to a large transaction database was very important. DSS users cannot remove themselves from the need to examine, verify, and communicate fundamental data. To be effective the DSS has to provide the means to access this elementary data in a timely fashion. We speculate that this will become a feature of most successful model-oriented DSS generators. That is, to be successful there will be pressure to link the DSS to the basic data processing of the organization. From a management perspective, this will result in a need to better coordinate DSS and MIS design efforts.

Fifth, the importance of addressing equity issues is stressed. The notion of equity in public policy is, in itself, a major research issue. This study suggests future DSS technology must enable the user to incorporate equity dimensions as well as activity and time dimensions. This indicates that public sector applications require a DSS generator that extends beyond the two dimensional framework currently represented by financially oriented DSS generators. The fact that DSS generators in the public sector must be at least three-dimensional increases demands for flexibility and sophisticated forms of presentation.

Finally, the benefits of DSS are difficult to assess a priori. The benefits of DSS will include such issues as support of organization change, support of individual learning, and improved management of the technological growth of the organization. This work indicated that significant system-wide impact occurred and should be explicitly recognized in the evaluation of the success or failure of the DSS effort. The DSS affected fundamental areas such as learning, organizational development, data processing, and decision process framing. It influenced user learning by providing the means to investigate the complexity of the problem in a systematic manner. It affected organizational development by unfreezing positions and attitudes concerning both the mission of the board and the structure of the allocation process. It affected data processing by providing the felt need and political support necessary to revamp data collection procedures and to increase the quality and integrity of their database. Finally, it provided the means to frame the decision as one of trade-offs between goals rather than increases or decreases in specific budget line items. This not only changed the allocation decision process but helped to institutionalize a goal-oriented planning process.

FOOTNOTES

1. The board's allocations budget is approximately $20 million; however, projections for budget cutbacks and inflation are significant, reducing these resources while various need assessments indicate increasing demand for service.
2. The transaction database contained over 500,000 records.
3. Introductory training sessions emphasized the underlying assumption of an interval scale implicit in the averaging of these important points.

REFERENCES

1. Alavi, M., and J. C. Henderson. "An Evolutionary Strategy for Implementing a Decision Support System." *Management Science* 27, no. 11, (November 1981), pp. 1309–23.
2. Alter, S. L. *Decision Support Systems: Current Practice and Continuing Challenges.* Reading, Mass.: Addison-Wesley, 1980.
3. Brill, E. D., Jr. "The Use of Optimization Models in Public Sector Planning." *Management Science* 25, no. 5 (May 1979), pp. 413–22.
4. Cohon, J., and D. Marks. "Multiobjective Screening Models and Water Resources Investments." *Water Resources Research* 9, no. 4 (1973), p. 826.
5. Delbecq, A., and A. H. Van De Ven. "A Group Process Model for Problem Identification and Program Planning." *Journal of Applied Behavioral Science* 7, no. 4 (July–August 1971), p. 466.
6. Delbecq, A. L.; A. H. Van De Ven; and D. H. Gustafson. *Group Techniques for Program Planning: A Guide to Nominal Group and Delphi Process.* Glenview, Ill.: Scott, Foresman, 1975.
7. Gustafson, D. H.; R. M. Shukla; A. L. Delbecq; and G. W. Walster.

"A Comparative Study of Differences in Subjective Likelihood Estimates Made by Individuals, Interacting Groups, Delphi Groups, and Nominal Groups." *Organizational Behavior and Human Performance* 9, no. 2 (April 1973), pp. 280–91.

8. Hammond, K. R. "Toward Increasing Competence of Thought in Public Policy Formation." In *Judgment and Decision in Public Policy Formation,* ed. K. R. Hammond, Boulder, Colo.: AAAS Selected Symposium, 1980.

9. Harrald, J.; J. Leotta; W. A. Wallace; and R. E. Wendell. "A Note on the Limitations of Goal Programming As Observed in Resource Allocation for Marine Environmental Protection." *Naval Research Logistics Quarterly* 25, no. 4 (1978), pp. 733–39.

10. Henderson, J. C., and D. A. Schilling. "Design and Implementation of Decision Support Systems in the Public Sector." College of Administrative Science Working Paper Series, WPS 81-77, Ohio State University, Columbus, 1981.

11. Henderson, J. C.; M. A. Showalter; and L. H. Krajewski, Jr. "An Integrated Approach for Manpower Planning in the Service Sector. *Omega* 10, no. 1 (January 1982).

12. Keen, P. G. W., and T. J. Gambino. "Building A Decision Support System: The Mythical Man-Month Revisited." In *Building Decision Support Systems,* ed. J. F. Bennett, Reading, Mass.: Addison-Wesley, 1982.

13. Keen, P. G. W., and M. S. Scott Morton. *Decision Support Systems: An Organizational Perspective.* Reading, Mass.: Addison-Wesley, 1978.

14. Lamm, R. A. "The Environment and Public Policy." In *Judgment and Decision in Public Policy Formation,* ed. K. R. Hammond, Boulder, Colo.: AAAS Selected Symposium, 1980.

15. Major, D., and R. Lenton. *Multiobjective Multimodel Riverbasin Planning: The MIT-Argentina Project.* Englewood Cliffs, N.J.: Prentice-Hall, 1978.

16. Ness, D. "Interactive Systems: Theories of Design." In *Joint Wharton/ONR Conference Interactive Information and DSS,* University of Pennsylvania, Philadelphia, November 1975.

17. Pressman, J., and A. Wildavsky. *Implementation: How Great Expectations in Washington Are Dashed in Oakland.* Oakland: University of California Press, 1973.

18. ReVelle, C. S.; D. Bigma; D. A. Schilling; J. A. Cohon; and R. Church. "Facility Location Analysis: A Review of Context-Free and EMS Models." *Health Services Research,* Summer 1977, pp. 129–47.

19. Rockart, J. F., and Flannery, L. S. "The Management of End User Computing." *Communications of the ACM* 26, no. 10 (October 1983), pp. 776–84.

20. Saladin, B. *A Methodology for the Allocation of Police Patrol Vehicles.* Unpublished doctoral dissertation, Ohio State University, Columbus, 1980.

21. Savas, E. S. "On Equity in Providing Public Service." *Management Science* 24, no. 8 (April 1978), pp. 800–8.

22. Schilling, D. A.; D. J. Elzing; J. A. Cohon; and C. S. ReVelle. "Design and Analysis of Location and Relocation Alternatives in a Fire Protection System." In *Proceedings of IEEE Modeling and Simulation Conference,* Pittsburgh, Pa., May 1980.

23. Schilling, D. A.; C. S. ReVelle; and J. L. Cohon. "An Approach to the Display and Analysis of Multiobjective Problems." *Socio and Economic Planning Science* 17, no. 2 (1983), pp. 57–63.

24. Sprague, R. H., and E. D. Carlson. *Building Effective Decision Support Systems,* Englewood Cliffs, N.J.: Prentice-Hall, 1982.

Chapter Six
Future Directions in DSS Technology

MICHAEL E. TREACY

1. INTRODUCTION

The impact of all information technologies is in large part a result of the vision we hold for their use. Until recently, our view of the potential of decision support systems (DSS) has been restricted by the relatively limited capabilities of the technology and by our conception of DSS as an individual support system. Rapid advances in the technology, most notably in the area of microcomputers, and greater understanding of the potential impacts of DSS on the nature of managerial work now promise a change in the future role of DSS.

For the past 15 years, decision support systems technology has evolved both steadily and predictably. Only recently have we seen rapid and revolutionary changes in DSS technology that have made obsolete many old concepts and assumptions about DSS capabilities. Understanding these recent changes and the future directions that they portend is one key to effectively managing the technology. Otherwise, one may continue to invest in an older generation of DSS capabilities that has significant limitations for leveraging a firm's productivity.

It is difficult to talk about decision support systems without acknowledging the definitional quagmire in which the term *DSS* exists. The fact that the definition of "decision support systems" remains problematic 15 years after the term was introduced by Gorry and Scott Morton (1971) is symptomatic of several prob-

Center for Information Systems Research Working Paper No. 123, Sloan School of Management, MIT, Cambridge, Mass., January 1985.

lems. First, this is still a relatively new area, and both researchers and practitioners are trying to understand what the DSS concept represents in terms of design alternatives and its impact on the organization. Second, the competitive nature of the technology marketplace encourages vendors to turn virtually any MIS concept into a marketing buzzword without concern for the confusion caused by its misuse. Finally, DSS is a multidisciplinary area drawing on fields such as behavioral decision theory, computer science, and systems analysis. Each discipline brings its own perspective and biases to the debate over the definition of DSS.

For our purposes, we can choose a fairly simple definition of DSS. We define a decision support system as a computer-based system used to support the needs of managers for data and analysis. This broad definition focuses on the functional capabilities of a support system and gives us wide latitude to explore alternative technologies.

Today, the evolution of data and analytic support is being driven by changes in the technology. We will be able to support new uses of systems and achieve new impacts on the business only if technology evolves to enable new types of systems. Therefore, understanding where the technology is going is fundamental to any discussion about the future of DSS. Paradoxically, for building systems today with existing technology, other issues such as needs assessment and design processes are more important.

2. DSS TECHNOLOGY TODAY

During the past 15 years, a host of decision support system software facilities have been developed that allow analysts and managers to develop, and use directly, decision support systems. Figure 1, adapted from Montgomery and Urban (1969), shows the capabilities that have been provided by different DSS generators.

A decision support system provides a manager with another source of information on his or her internal and external business environment. Through an interaction and display facility that may include a command and data query language, report writing, and color graphics facilities, the manager can access a base of data, perform statistical, arithmetic, and other data manipulation functions, and create explicit models of the firm, the competitors, and the industry and economy.

Figure 1 represents an ideal set of DSS generator capabilities. In practice, the majority of software is of one of two types that

FIGURE 1 The Montgomery–Urban Model of DSS Capabilities

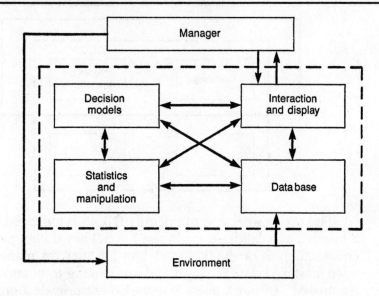

fall short of the ideal. Figures 2 and 3, adapted from Wurts (1981), indicate these groups.

The friendly, easy to learn and use, database management systems (DBMS) provide a manager with a facility for managing and accessing a large base of data, creating reports and graphs, and performing very limited analyses upon the data. They give managers the ability to choose the data that they wish to see and to format it in reports and graphs as they wish to see it.

FIGURE 2 Friendly Database Management Systems

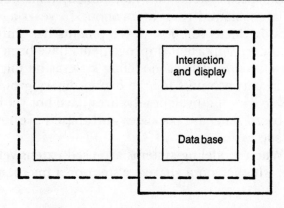

FIGURE 3   Spreadsheet Modeling Systems

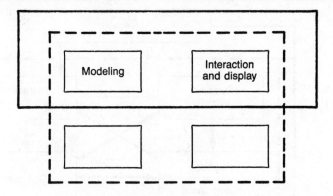

The major weakness of friendly DBMS is indicated in Figure 2 by what capabilities they do not have. They do not provide adequate analysis or explicit modeling facilities for managers who have mastered data retrieval and are looking to manipulate data for analysis. In short, query systems do not provide a growth path for the typical manager who learns through a DSS to perform increasingly sophisticated analyses.

Figure 3 indicates the other major class of DSS generator. A spreadsheet modeling system gives a manager the ability to define an explicit model of several interrelated variables and to calculate the results of the model over several time periods. The packages usually allow a manager to define and solve a model, perform sensitivity and risk analysis on it, and generate reports and graphs. They are particularly well tuned to financial modeling, but provide no support for traditional mathematical programming models. They do not, in general, manage a database or offer ad hoc analytic capabilities.

Database systems and modeling systems were first developed for large, shared computers about 15 years ago. In the last few years the locus for new developments has shifted to the microcomputer. Important improvements have been made in the ease of use of spreadsheet modeling systems on microcomputers and this in part accounts for the extraordinary growth of micro-based DSS activity. Equivalent advances have not yet been made in micro-based database packages and these have remained relatively less successful.

When modeling systems are used extensively in an organization, whether on a shared system or a micro, their use tends to

FIGURE 4 Individual DSS Developments

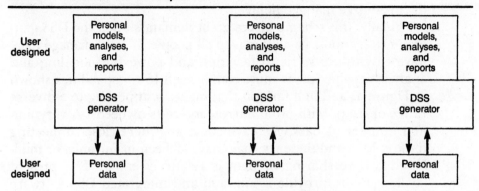

look something like Figure 4. Each user of the system acts quite independently, with his or her own data, reports, and models that are separately maintained from the rest. There usually isn't a database management system integrated with the modeling package, so data cannot be managed in a common, accessible pool.

Some companies have tried to create a degree of data and software commonality in their decision support systems environment. Instead of individual DSS development as shown in Figure 4, they have an organizational support system (Huber, 1982) that resembles Figure 5. This diagram illustrates three important features. First, users have a common decision support system generator. This facilitates sharing of models and analyses, reduces training needs, and helps create a mutually supportive environment among users. Second, users have a common base of data, designed and maintained with the support of information sys-

FIGURE 5 Organizational DSS Developments

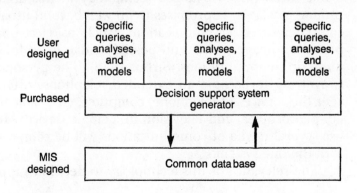

tems professionals. This facilitates sharing of data, reduces problems of redundancy and inaccuracy, and establishes elements of data resource management.

Finally, this scheme places great demands upon the DSS generator, for it must be all things to all people. It must manage data, have easy-to-use retrieval facilities, and powerful modeling and analysis capabilities. It must combine all four capabilities shown in Figure 1, and in a fashion that makes it appealing to a diverse range of users, with often narrow interests or needs. A very limited number of packages have come anywhere close to meeting these criteria and these packages have all been mainframe- or mini-based, where sharing of data is relatively easier. The present challenge is to provide a common and integrated DSS software architecture across a distributed hardware environment.

3. CHANGES IN SOFTWARE FUNCTIONALITY

In the area of software capabilities, there are three major trends. First, existing packages are becoming more comprehensive in terms of the four basic capabilities of DSS software: modeling, ad hoc analysis, database management, and interfaces. Packages that previously only had modeling and interface capabilities are adding data management and ad hoc analysis capabilities. Meanwhile, easy-to-use database management packages are improving their interfaces and adding modeling features. In short, DSS software packages are growing up to fill all of the four basic decision support capabilities. "Integrated" has become the catchword of the DSS software industry.

A second advance that will have a major impact on how we view and use decision support systems will be in the area of electronic messaging. Advanced technology in this area is just becoming available. It promises to go well beyond usual notions of computer-based communications (such as electronic mail) by providing image, voice, and possibly video in addition to alphanumeric communications (Sirbu, 1978). The personal computer is evolving to become an extended telephone, offering a manager the services of telephone, computer, electronic mail, facsimile, photocopier, and television in a single device. Messages that use several media of communications will be composed and sent with the one system.

The relevance of this technology to decision support systems

FIGURE 6   A Modified Model of DSS Capabilities

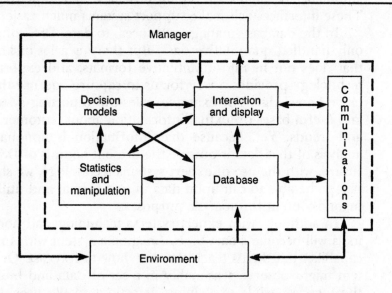

is that it represents a shift from early concepts of DSS that made no allowances for communications. The original idea of DSS, as represented in the Montgomery-Urban model did not explicitly consider the individual in an organizational context. Given this new electronic messaging technology, however, there is another capability of support systems that will grow up: communications support. Figure 6 includes the role of communications capabilities in the Montgomery and Urban framework.

Whether we call communications a subset of DSS or an allied capability is a semantic debate. Regardless, electronic messaging will be a major new technological capability that will impact how we view needs for support, how we design and implement systems, what impacts they have, and what policies we need to have in place to manage their development.

The third trend, one that is only beginning, is toward the use of "expert systems" technology to improve each of the four basic capabilities of DSS software. *Expert systems* is a branch of artificial intelligence that is concerned with building computer systems that display expert reasoning abilities (Davis, 1982; Winston, 1984; Hayes-Roth, Waterman, and Lenat, 1983). The DSS field is going to borrow from the tool kit that has been developed to build expert systems. For example, we will see much more intelligent interfaces, systems that try to understand what the user is attempting, or that will reshuffle menus, or provide help systems automatically, or ignore typing mistakes, or accept voice input. These interfaces will make support systems much easier to use.

In the database management area, to date, DSS software has only handled quantitative data. But there is a lot of knowledge that does not fit into quantitative formats, and expert systems technology provides a way for us to capture and use that qualitative knowledge. For example, sales-call reporting systems contain useful bases of textual information about customer histories and trends. Yet, because that information is nonquantitative, analysis of that data is outside the present bounds of DSS. In the future, with the use of expert systems technology, we should expect to be able to call upon data in text format and utilize its semantic content for analytic purposes.

In addition, with expert systems technology, ad hoc analysis tools will become smart tools. Imagine a system with forecasting capability that helps teach the user how to forecast. Or, the system might observe seasonality in a set of data and build it into the forecast, while explaining its actions to the user. Gale and Pregibon (1982) have built an expert regression system which "emulates some of the interaction between a client and an expert statistical consultant" (p. 110). Basic pro forma accounting models and standard accounting analyses will become a part of modeling systems. The knowledge represented by financial accounting interpretation can be built into software, using expert systems tools.

Over the past 20 years, a branch of set theory known as *fuzzy sets* has developed and is beginning to influence our ideas about modeling systems (Bellman and Zadeh, 1970). The opportunity is upon us to produce fuzzy modeling capabilities. These models will remove the traditional constraints that models must be precisely stated, that model rules must not conflict with each other, and that the logic of the model must be essentially complete. Fuzzy modeling will allow the user to externalize the sometimes fuzzy, incomplete, and inconsistent thinking or rules that most managers have to grapple with when making decisions.

Fuzzy models are used by managers all the time. For example, in a pricing decision, a manager might bring into play the following rules:

1. Our price should be about two times direct costs.
2. Our price should be just below our dominant competitor's price.

3. If our competitors' prices go too high, we should price for increased market share.

None of these statements is in a form precise enough to be used in a standard modeling system. Each statement begs for refinement. With a fuzzy modeling system, these statements form a model of the pricing decision that could be solved. The results of that solution clearly would not be satisfactory, but it is a useful starting point that prompts a manager for a more refined representation of his or her mental model.

Finally, communications capabilities can be significantly enhanced with expert systems technology. Effective communications comprises more than just the transportation of messages. Several communications functions require the intelligent application of knowledge about messages. For example, in telephone and mail systems, the functions of filtering and categorizing are essential for effective communications. Many of these functions can be incorporated into support systems, using expert systems technology.

4. CHANGES IN HARDWARE ENVIRONMENT

The evolution of DSS software functionality is complicated by the current major migration of software capabilities from the mainframe and minicomputer to the microcomputer (Healey, 1983). This is a major shift, one that may well move all analysis systems off shared systems in the next three years. From a software architecture standpoint, there are sound reasons for this migration.

As demonstrated by the phenomenal success of micro spreadsheet packages, ease of use is one of the most important technical features of management-oriented software packages. A key to ease of use is the degree of interactivity, for that determines the rate of feedback and responsiveness of the system (Doherty and Kelisky, 1979). Microcomputers provide very high limits on interactivity. Any location on the display of a microcomputer can be changed virtually as quickly as a primary memory location can be changed. Thus, the entire screen can be transformed in the blink of an eye. On a mainframe or minicomputer, highly interactive, easy-to-use interfaces cannot be delivered to asynchronous terminals because of the limited bandwidth between the screen and the processor. Even using a 9.6 kilobit connection, it takes two seconds to send a full screen of characters. Graphics take even longer.

Eventually, this handicap will eliminate the mainframe and minicomputer from decision support systems, except as data repositories and device managers on a network. How quickly this occurs will depend on how quickly IBM introduces subsequent generations of microcomputers, which will, ultimately, be many times more powerful than its original PC. Their introduction of the PC AT is an important step in this direction. The AT offers faster processing, much more memory, and expanded and faster secondary storage. It will enable an entirely new generation of decision support systems software to come to market within the next two years.

As a result, the only role left for the mainframe in the future of DSS will be that of a central data manager and as a manager of shared devices, such as printers and optical scanners. There is a serious question as to whether or not the software vendors now producing mainframe and minicomputer-based DSS generators will be able to develop products for the new marketplace that is evolving.

5. IMPACTS OF HARDWARE CHANGES UPON DATA ACCESS

At present, the decision support systems hardware environment can be characterized as one of double innocence. Mainframe and mini-based systems are almost completely separate from microcomputer systems, without sharing of data, software, or users. Figure 7 illustrates this. On the mainframe or minicomputer can be found friendly DBMS and modeling packages offering the usual run of capabilities: query, ad hoc analysis, and modeling. These software tools are often used as application generators to create reporting and consolidation systems that were once written in COBOL, but their main use is for decision support. Four major capabilities can be found on the microcomputer: spreadsheets (modeling), graphics, list management (a crude DBMS), and word processing.

There are two strategies among mainframe DSS software vendors that we have seen as a defensive reaction to the migration to the micro. One is to create microcomputer versions of DSS packages that previously existed only on the mainframe (Ferris,

FIGURE 7 **Existing DSS Software Architecture**

Mainframe/mini computer				

Query and analysis	Reporting system	Consolidation system	Modeling system
Friendly DBMS			
Operating system			

Operating system			
CALC	Graphics	List manager	WP

Micro computer

1983). The problem with this strategy is that typically the new micro products are merely replicas of the mainframe packages that fail to take advantage of the unique capabilities that a microcomputer affords, particularly for creating highly interactive interfaces. Outside their existing base of customers, these products are often completely uncompetitive.

The second strategy is to offer the microcomputer user a tailored terminal emulation capability. This turns the microcomputer into a smart terminal for accessing the mainframe or minicomputer resident software. Smart features, such as command editing, capturing output to floppy disks, and menu- and mouse-oriented command building, can be added by using the local power of the microcomputer. Some of these terminal emulators also provide file formatting capabilities, so that the user can bring data down to a microcomputer in a format used by microcomputer software.

The terminal emulation strategy is really a stopgap measure that allows mainframe software vendors to quickly announce microcomputer products. It is not a long-term solution. The major problem with this strategy is that the data link between mainframe or minicomputer and microcomputer is completely passive. A user who wishes to use data from a mainframe in his or her microcomputer's modeling package must: (1) invoke the terminal emulation facility, (2) use the mainframe package's command language to retrieve the appropriate data, (3) transfer the file in the correct format, (4) terminate the emulation facility, (5) invoke the modeling software, and (6) command the package to

FIGURE 8   *Emerging DSS Software Architecture*

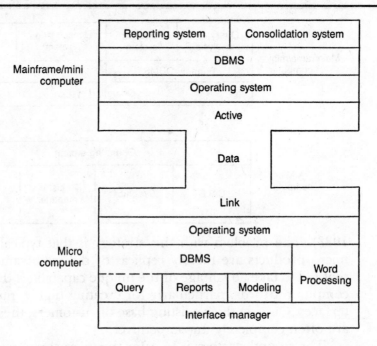

read in the transferred file. Preferable is to be able to call for the correct data while in the modeling package, using consistent commands.

A more sophisticated approach to linking micro-based DSS users to mainframe data is being taken by a few traditional DBMS vendors and is illustrated in Figure 8. The design involves three components: a mainframe- or minicomputer-based DBMS, a microcomputer-based DBMS, and software to join them together— what we call an active data link. The active data link maintains a directory of data available to the user on the mainframe system. If a microcomputer application makes a call to the micro DBMS for data that it has, the data is furnished. If data is requested that it does not have, the request is passed to the active data link, which checks the mainframe data directory, issues the appropriate procedure calls, receives the data from the mainframe, and passes it through the micro DBMS to the application. Thus, the mainframe DBMS appears as a virtual resource of the micro, an extension of the microcomputer's own database management system (Goldstein et al., 1984). The user has a unified view of both micro and mainframe resident data and does not need to be concerned with its location. To make this design work, the micro applications software for query, analysis, and modeling must be rewritten to run against the micro DBMS. For this reason, early products of this type have necessarily included a full suit of microcomputer applications.

Database packages are needed on microcomputers not primarily as stand-alone applications, but as systems software to enhance the integration of diverse applications software. For example, when a manager uses a set of applications packages such as graphics, spreadsheet, and word processing with DBMS capabilities behind them, data from one application remains available in the DBMS so that it can later be pulled into another application. In this case, the database management capabilities are being used behind the applications packages to integrate them.

The evolution of DSS functionality to incorporate multimedia communications capabilities will necessitate the development of systems for managing nonquantitative data in an office environment. Designs for these are only beginning to emerge (Ahlsen et al., 1984; Zdonik, 1983). Incorporating these designs into a distributed scheme has also been studied (Lyngbaek and McLeod, 1984). It may be several years before commercial systems are widely used.

A very important issue in this design is the development of standard interfaces between layers of software. Standards are crucial if a diversity of products are to work together. Standards can develop through cooperation of vendors and the scientific community or through the market power of a particular vendor (Sirbu and Zwimpfer, 1984). The open systems interconnection data communications standard developed by a subcommittee of the International Standards Organization is an example of the former (Folts, 1981). Microsoft's Disk Operating System (DOS) is an example of the latter (Microsoft Corp., 1983). For this next generation of DSS software, the major commercial DBMS vendors are best positioned to invoke de facto standards for data access.

6. THE EVOLUTION OF INTERFACE DESIGN

Yet another change we will see in DSS software comes about because of the revolution taking place in interface design. Traditionally, mainframe systems have been programming oriented, offering virtually no help to the user who lacks a conceptual understanding of how the data is stored in the computer, or who doesn't know how to respond to curt system prompts such as "ENTER." By following some fairly simple design rules, many of the more difficult features of traditional, programming-oriented interfaces can be eliminated (Branscomb and Thomas, 1984). But in the future we will see some very untraditional interfaces on database software packages, much like those that are now standard on microcomputer-based modeling software, such as Lotus 1-2-3.

Unlike a standard command-oriented DSS interface, the orientation of microcomputer-based modeling packages is always to show the results the user is seeking, while the algorithm that shows how the results were derived is suppressed (Kay, 1984). Unlike mainframe packages which traditionally have been programming oriented, the ease of use of such results-oriented interfaces significantly reduces the barriers to use for potential DSS users.

In present database query languages, the user must write the exact query for what is wanted if results are to be produced. No intermediate results are available, which makes it a process akin to target shooting. Only when the user aims correctly with the right query is the appropriate answer provided. Given the importance of data retrieval in decision support systems, existing software is frequently inadequate for the user's needs. But a new generation of visual retrieval languages will change that. It will open up ways of viewing data retrieval as a process of zooming in and out of a database until the right data are found.

The emergence of interface managers as separate software packages will facilitate the development of better interfaces on application packages. Interface managers sit "in front" of applications and provide window management and other tools that application developers can use to create friendlier interfaces (see Figure 8). In the future, a user will interact "through" an interface manager with a microcomputer-based application that relies upon a DBMS to manage its data. This is a far more complex systems software world than exists today on a microcomputer, but it is one that major vendors are actively trying to build because it will facilitate the development of more powerful applications with less effort.

7. IMPLICATIONS FOR SOFTWARE VENDORS

This vision of DSS in the future was not obtained by gazing deeply and intently into a crystal ball. It was formed through discussions with product strategists in several dozen leading and emerging DSS software companies. The best of the vendors have the power to create the future of DSS technology. For the rest, this forecast defines the emerging dimensions of future competition.

Four distinct classes of software are beginning to emerge: (1) distributed data management software, (2) microcomputer interface managers tightly coupled to operating systems, (3) applications software on the microcomputer that works in conjunction with the interface manager and local DBMS, and (4) applications development software on the mainframe for creating reporting and consolidation systems.

Distributed data management is a difficult technical problem. Major offerings in this area are likely to come from vendors of traditional transaction-oriented DBMS. These firms have products that can be adapted for use in a distributed system, they can acquire rights to a microcomputer DBMS, and they have the technical talent to build an active data link. Vendors of friendly DBMS presently used for DSS are in a relatively poorer technical position for making the transition. Their added value has not been the sophistication of their data management, but the ease of use of their interface. With query languages moving down to the microcomputer in much more visual and interactive forms, much of this value will be lost. Many of their products have neither the capacity nor the sophistication to be used as a central DBMS accessed by hundreds of microcomputers. Significant investments will have to be made. Where these firms do have an important edge over traditional DBMS vendors is in marketing. This is a very important advantage that may make it difficult for traditional DBMS vendors with sophisticated products to compete in the end user marketplace.

The marketplace for interface managers coupled to operating systems is coming down to a two-horse race. Microsoft, the owners of the Disk Operating System (DOS) have an announced product called Window. IBM, which is expected to make its move into operating systems shortly, has announced an interface manager called Topview. Which horse will ultimately win this race is an easy bet.

Of great interest over the next few years will be the application vendors such as Lotus and Ashton-Tate. These firms have tremendous marketing power, but little "systems" experience, so it may be difficult for them to compete in distributed data management software, except through a strategic alliance with a DBMS vendor. Follow-on innovations have been hazardous in microcomputer software and there is still room for new vendors to sweep them aside. The IBM AT hardware is of such power that it will facilitate a new generation of applications software that may obsolete present applications.

Finally, a safe harbor for battered mainframe software vendors may be found by some as mainframe applications development facilities. Demand for these systems is growing rapidly, as data processing organizations discover that large productivity gains can be made (Lientz and Swanson, 1980). Applications such as reporting and consolidation systems sit somewhere between a transactional or operational system and an end user facility. They are generally high maintenance, run infrequently, so that machine efficiency is not important, and written by IS professionals. Comprehensive mainframe DSS software, with a little adjustment, provides an excellent development environment for these systems.

Only a relatively small number of firms will be able to compete successfully in more than one of these software segments. Not only is the technology different in different segments, but the customer is different as well. For distributed database products, the primary prospects are the data resource manager and the DBMS technician. Applications software is sold to end users and their support professionals. Applications development facilities are bought by applications development staff within information systems. The development of accepted standards between classes of software will further the separation between these four submarkets.

8. IMPLICATIONS FOR MANAGEMENT POLICIES

Mainframe- and minicomputer-based decision support systems software is nearing the end of its life cycle. Nonetheless, corporations continue to purchase this software, though in declining quantities. These packages are purchased to maintain compatibility with existing systems, to avoid the risks of unproven, newer technology, and because many of the microcomputer-based options are still evolving or are not well known. In future years, these will rarely be satisfactory reasons for purchasing host-based DSS software.

The most common reason for continuing to build a mainframe- or minicomputer-based end user computing environment is that it preserves the value of the existing investments in older systems. This is true, but that value is maintained at the expense of even greater value that will be derived from a newer generation of microcomputer-based DSS technology. What will emerge over the next few years is a set of software capabilities that will lift support systems to a new plateau of impact. That level cannot be bridged from the mainframe base of DSS technology.

This is not to say that much of the investment in existing DSS systems cannot be preserved. Instead, it argues that preserving the existing investment should not be a goal or constraint in making future investments. A key observation is that newer technology will impact data management-oriented and modeling-oriented DSS software at different rates. Data management for shared databases logically should continue to reside on the mainframe, so companies that have built mainframe- or mini-based database-oriented systems will be in a much better position to integrate the new generation of DSS capabilities into their existing systems, thereby preserving their investments. With the analytic portion of decision support systems software moving to the microcomputer there will be a nice marriage between the old and new technologies. On the other hand, organizations with large installed bases of mainframe- and minicomputer-based modeling packages have a big job of database building ahead of them before they can take advantage of the new technologies. In this case, investments in early DSS will probably have to be written off.

Major errors in purchase decisions can be avoided if a firm's end user computing policies include a plan for the evolution of its technological infrastructure (Henderson and Treacy, 1984). The issue of technological infrastructure includes policies defining appropriate hardware, software, and communications equipment for the DSS environment. Any plan should include a forecast of technological developments and of the evolving needs of the organization. It should have a horizon of about five years and should set down a schedule for the phased introduction and assimilation of newer generations of technology as they come available.

Internal corporate standards are a key component of a technology plan for end user computing. Software standards promote the ability to share analyses and data and simplify support and training. But standards can also act as a barrier to newer, more innovative generations of technology. Standards can sensibly be used to phase in new technology. They should not be used to freeze it.

Successful new software products emerge as a response to pressures placed upon vendors by their competition and their customers. Most vendors strongly desire more help from their customers in shaping future product offerings, so that they can better meet the needs of the marketplace. Corporate customers that develop that dialogue with vendors can gain sharp insights into future directions in DSS technology. And that vision of the future, after all, is the basis for proactively managing corporate end user computing.

REFERENCES

Ahlsen, M.; A. Bjornerstedt; S. Britts; C. Hulten; and L. Soderlund. "An Architecture for Object Management in OIS." *ACM Transactions on Office Information Systems* 2, no. 3 (July 1984), p. 173–96.

Bellman, R. E., and L. A. Zadeh. "Decision Making in a Fuzzy Environment." *Management Science* 17, no. 4 (December 1970), p. B141–64.

Branscomb, L. M., and J. C. Thomas. "Ease of Use: A System Design Challenge." *IBM Systems Journal* 23, no. 3 (1984), p. 224–35.

Davis, R. "Expert Systems: Where Are We and Where Do We Go from Here?" *AI Magazine*, Summer 1982.

Doherty, W. J., and R. P. Kelisky. "Managing VM/CMS Systems for User Effectiveness." *IBM Systems Journal* 18, no. 1 (1979), p. 143–62.

Ferris, D. "The Micro-Mainframe Connection." *Datamation* 29, no. 11 (November 1983), p. 126–38.

Folts, H. C. "Coming of Age: A Long-Awaited Standard for Heterogeneous Nets." *Data Communications*, January 1981, p. 63–73.

Gale, W. A., and D. Pregibon. "An Expert System for Regression Analysis." *Computer Science and Statistics: Proceedings of the 14th Symposium on the Interface*, 1982, p. 110–17.

Goldstein, B. C.; A. R. Heller; F. H. Moss; and I. Wladawsky-Berger. "Directions in Cooperative Processing between Workstations and Hosts." *IBM Systems Journal* 23, no. 3 (1984), p. 236–44.

Gorry, A., and M. Scott Morton. "A Framework for Management Information Systems." *Sloan Management Review* 13 (Fall 1971), p. 55–70.

Hayes-Roth, F; D. Waterman; and D. Lenat. *Building Expert Systems.* Reading, Mass.: Addison-Wesley, 1983, 444 pp.

Healey, M. "Junking the Mainframe." *Datamation* 29, no. 8 (August 1983), p. 120–36.

Henderson, J. C., and M. E. Treacy. "The Management of End User Computing." CISR Working Paper No. 114, Sloan School of Management, MIT, Cambridge, Mass., April 1984.

Huber, G. P. "Organizational Information Systems: Determinants of Their Performance and Behavior," *Management Science* 28, no. 2 (February 1982), p. 138–55.

Kay, Alan. "Computer Software." *Scientific American* 251, no. 3 (September 1984), p. 52–59.

Lientz, B. P., and E. B. Swanson. "Impact of Development Productivity Aids on Application System Maintenance." *Database* 11, no. 3 (1980), p. 114–20.

Lyngbaek, P., and D. McLeod. "Object Management in Distributed Information Systems." *ACM Transactions on Office Information Systems* 2, no. 2 (April 1984), p. 96–122.

Microsoft Corporation. *Disk Operating Systems.* IBM Document No. 1502343, Boca Raton, Fl.: September 1983.

Montgomery, D., and G. Urban. *Management Science in Marketing.* Englewood Cliffs, N.J.: Prentice-Hall, 1969.

Sirbu, M. "Innovation Strategies in the Electronic Mail Marketplace." *Telecommunications Policy,* September 1978, p. 191–210.

Sirbu, M., and L. Zwimpfer. "Standards Setting for Computer Communications: The Case of X.25." CISR Working Paper No. 117, Sloan School of Management, MIT, Cambridge, Mass., September 1984.

Winston, P. H. *Artificial Intelligence.* Reading, Mass.: Addison-Wesley, 1984, 527 pp.

Wurts, J. S. "The Future of Financial Modeling Systems." In *Proceedings of a Conference on the Future of Corporate Planning and Modeling Software Systems, June 25–26, 1981,* Durham, N.C.: Duke University, 1981.

Zdonik, S. "Object Management System Supporting Concepts: Integrated Office Workstation Applications." Ph.D. dissertation, MIT, Cambridge, Mass., May 1983.

PART 2
EXECUTIVE
SUPPORT SYSTEMS

One important part of the management support systems puzzle is executive support systems (ESS) or executive information systems (EIS). While there is not yet a precise definition of ESS, the goal is clear: to help top management better manage the firm. The technology necessary to accomplish this goal varies, depending on the task to be performed, the organization, and the executive's style. Some top managers consider their electronic mail system an important ESS; others use complex modeling software to play "What if?" games for strategic planning.

The papers that follow in this section explore the questions of:

- What are ESS?
- How can ESS best be used by managers?
- How can we determine what an individual manager needs in ESS?
- How are ESS best implemented?
- Do we really understand how managers think?

In late 1985 most of these questions are still hotly debated. Yet it is critical to determine their answers since the ability to have a positive impact on the capabilities of the top managerial team can have profoundly beneficial effects on an organization.

The papers offered in this section represent some of the seminal thinking in the executive support field. "The CEO Goes On-Line" by Rockart and Treacy was one of the first works to discuss ESS as an area separate from management information systems in general and decision support systems, specifically. Through case-based research, the authors provide the first taxonomy of executive support systems and point out important differences in the design and use of these systems as opposed to traditional MIS. They also introduce the concept of a "third era" of computer usage: the information support era.

The second paper, "The Implementation of Executive Support Systems" by Levinson presents the key elements of effective development and utilization of ESS, over a three-phase life cycle for the implementation process. This framework is derived from extensive field research and illustrated with descriptions of five case studies. The author concludes with a discussion of the relationship between ESS and organizational change.

The next paper by Treacy, "Supporting Senior Executives' Models for Planning and Control," looks into the controversy of whether or not senior executives should be supported by formal modeling tools, by addressing three key areas:

- The nature of executive analytical needs.
- The criteria for evaluating alternative forms of support for the different analytical needs.
- Alternative forms of decision support systems.

The author details four types of analytic support appropriate in the context of the complexity and structure of the problem being addressed:

- Model-oriented DSS.
- Data-oriented DSS.
- Information support.
- Fuzzy modeling and expert support.

An important conclusion of this paper is that the concept of "models" or "modeling" should not be too narrowly defined. The implicit mental models in use by executives today are valuable and viable.

The final paper in this section is "A Survey of Current Trends in the Use of Executive Support Systems," by De Long and Rockart. The authors report on the results of a random survey of the *Fortune* 500, with the objective of describing the scope of actual ESS use today. The study finds that two thirds of the companies have computer-based executive support systems in at least a segment of the company and that there is diverse and widespread activity in this area. However, there are eight common issues which impair progress in ESS in the surveyed companies:

1. Political implications of computer access for executives.
2. The influence of existing users.
3. Data resource management.
4. Lack of an implementation methodology.
5. Poor existing hardware and software.
6. The role of management style in design, development, and use.
7. Support and training.
8. Security.

The study concludes that much is indeed happening in the "real world" in executive support systems. However, major issues exist which make it difficult to develop useful systems for senior management.

Chapter Seven
The CEO
Goes On-Line

JOHN F. ROCKART
MICHAEL E. TREACY

Computer terminals are no strangers to corporate offices. Clerks have had them for years. Middle managers are increasingly using them. So are key staff personnel. But the thought that the CEO and other top officers of a billion-dollar company might regularly spend time at their own terminals usually elicits an amused smile and a shake of the head. Somehow, the image of top executives hard at work at a keyboard just doesn't seem right.

After all, their day is supposed to be filled with meetings with key division officers, briefings, telephone conversations, conferences, speeches, negotiations. What is more, the classic research on what executives actually do shows them to be verbally oriented with little use of "hard" information. According to Henry Mintzberg, "A great deal of the manager's inputs are soft and speculative—impressions and feelings about other people, hearsay, gossip, and so on. Furthermore, the very analytic inputs—reports, documents, and hard data in general—seem to be of relatively little importance."[1]

But consider:

- Ben W. Heineman, president and chief executive of Northwest Industries, spends a few hours almost every day at a computer terminal in his office. Heineman accesses reports on each of his nine operating companies and carries out original analyses using a vast store of data and an easy-to-use computer language. The terminal has become his most important tool for monitoring and planning activities.

- Roger E. Birk, president of Merrill Lynch, and Gregory Fitzgerald, chief financial officer, have access via computer terminals in their offices to a large number of continually updated reports on the company's worldwide operations. The system, to which a graphics capability has recently been added, was initiated by the former president of Merrill Lynch and Secretary of the Treasury Donald T. Regan as a vehicle for quickly generating information on the latest financial developments.

- John A. Schoneman, chairman of the board and CEO of Wausau Insurance Companies, and Gerald D. Viste, president and chief operating officer, use an on-line database of information about their own business and those of competitors. At their terminals they develop numerical and graphic analyses that help determine the company's strategic direction.

- George N. Hatsopoulos, president of Thermo Electron, writes programs in the APL language to format data contained in several of his company's databases. As a result, he can quickly study information about company, market, and economic conditions whenever he desires.

Although these examples do not yet represent common practice for senior corporate officers, they do suggest a trend toward greatly increased computer use in top-executive suites. In fact, during the past two years we have studied some 16 companies in which at least one of the three top officers, most often the CEO, directly accesses and uses computer-based information on a regular basis. In the pages that follow we present a status report on this rapidly growing phenomenon.

AN INFORMATION SYSTEM FOR EXECUTIVES

Top managers' use of computers is spreading for three primary reasons: user-oriented terminal facilities are now available at an acceptable price; executives are better informed of the availability and capabilities of these new technologies; and, predictably, today's volatile competitive conditions heighten the desire among top executives for ever more timely information and analysis.

Whatever its specific causes, this trend is indisputably a measured response to a widely perceived need or set of needs. Our study indicates that the actual patterns of executive computer use represent variations on only a few basic themes. Though these patterns evolved independently and may appear quite different, their similarities are striking—so striking in fact that they suggest the emergence in a number of companies of a new kind of executive information support (or "EIS") system.

From our observations, we can generalize a simple model of EIS structure and development into which fit all the individual systems we have seen. This model helps illuminate both the process of executive information support and the factors that determine its success.

All EIS systems share . . .

. . . A Central Purpose

Obviously, the top executives who personally use computers do so as part of the planning and control processes in their organizations. The provision of information to senior management for such purposes is certainly nothing new; the reason for EIS systems is to support a more effective use of this information. Those managers with terminals of their own have decided that they need a better understanding of the workings of their corporations. To achieve this, they have sought out the individually tailored access to the broader, more detailed sweep of data that only computers can provide.

. . . A Common Core of Data

Although no two EIS systems are identical, each contains what we call a "data cube" (see Exhibit 1)—that is, data on important *business variables* (for example, the major general ledger accounting variables and, equally important, the nonfinancial substantive figures—such as unit sales by product line—that underlie and explain the accounting numbers) through *time* (budgeted, actual, and revised data on key variables is kept on a month-by-month basis for a number of past years, usually five, and is available in the form of projections for several years into the future) and by

EXHIBIT 1   THE DATA CUBE

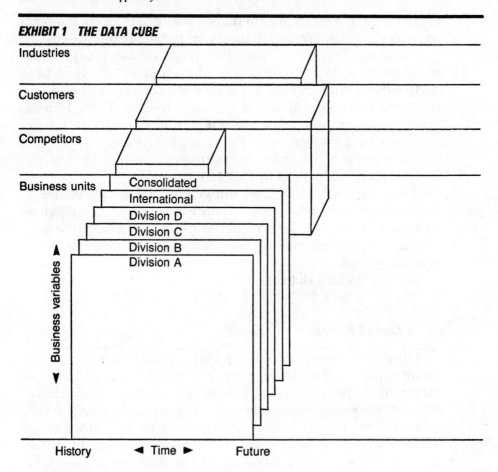

business unit (whatever the nature of those units—geographic, divisional, or functional).

What sets this data cube apart from information traditionally gathered by staff members and included in reports to top management is the sheer breadth of its cross-functional sources and the depth of its detail. With such inclusive information at their fingertips, executives can of course work through traditional accounting comparisons of "actual," "last year," and "budget" for a single business unit. But they can also look at a few variables, such as working capital and its major components, across time for a single subsidiary or at a single variable—say, a product line's performance in physical units as well as dollars—across all subsidiaries.

Further, a number of companies have extended these axes of

data to include information, however incomplete, on major competitors, key customers, and important industry segments.[2] Much of this information can be purchased today in the form of any of the several thousand machine-processable databases sold by information vendors. For competitive financial data, for example, one common source is Standard & Poor's Compustat tape, which provides 10 years of data on 130 business variables for more than 3,500 companies.

Operating data from a growing number of industries are readily available from industry associations or other published sources. Some of these sources—customer surveys, market sampling, and the like—are fairly "soft," but they are accurate enough for managerial planning and control purposes.

. . . Two Principal Methods of Use

The EIS systems in our study are used in two quite different ways by executives: (1) for access to the current status and projected trends of the business and (2) for personalized analyses of the available data. Let us look briefly at these two modes of use.

Status Access. When executives have "read only" access to the latest data or reports on the status of key variables, they can peruse the information requested but can do very little, if any, data manipulation. In industries where market conditions change rapidly, where there are many factors to watch, or where hour-to-hour operational tracking is important, the status access of this sort can be of great use. This is indeed the case at Merrill Lynch and at several other financial companies.

The status access approach also provides an easy, low-cost, and low-risk means to help an executive become comfortable with a computer terminal. At Owens-Illinois, for example, the first stage in the development of an EIS system will—for just these reasons—provide only status access for the CEO and other senior executives. Moreover, taking this approach can send a clear signal throughout an organization that top management intends to put more emphasis than it had in the past on quantitative analysis in the planning and control process. As one CEO put it, "The terminal on my desk is a message to the organization."

Personalized Analysis. Executives can, of course, use the computer not only for status access but also as an analytic tool. At Northwest Industries, Wausau, and Thermo Electron, senior managers have chosen the contents of the databases available to them and have learned to do some programming themselves. Instead of merely having access to the data, they are able to do creative analyses of their own.

The type of analysis performed differs from manager to manager. Some merely compute new ratios or extrapolate current trends into the future. Some graph trends of particular interest to gain an added visual perspective. Some work with elaborate simulation models to determine where capital investments will be most productive. All, however, enjoy a heightened ability to look at, change, extend, and manipulate data in personally meaningful ways. But to make this approach effective, executives must be willing to invest much of their own time and energy in defining the needed data and in learning what the computer can do.

. . . A Support Organization

Finally, all the systems we observed depend on the provision of a high level of personal support to their executive users. This support is essential if those systems are to have a fair chance to demonstrate their full potential. Users require at least some initial training and ongoing assistance with computer languages. And they need help in establishing and updating databases as well as in conceptualizing, designing, and improving their systems and their analyses.

In the organizations we observed, a group of EIS "coaches," often former consultants, gives EIS users continuing assistance. Their primary role is "to help" rather than "to do." Because such EIS coaches must be a different breed of expert from data processing analysts and because they need to be shielded from involvement in the normal run of EDP fire-fighting activities, the companies we studied have separated them organizationally from their regular data processing operations.

NORTHWEST INDUSTRIES: AN EXAMPLE

Perhaps the most impressive example of an EIS system, both in esign and use, is that at Northwest Industries (1980 sales: $2.9 billion). The development of this system began in 1976 when Heineman decided that he needed a specially tailored database to aid him in monitoring, projecting, and planning the progress of his nine operating companies. A great believer in the advantages of "not being the captive of any particular source of information," Heineman wanted to be able to analyze various aspects of the business himself but saw little opportunity to do so without a computer-based system to reduce data-handling chores.

In January 1977, the six top executives at Northwest were given access to an experimental system through which they could retrieve more than 70 reports and perform such limited analyses as compound growth calculations, variance analysis, and trend projections. By February, Heineman had reached the limits of the system's capabilities and was demanding more.

Additional capabilities came in the form of a new access and analysis language, EXPRESS, which facilitated not only simple file handling and data aggregation but also extensive modeling and statistical analyses of data series. To complement these improved capabilities, Northwest has since added to its executive database:

- 350 financial and operational items of data on planned, budgeted, forecasted, and actual monthly results for each operating company for the past eight and the next four years.
- 45 economic and key ratio time series.
- Several externally subscribed databases, including Standard & Poor's Compustat and DRI services.

Northwest's EIS system with its extensive and continually growing database is now used by almost all managers and executives at corporate headquarters to perform their monitoring and analytic functions. But the driving force behind the system and its most significant user remains Heineman. Working with the system is an everyday thing for him, a natural part of his job. With his special knowledge of the business and with his newly acquired ability to write his own programs, Heineman sees great value in working at a terminal himself rather than handing all assignments to staff personnel.

"There is a huge advantage to the CEO to get his hands dirty in the data," he says, because "the answers to many significant questions are found in the detail. The system provides me with an improved ability to ask the right questions and to know the wrong answers." What is more, he finds a comparable advantage in having instant access to the database to try out an idea he might have. In fact, he has a computer terminal at home and takes another with him on vacations.

Supporting Heineman and other Northwest executives are a few information systems people who function as EIS coaches. They train and assist users in determining whether needed data are already available and whether any additional data can be obtained. They also help get new information into the database, train users in access methods, and teach them to recognize the analytic routines best fitted to different types of analyses. Only for major modeling applications do these coaches actually take part in the system design and programming process.

What Top Managers Are Saying about EIS Systems

• The system has been of infinite help in allowing me to improve my mental model of the company and the industry we're in. I feel much more confident that I am on top of the operations of our company and its future path.

• Your staff really can't help you think. The problem with giving a question to the staff is that they provide you with the answer. You learn the nature of the real question you should have asked when you muck around in the data.

• It saves a great deal of the time spent in communicating with functional staff personnel. Today, for an increasing number of problems, I can locate the data I want, and I can develop it in the form I want, faster than I could describe my needs to the appropriate staffer.

• Some of my best ideas come at fallow times between five in the evening and seven the next morning. Access to the relevant data to check out something right then is very important. My home terminal lets me perform the analysis while it's at the forefront of my mind.

• Comparing various aspects of our company with the competition is a very fast way of defining the areas in which I should place most of my attention. The system allows me to do exactly that.

• I think graphically. It's so nice to be able to easily graph out the data in which I'm interested. . . . And it's especially nice to be able to adjust the display to see the data in the exact perspective that best tells the story.

• I've always felt that the answers were in the detail. Now, at last, I

THE PROMISE OF EIS SYSTEMS

Most of America's top managers still have no terminal-based access whatsoever. They find the idea of working at a terminal a violation of their managerial styles and their view of their roles. They are perfectly comfortable asking staff to provide both manual and computer-generated analyses as needed. What is more, EIS systems provide no clear, easily defined cost savings. In fact, we know of no system that a traditional cost/benefit study would justify in straight labor-saving terms. Why, then, are managers implementing them in growing numbers?

---

can pore through some of that detail. That's my style. It used to mean long nights and plenty of staff and lots of frustration. Now it's somewhat easier. And frankly, it also saves me a great deal of staff time that was formerly spent on routine charting and graphing.

• I bring a lot of knowledge to the party. Just scanning the current status of our operations enables me to see some things that those with less time in the company would not see as important. Although the resulting telephone calls undoubtedly shake up some of my subordinates, I think in the long run this is helpful to them, too.

• The system provides me with a somewhat independent source for checking on the analyses and opinions presented both by my line subordinates and by my functional staffs. There is a great deal of comfort in being relatively independent of the analyses done by others.

• By working with the data I originally thought I needed, I've been able to zero in on the data I actually need. We've expanded our database significantly, but each step has led to better understanding of our company and its environment.

• Frankly, a secondary, but very real, advantage of the use of the system by me is the signal it gives to the rest of the company that I desire more quantitatively oriented management of the organization. I want my subordinates to think more analytically, and they are. I feel we're on the way to becoming a significantly better-managed company.

EXHIBIT 2 A Conceptual Model of Executive Information Support

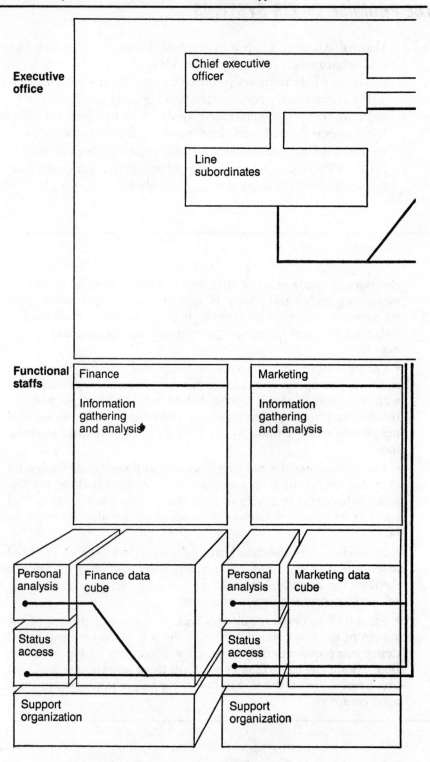

Executive office

Chief executive officer

Line subordinates

Functional staffs

Finance

Information gathering and analysis

Marketing

Information gathering and analysis

Personal analysis

Finance data cube

Personal analysis

Marketing data cube

Status access

Status access

Support organization

Support organization

EXHIBIT 2   *(concluded)*

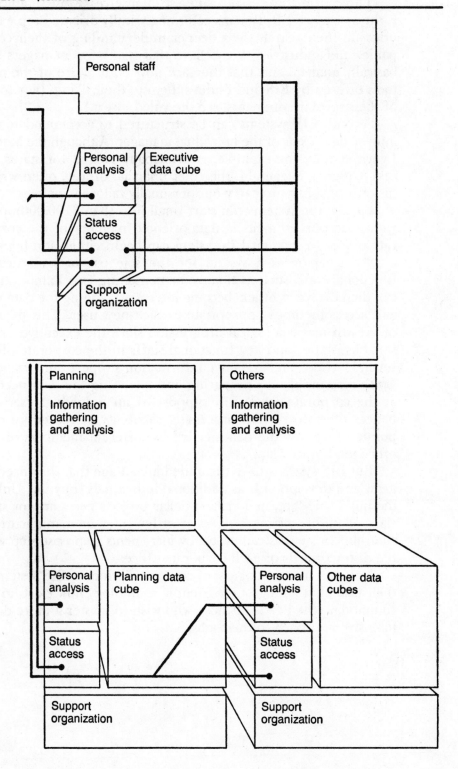

Three principal reasons suggest themselves. Most significant is the assistance EIS systems offer analytically oriented top executives in their search for a deeper understanding of their companies and industries. We believe that many top managers are basically analytic and that they are now both aware of the new tools offered by EIS and finding them to their liking. (For some of their specific comments, see the ruled insert.)

Second, EIS systems can be structured to accommodate the information needs of the individual manager. Although the Merrill Lynch system, for example, is principally geared for status access, Gregory Fitzgerald, the chief financial officer, often writes his own programs to carry out personally tailored analyses.

Finally, the systems can start small (less than $100,000), providing support to a single data-oriented member of the corporate office. In fact, an EIS system can begin either at a line-executive level or as a system for the sole use of a particular functional staff, such as finance or marketing (see Exhibit 2). It can then evolve as others become interested, adding the data sets and access methods appropriate to each new user. This pattern of growth marks a logical progression since the executives, personal assistants, and key functional staffs in the corporate office form, in effect, an "executive information support organization" *jointly* responsible for preparing and analyzing the data needed at the corporate level. EIS support of an individual user enhances the information processing capability of the entire corporate office, for the data needed by different members of the office tend to overlap.

But EIS systems have the added advantage that they need to grow and develop only as additional individuals "buy in." Unlike the huge, one-shot, multimillion-dollar projects necessary for such classic data processing systems as order entry or manufacturing control, EIS systems can evolve by increments in precise step with the distinct needs of each corporate office.

Not all senior managers, of course, will find an EIS system to their taste, but enough user-friendly technology now exists to accommodate the needs of those who wish to master a more data-intensive approach to their jobs.

> *I went to work now to learn the shape of the river; and of all the eluding and ungraspable objects that ever I tried to get mind or hands on, that was the chief. I would fasten my eyes upon a sharp, wooded point that projected far into the river some miles ahead of me, and go to laboriously photographing its shape upon my brain; and just as I was beginning to succeed to my satisfaction, we would draw up toward it and the exasperating thing would begin to melt away and fold back into the bank! If there had been a conspicuous dead tree standing upon the very point of the cape, I would find that tree inconspicuously merged into the general forest, and occupying the middle of a straight shore, when I got abreast of it! No prominent hill would stick to its shape long enough for me to make up my mind what its form really was, but it was as dissolving and changeful as if it had been a mountain of butter in the hottest corner of the tropics. Nothing ever had the same shape when I was coming downstream that it had borne when I went up.*
>
> From *Life on the Mississippi* by Mark Twain

FOOTNOTES

1. See Henry Mintzberg, "Planning on the Left Side and Managing on the Right," *Harvard Business Review* July–August 1976, p. 49.
2. For one method of defining those variables that should be included, see John F. Rockart, "Chief Executives Define Their Own Data Needs," *Harvard Business Review,* March–April 1979, p. 81.

Chapter Eight
The Implementation of Executive Support Systems

ELIOT LEVINSON

INTRODUCTION

Paul Dawson is President of Wellness, Inc., a health care distribution company. When Dawson took over the division two years ago, it was wracked by problems, losing market share, and its veteran sales force was not producing results. The firm was headed for its first loss in a decade. During the past year Dawson and his associates have utilized a computer-based executive information system to analyze their markets, reorganize their sales approach, restructure and sell off a part of a manufacturing unit, and change their product mix. Use of this tool has been instrumental in the turnaround of Wellness into a profitable company. In the process, Dawson has changed the culture of Wellness from a traditional sales organization to an analysis-oriented marketing organization. He has also restructured the organization to better fit the new direction. Employees of Wellness see the changes as a dramatic culture shift.

John Pepper is one of 18 group executives of a very large manufacturing firm. For the last 12 months Pepper has had a personal computer on his desk and one in his home. The personal computer is linked to several corporate databases, has word processing and electronic mail, Pepper's stock portfolio, spreadsheets, calendaring, document transfer capabilities, and allows him access to external databases and news services. Mr. Pepper has his secretary check the electronic mail and uses the personal computer to analyze his stock

Center for Information Systems Research Working Paper No. 119, Sloan School of Management, MIT, Cambridge, Mass., October 1984.

portfolio, but he is not using his support system to any large degree.

John Pepper and Paul Dawson both have executive support systems (ESS): terminal-based computer systems designed to aid senior executives in the management of the firm. The use of information technology at the top of the firm warrants study to provide insight into how the technology is changing the practice of management, as well as the processes and procedures in the firm.

The executives who sponsored the ESSs in this study view them as being of two types:

1. *Executive office automation* focusing on *efficiency,* emphasizing personal management and communication tools.
2. *Business-orieneted systems* focusing on *effectiveness,* emphasizing decision support tools based on a business problem.

The purpose of this paper is to describe these two types of ESS and to discuss the five key elements most effective in the development and utilization of ESS. Their interactive effects are not fully explicated in this discussion; rather, it allows for a clear understanding of the building blocks of executive support.

FRAMEWORK

The framework for this study attempts to explain the degree of usefulness executive support systems ultimately provide to their users. There are two components to the framework:

- The *key elements* component identifies those features of the ESS which distinguish successful from unsuccessful implementation efforts. These key elements were derived from observation of ESS in the firms we studied.
- The *time framework* addresses the stages of implementation.

The stage framework, combined with the key elements, allows determination of the importance of individual elements at different stages of implementation. The stage theory was developed and utilized by the Rand Corporation in the evaluation of technological innovations (Bikson, 1981). It is based on the premise that the utility of innovation is discovered and invented as it is utilized.

New technologies are never implemented as planned. To achieve successful implementation, both the technology and the organization must change and adapt to each other. To understand the implementation of ESS, a framework of the implementation process and of the components of executive support is helpful.

The five key elements that impact the effectiveness of ESS are:

1. The presence of a *business problem* or vision used to define the purpose of the system.
2. *Titular sponsorship* by a senior executive and *managerial sponsorship* by his delegate.
3. The organization of Management Information Systems (MIS) *computing groups* as effective support organizations that translate managerial needs into technical systems.
4. The existence of a well-defined, accessible *database*.
5. The effective *management of resistance* that occurs as the new systems change established procedures and reporting relationships.

These key elements are of varying importance at different stages of development and implementation of the system.

Figure 1, the matrix of key elements of executive support at different stages of development, provides the framework for understanding what is essential to the successful implementation of an ESS.

The implementation process is divided into a life cycle of three phases: organization, installation, and institutionalization.

The *organization* phase occurs before the ESS is implemented. The task in this period is to define the problem being solved, form the coalition of people necessary to undertake the project, determine what information is needed, and develop a sense of what the support will accomplish.

The *installation* phase is the actual undertaking of the project. During this period there are usually (1) technical problems, (2) organizational resistance issues that arise around unexpected startup problems and changes in procedures, and (3) adjustments needed to augment or decrease the scope of the system. There can be several iterations of a support system and changes in participation in it as it evolves. At the end of the installation period a decision is made to continue the use of the support system or to cease its use, either because it did not fulfill its initial

FIGURE 1

	Business Problem	Sponsorship	Computing Groups	Database	Management of Resistance
Organization	High	High	High	High	Low
Installation	Low	High	High	Low	High
Institution	Low	Low	High	High	Low

purpose, or the purpose, while met, did not provide the assistance originally anticipated.

The *institutionalization* phase is the period in which the system becomes incorporated as an ongoing part of organizational procedures. Institutionalization can occur in several ways: use of the system by successors to the original executive, diffusion of the system to other executives, and/or by changes in the work of subordinates and the structure and processes of the organization.

This implementation framework allows us to study executive support from its inception, through development to full usage. Concomitantly, it provides an aid to understanding when and why ESSs do or do not work as planned, are institutionalized, or are discarded.

METHODOLOGY

The research for this study comes from two sources: (1) in-depth case studies documenting the implementation of executive support systems in 5 firms over a two-year period; and (2) the regular monitoring of executive support activity in 20 firms. The majority of the systems were studied from planning phase through implementation.

Longitudinal studies were undertaken because it was presumed that usefulness of the support systems would be determined during their implementation, since planners, users, and those affected by the system had no previous experience with the innovation. It was also felt that different problems and processes would occur at various stages in the implementation process: specifically that the issues involved in the organization stage (pre-implementation), installation stage, and institutionalization (post-implementation) would be different and could modify the initial design of the support system.

The case study utilized interviews conducted on a regular basis in each of the five firms, with senior executives, MIS personnel and managers, and analysts who were affected by the system. In addition, records of all events which reflected the resource allocation, planning, execution, and use of the system were used with the interviews.

Third, a systematic tracking of decisions involved in the implementation of the support system was developed for each firm in order to facilitate comparison of the systems and to isolate the key factors that affected successful or problematic implementation of the system.

The contract with the other 15 firms consisted of three meetings per year with managers and MIS directors responsible for executive support systems and the ongoing monitoring of these systems. Following is a description of the five firms (names are disguised):

Manuco is a multinational manufacturing organization with stable leadership. Manuco has been affected severely in recent years by foreign competition and the need to modernize production processes. Executive support was called for by the chairman who felt that every group head should demonstrate the use of technology as an example for their organizations. Responsibility for development and execution of the support system was given to the MIS organization. The system consisted of a pilot program involving 18 executives and their secretaries, who were provided with various word processing, spreadsheet and communication tools. At the end of one year, the pilot program was ended and some of the executives returned their terminals.

Wellness is a manufacturing and distribution organization which had suffered a loss in profitability and market share. The support system was called for by the new CEO who was attempting to make the company more analysis and marketing oriented. At the end of two years the system had expanded from usage by eight executives to significantly affect the work of product managers and analysts. There are currently two subsystems of the executive support system: one for the marketing organization, and one for the sales organization. Significant changes have occurred in the product mix, organizational structure, incentive system, and middle management work, along with implementation of the support system. Currently there is concentration on a training program for managers, and reorganization of the database.

Smokestack is a basic manufacturing organization which was suffering large losses and near collapse. The support system was called for by the new chairman who was looking for a system to help him identify areas for cost control. Responsibility for the system was given to the CFO. Over the last two years there have been several attempts at limited executive support, including a personnel system, an acquisition model, a management reporting system, and a pricing model. Currently the CFO is establishing a budgeting model to be used by the senior five managers in making allocation decisions. During the last two years there has been an improvement in the financial position of the firm, but there have been several reorganizations, personnel changes, and divestitures.

International Products is a consumer products company responsible for the production, marketing, and sales of personal care products. The company has a long-established market share and is a leader in its industry. The support system was called for by the new CEO who was looking for a way to present complex data simply and wanted to identify changes in the firm's markets and bring divisions into line with the group's strategic plan. Responsibility for the ESS was given to the comptroller; initial users were the CEO and the comptroller. After two and a half years the system has moved down to the divisional presidents and is used by the financial staff. The system's range of applications has expanded to include all of the financial and much nonfinancial data. Executive support has also diffused to other groups of the company.

Toy Electric is the research and development group of a consumer electronics company which was undergoing a change in organizational structure. The chairman called for an ESS to be used in adding communication and personal management tools among the 30 vice presidents of the firm. Implementation of the support system was delegated to the MIS department for initial installation, which included 15 vice presidents and their secretaries, and utilized various communication applications. The project was doubled in size after the first year. At the end of the second year the pilot project was terminated.

The main body of this paper is organized as a discussion of the five individual key elements. In discussing each element, key issues will be presented and examples will be given showing how the various firms dealt with these issues at different stages of implementation.

The paper will close with a section that integrates the various elements and relates ESS to organizational change.

BUSINESS PROBLEM

Firms initiate ESS for three reasons: (1) to solve a business problem; (2) to make executives more efficient; or (3) symbolically to signal to the organization that technology should be employed. There is a distinct difference in the development and use of ESS in the firms where it is initiated as a problem-solving tool and where it is initiated for other reasons. The problem-solving systems begin small in number of applications and number of users, and then grow. They gradually evolve into planning systems. The efficiency systems begin with a larger number of users and atrophy. At the end of two years only the problem-initiated systems survived.

Organization Phase

The business problem is most important during the early stage of development of the support system. Two of the systems were established as crisis responses by new CEOs, who were looking to the new technology for an effective solution to dealing with serious problems. At Smokestack, the firm was losing $250 million a year and the chairman asked for a system which would allow him to control costs. At Wellness, sales had decreased substantially and the CEO wanted a database which would allow him to shift the company to an analytic marketing orientation.

At International, the division head knew that unless the company could come up with a clear strategic plan, and find better ways of communicating financial information, they were headed for hard times. He looked to ESS as a possible way of averting serious problems.

Clear expectations of the system's capabilities and benefits to the firm by the executive sponsor play an important role in its early development and ultimate utility. At Wellness and International, the sponsors defined their problem or organizational vision clearly and manageably so these issues were addressed. In both cases a critical success factors process was used with a small group of top management to clarify goals and specify the type of information executives needed. This process also served to establish a sense of mission within the organization. At Smokestack the function of the support system was initially more ambiguous. The early prototype was focused on cost problems but there was no clear direction because there were several other problems apparent at the same time. It was not until two years and three pilots later when executive support focused around the budgeting process, that the system began to function.

At Manuco and Toy, the ESS was not linked to business problems. Although Manuco had several long-standing business issues caused by its competitive situation, these were not employed as a catalyst for the executive support system. The only expectation set by the Chairman of Manuco was that senior executives should experiment with information technology and thus provide an example for people below them in their organization to use it. At Toy, the President wanted a machine for the 30 vice presidents and their secretaries which would help them communicate and manage their time better. In comparison to the effectiveness systems, the initial expectations of these systems were low, as they supported tasks peripheral to the core needs of the business.

Installation Phase

As implementation evolves through and beyond the installation period, the original business problem is not as important as it is in the organizational phase. During the installation phase at Wellness, the support system evolved to include more applications and receive use from lower levels in the organization. The focus of the system moved from present problems to planning of future products, and a component for the sales organization was added. At International, several financial, competitive, and nonfinancial databases were added to the initial support system and the executives of the divisions were put on the system.

Initially, executives use the support system to retrieve the management reports that they used to receive in hard copy. As the support systems evolve and their staffs develop competence in the use of decision support tools, the systems are increasingly used for "what if" queries and scenario building.

At Smokestack, the evolutionary design took the form of trial and error. Since the initial goals of the ESS were ambiguous, there were a series of support systems developed for various executives, including an executive personnel system, a pricing model, a management reporting system, and a plastics division model. None of these systems was totally successful and they reflected the ambiguity of the chairman in his initial call for executive support. They did, however, serve to expose senior executives to some of the possibilities of information technology.

The approach to ESS at Manuco and Toy during the installation phase could be termed the "portfolio approach." The Information Systems (IS) departments provided a range of applications such as electronic mail, calendaring, word processing, spreadsheets, automatic dialing, and corporate reports. The rationale was that with a wide choice of applications the executives would find something useful. At both firms, a significant number of executives utilized electronic mail, though a lack of people on the mail system at Toy made its use limited. Over time the usage of the communications tools diminished and only a small number of people used them.

The difficulty of implementing the efficiency systems can be attributed to the fact that senior executives have satisfactory support in the form of executive secretaries and assistants, and subordinates respond to their demands quickly. This differs from the business-problem-based systems where the information provided value added about a core concern of the business.

Institutionalization Phase

During the institutionalization phase, the raison d'être for ESS shifts from a business crisis to a combination of monitoring business health and looking toward the future.

At International, the President has used the ESS in assessing new ventures as a way of avoiding the decline of old products. At Wellness, the ESS is being used to make decisions about new-product development.

Another aspect of executive support in the institutionalization period is its linkage to core organizational processes. At Smokestack, it is utilized in the budgeting process, at International in strategic planning, and at Wellness in marketing and sales. It is interesting to note that those ESS which were not institutionalized were not linked to any core business function.

SPONSORSHIP

Sponsorship is the initiative role played by the senior executive in the design, development, and use of support systems. The executive's participation makes more of a mark on the implementation of ESS than on any other element in the initiation and execution of executive support. The sponsor's functions include:

- Initiating the demand for ESS.
- Establishing an organization to implement it.
- Defining its purpose.
- Evolving its usage.
- Utilizing its outputs.
- Moving it through the organization.

In the firms we have researched and worked with there have been a variety of patterns of sponsorship that include executives who view ESS as an essential management tool and those who see ESS as peripheral. There are executives who participate in the design, development, and evolution of the system, while others delegate it to the IS department. There are those who define the purpose of the system very early, while others discover its utility during implementation. The sponsorship role changes during the life of the support system. Initially, the titular sponsor—that executive who called for the system—is most important. As time moves on, an "operating sponsor," the person delegated to manage the installation and diffusion of the system, becomes most important.

Organizational Phase

The titular sponsor's motivation to call for ESS is spawned by two situations: (1) the combination of a crisis he or she wants to solve and being new to the job, or (2) a desire to have executives utilize computer technology as part of their daily work. The titular sponsors in this study divided into two categories. Those who called for effectiveness systems were all new to their jobs, looking for information to aid them in the solution of some problem, to provide a fast understanding of how the organization functioned, and to bring about organizational change. The sponsors who called for efficiency systems had been in their jobs longer and were motivated by a generalized desire to have other senior executives demonstrate modernity and work more efficiently by using technology.

After saying "I want one," the next step was defining what "one" was. At this stage there were a variety of responses by the sponsors. At Wellness, there was a problem–solution support system match. The CEO and his top managers went through a critical success factors process and defined the information needed to analyze their markets, assess performance of their products, and link the two to their sales territories. This exercise articulated a clear vision of where the management team was heading in aiming at high profit margin items. At Smokestack, the chairman and the head of decision support utilized a similar problem–solution match to develop a prototype system for cost control, but no other executives were involved. At International, the "discover as you implement" approach was used in defining the system. The comptroller, who had been developing accounts receivable and forecasting applications and the new CEO who was trying to find a way to easily communicate financial information requested that a computer graphics system be linked with the database.

At Manuco and Toy, the CEOs defined the support systems through delegation. At Manuco, the chairman stated that he wanted every group executive to have a computer on his desk, symbolizing to the rest of the organization that senior management was using technology, so they should. He then delegated sponsorship of the project to the IS organization. At Toy, the president asked an engineering group and then the MIS group to find a communications tool for senior executives which would combine a telephone and computer tools to help them with their management. In both cases the titular sponsor saw the support system as technical support and delegated its definition to technical organizations. This was in sharp contrast to the other three firms where the titular sponsors saw the systems as management tools and involved themselves and other executives in defining the systems.

Installation Phase

The role of sponsorship shifts from the titular sponsor to the operating sponsor as the task changes from envisioning the support system to installing it and evolving its usage within the organization.

The role of operating sponsorship is best demonstrated by its absence. At Smokestack, the chairman delegated installation of the project to the CFO who resigned, then to another vice president who was uninterested in the system. During this 15-month hiatus, the computing group initiated a series of less than successful support systems for division heads, and various vice presidents. A new CFO was then appointed who implemented a management reporting system for the group vice presidents (that had been stalled by his predecessor), and then the computing group, under the auspices of the CFO, developed a model to be used by all groups in the budget process. This model allowed the chairman and CFO to look at the relationships of the various groups as a value-added chain, something they had previously been unable to do. This budgeting model is becoming the ESS as it allows the senior management to look at individual businesses and their relationship to each other, which is the current central problem of the firm.

The comptroller at International represents a good example of operating sponsorship. He acted as the gatekeeper between the computing group and the president, made decisions regarding application development, linked the support system to the strategic planning process, and executed all of the applications so they were usable by other executives. As his primary contribution, the comptroller directed the financial analysts in learning to develop and utilize the ESS. He was also instrumental in diffusing ESS usage downward, into the various divisions of the group.

Sophisticated knowledge of computer technology was not a necessary condition for effective usage of the support system by senior executives. The ESS were very easy to use, with such features as menus, touch screens, and fourth generation languages. During the installation phase, the executives we observed learned to utilize the technology, usually beginning with retrieval of the standard reports they previously had received in hardcover. When more sophisticated tasks, such as querying and modeling, were demanded the executive had the system chauffeur-driven by one of his staff. The CEOs at Wellness and International both stated that ESS gave them an understanding of the dynamics of their businesses they had never had prior to the system's installation.

Institutionalization Phase

During the institutionalization phase of ESS, the sponsors became more users of the system's output and less directors of its development. By demanding a coherent set of information within an easily accessible, defined framework, these sponsors had driven the organizations under them to hire and train managers with computer skills who spent a significant part of their time inputting data to the system. At both Wellness and International, line managers and staff analysts adapted their work to the support system.

During the institutionalization period there are two processes which occur: (1) the ESS is diffused to other parts of the organization where new sponsors must adapt it to their needs, and (2) middle management is affected by having to fit analyses and reports into the framework of the support system in answering requests of their superiors.

The importance of new sponsorship can be seen at International. The MIS group disseminated the tools developed in the original division to another group. The group executive did not perceive the financial management tools as linked to his job, so what had been an ESS, became a middle management efficiency tool, helping the financial analysts in the new group to get their work done faster. At Wellness, and in the original group at International, the division heads and middle managers were highly affected by the ESS. The ESS imposed a discipline on the type of questions asked by senior executives of their subordinates, which in turn demanded that middle managers utilize computer-based skills and begin thinking in the framework of the ESS. In the three firms where problem-oriented ESS were established, the middle managers perceived their advancement as being linked to their ability to utilize decisions support tools.

ESS is an end user computing tool. The sponsor plays the key role in defining the use of the ESS so that it is used as a management tool. There were two patterns of sponsorship that delineated whether the ESS was ultimately useful as a management tool. One group of sponsors, exemplified by either the titular or operating sponsor in the effectiveness groups, saw the ESS as an extension of themselves and participated actively in its design and in the establishment of an organization to implement and manage it. Systems implemented under these sponsors reached full implementation. The other group delegated the design of the system to others, giving the message that they saw ESS as technical support rather than as a management tool.

There are two constructs that should be considered in understanding sponsorship. The first is that business crises or visions create effective sponsorship, and the second is that some executives, the *co-opters*, view the technology as a valuable phenomenon that must be turned to their advantage, while others, the *victims*, do not understand it and therefore manage it by delegating it to technical groups, and do not involve themselves in the process of implementation.

COMPUTING GROUPS

The role of computing groups is central to Executive Support Systems throughout the life cycle of implementation. The structure of the group, its relationship to management, and the approaches it uses in developing the support system at different stages of evolution significantly impact the effectiveness of the support system. ESS presents MIS with the extremes of the problems and opportunities associated with end user computing. The perceived power differential between general managers and MIS staff, combined with the differences in the nature of managerial and technical work, affect the process of defining and implementing easy to use, but complex, support systems.

In the various approaches that MIS or management take, there are three key factors to be controlled which affect implementation: (1) problem definition, (2) the type of ESS presented as the solution to the problem, and (3) the organizational sponsorship of the ESS. When all three factors are addressed, as in the case of management-generated support systems to solve a defined problem, the implementation process will move most effectively to meet expectations. When these expectations are not well defined, the ESS has less likelihood of being effective.

There are three types of IS organizations associated with ESS: the data processing (DP) group, the segmented group, and the integrated group, as shown in Figure 2.

The DP group differs little from the groups that constructed

FIGURE 2   Organization of MIS Groups

DP		Segmented		Integrated Managerial Group
Data Center	DP	Systems	End User	End-User
Office Automation		Development	Computing	Management
DSS				– – – –
Development				End-User
				Computing

---

transaction processing systems a decade ago, but they have since absorbed new technologies, including office automation and decision support. The DP groups approached ESS as a traditional systems development effort. The DP groups were staffed by people with strong technical backgrounds and had a product orientation. They took full delegated control of the projects rather than sharing decision making with management, and placed major emphasis on the development of hardware. The DP groups concentrated their effort more on the early phases of the project rather than on the installation phase of ESS.

In the segmented MIS organization, the end user computing function is autonomous: data processing is handled by one group, systems development by a second, and end user computing by a third.

An end user computing group differs from a traditional DP group in several respects:

1. They are service rather than product oriented. Their role is to help the end user accomplish his aims and establish the most appropriate hardware and software environments in which to do this. They do not "control" the system. From the outset it is clear that decisions concerning use of the system come from the end user. In two of our cases it was decided prior to beginning work that the system would be turnkeyed to the end user.

2. End user computing groups are staffed by people with a business background, or project teams are set up to include end user management.

3. End-user groups use an evolutionary design process which starts with a prototype and adds applications incrementally, as opposed to the traditional DP process of fully developing the system before usage.

The integrated MIS groups report directly to management as members of the executive's staff and have only a "dotted-line" relationship to the MIS organization. None of the groups we studied started as integrated groups, but evolved that way as the ESS implementation progressed. The staff within the integrated group is more managerial than technical in background and demonstrates consulting skills. However, they have a strong background in computer tools. They view information technology as the tool to accomplish a primary business task, such as financial planning or marketing.

The differences and similarities between the groups can be seen in their definition of, and approaches to, implementing ESS at different stages of development.

Organization Phase

The main task in the early stages of ESS is defining the problem to be worked with and choosing appropriate hardware and software. At Wellness, the end user computing group interviewed several subsidiary presidents to find a situation where an ESS would meet a need. They found a subsidiary where the new CEO was looking for a tool to change the focus of the company from sales to marketing. They conducted critical success factor interviews among the four senior executives to determine what information was needed and then developed a prototype of the marketing support system. At this point, Wellness committed the funding for the project and the Wellness management, jointly with the end user computing group, chose Express as the language for the ESS. A member of the end user computing staff was assigned at Wellness.

In contrast to Wellness, at Manuco executive support was given to an engineering group within the management systems organization which then developed technical specifications for personal computers to be used by executives. The project was then given to a newly formed marketing group within the information systems group which developed applications for an executive workstation. After the hardware had been ordered, the marketing group interviewed the 18 executives and their secretaries, who were designated as users. Unfortunately, they found out in the interviews that the hardware did not meet the work requirements of the executives.

The main differences between the approaches of the DP

groups and the end user organizations are that: (1) DP groups emphasized hardware, where the end user organizations concentrated on problem definition and software, and (2) the DP groups were delegated or took control of the project, where the end user groups shared decision making on the nature of the support system with line management.

Installation Phase

In the installation stage, the task of the computing groups is to get the system functioning and work through startup problems, modifying the system so it is of real utility to the users.

International presents a typical example of where an end user computing group worked on a parity basis with the International management, supplying half the manpower to teams developing different applications. After developing a prototype of a financial database with a financial analyst, the computing staff then went on to develop a nonfinancial database, an accounts receivable package, and a competitive database. They also helped select a graphics package but their choice for graphics was not the one finally chosen by International's management. The computing group at International combined a strategy of evolutionary design with participative decision making by the management group.

In contrast to International, the computing groups at Manuco and Toy were delegated more responsibility, but had less authority over the installation of the ESS. To cope with the ambiguity, the groups utilized a portfolio approach to the project. At Manuco, the MIS group decided that executives and their secretaries would utilize the following tools; word processing, calendaring, electronic mail, document transfer, Dow Jones, corporate reports, and spreadsheets. They placed all these applications on very easy-to-use menus and provided individual training to all the executives and secretaries involved. Their rationale was that out of the sumptuous buffet of software the executives would choose something. Although secretaries did utilize the system, only four executives used it regularly and the computing group was unable to get access to the executives to train them, or to divisional data, which might be of assistance to the executives. Another aspect of the DP group's approach was an emphasis on the computer interface. At Toy, the hardware, which was a combination of telephone and computer, took only an hour to learn to use, and at Manuco considerable effort was placed on establishing one-button access to any application faced with low usage. As a solution, the computing groups continued to expand the portfolio and the number of installations.

With both the end user and DP groups, emphasis was placed on user training during the installation phase. At International and Wellness, the computing group saw its function as developing expertise within the executive staff, and at Manuco and Toy the emphasis was placed on user-seductive software which could be of immediate utility to the executive. At Smokestack, effort was made to provide executives with easy-to-use management reports. The training efforts were more successful when aimed at staff people than at the executives themselves.

Institutionalization Phase

During the institutionalization phase of implementation, the tasks for the computing groups are to disseminate the system either downward and diffuse within the organization, or across other divisions, and to establish a standardized environment for operation of the system.

The efficiency-oriented communication systems ceased to exist after the installation phase. At Manuco and Toy the support systems had been labeled as pilots, and both firms declared victory and ceased operation. At the other three firms the support systems became embedded within the organization.

In all three firms the computing groups moved toward being more integrated into the user organization. At Smokestack, the computing group moved from de facto reporting to MIS, to reporting to the CFO. At International, the comptroller's staff took over operation of the support system and the computing group disseminated the applications to four other divisions. At Wellness, the computing organization lost its reporting independence from MIS, but became fully integrated within subsidiary management. At both Wellness and International, the support system affected the jobs of middle managers and analysts within the organization, and training programs were established to provide these managers with the necessary skills in use and growth of the technology. At Wellness, the increase in breadth and depth of the system necessitated a reconstruction of the database which was given to the computing group.

At Smokestack, the integration occurred around a central

corporation-wide budgeting process. The computing group, as delegate for the CFO, developed a budgeting model which affected all groups in the corporation. They are currently in the process of training the various financial staffs in use of the tool.

In summary, the computing group is an important factor in executive support since they affect the implementation at all stages, and have considerable daily contact with the nuts and bolts of the system. The role of the computing groups changes during the process of implementation from problem definer, to implementor, to maintainer and diffuser of systems. The computing groups which were most successful appear to have shared decision making more with management than those which were delegated more responsibility for the implementation.

The discussion of computing groups as a factor illustrates the problem of separating out factors. It is obvious that the kind of management sponsorship and problem definition greatly affect the role of the computing group. It is not coincidence that computing groups were more effective when business problems catalyzed initiation of the system, and managerial sponsorship was active. However, the ability of computing groups to capitalize on those opportunities depends on their structure and skills.

DATABASES AND NETWORKS

The existence, usability, and development of databases were major factors in the building of ESS. Existing databases were a necessary but not sufficient condition for the installation stage of the effectiveness-oriented systems and became important again in the institutionalization phase. The pre-existence of a community of users is as necessary a condition for communication-oriented support systems as databases are for business-problem-based systems, since being accustomed to the technology speeds the implementation process. The existence of databases and a community of users demonstrates a seeding of technology within the firm that prepares it for the growth of support systems. During the last phase of implementation, databases become important as diffusion of ESS from one division to others and to the corporate office demands the creation of a data warehouse and the establishment of common conventions surrounding data management.

Organizational and Installation Phase

Business-problem-based ESS demand the presence of information on which alternative scenarios for decisions can be made against past performance, and categories of information may be compared to each other. In two of the firms we studied, Wellness and International, the use of information technology was well developed. This indicated that managers had been exposed to information technology and that historical databases on matters central to the firm were usable. In contrast, information systems had been given very low priority at Smokestack prior to the arrival of the new management. At the beginning of the implementation process, the computing group found that all financial accounting had been decentralized to the subsidaries, rendering financial data incomparable. The centralization of accounting practices and the development of a common general ledger system was necessary before financial data could be developed for an ESS. The development of these systems took 18 months and made the initial concept of a cost control ESS unfeasible. Smokestack was able to establish a management reporting system and then a budget model only after the data requirements between divisions had been standardized and the consolidated reporting system needed for the database was established.

In the communication-oriented ESSs, the executives need the people they communicate with linked to them on the system. If the people in the executive's communication community do not use or are not on the system, then the executive cannot gain the benefits of using such efficiency-oriented communication tools as electronic mail. At both Manuco and Toy, it was found that executives communicated downward to their subordinates. In both firms, the support systems were organized horizontally to other executives and subordinates were not originally on the system. This limited the utility that the systems could have.

Manuco provides a good example of what occurs when databases cannot be compared or utilized across different groups. The firm had over 50 separate divisional and staff databases but the databases could not be used in concert. This caused considerable difficulty for the policy-oriented group executives who complained that the ESS could only be of help to them in their work if they could utilize and compare information across divisions and groups. This example illustrates why three of the firms spent considerable time and effort in selecting database management systems that created relational databases.

Institutionalization Phase

The databases for ESS are often, though not exclusively, extracts of corporate transaction systems. During the institutionalization period, ESS diffuses into other divisions and staffs, and usage within corporate subgroups increases. It is necessary to establish corporation-wide systems that allow for easy transfer of data. The two firms we have studied that have reached the institutionalization stage have approached the problem of standardization by establishing corporate data warehouses from which data can be extracted for individual support systems and by establishing common database management systems which all divisions and subsidiaries must use.

THE MANAGEMENT OF RESISTANCE

Resistance to a new technology is a normal phenomenon. Resistance can be either an act to protect one's domain or simply "why should one change unless the new way is better?" Resistance to ESS occurred during the installation period in all companies. It took the form of nonusage of the system, active resistance, and withholding. Resistance can slow down or cripple installation of an ESS. Where the ESSs were installed well, resistance was effectively managed.

Installation Phase

In efficiency-based systems, the resistance took the form of nonusage of the system. Toy Electric provided a good example of this passive resistance. The executives already had good support in place; secretaries to pass and screen their messages, administrative assistants to do budgets. The resistance was expressed by both secretaries and executives. In responding to questionnaires, they said the system was fine, and asked for minor modifications, but they didn't use the system, because the questionnaires addressed interface rather than compatibility of work issues. In this way they satisfied the perceived desire of the CEO to provide personal management tool, and then proceeded to work as they liked. At Wellness, the problem of nonusage was dealt with by the president inviting other executives to attend training sessions with him.

Active resistance was evident at Smokestack. The DSS group developed an easy-to-use personnel query system for the vice president of personnel. He used the system for three weeks and then gave it to his own systems person to operate. The systems person claimed that the new system was inadequate and not as complete as the complex personnel information system already in existence. He was, however, the only one in the corporation who could operate the older system, where the new, simpler system was usable by anyone.

A third form of resistance, withholding, is based on the "information is power" principle. At Manuco, the MIS people were unable to obtain several divisional databases which would have been helpful to group executives in policy planning because the divisions did not want their data on a common system.

At International, the divisional presidents were reluctant to provide information for the ESS because they thought their autonomy would be affected. A frank discussion around critical success factors was held between the divisional executive and group president, allowing resistance to be dealt with by negotiation. This is a good example of how resistance can be dealt with. Because participation in designing the system was high, end users perceived it as a central tool to their success rather than an infringement on their autonomy, and resistance was managed.

PUTTING THE PIECES TOGETHER

Figure 3 shows definite patterns in the relationship between the number of elements that are managed well during the implementation process and the effectiveness of the ESS. Wellness and International had all the elements present early and promptly and have the most successful implementations to date. Manuco and Toy had fewest elements present, the most problems, and ceased the implementation process prior to institutionalization. The primary messages that come out of the chart are that *business-oriented systems function better than efficiency-oriented systems* and that the greater the number of elements present, the more likely the support system is to meet the executive's needs. This is exemplified in the case of Smokestack where the initial absence of operating

---

FIGURE 3

	Toy	Manuco	Wellness	Smokestack	International
Defined business problem			X	X*	X
Titular sponsorship	X	X	X	X	X
Operating sponsorship			X	X*	X
End User organization		X	X	X	X
Database			X		X
Management of resistance			X	X*	X

---

*Late.

sponsorship and databases significantly retarded development of the implementation.

ESS AND ORGANIZATIONAL CHANGE

ESS is often a lever for organizational change. This change tends to be associated with a new leader's vision of how he wants his organization to function. The ESS becomes an extension of the leader. It is one of the tools he uses in bringing about a restructuring of the organizational mission. The reports and data in the ESS are the message to the rest of the organization of what indicators count, and the staff who manage the ESS become the gatekeepers of information.

The relationship of executive support and organizational change was clear in this sample. The three executives who sponsored effectiveness-oriented systems had been in their jobs less than a year. They all said that after spending several months getting accustomed to their jobs they developed a vision of where they wanted to move the organization. At International, Peter Dewey saw a need to focus the corporation on its future. This meant finding ways to communicate critical information to the top of the organization and to bring the divisions in his group into line with a strategic plan. Dewey perceived the firm as complacent due to past success, and unrealistic about its future. He also felt that the changes had to be brought about carefully, since theirs was a long history of decentralization of the subsidiaries and no immediate crisis to justify participants' action. He was also conscious that as a group executive he had limited staff and it was not fruitful to involve himself in the nitty gritty operations of his divisions. He saw his increase in effectiveness in being able to make his divisions, and the upper management of the corporation, focus on strategic planning. For Dewey the presentation form of information became very important. He felt that graphics allowed people to see trends clearly and avoided being buried in numbers and paper. This fit his role perception of communicating crucial information and goals upward to the chairman and down to his divisions. He also utilized the critical success factors process in bringing his division presidents into agreement with the strategic plan and established a graphic reporting system linked to that plan. Dewey's vision was one which he saw as gradually moving International to its future rather than reacting to crisis. At this point the divisions have institutionalized reporting which addresses the strategic goals.

When Paul Dawson assumed the helm at Wellness he knew that the traditional sales orientation was not working any more. Dawson had a vision of changing Wellness into a firm that was analytically marketing based. Dawson established his ESS with a marketing database and simultaneously established a market research group directly below him to run the system. He changed the bonus structure for his managers from one where they got bonuses by meeting quota on any products to one where they had to meet quota on all product lines. In the last year Dawson has restructured the division, amalgamating units and dropping product lines, forcing them to use the system. He has also focused his sales effort on a different market segment. In Dawson's case the ESS can be seen as one of the tools in a tool kit for changing the operation and culture of Wellness.

It is worth noting that a significant difference between the ESS systems which are business-problem-based and linked to visions of change and those systems which are oriented to personal management and efficiency is that the communications-based systems are not driven by a vision of organizational change. This may make them more difficult to implement because the executive is actually viewing the system as office equipment, a typewriter or dictaphone, rather than as a central part of his business.

Chapter Nine
Supporting Senior Executives' Models for Planning and Control

MICHAEL E. TREACY

1. INTRODUCTION

By now the successful use of models in corporate decision making is well documented and easily observable. McInnes and Carleton (1982), Grinyer and Wooller (1978), Naylor and Schauland (1976), and Traenkle et al. (1975) have all observed the accelerating use of decision support system (DSS) modeling packages. Most of these models are built and used by mid-level analysts to support functional needs in finance, marketing, operations management, and corporate planning. Very few explicit—or formal—models appear to be built or used by senior executives (Rockart and Treacy, 1982). If these are the people responsible for the formulation of broad strategies and the design of organizational control mechanisms, then it follows that explicit modeling has not had as much impact upon these areas as some proponents would desire.

Yet, these senior executives use models for planning and control. Their models are intuitive and implicit. They are mental representations of reality—abstractions of complex decision contexts—that executives use to simplify the decision process, to identify important variables, and to generate and evaluate alter-

Center for Information Systems Research Working Paper No. 125, Sloan School of Management, MIT, Cambridge, Mass., June 1985.

FIGURE 1 *Analyzing Sales Data with Implicit Models*

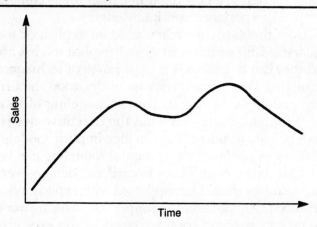

natives. They are not usually put down on paper, built into a computer program, analyzed quantitatively, or even viewed as models, but they are models. They are often simple and inelegant and may bear little relationship to "good theory," but they are arguably the most important models for planning and control, because they are powerful and they get used. As one executive put it:

> I bring a lot of knowledge to the party. Just scanning the current status of our operations enables me to see some things that those with less time in the company would not see as important. (Rockart and Treacy, 1982)

This executive clearly has many well-developed implicit models of his operation. These models allow him to quickly assess new information that someone less experienced would have to formally analyze. Figure 1 illustrates this point. Looking at the sales performance reflected in the trend line, one might ask: How well is this company doing? One reaction is that the firm is in trouble because sales are declining. This conclusion is derived from a commonly held implicit model that sales are always rising in a healthy company.

But what if the time frame represented is only 12 months? Then the sales pattern may simply indicate seasonality, and a more complex informal model is required to interpret the data. An experienced executive looking at these numbers may actually see a very healthy situation because his or her model of expected sales was much lower. This example illustrates that data only becomes information when it is interpreted through some implicit model. These models are nothing other than the accumulation of an individual's experience and knowledge.

Does the executive really need an explicit or formal model to understand his or her operations? Explicit models are easily shared and they can be analyzed using a range of techniques. Some would argue that even a manager who understood the firm's operations very well could benefit by formal modeling of those operations. Others might argue that what the executive needs is not formal models, but support for his or her implicit modeling, so that the weaknesses of this abstract mental modeling can be reduced.

This paper contributes toward the debate over whether senior executives should be supported with explicit models or by other measures. Our position is a simple one. The answer depends upon the type of decision contexts faced by the executive. We analyze the nature of explicit and implict models and alternatives for supporting these different modeling processes. To accomplish this, the rest of the paper is divided into several sections. Section 2 discusses the nature of executive analytic needs and concludes that senior executives' most important problems are complex and unstructured and that complete and formal analyses of these problems are not always possible. The section closes with a simple categorization of analyses that is later used to discuss alternate types of support systems.

Section 3 develops a set of criteria for evaluating the appropriateness of alternate forms of support for the different analytic needs of senior executives. This is done by examining the potential problems that each form of analysis may incur, for a major objective of support systems is to alleviate or avoid such problems.

The final section discusses alternate forms of decision support systems. These different forms derive from differences in DSS tools, so some time is devoted to a discussion of these tools. One conclusion drawn in this section is that new, emerging forms of modeling, such as fuzzy modeling, may provide support for many of senior executives' most important analytic problems.

2. THE NATURE OF SENIOR EXECUTIVE ANALYSIS

There is a lot of use of formal models for planning and control in organizations, but little use of them by senior executives. Several explanations suggest themselves. It may be that senior executives do not possess the necessary skills for model building and analysis or for using a computer. But Rockart and Treacy have found that even among senior executives who use computers for analytic support there is little use made of explicit models (1981, 1982). It may be that executives don't need formal models; or that their information requirements are simple enough that ad hoc analysis is sufficient. Or, it may be quite the opposite, that the problems they confront are too complex for explicit modeling to be of much benefit. This third possibility we believe is often closest to the truth.

Much has been written about the roles and information needs of senior executives. Mintzberg (1973) observed that senior managers are often dealing with overwhelming complexity under great time pressure. He found that computer-generated information was of little use to these people. They preferred current and timely information that could be obtained only through informal channels. Gorry and Scott Morton (1971) built upon Anthony's (1965) framework and characterized the role of senior executives as strategic and largely unstructured. They require support for defining problems, generating alternative solutions, and evaluating them against strategic criteria.

Most of the important planning and control issues that senior executives must face, such as the creation of plans, the control of subordinates, or the analysis of competitive advantage, are highly dependent upon the exact context of the problem. They deal with unique problems for which there are no standard operating procedures. Sufficient and complete knowledge of these problems is very difficult to obtain. Therefore, senior managers must often work under great uncertainty. There is no "normative" approach to planning and control; there is no clear set of decisions which arise in the course of this process. Rather, data concerning both past and current results, as well as future plans, are scanned and analyzed, and a set of ad hoc, highly variable decision opportunities occur. As Charles Hitch (1957) observed some years ago:

> The sort of simple explicit model which operations researchers are so proficient in using can certainly reflect most of the significant factors influencing traffic control on the George Washington Bridge, but the proportion of the relevant reality which we can represent by any such model or models in studying, say, a major foreign policy decision, appears to be almost trivial. (p. 718)

FIGURE 2   Four Types of Analytic Situations

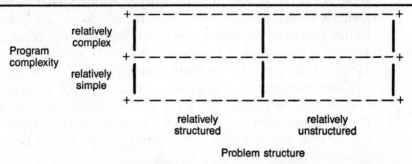

Adding to the difficulties of a lack of structure and great uncertainty is what Bellman (1957) calls "the curse of multidimensionality." Managers may aspire to plan and control their firms for the single objective of long-term profitability, but in practice they require many operational objectives, such as present period profit plans and gaining X percent of market share, as milestones along the way. These operational objectives are not independent and their relationship to the overall objective of long-run profits is often not well understood. Thus, there is further uncertainty introduced by multiple and fuzzy evaluation criteria.

We may conclude that the most important problems of planning and control faced by senior executives are complex and relatively unstructured. These two characteristics, complexity and structure, define a categorization of analytic situations that is helpful in discussing alternate ways of supporting senior executives. In Figure 2 we have illustrated this categorization. For expository purposes, quadrants have been used to define four types of analytic situations. The qualifier *relatively* has been used to indicate that there are not clear demarcations between these categories.

The important problems of planning and control faced by senior managers are analytic situations illustrated in the upper right quadrant: they are complex, relatively unstructured problems.

In the lower left quadrant are analytic situations where the extent of knowledge about the problem is relatively complete and the problem is not very complex. In such situations, problem solving is fairly easy and standard operating procedures can often be routinely applied. In the upper left quadrant are analytic situations that are relatively well structured, but complex. For these problems, standard operating procedures or rules of thumb are often inadequate. Formal analysis, typically in the form of an explicit model, is required to integrate many pieces of information in a structured way.

The difference between the two types of relatively well-structured problems can be illustrated with the problem of inventory reordering. This problem can be viewed as a simple one, to which rules of thumb such as economic order quantity can be applied, or as a complex problem, for which formal models are needed to pull all relevant information together. Material requirements planning is an example of the latter view of the problem. It can be implemented only with the aid of large, formal models. Which view is appropriate for structured problems depends primarily upon the level of effort one wishes to expend to generate a satisfactory solution. For unstructured problems, it also depends upon what is and is not known about the problem.

It is evident from the preceding examples that some problems can be viewed as fitting in any of the four quadrants of Figure 2. An inventory problem can be simple or complex, depending upon how it is viewed, and the greater one's experience and understanding of such problems, the more structure they appear to have. The more unstructured the problem area, the less able are we to provide a complete representation; the more complex the problem area, the more important it is to provide a valid formal analysis. Thus, given a choice, one would opt for the most complete analysis and perhaps a formal analysis, but senior executives, by the nature of the problems they face, are not often given a choice.

For each of the analytic situations illustrated in Figure 2, different analytic approaches can be applied. In particular, one can choose to apply explicit or implicit models to any of these types of problems. Which form of modeling is most appropriate for each type of analytic situation is examined in the next section by developing a list of strengths and weaknesses for each analytic approach. These lists are also used in the subsequent section to determine which form of support system is most appropriate for each type of analytic situation.

3. POTENTIAL PROBLEMS WITH EXPLICIT AND IMPLICIT MODELS

A list of criteria for good models has been developed by Little (1970). Good models are simple, robust, easy to control, adaptive, easy to communicate with, and as complete as possible. By these criteria, implicit mental models can be good models. They are simple, or at least simple enough that they can be carried around in a person's head. They can be robust. The mental models of experienced executives have been derived from observing complex relationships and events over many years. Subtle relationships, exceptional cases, and critical assumptions can all be part of a good mental model. These implicit models are also easy to control. And one can use them in many ways—to examine alternate scenarios, as part of a larger analytic process, or in conjunction with current information. Mental models are adaptive. If observation negates part of a manager's model, it will probably be modified to account for what was observed. They are as complete as possible, as complete as a manager has been able to comprehend.

Little's criteria for good models, however, can be interpreted another way. They can be viewed as a list of the potential problems introduced when implicit mental models are made explicit. This would account for why mental models so easily meet Little's criteria. Formal models tend to be complicated; they can sometimes give absurd results when certain complexities are missing. They can only be controlled and exercised through whatever facilities are built into the modeling system. They usually are difficult to adapt to other situations and to new information. And explicit models certainly are not easily communicated with by a typical manager unaccustomed to their use.

Not all formal models are this bad. Little provided a list that helps to pick out the good ones. But, in general, formal models suffer more of these ills than do informal models. Or, at least their shortcomings are more obvious. That is why model management is an important and new area of research for those committed to formal models. Konsynski and Dolk (1982), Elam et al. (1980), and Will (1975) each present conceptual schemes for modeling systems that would help automatically to reduce some of the problems with explicit models. If these ideas could be implemented, then we might see more managers approaching problems using formal modeling methods because they would be perceived as more valuable relative to implicit mental models.

Perhaps the most important limitation of mental models is that they do not handle complexity well. It is difficult to mentally integrate complex relationships between variables. Our mental capacities can handle a remarkably broad range of knowledge, but people are not particularly good integrators of that knowledge.

A second problem with these implicit models is that they are hard to manipulate. Once a model adequately describes a phenomenon, one might like to use it to predict or to optimize some aspect of the phenomenon. This requires manipulation of the model, trying alternative scenarios, assessing the impact of uncertainty, and all the other techniques that have become familiar through line-oriented modeling systems (i.e., electronic spreadsheets). This cannot be done as easily with implicit models as with a formal mathematical model.

Another problem with mental models is that they are difficult to share with others. And it is even harder to convey the supporting evidence for the model because it is often intangible and gathered through years of experience. This is an important problem because the process of management planning and control is a large and widespread undertaking. It requires specialists in particular areas, such as strategic planning, accounting, and finance. In addition, it requires the insight, analysis, and guidance which can only be provided by senior line management. Thus, it is a shared activity, involving many different actors with only partly shared perspectives.

A fourth problem with implicit models stems from the first and second problems. Mental models are difficult to validate. If they cannot be easily manipulated and if they cannot be easily shared with others, then they are also difficult to test against impartial evidence. We know that people are imperfect information processors. This may result in imperfect, perhaps badly flawed mental models. Without proper validation, these flaws may not surface.

Finally, implicit models are vastly underutilized. Managers often know much more about situations than they bring to the decision-making processes of planning and control. There is a major, uncatalogued resource out there that is not being adequately utilized.

In Figure 3 we have summarized the preceding discussion as a list of the primary potential problems with formal and mental models. A major objective of a support system for executive modeling is to alleviate some of these problems.

4. ALTERNATE FORMS OF ANALYTIC SUPPORT

Among all the buzzwords, jargon, and acronyms of the information systems field, decision support systems (DSS) has proven

---

FIGURE 3   Primary Potential Problems with Formal and Informal Models

Formal Models:	• Complicated and hard to understand. • Difficult to make robust. • Difficult to control. • Difficult to adapt. • Difficult to communicate with.
Mental Models:	• Do not handle complexity well. • Difficult to manipulate. • Difficult to share. • Difficult to validate. • Uncatalogued and underutilized.

---

to be a term of practical and philosophical substance. As a practical matter, DSS focuses on the analysis of data and explicit modeling of the business and its environment. A manager is viewed not as a passive consumer of information, but as an active participant in the development and use of his or her personalized, supporting computer system. Thus, user control over, not just involvement in, the DSS development process is a fundamental tenet of the approach. Adaptive and evolutionary design are necessary to fit a system to a manager's job. Adaptive design and user control require that the process of support begin with the user's perspective, supporting those parts of the job that the manager wants to maintain, and evolve in the direction that he or she desires. The user is assumed to be knowledgeable about his or her role and, if provided with the appropriate data, software tools, training and guidance, will evolve toward better management. It is the information systems equivalent to Lindblom's (1959) "muddling through." This noninvasive, adaptive philosophy has been key to DSS's extraordinary practical success.

During the past 10 years, a host of decision support systems (DSS) generators and software packages have been developed that allow analysts and managers to develop and directly use decision support systems. The differences among the major categories of packages define the alternative forms of analytic support presently available. Figure 4, adapted from Montgomery and Urban (1969), shows the capabilities that have been provided by different DSS generators.

A decision support system provides a manager with another source of information on his or her internal and external business environment. Through an interaction and display facility that may include a command language and query, report writing, and

FIGURE 4 **Comprehensive DSS Generator Capabilities**

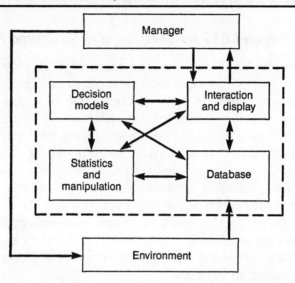

color graphics facilities, the manager can access a base of data, perform statistical, arithmetic, and other data manipulation functions, and create explicit models of his or her firm, competitors, industry, and the economy.

Figure 4 represents an ideal set of DSS generator capabilities. With these capabilities it is now possible to build many different types of support systems. The question we face is: Which form of support is best for each of the different analytic situations discussed in Section 2? In Figure 5, four different forms of support are indicated for the four analytic situations. In the rest of this section we will describe each of these forms of support and ex-

FIGURE 5 **Four Types of Analytic Support**

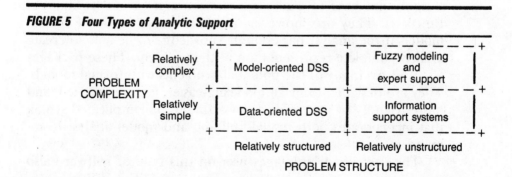

plain how they relieve the potential problems of explicit and implicit models discussed in the last section.

4.1 Model-Oriented DSS for Complex, Well-Structured Problems

Complex problems that are relatively well structured are better analyzed with formal explicit models. In a well-structured problem area, there is enough knowledge to construct a fairly complete representation of the problem context. Hence, formal modeling is possible and for significant problems it is the analytic approach of choice. A system to support the analysis of complex, well-structured problems should be aimed toward providing a formal modeling environment in which modeling is easier and potential problems are reduced.

Many of the decision support system generators presently available are focused on just such a form of support. The capabilities of these line-oriented modeling packages are diagrammed in Figure 6.

A line-oriented modeling system, more commonly known as an electronic spreadsheet, gives a manager the ability to define an explicit model of several interrelated variables and calculate the results of the model over several time periods. Typically, the packages allow the user to easily manipulate the model, to test alternate assumptions and scenarios, and to perform sensitivity analyses. These are line-oriented systems in the sense that the model is defined line by line, with each line representing another variable. The packages usually allow a manager to define, solve, and analyze a model and generate reports and graphs. They do not, in general, manage a database or offer ad hoc analytic capabilities.

These line-oriented modeling systems have won many supporters, but they are still not user-friendly enough to have gained a significant base of senior executive users, except in financial functions. They are, however, ideal for the creation of formal models if the analyst has enough knowledge to be able to create a fairly complete representation of the problem. These packages also address many of the potential problems with formal models. They are designed to make modeling easier, less complicated, and more friendly by providing a powerful but uncomplicated syntax that incorporates both model building and model analysis commands.

The command languages used in this type of software also

FIGURE 6 **Line-Oriented Modeling Systems**

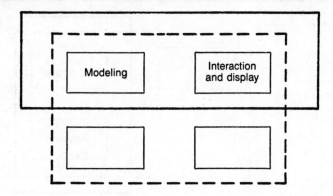

make it easier to control models. Changing data values, performing different analyses, and changing the format of printouts are all easier with these packages than with a standard programming language. Because the models are syntactically less complicated and easier to understand, they are also easier to adapt.

The one potential problem that these packages do not help to alleviate is the difficulty in making formal models robust. For example, this software might be used to create a sales forecasting model, but because the package is only a language and has no built-in intelligence about sales forecasting, it can in no way assure that the model is correct.

These line-oriented modeling systems are used extensively for accounting-based models in fairly well-understood areas, such as financial evaluation of projects, budgeting, and consolidation analysis. Most managers understand enough accounting to be able to evolve useful and usable financial models through an interactive process of model building and analysis. Thus, one way that the potential semantic problems of formal models have been overcome is by basing the models upon well-understood accounting principles.

4.2 Data-Oriented DSS For Simple, Well-Structured Problems

Simple and well-structured problems are fairly easy to support. In monitoring and tracking sales, for example, what managers need is access to data that they can use to trigger rules of thumb or standard operating procedures. This is the type of support of-

FIGURE 7   Friendly DataBase Management Systems

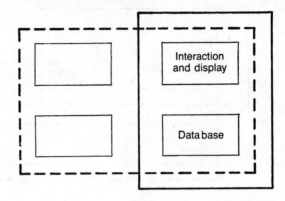

fered by data-oriented DSS. These systems are built to provide managers with ready access to a predefined base of data. They are often used as supplements for paper-based reporting systems because they offer more flexible reporting formats as well as a limited set of analytic tools. These systems are used to support monitoring in areas where an executive has a fairly well-formed mental model of expected performance. But because the data covers only a limited area and analytic tools are also limited, data-oriented DSS are only appropriate for recurring, reasonably structured problem areas such as monitoring performance versus budget.

The software that data-oriented decision support systems are based upon is quite different from the software used for model-oriented systems. They are usually called "friendly" (that is, easy to learn and use) database management systems (DBMS). The capabilities of this class of software are illustrated in Figure 7. Some well-known products in the marketplace are FOCUS, RAMIS, NOMAD, and DBASEII. These packages provide a manager with a facility for managing and accessing a large base of data, creating reports and graphs, and performing very limited analysis upon the data. They give managers the ability to choose the data that they wish to see and to format it in reports or graphs as they wish to see it. Unfortunately, as with much of the line-oriented modeling software, the user interfaces for these database packages are not yet friendly enough to encourage widespread use by executives.

FIGURE 8   Information Support Systems

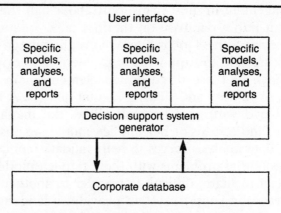

4.3 Information Support for Simple, Unstructured Problems

Even for relatively simple problems, the more unstructured they are, the more difficult it becomes to predefine the data and reports that are appropriate for support. Concurrently, the implicit mental models that are used to address problems such as succession planning or how a firm is doing relative to its competition become subject to questionable validity, manipulability, and shareability. Support for simple but unstructured problems must be based upon at least three design elements: (1) a large base of data, (2) a set of ad hoc analytic tools, and (3) sharing of the system by managers with common information needs. These design elements define an information support system, which is the most widely implemented form of support for senior executives.

In an increasing number of companies, a level of data and software commonality has been established; their information support systems resembles Figure 8. Bases of data have been established for groups of individuals who naturally draw upon the same type of data. In one company, the strategic planners and controllers created one base of data, while the marketing managers and market researchers created another. At Northwest Industries in Chicago, corporate staff and executives all draw from one base of data (Rockart and Treacy, 1982). In both firms, it was the managers and analysts who established what data would be in the databases and what data definitions would be used. And, despite the common databases, in every case the users also maintain their own personal data files.

These databases evolve. With present information requirements analysis techniques and with the existing state of data management in most firms, only about half the needed data can be put into a database on the first pass. In addition, the nature of the executive's job is one of constant change and new data are often needed to support new problems and opportunities.

Each of these three design elements helps to reduce problems of validity and sharing mental models. A large base of data combined with analytic tools allows the manager to build, explore, and test his or her implicit models against the data. In this way, data analysis serves to help validate mental models. One of the potential problems with these implicit models is that they are difficult to share, difficult to transfer to another person. A shared information support system provides a language and a medium for communicating implicit models. If managers support their implicit models through a system, then the models become more transferable with the sharing of data and analysis.

The software that underlies information support systems must have both data management and ad hoc analysis capabilities. The packages must be comprehensive and contain all the elements shown in Figure 4.

4.4 Fuzzy Modeling and Expert Support for Complex and Unstructured Problems

Most implicit mental models are fuzzy, but computer-based modeling systems are precise. Until we can develop fuzzy modeling systems, most of the useful, computer-based support for implicit models will be provided through data retrieval, analysis, and the transforming of data into different formats. Fuzzy modeling systems will allow a manager to externalize crude, incomplete, and inconsistent internal models without having to translate them into complete and internally consistent models like those found in model-oriented DSS.

Fuzzy models are used by senior managers all the time. For example, in a pricing decision, a manager might bring into play the following rules:

1. Our price should be about two times direct costs.
2. Our price should be just below our dominant competitor's price.

3. If our competitor's prices go too high, we should price for increased market share.

None of these statements is in a form precise enough to be used in a standard formal modeling system. Each statement begs for refinement. With a fuzzy modeling system, however, the above statements form a model of a pricing decision that could be solved. The results of that solution clearly would not be satisfactory, but it is a useful starting point that prompts the manager for a more refined representation of his or her mental model.

Fuzzy models are ideally suited to complex and relatively unstructured problems, the type of problems that senior executives must commonly deal with. These models have the power of formal modeling systems to handle complexity. But, conceptually, fuzzy models compensate for many of the potential flaws of formal models such as the requirements for completeness, precision, and consistency.

Fuzzy modeling systems can create and analyze models that are incompletely specified, internally inconsistent, or ambiguous in their causality. The systems compensate for these flaws in the models by intelligently choosing assumptions that will allow the model to be analyzed. Along with the results, these assumptions are automatically added to the model and shown to the manager who can modify them for futher analysis.

The development of fuzzy modeling systems might sound as if it is many years away. It is not. The technology for fuzzy modeling has been developed in the artificial intelligence community and is becoming widely available. One product already has an approximate reasoning capability that provides some fuzzy modeling features.

Another important development from the artificial intelligence community, relevant to the support of relatively complex and unstructured decision situations, is human expert systems. To date, such systems have been oriented toward replicating expert capabilities on a computer. A recent development has been to reorient the applications toward providing computer-based expert assistants that can support rather than replace a decision maker. For example, one company has developed "smart" statistical tools. When a computer is given sales data, for instance, the system will analyze the characteristics of the data, taking into account such things as seasonality, and will then choose the most appropriate sales forecasting tool.

The conceptual underpinnings of expert support systems have been developed under the rubric of "model management systems." According to Elam et al. (1980), a model management system

> can be viewed as a system that dynamically constructs a decision aid in response to a particular problem. This is accomplished by drawing on a knowledge base of models that captures the technical expertise of a management scientist plus an understanding of the basic activities involved in a given decision-making environment.

These fuzzy modeling and expert support tools are not yet available. It is little wonder, therefore, that we have had difficulty supporting the modeling needs of senior executives faced with complex and unstructured problems. Of the three other forms of support, information support systems are the most popular for executive support systems because they offer meaningful support for a manager's implicit mental models. But, information support fails as a support mechanism for complex problems. That is why many senior managers might feel that executive support cannot help them with their "real" problems, their complex problems. For them, we must wait a little longer for the emergence of some "real" executive support tools.

While we are waiting, it benefits us not to think too narrowly about models or modeling systems. In reading some of the literature on models used for planning and control, one might assume that all important models are explicit, mathematical representations of problems in a spreadsheet format. This paper has explored another type of model—implicit models—and how to best support managers' uses of them. As support technology evolves, it will challenge us to rethink our concept of a model and its role in managerial decision making.

REFERENCES

Anthony, R. N. *Planning and Control Systems: A Framework for Analysis.* Boston: Division of Research, Harvard Graduate School of Business Administration, 1965.

Bellman, R. E. *Dynamic Programming.* Princeton, N.J.: Princeton University Press, 1957.

Elam, J.; J. Henderson; and J. Miller. "Model Management Systems: An Approach to Decision Support in Complex Organizations." In *Proceedings of the Conference on Information Systems,* 1980, pp. 98–110.

Gorry, G. A., and M. S. Scott Morton. "A Framework for Management Information Systems." *Sloan Management Review* 13, no. 1 (Fall 1971), pp. 55–70.

Grinyer, P. H., and J. Wooller. *Corporate Models Today: A New Tool for Financial Management,* 2d ed. The Institute of Chartered Accountants in England and Wales, London, 1978.

Hitch, C. J. "Operations Research and National Planning—A Dissent." *Operations Research* 5 (October 1957).

Konsynski, B., and D. Dolk. "Knowledge Abstractions in Model Management." Working paper, MIS Department, University of Arizona, Tucson, 1982.

Lindblom, C. E. "The Science of 'Muddling Through'." *Public Administration Review* 19 (1959), pp. 79–88.

Little, J. D. C. "Models and Managers: The Concept of a Decision Cal culus." *Management Science* 16, (April 1970), pp. B466–85.

McInnes, J. M., and W. J. Carleton. "Theory, Models and Implementation in Financial Management." *Management Science,* 28, no. 9 (September 1982), pp. 957–78.

Mintzberg, H. *The Nature of Managerial Work.* New York: Harper & Row, 1973.

Montgomery, D. B., and G. L. Urban. *Management Science in Marketing.* Englewood Cliffs, N.J.: Prentice-Hall, 1969.

Naylor, T. H., and H. Schauland. "A Survey of Users of Corporate Planning Models." *Management Science,* 22, no. 9 (May 1976), pp. 927–37.

Rockart, J. F., and M. E. Treacy. "The CEO Goes On-Line." *Harvard Business Review* 60, no. 1 (January–February 1982), pp. 82–88.

Rockart, J. F., and M. E. Treacy. "Executive Information Support Systems." CISR Working Paper No. 65, Center For Information Systems Research, Sloan School of Management, MIT, Cambridge, Mass., 1981.

Traenkle, J. W.; E. B. Cox; and J. A. Bullard. *The Use of Financial Models in Business.* New York: Financial Executives' Research Foundation, 1975.

Will, H. "Model Management Systems." In *Information Systems and Organizational Structure,* ed. Grochla and Szyperski, Berlin: de Gruyter, 1975.

Chapter Ten
A Survey of Current Trends in the Use of Executive Support Systems

DAVID W. DE LONG
JOHN F. ROCKART

INTRODUCTION

Since 1979 there has been a small but growing amount of research done on the evolution of executive support systems (ESS). These systems have been defined as "terminal-based computer systems designed to aid senior executives in the management of the firm" (Levinson). Virtually all ESS research (e.g., Rockart and Treacy, 1981; Levinson) has been an attempt to develop an understanding of what executive support systems are, how they are implemented, and how they are actually used. The authors have drawn conclusions about ESS from a relatively limited set of companies that have pioneered in the development of systems to support top management.

Partly because of the limited evidence, much argumentation exists as to the efficacy and future path of executive support systems. Rockart and Treacy observed in 1980 that the ESS phenomenon was growing. Others, however, (Dearden, Naylor, Kiechel, Hollis) have since suggested that the idea of a senior ex-

Center for Information Systems Research Working Paper No. 121, Sloan School of Management, MIT, Cambridge, Mass., November 1984.

ecutive using a computer terminal makes little, if any, sense, and that only a few very unusual top managers will have them on their desks. Despite these negative predictions, the management literature and the popular business press continues to report on an increasing number of senior executives who are making use of computer terminals (Perham, Whiteside, Nulty, Steinhart, Verespej, Davis). What has been missing up to this point is any evidence concerning the actual prevalence and use of ESS in organizations. How many top executives are using computers to help manage their businesses? What are they using the terminals for? And, what is the impact of ESS?

The purpose of the study reported on here was to gain some insights into these questions, by providing data from which to draw rough conclusions about the proliferation and use of ESS. A second objective was to identify some of the emerging issues and concerns that could be the focus of future ESS research.

This survey is just one part of a multistage study into the current state of executive support systems. The objective of this research is to gain a descriptive understanding of the systems now in existence—the ways in which ESS are being used, their strengths and weaknesses, and the users' views of the systems. In the end we hope this analysis will produce conclusions about senior management's use of computers which will be of value both in designing future ESS and in understanding the impact of the technology on the ways in which senior executives will manage their organizations in the future.

METHODOLOGY

The 50 corporations chosen for this study represent a 10 percent random sample of the 1984 *Fortune 500* list. In each case, we contacted either the senior computer executive in the corporation, or the information systems person capable of providing the best overview of the firm's activity in the area of computer-based executive support systems. At the outset of each telephone interview, the interviewees were told that their responses were confidential and that they would be sent a copy of the final report. Interviews were conducted between July 1 and September 15, 1984, with 45 firms responding and 5 choosing not to participate.

The problems with telephone interviews are well known, and

the results shown here must be treated with care. However, some interesting data emerged. In addition, several qualitative themes were noted time and time again, and we believe they are worth reporting.

The interviews ranged from 5 to 30 minutes in length, depending on the amount of ESS activity in the respondent's firm and the willingness of the subject to talk about the applications and their impacts. The average interview took 20 minutes. The questions used came from an interview outline, but not every question was covered in each interview because of interviewee time constraints and reluctance to discuss particular items.

The qualifying question used at the outset of each interview was: "Does your company have computer-based executive support systems?" Then, the interviewer read the following: "For this study, we define 'executive support systems' as the routine use of a computer terminal for any business function. The users are either the CEO or a member of the senior management team reporting directly to him (or her). Executive support systems can be implemented at the corporate and/or divisional level."

One of the problems with any study of "executive support systems" is that there is still great confusion about what really constitutes such a system. What one information systems executive might define as "executive support," another would discount as "just electronic mail" or "just a personal computer." Because this concept is evolving so fast and in so many different ways, our first objective was simply to determine whether or not a corporation's top executives had terminals on their desks. Then, we could begin to determine the system's capabilities, degree of use, and impact on the organization.

FINDINGS

Three significant findings emerged from the interviews:

- About two thirds of the companies had some activity going on in the area of computer-based executive support.
- The type of use and expected organizational impact varied widely. In only 3 companies was ESS usage described as "high." Another 14 reported "moderate" use.
- Several key issues appeared repeatedly throughout the interviews. Most point the way to critical areas for further re search in the ESS area.

EXHIBIT 1   Capabilities/Users

	Ranges of Use			
System Capability	Entire Corporate/ Divisional Office	A Few Users	An Individual	Total
Office Automation	2	10	0	12
Status Access	2	9	2	13
Query and Analysis	1	10	3	14
Totals	5	29	5	39

Widespread and Diverse Activity

In 30 corporations out of the 45 responding in our survey, at least one executive, at either the corporate or divisional level, had a computer terminal on his or her desk. As Exhibit 1 shows, in most cases (29), computer terminals are appearing on the desks of "a few users" in the corporation, as opposed to individual or office-wide applications. (Note the total number of systems, 39, exceeds the number of corporations where executives have terminals, 30, because some firms have multiple systems with different capabilities.)

There are essentially three classifications of capabilities: office automation, status access, and query and analysis. Often, specific systems offer capabilities from a combination of the three classifications.

"Office automation" generally means terminal-based access to functions such as electronic mail, calendaring, and word processing. The executive's terminal is usually networked to others in the company, although in 4 of the 12 firms in this category ex-

EXHIBIT 2   Capabilities/Architecture

	Architecture	
	Networked*	Stand-Alone
Office Automation	8	4
Status Access	13	0
Query and Analysis	5	9
Totals	26	13

System Capability

*This includes personal computers or terminals that are linked to mainframes, as well as PCs that are linked to other PCs.

ecutives were using stand-alone personal computers (see Exhibit 2). Office automation applications are generally designed to make the executive more efficient, and do not provide analytic capabilities. Although unreported in previous research (e.g., Rockart and Treacy, 1981), the use of terminals for communication purposes (e.g., electronic mail) appears now to be a significant factor in the evolution of ESS.

"Status access" applications give a manager the ability to access a predetermined and preformatted set of reports through a terminal. The data used to generate status access reports may be updated hourly or quarterly, depending on the particular system, but the significant thing about these reports is that their formats are static and the numbers of reports available is finite. Unlike reports generated by query-based systems, the data cannot be manipulated or broken down further.

"Query and analysis" is the ability to perform random and

unstructured "what if" and other analysis. One means of doing this is through analytical tools which access corporate or divisional databases. Also included in this category are the capabilities provided by the spreadsheet packages such as Lotus 1-2-3, which are available on personal computers, and which may or may not be linked to corporate databases. In fact, 9 of the 14 systems found in this category are stand-alone microcomputers using spreadsheet packages. The ability to do ad hoc querying in extensive corporate databases, which is what many writers have in mind when they discuss "executive support systems," is still relatively rare at the executive level. Reasons cited for this include difficulties in aggregating production databases, problems in developing the software for effective access to data on mainframes, and the political ramifications of providing such access for top management.

Of the 30 companies where executives have computer terminals on their desks, the most common user is, as expected, the chief financial officer (37 percent), followed closely by the group vice presidents (33 percent) and the CEO or chairman of the board (30 percent). In one company or another, terminals are found on the desks of virtually all types of functional vice presidents at the corporate level. It is worth noting, however, that ESS use by an entire management team, at either the corporate or divisional level, is still relatively rare.

Limited Use

The most obvious finding in terms of the "degree of use" of the systems, as illustrated in Exhibit 3, is that only in a very few cases (3 of 39) is the use of computer terminals considered "high" (daily use). A significant number of the systems get "moderate" (i.e., several times a week) use. While only six systems fell into the "low" (infrequent or no use) category, it is also likely that a majority of the "don't know/didn't comment" responses would fall into the "low" use category. Our guess is that if key I/S managers do not know or do not feel informed enough to comment on use, then the systems probably are not very active.

As might be expected, there is a very strong correlation (the figures are identical except for one company) between the interviewer's impression of the impact of use (Exhibit 4) and the degree of use (Exhibit 3). Data in Exhibit 4 shows that executive computer use is not yet having a significant direct impact on the

EXHIBIT 3   Degree of Use

	Degree Used			
System Capability	High	Moderate	Low	Don't Know/ Didn't Comment
Office Automation	0	4	3	5
Status Access	0	5	2	6
Query and Analysis	3	5	1	5
Totals	3	14	6	16

way most organizations are managed. Instead, there appears to be tremendous variability in both use and impact, with comments ranging from "no discernible impact" to "the system has changed the way he does business."

EMERGING ISSUES

Although a telephone survey is a limited research instrument, a series of issues were raised so consistently by those interviewed that they deserve special mention and further attention.

Political Implications

The first and most critical issue is the political implications of increasing access for senior managers to unfiltered operations data.

EXHIBIT 4   Impact of Use on the Organization

		Impact		
System Capability		Extensive	Moderate	Low	Don't Know/ Didn't Comment
Office Automation		0	5	4	3
Status Access		0	5	2	6
Query and Analysis		3	3	1	7
Totals		3	13	7	16

In one corporation, executives now have on-line access to operational reports from the divisions two days after the monthly books close. Previously, it had taken 20 days to get the same information. "Our ESS has made the division people aware that they are under far more scrutiny than before. The feedback comes much faster," said the corporation's I/S executive.

At this company, on several occasions the vice president of finance has seen data on the screen, run off a hard copy, redpenciled it, and mailed it off to financial VPs at division level, demanding explanations for certain numbers. The divisional VPs were taken aback at how fast the corporate level could now react to the numbers—sometimes even before they were seen in their paper formats in the divisions. Subsequently, the divisions have asked that the ESS be installed at their level, so they could anticipate questions from corporate management.

This situation is typical of the kinds of problems more and more organizations are going to face as ESS technology spreads. "Who controls the data is the key issue in ESS. The question is who gets what data and when," said one I/S manager in a natural resources corporation.

To deal with this issue, the manager of electronic office systems in a telecommunications company said his firm had appointed a "database manager" at the executive level to address questions of data ownership. This person manages access to corporate data. "We had to ask: does the controller in the organization own the financial data? We decided the data belongs to the company, not the function," he said.

Data ownership and data access issues can have significant impact on the actual data "reported" in the corporation. "The staff used to have more time to review data and launder it," said the manager of I/S planning for a large manufacturing company. "Now the VP sees raw data." In other organizations, however, the "laundering" process has merely been speeded up because the data still moves up through the management hierarchy.

Influencing Computer Use

There is another side, however, to the proliferation of terminals at the top of organizations. Once executives begin using terminals, or at least having them on their desks, the use of computers by their subordinates increases significantly. "The chief benefit of the executives' use of computers is that they make it easier for subordinates to buy systems because now the boss understands the benefits," said one I/S executive. In another corporation, a senior executive forced his staff to get terminals saying, "If I send an electronic mail message, I expect a response." In cases where the systems are being used regularly by top management to monitor performance data, lower level managers are demanding access to the system so they can see the data their superiors are getting. "If you're not on the system, you're not in the ball game," commented one interviewee.

Data Management Difficulties

The politics of increased data access for top management are not, however, the only barrier to making data available. Aggregating, accessing, and managing production databases in a corporation with multiple divisions is proving to be the biggest physical road-block to ESS development. Problems with aggregating noncompatible databases and inconsistent data elements, combined with frequent resistance and outright refusal to make this data available to top management, make data access a major issue that will have to be addressed if executive support systems are to be effective.

Implementation Problems

Another major barrier to the effective development of ESS is the lack of a well-understood implementation process. Unlike the processes for implementing more traditional transaction processing or decision support systems, which are well documented, executive support implementation methodologies are not yet well understood.

Four reasons for implementation problems were frequently mentioned. First, ESS is a relatively new concept, and literature on the subject is still scarce. Second, each system must be designed to meet different needs, fit a unique culture, and draw from differently structured databases. Third, each system is shaped by the management style of the user and requires a significant time investment from that user during the design stage and in actually learning to use the system. Finally, there is a tendency to draw upon old I/S development processes, which are actually counterproductive for implementing ESS. Evidence of the implementation problems can be found in comments made during the interviews: "We hope management will come back and tell us what they really need." "The CFO likes the system we gave him and says he wants 'more.' But he hasn't told us what 'more' means."

"It's not resistance. It's just that executives don't know yet how to use the system and what they can get out of it. Right now they are reluctant to use it, but once people get used to the system, it will spread like wildfire." "We developed a system, but the executives don't use it much." Why? "There are some cultural problems."

All of these statements are evidence of the confusion or ignorance that exists around the implementation process needed for executive support systems. I/S people, for the most part, have not previously been asked to develop information systems from a senior management perspective. And top management has not

EXHIBIT 5   System Initiator/Degree of Use

	Initiator		
System Use	I/S Generated	Management–I/S Combo	Management Generated
High	0	0	3
Moderate	1	4	4
Low	2	0	1
Totals	3	4	8

Note: The "N" here is 15 since the data necessary to determine who initiated the ESS and what its use has been was only available for 15 systems.

thoroughly considered what information will provide the most leverage for managing and thinking about the business.

One implementation hypothesis presented in previous studies (Rockart and Treacy; Levinson) received some backing in the survey. Although the numbers are small and the data subjective, 87 percent of the systems initiated by the executives themselves receive "moderate" to "high" use (Exhibit 5). Only one third of the systems "sold" to top management by I/S were in the "moderate" category. None received a "high" degree of use.

Hardware and Software Capabilities

Another barrier to ESS is the lack of hardware and software capabilities needed to handle the special requirements of an ESS. Vendors will often claim that their software can meet the specs of systems designed to support top management, but user experience suggests otherwise. System components for an acceptable ESS are still hard to find and respondents' comments illustrate the problem:

> We don't have a delivery system that can synthesize and summarize data and hand the executive the information he needs. Finding software packages that can integrate data from many databases is the biggest barrier to ESS.

> Our first project is to find a software package that will allow the company to get at financial data very flexibly on a PC or terminal.

> We won't have an ESS until we find a link to our mainframe financial data. Once that software is found and implemented, our executives will begin to use the system for decision support.

Never before has the technology been called on to be so integrated, so transparent, and so fast. While much of the necessary hardware and software does exist, it is very difficult to find and implement the component pieces for a customized system that can suit the whims and needs of individual executives. As a result, the technology utilized frequently falls far short of user expectations. The flurry of companies, however, now addressing this issue—Metaphor, Boeing EIS, Pilot Software, etc.—suggests the presence of a significant marketplace and a possible solution for this problem.

Management Style

Data access and technical problems notwithstanding, the factor that ultimately separates ESS from all other management-oriented computer applications is the role management style plays in the design, development, and use of an executive support system. It is the management style of individual executives which dictates the use and non-use of computer terminals and the need for specific applications. Executives whose personal style calls for lots of face-to-face communication, while leaving analysis to their staffs, will continue to resist ESS. So will those who do not type and who fear being embarrassed by the computer. Said one I/S manager, "There are several executives here who would love to have an ESS, but they won't move because of their sensitive egos and fear of criticism."

A respondent at one high tech corporation said, "Our top management has little interest in ESS. They see no need to become terminal operators. At best they will become casual users."

At another firm, executive responses to a new ESS ranged from: "Train my secretary," to "I only want to have to push one button," to "I want the capabilities, but I don't have time to learn the system."

It is clear that a large number of senior executives, for many rational reasons, are not turning to terminal usage. Nor will they be pushed, said the I/S manager at a forest products company: "If you think you can sell an executive by jamming the system down his throat, you are very wrong."

User Support

User support is clearly a critical factor in determining the success of the technology because it is essential for dealing with management resistance to ESS. Asked about the type of support currently provided for executives, 15 of 19 respondents listed "one-on-one" or "coaching" as the primary type of support provided. Sometimes this lesson is only learned through experience. An I/S manager commented, "We've relied on one executive vice president to use the computer, giving him very easy software packages. But he has just not used the spreadsheets on his own, as we thought he would. The support will have to be much more intense."

Security

Once executive support systems are in place, a new problem arises—security. Security is a very big issue because of the sensitivity of the files (e.g., strategic plans, executive bonuses) created and accessed by users. Some firms have dealt with the problem head on. One company, for example, has three to five levels of passwords for ESS users. Other firms are feeling vaguely uneasy about the security issue, but are not sure what to do about it. "Because we have a centralized DP operation, there are lots of concerns about localized PC applications and the resulting questions of security," said the director of corporate computing for a major engine manufacturer. "There's lots of talk and worry, but no action as yet."

EXHIBIT 6   Future ESS Plans

		Plans			
System Capability	Charging Ahead	Moving Ahead Slowly	"In Limbo"	No Plans	Insufficient Data
Office Automation	0	2	1	1	1
Status Access	2	6	2	0	1
Query and Analysis	3	10	0	1	0
No ESS	1	2	0	10	2
Totals	6	20	3	12	4

Note: In firms that had multiple systems or where systems had multiple capabilities, such as office automation *and* status access, future plans were recorded here only under the more advanced capability. Thus, the multiple systems or capabilities represented in Exhibits 1–4 (totaling 39) are not counted here, and each firm is only represented once.

THE FUTURE

Future plans for executive support systems in the corporations studied range from none to extensive. According to our interviews, 23 of the 30 firms that currently have some executive support systems in place intend to provide additional ESS capabilities. In addition, 3 of the 15 firms that are currently without any ESS have plans to initiate executive systems (see Exhibit 6).

Of the 30 firms that currently have some ESS activity, 18 continue to move ahead slowly in this area, while 5 corporations are "charging ahead" with ESS development. The future plans for 3 remain "in limbo," and 2 companies have no plans to expand their current ESS efforts. Not surprisingly, in the 5 companies where ESS development is "charging ahead," the systems received early and strong top management involvement and direction.

It appears that, with more than half of the respondents planning some type of additional ESS activity in the future, the use of computers by senior executives will continue to increase in the next few years. As with earlier generations of computer applications, however, the spread of ESS will not be uniform. Our understanding of these systems is primitive. Much more needs to be learned about issues such as the effects of senior management style on ESS, the managerial tasks that are most appropriate for these systems, what comprises an effective implementation methodology, and—perhaps most significantly—the impact of these systems on the organization.

REFERENCES

Davis, David. "SMR Forum: Computers and Top Management." *Sloan Management Review,* Spring 1984.

Dearden, John. "SMR Forum: Will the Computer Change the Job of Top Management?" *Sloan Management Review,* Fall 1983.

Hollis, Robert. "Real Executives Don't Use Computers." *Business Computer Systems* 3, no. 7 (July 1984).

Kiechel, Walter. "Why Executives Don't Compute." *Fortune,* November 14, 1983.

Levinson, Eliot. "The Implementation of Executive Support Systems." CISR Working Paper No. 119, Center for Information Systems Research, Sloan School of Management, MIT, Cambridge, Mass., October 1984.

Naylor, Thomas H. "Decision Support Systems or Whatever Happened to M.I.S.?" *Interfaces* 12, no. 4 (August 1982).

Nulty, Peter. "How Personal Computers Change Managers' Lives." *Fortune,* September 3, 1984.

Perham, John. "The Computer and the Top Honcho." *Dun's Business Month,* 121, no. 5 (May 1983).

Rockart, John F., and Michael E. Treacy. "Executive Information Support Systems." CISR Working Paper No. 65, Center for Information Systems Research, Sloan School of Management, MIT, Cambridge, Mass., November 1980.

Rockart, John F., and Michael E. Treacy. "The CEO Goes On-Line." CISR Working Paper No. 67, Center for Information Systems Research, Sloan School of Management, MIT, Cambridge, Mass., April 1981.

Rockart, John F., and Michael E. Treacy. "The CEO Goes On-Line," *Harvard Business Review*, January–February 1982.

Steinhart, Jim. "The Computer and the Boss." *Executive* 26, no. 4 (April 1984).

Whiteside, David. "Computers Invade the Executive Suite." *International Management* (European edition) 38, no. 8 (August 1983).

PART 3
DEFINING MANAGEMENT INFORMATION NEEDS

This section presents three major papers dealing with the Critical Success Factor (CSF) concept. Since the original article appeared in the *Harvard Business Review* in 1979, the CSF approach has become a widely used method in the information systems field. The concept is simple, yet powerful, and readily understood by management. Critical success factors are those few essential areas of importance which must go well in order for the business to succeed.

The first paper here is the original, introductory article, "Chief Executives Define Their Own Data Needs." The basic concept is presented and illustrated with examples. Four prime sources of CSFs are described:

- The structure of the industry.
- The competitive strategy and industry position of an organization.
- Environmental factors.
- Temporal factors.

In response to requests for greater detail than found in this paper, a "how to" paper was written, titled, "A Primer on Critical Success Factors." It can be found in the appendix of this volume.

The use of the CSF concept has grown rapidly and it is currently one of the most widely used information systems planning methods. Its use has been extended to both technology systems planning in general, and corporate strategic planning. The next two articles illustrate and extend its use.

"Engaging Top Management in Information Technology" by Rockart and Crescenzi illustrates how the CSF concept was used in one corporation to fully involve the key top managers in the planning activity. This paper also introduces three new concepts which are being successfully integrated with the original CSF method:

- Focusing workshops—in which the CSFs obtained from individual interviews are reviewed, discussed, and agreed upon by the interviewees.
- Decision scenarios—in which the managers are presented with paper mock-ups of proposed reports from the systems to be developed to aid decision making.
- Prototyping—through which the organization can quickly experience the benefits of the planned system, at minimal initial investment.

The final paper in this section is "A Planning Methodology for Integrating Management Support Systems," by Henderson, Rockart, and Sifonis. This article adds to the CSF concept a process for understanding the assumptions which underlie managerial beliefs concerning what is critical. These assumptions and CSFs are then used as a diagnostic tool for building a strategic information planning framework.

The case study interviewees found this extension of the CSF concept to be valuable and useful in integrating the various pieces of their information systems plan. In addition, the model serves to link the strategic data needs of top management with the operational and technical needs of information systems management.

Chapter Eleven
Chief Executives Define Their Own Data Needs

JOHN F. ROCKART

He could have been the president of any one of a number of successful and growing medium-sized companies in the electronics industry. He had spent the previous day working to salt away the acquisition of a small company that fitted an important position in the product line strategy he had evolved for his organization. Most of this day had been spent discussing problems and opportunities with key managers. During both days he had lived up to his reputation of being an able, aggressive, action-oriented chief executive of a leading company in its segment of the electronics field.

Unfortunately, the president had chosen the late afternoon and early evening to work through the papers massed on his desk. His thoughts were not pleasant. His emotions ranged from amusement to anger as he plowed through the papers. "Why," he thought, "do I have to have dozens of reports a month and yet very little of the real information I need to manage this company? There must be a way to get the information I need to run this company!"

In effect, he was expressing the thoughts of many other general managers—and especially chief executive officers—whose needs for information are not as clearly determined as are those of many functional managers and first-line supervisors. Once one gets above the functional level, there is a wide variety of information that one might possibly need, and each functional specialty has an interest in "feeding" particular data to a general manager. As in this case, therefore, a massive information flow occurs. This syndrome is spelled out with differing emphases by the recent comments of two other chief executives:

> The first thing about information systems that strikes me is that one gets too much information. The information explosion crosses and criss-crosses executive desks with a great deal of data. Much of this is only partly digested and much of it is irrelevant.[1]

> I think the problem with management information systems in the past in many companies has been that they're overwhelming as far as the executive is concerned. He has to go through reams of reports and try to determine for himself what are the most critical pieces of information contained in the reports so that he can take the necessary action and correct any problems that have arisen.[2]

It is clear that a problem exists with defining exactly what data the chief executive (or any other general manager) needs. My experience in working with executives for the past decade or more is that the problem is universally felt—with individual frustration levels varying, but most often high.

In this article, I will first discuss four current major approaches to defining managerial information needs. Next, I will discuss a new approach developed by a research team at MIT's Sloan School of Management. Termed the "critical success factor (CSF) method," this approach is being actively researched and applied today at the MIT center. Finally, I will describe in detail this method's use in one major case as well as provide summary descriptions of its use in four other cases.

CURRENT PROCEDURES

In effect, there are four main ways of determining executive information needs—the *by-product* technique, the *null* approach, the *key indicator* system, and the *total study* process. In this section of the acticle, I will offer a brief synopsis of each of these and discuss their relative strengths and weaknesses.

By-Product Technique

In this method, little attention is actually paid to the real information needs of the chief executive. The organization's computer-based information process is centered on the development of operational systems that perform the required paperwork processing for the company. Attention is focused, therefore, on systems that process payroll, accounts payable, billing, inventory, accounts receivable, and so on.

The information by-products of these transaction-processing systems are often made available to all interested executives, and some of the data (e.g., summary sales reports and year-to-date budget reports) are passed on to top management. The by-products that reach the top are most often either heavily aggregated (e.g., budgeted/actual for major divisions) or they are exception reports of significant interest (e.g., certain jobs now critical by some preset standard). All reports, however, are essentially by-products of a particular system designed primarily to perform routine paperwork processing.

Where the information subsystem is not computer-based, the reports reaching the top are often typed versions of what a lower level feels is useful. Alternatively, they may be the ongoing, periodically forthcoming result of a previous one-time request for information concerning a particular matter initiated by the chief executive in the dim past.

Of the five methods discussed herein, the by-product approach is undoubtedly the predominant method. It leads to the welter of reports noted in the introductory paragraphs of this article. It has the paper-processing tail wagging the information dog.

The approach is, however, understandable. Paperwork must be done and clerical savings can be made by focusing on automating paper-processing systems. It is necessary to develop this class of data processing system to handle day-to-day paperwork. However, other approaches are also necessary to provide more useful management information.

Null Approach

This method is characterized by statements that might be paraphrased in the following way: "Top executives' activities are dynamic and ever changing, so one cannot predetermine exactly what information will be needed to deal with changing events at any point in time. These executives, therefore, are and must be dependent on future-oriented, rapidly assembled, most often subjective, and informal information delivered by word of mouth from trusted advisers."

Proponents of this approach point to the uselessness of the reports developed under the by-product method just noted. Having seen (often only too clearly) that (1) the *existing* reports used by the chief executive are not very useful, and (2) he, therefore, relies very heavily on oral communication, advocates of this approach then conclude that all computer-based reports—no matter how they are developed—will be useless. They look at inadequately designed information systems and curse all computer-based systems.

Proponents of the null approach see managerial use of information as Henry Mintzberg does:

> It is interesting to look at the content of managers' information, and at what they do with it. The evidence here is that a great deal of the manager's inputs are soft and speculative—impressions and feelings about other people, hearsay, gossip, and so on. Furthermore, the very analytical inputs—reports, documents, and hard data in general—seem to be of relatively little importance to many managers. (After a steady diet of soft information, one chief executive came across the first piece of hard data he had seen all week—an accounting report—and put it aside with the comment, "I never look at this.")[3]

To some extent, this school of thought is correct. There is a great deal of information used by top executives that must be dynamically gathered as new situations arise. And, most certainly, there are data that affect top management which are not computer-based and which must be communicated in informal, oral, and subjective conversations.

There are, however, also data that can and should be supplied regularly to the chief executive through the computer system. More significantly, as I will note later on, it is also important to clearly define what informal (*not* computer-based) information should be supplied to a top executive on a regular basis.

Key Indicator System

A clear contender today for the fastest growing school of thought concerning the "best" approach to the provision of executive information is the key indicator system. This procedure is based on three concepts, two of which are necessary and the third of which provides the glamour (as well as a few tangible benefits).

The first concept is the selection of a set of key indicators of the health of the business. Information is collected on each of these indicators. The second concept is exception reporting—that is, the ability to make available to the manager, if desired, only those indicators where performance is significantly different (with significance levels necessarily predefined) from expected results. The executive may thus peruse all the data available *or* focus only on those areas where performance is significantly different from planned.

The third concept is the expanding availability of better, cheaper, and more flexible visual display techniques. These range from computer consoles (often with color displays) to wall-size visual displays of computer-generated digital or graphic material. A paradigm of these systems is the one developed at Gould, Inc., under the direction of William T. Ylvisaker, chairman and chief executive officer. As *Business Week* reports:

> Gould is combining the visual display board, which has now become a fixture in many boardrooms, with a computer information system. Information on everything from inventories to receivables will come directly from the computer in an assortment of charts and tables that will make comparisons easy and lend instant perspective.
>
> Starting this week Ylvisaker will be able to tap three-digit codes into a 12-button box resembling the keyboard of a telephone. SEX will get him sales figures. GIN will call up a balance sheet. MUD is the keyword for inventory.
>
> About 75 such categories will be available, and the details will be displayed for the company as a whole, for divisions, for product lines, and for other breakdowns, which will also be specified by simple digital codes.[4]

At Gould, this information is displayed on a large screen in the boardroom, and is also available at computer terminals. The data are available in full, by exception, and graphically if desired.

As in most similar key indicator systems I have seen, the emphasis at Gould is on financial data. Daniel T. Carroll, reporting on Gould's system in mid-1976, described the system's "core report."[5] The report, available for each of Gould's 37 divisions, provides data on more than 40 operating factors. For each factor, current data are compared with budget and prior year figures on a monthly and year-to-date basis. The report, as noted by Carroll, is ever changing, but its orientation toward "profit and loss" and "balance sheet" data, as well as ratios drawn from these financial data, is evident.

Total Study Process

In this fourth approach to information needs, a widespread sample of managers are queried about their total information needs, and the results are compared with the existing information systems. The subsystems necessary to provide the information currently unavailable are identified and assigned priorities. This approach, clearly, is a reaction to two decades of data processing during which single systems have been developed for particular uses in relative isolation from each other and with little attention to management information needs. In effect, this approach was developed by IBM and others to counter the by-product method previously noted.

The most widely used formal procedure to accomplish the total study is IBM's Business Systems Planning (BSP) methodology. BSP is aimed at a top-down analysis of the information needs of an organization. In a two-phase approach, many managers are interviewed (usually from 40 to 100) to determine their environment, objectives, key decisions, and information needs. Several IBM-suggested network design methods and matrix notations are used to present the results in an easily visualized manner.

The objectives of the process are to develop an overall understanding of the business, the information necessary to manage the business, and the existing information systems. Gaps between information systems that are needed and those currently in place are noted. A plan for implementing new systems to fill the observed gaps is then developed.

This total understanding process is expensive in terms of manpower and all-inclusive in terms of scope. The amount of data and opinions gathered is staggering. Analysis of all this input is a high art form. It is difficult, at best, to determine the correct level of aggregation of decision making, data gathering, and analysis at which to work.

Yet the top-down process tends to be highly useful in most cases. The exact focus of the results, however, can be biased either toward top management information and functional management information or toward paperwork processing, depending on the bias of the study team. I have not seen a BSP study that gives priority to top executive information in the study's output.

The design, cleaning up, and extension of the paper-processing information network is too often the focus of the study team.

Each of the four current procedures just discussed has its advantages and disadvantages. The by-product technique focuses on getting paperwork processed inexpensively, but it is far less useful with regard to managerial information. It too often results in a manager's considering data from a single paperwork function (e.g., payroll) in isolation from other meaningful data (e.g., factory output versus payroll dollars).

The null approach, with its emphasis on the changeability, diversity, and soft environmental information needs of a top executive, has probably saved many organizations from building useless information systems. It, however, places too much stress on the executive's strategic and person-to-person roles. It overlooks the management control role of the chief executive, which can be, at least partially, served by means of routine, often computer-based, reporting.[6]

The key indicator system provides a significant amount of useful information. By itself, however, this method often results in many undifferentiated financial variables being presented to a management team. It tends to be financially all-inclusive rather than on-target to a particular executive's specific needs. The information provided is objective, quantifiable, and computer stored. Thus in the key indicator approach the perspective of the information needs of the executive is a partial one—oriented toward hard data needs alone. More significantly, in its "cafeteria" approach to presenting an extensive information base, it fails to provide assistance to executives in thinking through their real information needs.

The total study process is comprehensive and can pinpoint missing systems. However, it suffers, as noted, from all of the problems of total approaches. There are problems concerning expense, the huge amount of data collected (making it difficult to differentiate the forest from the trees), designer bias, and difficulty in devising reporting systems that serve any individual manager well.

NEW CSF METHOD

The MIT research team's experience in the past two years with the critical success factors (CSF) approach suggests that it is highly effective in helping executives to define their significant information needs. Equally important, it has proved efficient in terms of the interview time needed (from three to six hours) to explain the method and to focus attention on information needs. Most important, executive response to this new method has been excellent in terms of both the process and its outcome.

The actual CSF interviews are usually conducted in two or three separate sessions. In the first, the executive's goals are initially recorded and the CSFs that underlie the goals are discussed. The interrelationships of the CSFs and the goals are then talked about for further clarification and for determination of which recorded CSFs should be combined, eliminated, or restated. An initial cut at measures is also taken in this first interview.

The second session is used to review the results of the first, after the analyst has had a chance to think about them and to suggest "sharpening up" some factors. In addition, measures and possible reports are discussed in depth. Sometimes, a third session may be necessary to obtain final agreement on the CSF measures-and-reporting sequence.

Conceptual Antecedents

In an attempt to overcome some of the shortcomings of the four major approaches discussed earlier, the CSF method focuses on *individual managers* and on each manager's *current information needs*—both hard and soft. It provides for identifying managerial information needs in a clear and meaningful way. Moreover, it takes into consideration the fact that information needs will vary from manager to manager and that these needs will change with time for a particular manager.

The approach is based on the concept of the "success factors" first discussed in the management literature in 1961 by D. Ronald Daniel, now managing director of McKinsey & Company.[7] Although a powerful concept in itself for other than information systems' thinking, it has been heavily obscured in the outpouring of managerial wisdom in the past two decades. It has been focused on and clarified to the best of my knowledge only in the published work of Robert N. Anthony, John Dearden, and Richard F. Vancil.[8]

Daniel, in introducing the concept, cited three examples of major corporations whose information systems produced an extensive amount of information. Very little of the information, however, appeared useful in assisting managers to better perform their jobs.

To draw attention to the type of information actually needed to support managerial activities, Daniel turned to the concept of critical success factors. He stated,

> A company's information system must be discriminating and selective. It should focus on "success factors." In most industries there are usually three to six factors that determine success; these key jobs must be done exceedingly well for a company to be successful. Here are some examples from several major industries:
> - In the automobile industry, styling, an efficient dealer organization, and tight control of manufacturing cost are paramount.
> - In food processing, new product development, good distribution, and effective advertising are the major success factors.
> - In life insurance, the development of agency management personnel, effective control of clerical personnel, and innovation in creating new types of policies spell the difference.[9]

Critical success factors thus are, for any business, the limited number of areas in which results, if they are satisfactory, will ensure successful competitive performance for the organization. They are the few key areas where "things must go right" for the business to flourish. If results in these areas are not adequate, the organization's efforts for the period will be less than desired.

As a result, the critical success factors are areas of activity that should receive constant and careful attention from management. The current status of performance in each area should be continually measured, and that information should be made available.

As Exhibit 1 notes, critical success factors support the attainment of organizational goals. Goals represent the end points that an organization hopes to reach. Critical success factors, however, are the areas in which good performance is necessary to ensure attainment of those goals.

Daniel focused on those critical success factors that are relevant for *any* company in a particular industry. Exhibit 1 updates Daniel's automobile industry CSFs and provides another set of CSFs—from the supermarket industry and a nonprofit hospital.

As this exhibit shows, supermarkets have four industry-based CSFs. These are having the right product mix available in each local store, having it on the shelves, having it advertised effectively to pull shoppers into the store, and having it priced correctly—since profit margins are low in this industry. Super-

EXHIBIT 1   How Attainment of Organizational Goals Is Supported by CSFs

Example	Goals	Critical Success Factors
For-profit *Concern*	Earnings per share Return on investment Market share New product success	*Automotive Industry* Styling Quality dealer system Cost control Meeting energy standards
		Supermarket Industry Product mix Inventory Sales promotion Price
Nonprofit *Concern*	Excellence of health care Meeting needs of future health care environment	*Government Hospital* Regional integration of health care with other hospitals Efficient use of scarce medical resources Improved cost accounting

markets must pay attention to many other things, but these four areas are the underpinnings of successful operation.

Writing a decade later, Anthony and his colleagues picked up Daniel's seminal contribution and expanded it in their work on the design of management control systems. They emphasized three "musts" of any such system:

> The control system *must* be tailored to the specific industry in which the company operates and to the specific strategies that it has adopted; it *must* identify the 'critical success factors' that should receive careful and continuous management attention if the company is to be successful; and it *must* highlight performance with respect to these key variables in reports to all levels of management.[10]

While continuing to recognize industry-based CSFs, Anthony et al. thus went a step further. They placed additional emphasis on the need to tailor management planning and control systems to both a company's particular strategic objectives and its particular managers. That is, the control system must report on those success factors that are perceived by the managers as appropriate to a particular job in a particular company. In short, CSFs differ from company to company and from manager to manager.

Prime Sources of CSFs

In the discussion so far, we have seen that CSFs are applicable to any company operating in a particular *industry*. Yet Anthony et al. emphasized that a management control system also must be tailored to a particular *company*. This must suggest that there are other sources of CSFs than the industry alone. And, indeed, there are. The MIT team has isolated four prime sources of critical success factors:

1. Structure of the particular industry.

As noted, each industry by its very nature has a set of critical success factors that are determined by the characteristics of the industry itself. Each company in the industry must pay attention to these factors. For example, the manager of *any* supermarket will ignore at his peril the critical success factors that appear in Exhibit 1.

2. Competitive strategy, industry position, and geographic location.

Each company in an industry is in an individual situation determined by its history and current competitive strategy. For smaller organizations within an industry dominated by one or two large companies, the actions of the major companies will often produce new and significant problems for the smaller companies. The competitive strategy for the latter may mean establishing a new market niche, getting out of a product line completely, or merely redistributing resources among various product lines.

Thus for small companies a competitor's strategy is often a CSF. For example, IBM's competitive approach to the marketing of small, inexpensive computers is, in itself a CSF for all minicomputer manufacturers.

Just as differences in industry position can dictate CSFs, differences in geographic location and in strategies can lead to differing CSFs from one company to another in an industry.

3. Environmental factors.

As the gross national product and the economy fluctuate, as political factors change, and as the population waxes and wanes, critical success factors can also change for various institutions. At the beginning of 1973, virtually no chief executive in the United States would have listed "energy supply availability" as a critical success factor. Following the oil embargo, however, for a considerable period of time this factor was monitored closely by many executives—since adequate energy was problematic and vital to organizational bottom-line performance.

4. Temporal factors.

Internal organizational considerations often lead to temporal critical success factors. These are areas of activity that are significant for the success of an organization for a particular period of time because they are below the threshold of acceptability at that time (although in general they are "in good shape" and do not merit special attention). As an example, for any organization the loss of a major group of executives in a plane crash obviously would make the "rebuilding of the executive group" a critical success factor for the organization for the period of time until this was accomplished. Similarly, while inventory control is rarely a CSF for the chief executive officer, a very unusual situation (either far too much or far too little stock) might, in fact, become a high-level CSF.

Like Organizations, Differing CSFs

Any organization's situation will change from time to time, and factors that are dealt with by executives as commonplace at one time may become critical success factors at another time. The key here is for the executive to clearly define at any point in time exactly those factors that are crucial to the success of his particular organization in the period for which he is planning.

One would expect, therefore, that organizations in the same industry would exhibit different CSFs as a result of differences in geographic location, strategies, and other factors. A study by Gladys G. Mooradian of the critical success factors of three similar medical group practices bears this out.[11] The medical group practices of the participating physicians were heterogeneous with regard to many of these factors. Each group, however, was well managed with a dynamic and successful administrator in charge.

Mooradian defined the CSFs through open-ended interviews with the administrator of each group practice. She then asked the managers to define their critical success factors and to rank them from most important to least important. Finally, to verify the factors selected, she obtained the opinions of others in the organization.

Exhibit 2 shows the administrators' key variables for the three group practices, ranked in order as perceived by the managers of each institution. It is interesting to note that several of the same variables appear on each list. Several variables, however, are unique to each institution. One can explain the difference in the

---

EXHIBIT 2 **Critical Success Factors for Three Medical Group Practices**

	Clinic #1	Clinic #2	Clinic #3
Most Important	Government regulation	Quality and comprehensive care	Efficiency of operations
	Efficiency of operations	Federal funding	Staffing mix
	Patients' view of practice	Government regulation	Government regulation
	Relation to hospital	Efficiency of operations	Patients' view of practice
	Malpractice insurance effects	Patients' view of practice	Relation to community
	Relation to community	Satellites versus patient service	Relation to hospital
		Other providers in community	
Least Important		Relation to hospital	

CSFs chosen by noting the stages of growth, location, and strategies of each clinic:

- The first medical group is a mature clinic that has been in existence for several years, has a sound organization structure, and has an assured patient population. It is most heavily concerned with government regulation and environmental changes (such as rapidly increasing costs for malpractice insurance), which are the only factors that might upset its highly favorable status quo.
- The second group practice is located in a rural part of a relatively poor state. It is dependent on federal funding and also on its ability to offer a type of medical care not available from private practitioners. Its number one CSF, therefore, is its ability to develop a distinctive competitive image for the delivery of comprehensive, quality care.
- The third clinic is a rapidly growing, new group practice, which was—at that point in time—heavily dependent for its near-term success on its ability to "set up" an efficient operation and bring on board the correct mix of staff to serve its rapidly growing patient population.

In looking at these three lists, it is noticeable that the first four factors on the mature clinic's list also appear on the other two lists. These, it can be suggested, are the all-encompassing industry-based factors. The remaining considerations, which are particular to one or the other of the practices but not to all, are generated by differences in environmental situation, temporal factors, geographic location, or strategic situation.

CSFs at General Manager Level

To this point, I have discussed CSFs strictly from the viewpoint of the top executive of an organization. Indeed, that is the major focus of the MIT research team's current work. It is, however, clear from studies now going on that CSFs, as might be expected, can be useful at each level of general management (managers to whom multiple functions report). There are significant benefits of taking the necessary time to think through—and to record—the critical success factors for each general manager in an organization. Consider:

- The process helps the manager to determine those factors on which he or she should focus management attention. It also helps to ensure that those significant factors will receive careful and continuous management scrutiny.
- The process forces the manager to develop good measures for those factors and to seek reports on each of the measures.
- The identification of CSFs allows a clear definition of the amount of information that must be collected by the organization and limits the costly collection of more data than necessary.
- The identification of CSFs moves an organization away from the trap of building its reporting and information system primarily around data that are "easy to collect." Rather, it focuses attention on those data that might otherwise not be collected but are significant for the success of the particular management level involved.
- The process acknowledges that some factors are temporal and that CSFs are manager specific. This suggests that the information system should be in constant flux with new reports being developed as needed to accommodate changes in the organization's strategy, environment, or organization structure. Rather than changes in an information system being looked on as an indication of "inadequate design," they must be viewed as an inevitable and productive part of information systems development.

- The CSF concept itself is useful for more than information systems design. Current studies suggest several additional areas of assistance to the management process. For example, an area that can be improved through the use of CSFs is the planning process. CSFs can be arrayed hierarchically and used as an important vehicle of communication for management, either as an informal planning aid or as a part of the formal planning process.

Let me stress that the CSF approach does not attempt to deal with information needs for strategic planning. Data needs for this management role are almost impossible to preplan. The CSF method centers, rather, on information needs for management control where data needed to monitor and improve existing areas of business can be more readily defined.

ILLUSTRATIVE CSF EXAMPLE

Let us now turn to an example of the use of this approach. The president referred to at the start of this article is real. He is Larry Gould, former president of Microwave Associates, a $60-million sales organization serving several aspects of the microwave communication industry.[12] When he first looked carefully at the "information" he was receiving, Gould found that some 97 "reports" crossed his desk in a typical month. Almost all were originally designed by someone else who felt that he "should be receiving this vital data."

However, the reports provided him with virtually nothing *he* could use. A few gave him some "score-keeping data," such as the monthly profit statement. One or two others provided him with bits and pieces of data he wanted, but even these left major things unsaid. The data were either unrelated to other key facts or related in a way that was not meaningful to him.

The concept of critical success factors sounded to him like one way out of this dilemma. He therefore, with the MIT research analyst, invested two two-and-a-half-hour periods in working through his goals, critical success factors, and measures. First, he noted the objectives of the company and the current year's goals. Then, he went to work to assess what factors were critical to accomplish these objectives.

EXHIBIT 3   CSFs Developed to Meet Microwave Associates' Organizational Goals

Critical Success Factors	Prime Measures
1. Image in financial markets	Price/earnings ratio
2. Technological reputation with customers	Orders/bid ratio Customer "perception" interview results
3. Market success	Change in market share (each product) Growth rates of company markets
4. Risk recognition in major bids and contracts	Company's years of experience with similar products "New" or "old" customer Prior customer relationship
5. Profit margin on jobs	Bid profit margin as ratio of profit on similar jobs in this product line
6. Company morale	Turnover, absenteeism, etc. Informal feedback
7. Performance to budget on major jobs	Job cost budgeted/actual

Factors & Measures

The seven critical success factors Gould developed are shown in Exhibit 3, along with from one to three prime measures for each factor (although he also developed some additional measures). The reader should note that this specific set of CSFs emerged only after intensive analysis and discussion. At the end of the first meeting, nine factors were on Gould's list. By the end of the second meeting, two had been combined into one, and one had been dropped as not being significant enough to command ongoing close attention.

Most of the second interview session centered on a discussion of the measures for each factor. Where hard data were perceived to be available, the discussion was short. Where softer measures were necessary, however, lengthy discussions of the type of information needed and the difficulty and/or cost of acquiring it often ensued. Yet convergence on the required "evidence" about the state of each CSF occurred with responsible speed and clarity in each case. Some discussion concerning each CSF and its measures is perhaps worthwhile. Consider:

1. Image in financial markets.

Microwave Associates is growing and making acquisitions as it seeks to gain a growth segment of the electronics industry. Much of the company's growth is coming from acquisitions. Clearly, the better the image on Wall Street, the higher the price–earnings ratio. The measure of success here is clear: the company's multiple vis-à-vis others in its industry segment.

2. Technological reputation with customers.

Although Microwave Associates has some standard products, the majority of its work is done on a tailor-made, one-shot basis. A significant number of these jobs are state-of-the-art work that leads to follow-on production contracts. To a very large extent, buying decisions in the field are made on the customer's confidence in Microwave's technical ability. Sample measures were developed for this CSF. The two measures shown in this exhibit are at the opposite extremes of hard and soft data. The ratio of total orders to total bids can be easily measured. While this hard measure is indicative of customers' perception of the company's technical ability, it also has other factors such as "sales aggressiveness" in it.

The most direct measure possible is person-to-person interviews. Although this measure is soft, the company decided to initiate a measuring process through field interviews by its top executives. (Other measures of this CSF included field interviews by sales personnel, assessment of the rise or fall of the percentage of each major customer's business being obtained, and so forth.)

3. Market success.

On the surface, this CSF is straightforward. But, as shown by the measures, it includes attention to *current* market success, as well as the company's progress with regard to significant *new* market opportunities (e.g., the relative rate of growth of each market segment, opportunities provided by new technology, and relative—not just absolute—competitive performance).

4. Risk recognition in major bids and contracts.

Because many of the jobs accepted are near or at the state of the art, controlling the company's risk profile is critical. As noted in the exhibit, a variety of factors contribute to risk. The measurement process designed involves a computer algorithm to consider these factors and to highlight particularly risky situations.

5. *Profit margin on jobs.*

When profit center managers have low backlogs, they are often tempted to bid low to obtain additional business. While this procedure is not necessarily bad, it is critical for corporate management to understand the expected profit profile and, at times, to counter lower-level tendencies to accept low-profit business.

6. *Company morale.*

Because of its high-technology strategy, the company is clearly heavily dependent on the esprit of its key scientists and engineers. It must also be able to attract and keep a skilled work force. Thus morale is a critical success factor. Measures of morale range from hard data (e.g., turnover, absenteeism, and tardiness) to informal feedback (e.g., management discussion sessions with employees).

7. *Performance to budget on major jobs.*

This final CSF reflects the need to control major projects and to ensure that they are completed on time and near budget. Adverse results with regard to timeliness can severely affect CSF #2 (technological perception), and significant cost overruns can similarly affect CSF #1 (financial market perception). In general, no single job is crucially important. Rather, it is the *profile* of performance across major jobs that is significant.

Reports & Subsystems

Given the foregoing CSFs and measures, the next step was to design a set of report formats. This step required examination of both existing information systems and data sources.

For the soft, informal, subjective measures, this process was straightforward. Forms to record facts and impressions were designed so as to scale (where possible) perception and highlight significant soft factors.

For some of the hard computer-based measures, existing information systems and databases supplied most of the necessary data. However, in every case—even where *all* data were available—existing report forms were inadequate and new reports had to be designed.

Most important, however, two completely new information subsystems were needed to support the president's CSFs. These were a "bidding" system and a vastly different automated "project budgeting and control" system. (Significantly, each of these subsystems had been requested many times by lower-level personnel, who needed them for more detailed planning and control of job bidding and monitoring at the product-line manager and manufacturing levels.) Subsequently, these subsystems were placed at the top of the priority list for data processing.

In summarizing the Microwave case, it is clear that the exercise of discovering information needs through examination of the chief executive's critical success factors had a number of specific benefits. All of the seven general advantages of the CSF method for information systems development previously noted applied to some extent. However, the importance of each of these varies from organization to organization. At Microwave, the most striking advantages were:

- The conscious listing (or bringing to the surface) of the most significant areas on which attention needed to be focused. The process of making these areas *explicit* provided insights not only into information needs, but also into several other aspects of the company's managerial systems.
- The design of a useful set of *reports* to provide the information needed for monitoring ongoing operations at the executive level. (There clearly were other data needed—i.e., for developing strategy, dealing with special situations, and so on.) The CSF route, however, focused on the data needed for the ongoing "management control" process, and this need was significant at Microwave.
- The development of *priorities* for information systems development. It was clear that information needed for control purposes by the chief executive should have some priority. (It also highlighted priorities for other management levels.)
- The provision of a means of hierarchical *communication* among executives as to what the critical factors were for the success of the company. (Too often, only goals provide a major communication link to enhance shared understanding of the company and its environment among management levels.) This hierarchical approach provided another —and we believe more pragmatic and action-oriented— means of communication. At Microwave, there is a current project aimed at developing and sharing CSFs at the top four management levels.

Other Case Examples

The critical success factors developed in four other cases provide useful additional background for drawing some generalizations about the method and executive information needs. These CSFs are arrayed in Exhibit 4.

Major Oil Company

The chief executive of this centralized organization responded quickly and unhesitatingly concerning his critical success factors. His goal structure was oriented toward such traditional measures as increasing return on investment, increasing earnings per share, and so forth. Yet he felt there were two major keys to profitability in the future. One was to improve relationships with society as a whole and with the federal government in particular. The other was the urgent need to provide a broader base of earnings assets in petroleum-shy future decades.

As a result of this view of the world, the CEO had initiated major programs to develop new ventures and to decentralize the organization. To facilitate the acquisition process, emphasis was placed on cash flow (liquidity) as opposed to reported earnings. In addition, prime attention was given to understanding and improving external relationships.

All of these efforts are reflected in the company's critical success factors shown in Exhibit 4. Progress in each of these areas is monitored weekly. CSFs #1, #3, and #4 are reported on with regard to both actions taken and the appropriate executive's subjective assessment of results attained. Liquidity measures are provided by computer output. New-venture success is now assessed by a combination of hard and soft measures.

Store Furnishings Manufacturer

This midwestern company has three major product lines. The largest of these is a well-accepted but relatively stable traditional line on which the company's reputation was made (product line A). In addition, there are two relatively new but fast-growing lines (B and C). The president's preexisting information system was a

---

EXHIBIT 4   CSFs in Four Cases

Chief Executive of a Major Oil Company

1. Decentralize organization.
2. Improve liquidity position.
3. Improve government/business relationships.
4. Create better societal image.
5. Develop new ventures.

Director of a Government Hospital

1. Devise method for obtaining valid data on current status of hospital operations.
2. Devise method for resource allocation.
3. Manage external relationships.
4. Get acceptance of concept of regionalization by all hospital directors.
5. Develop method for managing regionalization in government hospital group.
6. Strengthen management support, capability, and capacity.
7. Improve relationship with government department central office.
8. Meet budgetary constraints.

President of a Store Furnishings Manufacturer

1. Expand foreign sales for product lines B and C.
2. Improve market understanding of product line A.
3. Redesign sales compensation structure in three product lines.
4. Improve production scheduling.
5. Mechanize production facilities.
6. Strengthen management team.

Division Chief Executive of an Electronics Company

1. Support field sales force.
2. Strengthen customer relations.
3. Improve productivity.
4. Obtain government R&D support.
5. Develop new products.
6. Acquire new technological capability
7. Improve facilities.

---

combination of monthly financial accounting reports and several sales analysis reports.

The president's critical success factors directly reflected the changing fortunes of his product lines. There was a need to concentrate on immediate foreign penetration (to build market share) in the two "hot" lines. At the same time, he saw the need to reassess the now barely growing line on which the company was built three decades ago.

Equally significant, whereas direct selling had been the only feasible mode for the traditional line, the new lines appeared to respond heavily to trade advertising to generate both leads and, in some cases, direct-from-the-factory sales. Because margins are relatively tight in this competitive industry, one factor critical to the company's success with this new product structure, therefore, was a redesign of the sales compensation structure to reflect the evidently diminished effort needed to make sales in the new lines.

A similar need for cost-consciousness also dictated attention to the CSFs of production scheduling efficiency and productivity improvements through the increasing mechanization of production facilities. Finally, strengthening the management team to take advantage of the opportunities presented by the new product lines was felt to be critical by this president.

The analysis of CSFs in this case indicated a need for two major changes in formal information flow to the president. Subsequently, a far more meaningful production reporting system was developed (to support CSF #4), and a vastly different sales reporting system emphasizing CSFs #2 and #3 was established.

Government Hospital

The CSFs for the director of a government hospital reflect his belief in the need for his organization to radically restructure itself to adapt to a future health care environment perceived as vastly different. He believes that his hospital and his sister government agency hospitals must provide specialized, cost-conscious, comprehensive health care for a carefully defined patient population. Moreover, this care will have to be integrated with that provided by other government hospitals and private hospitals within the region of the country in which his hospital exists.

The director's critical success factors are thus, as shown in Exhibit 4, concerned primarily with building external links and managing cooperation and resource sharing within the set of eight government agency hospitals in his region. The director is also concerned with the development of adequate data systems and methods to manage effective and efficient use of scarce medical resources.

The organization currently has only minimal management information—drawn in bits and pieces from what is essentially a financial accounting system designed primarily to assure the safeguarding and legal use of government funds. The director's desire to get involved in a CSF-oriented investigation of management information needs grew from his despair of being able to manage in the future environment with existing information.

The MIT research team is currently conducting a study involving CSF-based interviews with the top three levels of key managers and department heads in the hospital. Their information needs are heavily oriented toward external data and vastly improved cost accounting.

Major Electronics Division

This decentralized electronics company places return-on-investment responsibility on the top executive of a major division. His first two CSFs indicate his view of the need for an increasing emphasis on marketing in his traditionally engineering-oriented organization. As Exhibit 4 shows, his CSFs #3, #6, and #7 are oriented toward the need for more cost-effective production facilities.

Equally important is his attention to new product development (CSF #5) in a fast-moving marketplace. In conjunction with this, CSF #4 reflects his view that a healthy portfolio of government R&D contracts will allow a much larger amount of research to be performed, thereby increasing the expected yield of new ideas and new products. Thus he spends a significant share of his time involved in the process of assuring that government research contracts are being avidly pursued (although they add relatively little to his near-term bottom line).

Efforts to improve the information provided to this division manager have revolved primarily around making more explicit the methods of measuring progress in each of these CSF areas. More quantitative indexes have proved to be useful in some areas. In others, however, they have not improved what must be essentially "subjective feel" judgments.

SUPPORTIVE CSF INFORMATION

Previously, I discussed the advantages (both general and specific to one case) of using the CSF process for information systems design. Additionally, some important attributes of the types of information necessary to support the top executive's CSFs can be drawn from the five examples. Consider:

1. Perhaps most obvious, but worth stating, is the fact that traditional financial accounting systems rarely provide the type of data necessary to monitor critical success factors. Financial accounting systems are aimed at providing historical information to outsiders (e.g., stockholders and others). Only very occasionally is there much overlap between financial accounting data and the type of data needed to track CSFs. In only one of the companies studied was financial accounting data the major source of information for a CSF, and there for only one factor. However, the need for improved *cost* accounting data to report on CSFs was often evident.

2. Many critical success factors require information external to the organization—information concerned with market structure, customer perceptions, or future trends. Approximately a third of the 33 CSFs in the five examples fit this description. The data to support these CSFs are not only unavailable from the financial accounting system but, in the majority of cases, are also unavailable as a by-product of the organization's other usual day-to-day transaction-processing systems (e.g., order entry, billing, and payroll). The information system must therefore be designed, and the external information consciously collected from the proper sources. It will not flow naturally to the CEO.

3. Many other CSFs require coordinating pieces of information from multiple data sets that are widely dispersed throughout the company. This is perhaps best noted in the Microwave case, but it is a recurrent feature in all companies. This situation argues heavily for computer implementation of database systems that facilitate accessing multiple data sets.

4. A small but significant part of the information concerning the status of CSFs requires subjective assessment on the part of others in the organization, rather than being neatly quantifiable. About a fifth of the status measures at the companies studied require subjective assessment. This is significant managerial data, and top executives are used to these soft but useful status measures.

(However, it should be noted, many more of the measures at first devised were subjective. It takes considerable work to find objective measures, but in more instances than originally perceived, suitable objective measures are available and can be developed.)

5. Critical success factors can be categorized as either the "monitoring" or the "building" type. The more competitive pressure for current performance that the chief executive feels, the more his CSFs tend toward monitoring current results. The more that the organization is insulated from economic pressures (as the government hospital was) or decentralized (as the oil company was becoming), the more CSFs become oriented toward building for the future through major change programs aimed at adapting the organization to a perceived new environment.

In all cases that I have seen thus far, however, there is a mixture of the two types. Every chief executive appears to have, at some level, both monitoring and building (or adapting) responsibilities. Thus a great deal of the information needed will not continue to be desired year after year. Rather, it is relatively short-term "project status" information that is needed only during the project's lifetime. Periodic review of CSF's will therefore bring to light the need to discontinue some reports and initiate others.

> *The critical power . . . tends to make an intellectual situation of which the creative power can profitably avail itself . . . to make the best ideas prevail.*

From Matthew Arnold, *The Function of Criticism at the Present Time* (1864).

FOOTNOTES

1. Interview with Anthony J. F. O'Reilly, president of H. J. Heinz Co., *M.I.S. Quarterly,* March 1977, p. 7.

2. Interview with William Dougherty, president of North Carolina Bank Corporation, *M.I.S. Quarterly,* March 1977, p. 1.

3. See Henry Mintzberg, "Planning on the Left Side and Managing on the Right," *Harvard Business Review,* July–August 1976, p. 54.

4. "Corporate 'War Rooms' Plug into the Computer," *Business Week,* August 23, 1976, p. 65.

5. Daniel T. Carroll, "How the President Satisfies His Information Systems Requirements," published in *Society for Management Information Systems Proceedings,* 1976.

6. Management control is the process of (a) long-range planning of the activities of the organization, (b) short-term planning (usually one year), and (c) monitoring activities to ensure the accomplish-

ment of the desired results. The management control process thus follows the development of major strategic directions that are set in the strategic planning process. This definition roughly follows the framework of Robert N. Anthony, *Planning and Control: A Framework for Analysis* (Boston: Division of Research, Harvard Business School, 1965).

7. See D. Ronald Daniel, "Management Information Crisis," *Harvard Business Review*, September–October 1961, p. 111.

8. See Robert N. Anthony, John Dearden, and Richard F. Vancil, "Key Economic Variables," in *Management Controls Systems* (Homewood, Ill.: Richard D. Irwin, 1972), p. 147.

9. Daniel, "Management Information Crisis," p. 116.

10. Anthony, Dearden, and Vancil, "Key Economic Variables," p. 148.

11. Gladys G. Mooradian, "The Key Variables in Planning and Control in Medical Group Practices," Unpublished master's thesis, Sloan School of Management, MIT, Cambridge, Mass., 1976.

12. Since this was originally written, Gould has assumed the position of chairman of the board at M/A-COM, Inc., a holding company of which Microwave Associates is a subsidiary.

Chapter Twelve
Engaging Top Management in Information Technology

JOHN F. ROCKART
ADAM D. CRESCENZI

During the past three decades, innumerable systems have been computerized to improve efficiency in accounting and operational activities. More recently, decision support systems (DSSs) have come into their own and are flourishing in many companies. Now, with the advent of the personal computer, computer-based assistance for all functions of the business is becoming widespread in a number of corporations.

In the midst of this computer-based explosion, however, one significant ingredient has been noticeably missing. For the most part, top management has stood—uninvolved—at the sidelines. Senior executives have merely been spectators in the development and use of information systems. With a few notable exceptions, they have given little thought to improving corporate effectiveness through their own involvement in systems planning and priority setting.

Until very recently, this posture made some sense: information systems were considered primarily paperwork-processing systems, which were thought to have very little impact on organizational success or failure.

Today, however, managers are confronting forces which are

indicating that widespread change is imminent. These forces include: recognition of the limits to growth in the "smokestack industries"; competition to find strategic niches; and new organization structures, which will often lead managers to unfamiliar territories. Thus, executives are eager to obtain the right information that will help them *manage change*.

HOW INFORMATION TECHNOLOGY CAN HELP MANAGEMENT

The movement of information systems hardware and software capabilities from merely facilitating the automation of clerical tasks to providing direct on-line support for decision making and other managerial processes has opened up new ways for top executives to view their information needs. Today, information technology (IT) gives managers an opportunity (1) to improve delivery of their products and services and (2) to potentially increase their effectiveness and productivity in *managing* the businesses.

Finally, and, perhaps, most important, the new information/communication technology is having a significant impact on *business strategy* itself. For example, such companies as Merrill Lynch, American Hospital Supply, and McKesson have demonstrated that significant competitive advantages can be gained through judicial use of new technology.[1]

Clearly, it is time for top management to get off the sidelines. Recognizing that information is a strategic resource implies a clear need to link information systems to business strategy, and, especially, to ensure that business strategy is developed in the context of the new IT environment. In short, senior executives are increasingly feeling the need to become informed, energized, and engaged in information systems.

Our tenet in this article is that active engagement of top management with information systems is highly desirable in organizations of every size. Through a case study of Southwestern Ohio Steel (SOS), we present a three-phase process that we believe is instrumental in engaging top executives. The process is based on three major concepts:

- Critical Success Factors: to engage management's attention and ensure that the systems meet the most critical *business* needs.

- Decision Scenarios: to demonstrate to management that the systems to be developed will aid materially in the decision-making process.
- Prototyping: to allow management to quickly reap system results which are to be a part of the development process, and to minimize initial costs.

Tying these three concepts together in a single development process accomplishes two major ends. First, it engages top management in the information systems planning process in a manner that is managerially meaningful. Second, it keeps management's attention and involvement throughout a rapid development process, since the systems priorities are targeted to support their decision-making processes.

SOUTHWESTERN OHIO STEEL: A CASE STUDY

Southwestern Ohio Steel is one of the top three steel service centers in the U.S., with sales of approximately $100 million. Located in Hamilton, Ohio, with a processing plant in Middletown, Ohio, it employs more than 400 people. SOS is in the business of purchasing steel of differing quality, including primes and seconds as well as overruns, from major steel companies and selling it directly to hundreds of customers throughout the Midwest and contiguous states. The majority of the steel is processed (e.g., slitted, sheared) to some extent at the SOS plant before it is shipped to customers. By paying close attention to merchandising and manufacturing processes, SOS has developed an image of quality and service to both its customers and suppliers. A key contributor to SOS's image is its capability to provide customized products quickly as a result of extreme flexibility in its production schedule.

A Changing Environment

In early 1982, SOS utilized its existing computer installation to perform only routine accounting functions. However, several factors convinced management that a major review of its information systems capability was needed. These factors included:

- The company's planning process indicated that, despite possible stagnant growth in the steel industry, SOS could be expected to continue to grow significantly. Steel service centers were becoming an increasingly accepted and utilized service by American industry. Service centers' share of the steel end-market had grown from 17 percent in 1960 to 23 percent in the early 80s and was expected to be in the high 20s by 1990. Two competitive advantages facilitated SOS's decision. First, the steel centers' ability to hold and preprocess steel vastly decreased the inventories needed to be maintained by their customers. Second, as more firms turned to the essentials of Japanese management, a growing trend toward "just-in-time" delivery-oriented steel manufacturers was gaining a competitive edge over the less delivery-oriented ones.

These very positive factors, however, were in turn making the steel service center business increasingly complex. Thus, the complexity of inventory and manufacturing management at SOS had grown significantly. With customers maintaining lower inventory levels, a vastly increased number of "hot orders" (or next-day delivery) was complicating plant operations. In addition, an increasing number of SOS customers were using manufacturing requirements planning (MRP) systems and were, therefore, calling for smaller lots and more frequent deliveries.

- At SOS, the information systems capability was strained. While existing systems, which were installed by the company's accounting firm, were doing a superb job of providing the accounting personnel with data, all key managerially oriented information remained manual.

- Finally, SOS's management team was changing. The first-generation management of the family-owned organization was giving way to a newer, younger managerial team, two of whom were sons of the original top management. Still, there was a need for departing key executives to pass on knowledge and to build into the systems some of the expertise and perspectives they gained over a number of years.

Management's first impulse was to turn to a consulting firm it had used in the past. However, the solution this firm proposed came as a shock to the senior executives of the steel firm. It was a series of on-line computerized information systems based on 'tried-and-true" conventional systems design and implementation processes. The cost was estimated at $2.4 million over the course of four years. Furthermore, major results and benefits would not be apparent until after the fourth year.

Management, therefore, rejected this approach. All members of the management team felt quite uncomfortable with the price tag, timeframe, and overall risk associated with the project. *Most important,* the exact tie between the systems proposed and the real needs of the business was unclear.

At this point, Tom Heldman, the chief financial officer, embarked on a search: "I wasn't quite sure what I wanted. But I knew there had to be a more creative approach toward assisting top management to understand its systems needs and to bring up systems more quickly, with reduced risk and cost." Heldman found what he wanted in the process described below.

A Three-Phase Process for Managerial Involvement

Figure 1 outlines the three major phases of the process used at Southwestern Ohio Steel. Each phase has two or three subparts and a particular "key technique" associated with it. The three techniques are what assure managerial involvement from the earliest planning stages through a very interactive implementation process. The three phases are:

- Linking information systems to the management needs of the business. Utilizing *critical success factors,* management develops a clear definition of the business and comes to an agreement on the most critical business functions. In addition, management takes a first cut at stating its information systems needs in these critical areas.
- Developing systems priorities and gaining confidence in the recommended systems. Using the key technique *decision scenarios,* management develops an understanding of how these systems, which were defined in phase one, would deliver the necessary information to support key decisions.
- Building low-risk, managerially useful systems. Utilizing the key technique *prototyping,* initial, partial systems are built and brought up very quickly at low cost. In working with early, limited—but operational—versions of these systems, management is able to grasp more fully their usefulness and to authorize, with significantly greater comfort, continued system development. As a by-product, initial financial benefits from these systems are received very quickly.

FIGURE 1   A Three-Phase Process for Managerial Involvement

Phase One: Linking information systems to the management needs of the business. Key technique: critical success factors process

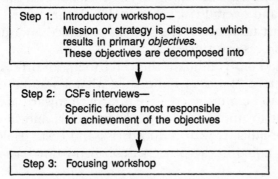

Step 1:   Introductory workshop—
          Mission or strategy is discussed, which results in primary *objectives*.
          These objectives are decomposed into

Step 2:   CSFs interviews—
          Specific factors most responsible for achievement of the objectives

Step 3:   Focusing workshop

Phase Two: Developing systems priorities and gaining confidence in recommended systems. Key technique: decision scenarios

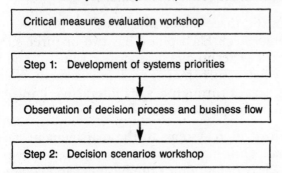

Critical measures evaluation workshop

Step 1:   Development of systems priorities

Observation of decision process and business flow

Step 2:   Decision scenarios workshop

Phase Three: Rapid development of low risk, managerially useful systems. Key technique: prototype development, implementation, use, and refinement

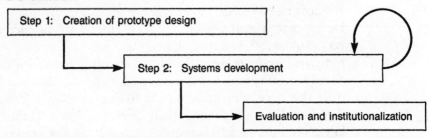

Step 1:   Creation of prototype design

Step 2:   Systems development

Evaluation and institutionalization

Phase One: Linking Information Systems to the Business

This phase emphasizes understanding the business, focuses on the few factors that drive the business, and actively engages management in the process. Only at the very end of this phase is the initial *link* made to information requirements for the key areas of the business. As Figure 1 shows, the first phase is divided into three steps: (1) an introductory workshop, (2) critical success factors (CSFs) interviews, and (3) an all-important "focusing workshop" in which the results of the interviews and their implications are evaluated and discussed very thoroughly.

Step 1: Introductory Workshop.　Five key members of the SOS management team participated in this workshop. They were William Huber, chairman of the board; Joseph Wolf, president; Tom Heldman, vice president of finance; Jacque Huber, vice president of sales; and Paul Pappenheimer, vice president of materials.

In the first workshop session, the consultants—having already completed their introductory "homework" about the company—presented the three-phase-process approach to determine what the company's information needs would be. The CSF method and the prototype concept were also described here. The major step was to discuss and agree upon company objectives.

William Huber found this approach very much to his liking, even though he was initially skeptical. Before the workshop, he told Heldman: "Don't let anybody ask me what information I need. People don't know what they need." Nonetheless, the approach of developing information systems based on the *understandable* information imperatives of critical business functions, not on vaguely guessed at information "needs," caught his attention. Consequently, he became an active and influential participant throughout the workshop, passing on to the younger management team much knowledge which he had acquired in the several decades of his managing the business.

Four benefits emerged from the workshop:

1. A *managerial* perspective for systems development—that is, one of linking information systems needs and priorities to the most important business activities of the executives—was established.
2. An initial step was made toward the establishment of business priorities through the definition—essentially, a redefinition—of corporate goals.
3. Active involvement of the key member of the executive team, the chairman of the board, was obtained.
4. The techniques that were to be utilized during the process were explained to the SOS executives.

Step 2: CSFs Interviews.　The critical success factors method is a technique designed to help managers and system designers identify the management information necessary to support the key business areas.[2] For an individual manager, CSFs are the few key areas in which successful performance will lead to the achievement of the manager's objectives. In effect, critical success factors are the *means* to the objectives—which are the desired *ends*. On a corporate level, CSFs are the key areas on which the company must focus in order to achieve its objectives.

The CSF interview process is designed to have each manager explicitly state those factors which are critical, both for himself and for the corporation. By voicing these CSFs, managers are able to sharpen their understanding of the business's priority areas. The ways in which the CSFs might be measured are also discussed, which leads to considering what information is necessary.

At SOS the 5 key executives and 10 other key managers were interviewed. In addition to further communicating the desire to link all systems development strongly to the needs of the business, the interviewing process also helped to clarify the understanding of the business, the role of each individual, and the culture of the organization.

Step 3: Focusing Workshop. Preparation for the focusing workshop on management's part consists of reading interview summaries, which are then distributed after they have been reviewed by the individual participants. At the workshop, the consultants present a "strawman" of corporate mission, objectives, and CSFs—all constructed from the analysis of the introductory workshop and interviews. The strawman provides a basis for extended, often intense, discussion and the key to uncovering varying perceptions and disagreements among the management team. This is the most significant and difficult step in the first phase, for different individual perspectives, managerial loyalties, and desires emerge. Thus, leadership by corporate management is essential in untangling the myriad of differences and focusing on the core elements of the business. The end result is agreement on what the company's mission and goals are.

During the focusing workshop at SOS, corporate objectives developed in the introductory workshop were reaffirmed. Most of these objectives were related to financial and marketing aspects of the business. From a set of 40 initially suggested critical success factors, which were obtained through the interviews, 4 CSFs emerged:

- Maintaining excellent supplier relationships.
- Maintaining or improving customer relationships.

- Merchandising available inventory to its most value-added use.
- Utilizing available capital and human resources efficiently and effectively.

As Tom Heldman notes: "This is the key meeting. The interviews are merely a preliminary, a 'softening-up' process in which managers get an initial opportunity to think deeply about the corporation, as well as to develop relationships with the consultants."

In the course of the focusing workshop, what had previously been implicit was made explicit—sometimes with surprising, insightful results. In Jacque Huber's words: "We all knew what was critical for our company, but the discussion—sharing and agreeing—was really important. What came out of it was a minor revelation. Seeing it on the blackboard in black and white is much more significant than carrying around a set of ideas which are merely intuitively felt."

Another SOS executive portrays the managerial insights gained from focusing on the organization's CSFs in a somewhat different way: "During the meeting, our concept of our organization structure went from an organization chart that looked like [Figure 2a] to one that looked like [Figure 2b]. This was important. It affected our system's design enormously. More importantly, it has affected the way we manage the business."

Although the interpersonal skills and business knowledge of the consulting team running the focusing workshop are very significant, the workshop technique itself readily captures the attention and involvement of the management team and eases the seminar leadership job. Again, Heldman sums it up: "Focusing on 'what makes the company a success' intrigued almost all of top management. It appealed to a group of good managers, allowing them to engage in a discussion of what they knew best and what seemed important to them."

Phase Two: Developing Systems Priorities

In the second phase, another workshop is held to define the set of measures that would be used to evaluate the CSFs (see Table 1). The measures are hard and soft data which managers use to monitor the performance and behavior of each CSF. In the SOS workshop, for example, current measures and data used for

FIGURE 2a

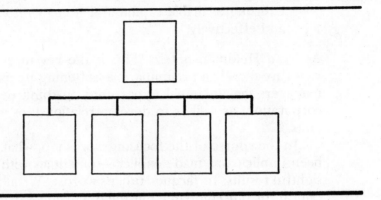

FIGURE 2b

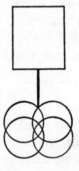

decision making were examined through observations of business activities.

Finally, initial steps are taken to assess from management's viewpoint the implications of the set of objectives, CSFs, and measures for information systems priorities. As Figure 1 illustrates, phase two has two major steps: (1) the development of systems priorities and (2) the gaining of managerial confidence, through the use of decision scenarios, that the systems priorities will support key decisions.

Step 1: Development of Systems Priorities. At the same time that the results of the interviews and sessions were being reviewed, the project team began studying the business in more depth. At the end of this period, three distinct systems priorities that would support the fundamental managerial processes were identified: the buying and inventory process, the marketing of steel, and the production scheduling process.

An analysis of these three proposed systems showed that each

TABLE 1   Measures of One CSF

CSF	Measures	Data Type	Current Measure
Customer relations	Volume	H	M
	Inquiries	H	M
	Order/bid ratio	H	M
	Complaints and/or rejections of materials	H	M
	Customer turnover or lost accounts	H	M
	Decline in volume with customer	H	M
	Program account actual volume versus customer and SOS forecasts	H	A
	New accounts	H	M
	Conversions to program accounts	H	U
	On-time delivery:	H	A
	—To first promise date		
	—To final need date		
	Trends in credit rejections	H	U
	Tone of voice (*especially during late delivery calls*)	S	A
	Finance and credit *"handling"* feedback	S	A

Key:
H = Hard.   A = Data available.
S = Soft.   U = Data unavailable.
M = Measured.

would significantly affect the CSFs of the firm. Inventory management would affect all of the CSFs, especially supplier relationships and efficient use of resources. The marketing system would have a direct impact on customer relationships and merchandising. Finally, production scheduling would be significant with regard to the critical areas of efficient and effective use of resources, merchandising, and customer relationships.

In general, the transition from a business focus on objectives and CSFs to one on systems definition is not a straightforward, simple process; it is more an art form than a science. In other words, such a transition relies heavily on the technical expertise, systems knowledge, and all-around expertise of the design team. But at SOS, as in other cases in which we have been involved, the significant *systems* needs were strongly indicated from the preceding *managerial* discussion of goals, CSFs, and measures.

Step 2: Decision Scenarios Workshop.   While observing the key managers in their daily activities, the project team noted recurring decisions along with the questions managers asked of themselves and others in order to make these decisions. From these

TABLE 2A   A Sample Decision Scenario

Purchasing Scenario:

The inventory manager receives a call from a supplier offering an extremely attractive purchase opportunity: a 15-ton slab which can be rolled to any width from 57¼ to 59¾ in either cold rolled or galvanized prime coil. The price is 19 cents per pound.

Questions Asked:

What does the economy look like overall?

How have orders been keeping up?
—Are contract customers meeting expectations/using their reserves?
—What was last week's order volume in prime roll?*

What are prime cold roll inventory levels?*
—Are we particularly low in any gauge?
—Have we been too high in this area?
—What can I expect to use in the next two months?

What is the supplier's situation?
—Is this a "once-in-a-lifetime" situation?
—How badly do they need us here?
—Is this price likely to be offered again?

What have I paid for this item in the past?*

Who will get it if we refuse it?

*Denotes questions that can be answered by the proposed system.

"decision situations," a set of "decision scenarios" was developed. Each decision scenario was concerned with a particular managerial event and the questions which might have been instrumental in the formulation of a decision. All relevant questions, both those which could be answered by computer-based data and those which could not, were included in the scenario.

In another session, the three proposed prototype systems were outlined to the managerial team. This particular session, however, centered on the "decision scenarios." A sample decision scenario is presented in Tables 2a and 2b. By working through a series of scenarios, the managers were able to gain a much greater familiarity with and insight into the workings of the proposed systems. They were able to see what questions would be answered by the new systems, what questions would not be answered, and how the data would be presented through "paper models" of proposed screen formats.

During this session, the technical environment necessary to support the systems, the necessary data in the system, and the source and frequency of data collection were also discussed. After

---

TABLE 2B   Paper Model of Output: Inventory Levels

To Review cold rolled steel inventory levels:
Product Description—CR
Grade—   SOS
Gauges*—   ALL

Gauge†	On Hand	On Order	Total	Available to Promise‡	Percent Available to Promise	Last Month Sales	Weeks of Sales§
.022	232	51	283	35	12	50	25
.026	636	0	636	101	16	135	20
.032	1,450	474	2,014	234	12	328	27
.044	6,213	1,352	7,565	945	13	1,324	25
.055	5,769	1,256	7,025	939	14	1,229	25
.068	192	87	279	0	0	41	30
.097	143	0	143	0	0	31	20
.112	67	0	67	0	0	14	21
Total	14,792	3,220	18,012	2,250	12.5	3,152	—

*A specific gauge (i.e., *.031*), range of gauges (i.e., *.031, .044*), all gauges = *ALL.*
†Gauges without inventory do not appear.
‡Neither reserved for program account nor assigned.
§On hand plus on order less open orders (last month's sales/days in month: Column 7).

the SOS management confirmed that the systems were appropriate, the project team began working on the design details of each system.

Phase Three: Creating Prototypes and Implementing Actual Systems

As Figure 1 shows, the final phase of the process contains two major steps: (1) the creation of an initial, detailed prototype design and (2) actual systems development.

Step 1: Creation of a Prototype Design. Even after the systems are agreed upon, the exact method of prototyping must be decided and the right *type* of prototype must be selected. So far, it appears that there are three significantly different kinds of prototypes: an information database, a pilot system, and a "classical" prototype. Interestingly enough, all three prototypes were called for at SOS.

- *An information database for marketing support.* By its very nature, an information database, which is a collection of data made accessible to users, is a prototype. No matter how carefully designed the initial system is, it is impossible to have a manager define the exact information he or she will use to make decisions. Most decision-making processes are tenuously understood at best, and knowledge of the data needed for them previous to automation is incomplete. Moreover, as a manager uses a database, he or she gains further insight into both the data he or she *really* needs and the methods of access that he or she desires in order to utilize that data.

At SOS, sales support was provided by an information database originally designated to include information on customers, potential customers, open orders, and accounts receivable. The majority of the CSF measures stated in Table 1 were included in one form or another. This prototype was, in current parlance, a decision support system.

- *A pilot system for inventory management.* Pilot systems and pilot plants have been built as part of research and development processes for decades. These systems are a miniature replication of the final production plan. Tests are made to make sure that the pilot will perform the needed function. If all goes well, the process is then expanded in scale to the full production system. The "pilot" class of prototype works similarly: a piece of an entire system with all its functions is developed. The pilot that was developed at SOS was an inventory management system: one separable segment of the inventory, approximately 15 percent, was initially put on the computer.

- *A classical prototype: production scheduling.* A prototype system—which, according to the dictionary definition, "exhibits the *essential features* of a later type"[3] [emphasis added]—is built with an initial fundamental, yet incomplete, set of functions. The prototype system is then exercised to illustrate what it can do. Its functionality is expected to increase later on.[4]

    At SOS, a production scheduling prototype was designed to allow managers to queue work at machines, generate schedules based on job priorities, and minimize setup time. In DSS mode, the computer performs some functions automatically and interacts with schedulers to perform other functions. Increased functionality is continually being built into the prototype.

A major feature of each of the prototype systems developed at SOS is its ability to provide some data for *all levels* of manage-

FIGURE 3   Management Support System (MSS)

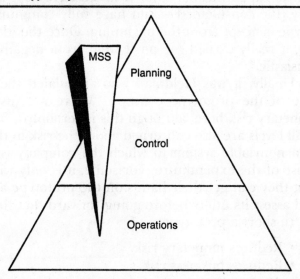

ment. (Most systems that are routinely developed today emphasize only a single level management function—for example, operational control, management control, or strategic planning.)[5]
At SOS, however, a top-down managerial approach ensures that
the systems not only contain the relevant data for operational
purposes but also provide the raw material necessary for managers to make decisions regarding management control applications and strategic planning. Figure 3 shows that emphasis is
placed on the last two functions, which is indicated by the heavy
wedge of the slice at the top of the figure.

At SOS, not all of the key executives were committed until
after the prototyping concept was fully evident. Although most
of them, during the CSF phase, were intrigued, and even excited
with the idea of actually linking systems to *business* needs, Paul
Pappenheimer, for one, was not. He remained skeptical: "I had
heard of a great number of computer horror stories," he recalled. He was fearful that control of the inventory would be lost
in the conversion process and that the computer could not support his somewhat unique inventory needs. (Each *item* of inventory is different at SOS in that it varies in quality, size, and many
other attributes. Each steel coil needs a full description.) It was
not until decision scenarios were utilized and an early prototype
design was well under way that Pappenheimer fully understood
the prototype approach and felt comfortable with it. He finally
perceived the prototype concept as a means of lowering the com-

pany's (and his) risks to an acceptable level. Recalling his experience, Pappenheimer says: "I would have slept better at night if they [the consultants] would have fully communicated the prototype concept from the beginning. Once the idea finally struck me, it really turned me on. I went from negative to highly enthusiastic."

Finally, it was Heldman who articulated the unique advantage of the prototype concept: "We're not just talking about monetary risk here, although this is certainly a factor. Managers at all levels are also concerned about the risk in the development of a nonviable system to which the company is committed because of the expenditure. For some, it is only when they realize that they can get their hands on the prototype at an early stage and assess its utility before going forward that they can relax."

In short a prototype:

- Reduces monetary risk.
- Reduces business risk.
- Allows a manager to inspect, work with, and shape the product as it is being developed to a point where he or she feels comfortable with it in all dimensions.

Step 2: Systems Development.   Actual development of all of the prototypes was done on an IBM System 38, utilizing RPGIII. The system now has 28 terminals with additional terminals on order. The final detailed design and programming were performed by the SOS staff with the aid of an outside programmer who was proficient in RPGIII. The initial prototype development period was short for all systems. For example, the initial inventory prototype was up in two months. After three months of operation, a significant redesign added new functions. This redesign process was repeated again after an additional six months, fully illustrating the concept of "evolutionary design."[6]

The systems are now used by operational personnel and managers at all levels. Some standard reports are issued, but most of the interaction is through menu-based interactive processing. More significant, today a number of SOS personnel at all levels are learning the available query language for the System 38 which will allow them to interrogate the files on their own. In fact, one of the first persons to attend the query school and to use the facility actively was Jacque Huber: "If I could tell a staff person what I wanted in the past, I can write my query today. I get my answers faster."

Summary

Figure 1 summarizes the three-phase process as perceived by the SOS management. The figure, however, does not show the considerable "backroom" effort that was made by both the consultants and the systems developers. It should be stressed that it is imperative that the consultants gain some background knowledge about the company before the first phase. There is also a need for them to understand the details of some of the operational activities before the prototypes are sketched out. These behind-the-scenes steps are necessary if one wishes to implement this three-phase process. (The actual creation of databases and the development of control procedures to assure the appropriate updating of data must be carried out by operational personnel during the prototype system development stages.)

The Benefits of the Three-Phase Process

Much has been accomplished at SOS through the use of this process. On one level, all three systems are up and functioning, thereby providing the usual advantages of computerizing marketing data, inventory control, and production scheduling. The advantages gained include:

- *Immediate access to order status.* "Now," says saleswoman Brenda Grant, "you can check exactly where your order is in the production system while keeping the customer on hold. You don't have to check with the plant and then make those long-distance calls back." Both internal and external telephone tag is avoided. Another salesman comments: "With the new system, what used to take an hour now takes only a minute or two."

- *A significant increase in the number of sales calls that can be made per salesperson.* Time which used to be "wasted" in answering customer queries and in searching for raw material inventory status has been eliminated. In addition, customer and prospect data, which are available in the marketing information database, enable salespeople to prepare for "cold calls" more efficiently.

- *Improved understanding of customers.* By using the available query system, Jacque Huber and the sales personnel are able to analyze customer buying patterns to improve production efficiency.

- *Improved management of slow-moving inventory.* Both visibility into the entire inventory status and analytic capability make this kind of management possible. Pappenheimer cites the particular ability to get to past usage data which "previously were only in my head."
- *More accurate inventory control.* John Antes, manager of inventory and material assignment, says: "The computer is faster and more accurate. There are controls and validations. There were some errors before with the manual system.
- *Improved production scheduling.* Greg Parsley, manager of the first shift in the plant, notes: "The system allows us to foresee problems and to react to them sooner. Before, we never knew where we would be in the future until we were there."
- *Reduction in plant personnel.* With the introduction of the system, plant management has reduced its staff while still maintaining the workload. A combination of factors made this possible: improved scheduling, reduced need to interact with sales personnel, reduced time in searching for or correcting lost or inaccurate paper work, and improved visibility into aspects of the plant.

On a more significant level, the three-phase process has strongly affected the management team in a very positive way. The questions one asks in evaluating a system are:

1. Did it work? Was something beneficial accomplished?
2. What is management's attitude?
3. Is management moving ahead?

The answer to the first question is given in the section above. As to the second question, there is a clear sense of both success and comfort in the top management team at SOS today. As Wolf, the president, notes: "Our good feelings today come from an approach to information systems which is based on managing the business." Jacque Huber says that the SOS management team, which initially was highly nervous that it would "mess with something that works" and "lose control," was able to "come together," through this process, on a systems plan. In addition, he says: "We have achieved in nine months at far lower cost what we expected would take six years under the previously proposed plan." Managerial attitude also appears to have been affected by four other results of the process:

1. A *sharper focus* in the minds of all top managers on the few important things to which they must direct their attention.
2. An *increased understanding* of the interdependence of the various parts of the business and the ability, through the computer system, to take advantage of this knowledge.
3. The *transfer of a sizable segment of this knowledge* from the retiring chairman to the younger management team which was made possible through the multiple workshops in which various aspects of the business, particularly the most critical ones, were discussed. For Heldman, who was the newest member of the management team, "the insights gained into the company" were extremely useful. He further notes: "I would believe that for any information systems officer who may have been slightly on the 'outside,' this process would provide tremendous insights into the company and the ways in which top management thinks."
4. The *direct terminal-based access* that management now has to data on various aspects of the status of the company. Huber and Pappenheimer rely on this daily.

It is also clear that the process will have a continuing effect on the company. For example:

- The three existing prototype systems are continually being expanded on in scope and functions.
- CEO Wolf has just commissioned a prototype system to develop a "cost model" for SOS—a system which he will be able to access directly.
- Additional personnel are being sent to "query" school.
- CSF use is being extended. Jacque Huber states: "A good manager and his team can use CSFs in all phases of business activity. What is needed is a broad educational program to introduce and promote the concepts of CSFs. I plan to introduce CSFs to my sales managers soon."

Can the Process Work in Other Companies?

Is the process replicable in other companies? SOS is a medium-sized company in a single industry with a capable management team. (It goes without saying that good management *is* necessary, for no consulting team can help inadequate management develop a clear focus.) However, this process does not only work in medium-sized single industries. Index Systems Inc., for example, has utilized the CSF and prototyping phases many times with management teams in half-billion-dollar companies and divisions of multibillion-dollar organizations. Decision scenarios, the newest input into the process, also appear to be working well in other organizations.

It should be stated that we believe this process will *not* work at all times in all companies. Timing is key. Management must be ready to be involved. Competitive pressures, a felt need to rethink computer priorities, or sheer awareness of the increasing strategic importance of information systems are all among a long list of factors on which the outcome of the process is dependent. Given that these conditions are increasingly evident in many organizations, successful implementation of the process occurs because of the following:

- *An easy and quick link to top management is made.* As Jacque Huber notes: "The businessman can relate to CSFs. They make sense. They are a natural extension of objectives and the planning process."

- *Management focuses on those areas of the business it deems important. Thus management feels comfortable about building information systems to support these areas.* Huber again states: "The businessman needs to be reminded to focus on the means after the ends have been determined. The CSFs process is the best focusing device I have ever been exposed to."

- *Real management involvement is engaged.* Heldman notes: "Most top executives really only provide token 'support' for information systems. In this process, management spent considerable time talking about its own business. They were involved. And a great amount of energy of the executive group went into the process. Token 'support' is not enough. One winds up with systems that do not affect the guts of the business."

- *The consultants (whether internal or external) gain significant insight into the business and therefore are more effective.* In addition to providing managerial focus, this process enables the system designers to better understand management and its needs. Several days of managerial interaction centered on the business itself provide a wealth of company-specific knowledge. As Pappenheimer notes: "The previous consultants who submitted the $2.4-million bid never grasped the business. They were working from an information technology and systems capability viewpoint, rather than from a business perspective. Index grew to know us."

- *Finally, managers recognize that this process involves lower risk.* There is a strong managerial bias against committing vast sums of money in areas which one does not fully understand. The CSFs provided the knowledge confirming why the systems should be developed. Decision scenarios convinced management that the particular systems would provide the information they needed to ask major questions at all levels of management. And the prototypes made it possible for management to see what the systems' capability would be on a small scale before they committed all the funds to the project.

In summary, Heldman states: "The organizational impact and change as a result of the systems have been profound. In a year when our marketplace is collapsing, we have been able to stay ahead, respond, and serve our customers better. This is a success story."

Acknowledgement. The process illustrated here was carried out at SOS under the direction of Thomas Heldman, chief financial officer. The work was shared by Index Systems Inc., a consulting organization, and SOS personnel. This article is based on data from SOS, Index, and a two-day evaluation interview process carried out by the personnel at the Center for Information Systems Research (CISR) of the Sloan School of Management, MIT.

FOOTNOTES

1. J. F. Rockart and M. S. Scott Morton, "Implications of Changes in Information Technology for Corporate Strategy." *Interfaces,* January–February 1984; "Foremost-McKesson: The Computer Moves Distribution to Center Stage," *Business Week,* December 7, 1981, pp. 115–22.

2. J. F. Rockart, "Chief Executives Define Their Own Data Needs." *Harvard Business Review,* March–April 1979, pp. 81–93; C. V. Bullen and J. F. Rockart, "A Primer on Critical Success Factors." CISR Working Paper No. 69, MIT, Cambridge, Mass., June 1981.

3. *The Random House Dictionary of the English Language: The Unabridged Edition.* New York: Random House, 1966, p. 1156.

4. R. A. Carpenter, "Designing and Developing Adaptive Information Systems." *Computer Technology Review*, Spring–Summer 1982, pp. 19–28.

5. The typology is taken from R. A. Anthony, *Planning and Control: A Framework for Analysis*. Cambridge, Mass.: Division of Research, Harvard Business School, 1965.

6. J. C. Henderson and M. A. Alavi, "An Evolutionary Strategy for Implementing a Decision Support System." *Management Science*, November 1981, pp. 1309–23.

Chapter Thirteen
A Planning Methodology for Integrating Management Support Systems

JOHN C. HENDERSON
JOHN F. ROCKART
JOHN G. SIFONIS

1.0 INTRODUCTION

In recent years, the impact of information technology on organizations has been extensive. Driving forces include the rapidly improving price/performance ratio of technology and a general increase in computer literacy. Perhaps most significantly, the role of technology in establishing competitive advantage is emerging as a new and powerful driving force. Rockart and Scott Morton (1983), Parsons (1983), and others have stressed several alternative approachs by which competitive advantage can be achieved through technology. A common theme among all advocating this concept is the importance of strategic information systems planning and the need to link the information systems plan to the strategic business plan.

Of particular interest to most organizations is how this investment in information technology will support and improve the productivity of professionals. The rapid influx of microcomputers (Quillard et al., 1983; Henderson and Treacy, 1984) into organizations is one response for better support of managers and

Center for Information Systems Research Working Paper No. 116, Sloan School of Management, MIT, Cambridge, Mass., September 1984.

professional staff. The concepts of Decision Support Systems (DSS) and Executive Support Systems (ESS) have been widely accepted and organizations are investing significant capital into development efforts to build these systems. Just in terms of numbers, the growth of end users has dramatically increased the resources directed toward management support systems. And yet, trends clearly suggest that many of these systems, while initially viewed as stand-alone, will ultimately increase requests for access to corporate databases and improved communications. The investment in management support systems will directly impact the investment in the large transaction systems that make up the technological infrastructure of the firm. Research suggests a key to success for DSS and ESS rests on the ability to link these support systems to the traditional system infrastructure (Henderson and Schilling, 1984). Given the magnitude of the investment and the potential for strategic impact, there is a need for a strategic planning methodology that can achieve the following goals:

1. Provide a linkage between the strategic business plan and strategic information systems plan.
2. Provide a means to coordinate the investment in a range of management support systems[1] that are responsive to management needs.
3. Provide a basis for understanding data as a corporate resource through the construct of a strategic data model.

These goals are not new. In fact, they reflect an evolution in the management of information technology from a perspective that is technically oriented to one that is business oriented. This evolution has produced many design methodologies, each attempting to address one or more of these goals.

This paper discusses an extension to the Critical Success Factor (CSF) planning methodology that provides a basis for achieving these goals.

The CSF methodology has proven an effective approach for introducing a top management perspective and, hence, strategic direction into information systems planning. Cresap et al.'s recent survey (1983) of information system planning methodology shows CSF second to BSP (Business Systems Planning) in terms of actual usage.

The CSF methodology has been used to identify the management needs that must be addressed through investments in Management Information Systems (MIS). More recently it has been used to identify DSS prototyping opportunities (Rockart and Crescenzi, 1984). The extension described and illustrated herein will also address needs for executive support and provide important input into the development of a strategic data model for the firm. The former provides for both enhanced management support and, often, an additional mechanism to link the strategic information systems plan to the strategic business plan. The latter provides a means to coordinate investments across the range of management support systems and establishes a foundation for managing data as a corporate resource.

Section 2 of this paper provides a description of the original CSF methodology and a definition of management support systems. Section 3 details the extended methodology, indicating how the new approach achieves the goals discussed earlier. Section 4 describes an application of the extended methodology and discusses the benefits of the new approach based on this experience. Finally, Section 5 provides general conclusions.

2.0 THE ORIGINAL CRITICAL SUCCESS FACTOR METHOD

2.1 Information Systems Planning Using Critical Success Factors

Rockart (1979) developed the CSF approach as a means to understand directly the information requirements of the Chief Executive Officer. He defined CSFs as "those few critical areas where things must go right for the business to flourish." Bullen and Rockart (1981) elaborated on the methodology, providing a means to use CSFs at any organizational level and to derive management information systems requirements. Boynton and Zmud (1984) provide a detailed analysis of the use of CSFs as an information planning methodology. They conclude the CSF approach is very effective.

A key aspect of the CSF approach is to elicit success factors that directly affect an individual's ability to achieve his or her goals. This individual-based approach provides two key advantages. First, since the goals of key stakeholders (e.g., top management) form the basis for the CSF analysis, the methodology will directly identify how MIS investments can be responsive to management needs. As Mason and Mitroff (1980) point out, organizations do not have goals, people have goals. Thus, the CSF approach creates an effective context or starting point for the planning process.

Second, to the extent that management goals are linked to

the business strategy, or mission, the CSF approach will identify MIS investments that are also linked to the business strategy. As will be discussed later, the CSF approach provides another means to strengthen this goals-strategy linkage. King and Zmud (1982) have suggested such linkages should reflect a need to manage MIS functions as well as general MIS resources. Boynton and Zmud (1984) argue a CSF-based approach provides a means to address both of these needs. Ferguson and Dickinson (1982) suggest CSFs provide a method to establish guidelines for monitoring and controlling organizational activities. Munro and Wheeler (1980) draw a direct linkage between the CSF method and other methods to develop corporate strategy. In fact, the CSF approach is consistent with many of the current strategic planning methodologies. For example, the stakeholder methodology proposed by Mitroff and Emshoff (1979) utilizes the goals of key stakeholders as the context for strategic planning. This method attempts to narrow the planning focus by examining critical assumptions. Extensions of this approach are discussed by Mason and Mitroff (1981). More generally, the notion of prioritizing or focusing on the critical opportunities to achieve strategic advantage has long been recognized and is quite consistent with the CSF approach. Thus, its wide acceptance by planners is not surprising.

The CSF approach does have limitations. Davis (1979) suggests three possible areas of concern: (1) the dependence on skilled analysts; (2) the risk of analyst bias introduced by the interview process; and (3) the possibility that CSFs overemphasize current concerns and crises and thus may not address the full range of organizational needs.

As Boynton and Zmud (1984) note, the concern relative to dependence on skilled analysts is common to most, if not all, strategic planning methodologies. Munro and Wheeler (1980) indicate the CSF process produces consistent results and, thus, the issue of bias appears to be of less concern. Boynton and Zmud (1984) support this finding. The issue of focusing on narrow, perhaps inappropriate, factors is still an area of concern. Rockart (1979) suggests a corollary to this: CSFs are time dependent. Thus, even if the appropriate factors are identified, events may alter the criticality of these factors. One major contribution of the extension proposed herein is to provide a direct means to validate the proposed CSFs and to provide an "early warning" mechanism to alert management to change in what is critical.

2.2 Management Support Systems

In many respects, the field of information systems management can be characterized by an evolution in its areas of study. The earliest focus of study was on introducing and automating clerical systems. These efforts led to the concept of management information systems (MIS) as a type of management support system. MIS systems are typically characterized as related to the development of the reports necessary to manage well-specified, structured activities. These activities have clear benefits or products which can be achieved through the design and implementation of an MIS. The implementation of large transaction systems such as order entry, coupled with the capability to extract information for management, is the classical domain of MIS. Such systems have historically had an impact on low-level management, since these individuals carry the responsibility for overseeing the day-to-day structured activities of the firm. Aggregrated reports and ad hoc query of the systems have produced useful, but somewhat narrow, support for high-level management. A primary objective of the CSF methodology is to understand better how these types of systems can be designed to yield enhanced support of middle- and upper-level management.

A major evolution in information systems study centered around Decision Support Systems (DSS) (Keen and Scott Morton, 1978). This type of management support system addresses semistructured decisions where the key benefits lie in qualitative improvements in the decision process. The systems need to be interactive and highly flexible and, hence, require different technology and design methodologies. DSS systems are still task specific, although the semistructured nature of the decision process is the key unit of analysis rather than a standard operating procedure. As might be expected, these systems have had their major impact on middle-level management and professional staff. They find their way to top executives most often through these types of intermediaries.

A third and fairly recent area of study concerns Executive Support Systems (ESS). These are systems used directly by senior executives. They address a broad range of issues and take on different technological characteristics then DSS. Further, they have significant implications for organization support structures; so while they are process oriented like DSS, their effective implementation generates unique problems (Rockart and Treacy, 1982). Obviously the key benefits center around improving the effectiveness of these top executives.

While this evolution has often carried with it attempts to define these different systems in a specific, mutually exclusive manner, Scott Morton (1983) argues they in fact form a range of management support systems with significant areas of overlap. This suggests a need to coordinate investment across this range of systems so that each system can contribute directly to achieving corporate strategy. Henderson and Schilling (1984), for example, discuss the interdependencies between DSS and MIS and suggest the introduction of DSS can have major strategic impact on the firm.

While progress has been made with respect to linking investments in MIS to the business strategy, little or no efforts have been made to develop methods that produce coordinated plans that span the range of management support systems. Providing such a method is a second major goal of the proposed extension of the CSF approach.

3.0 EXTENDED CSF: A STRATEGIC PLANNING FRAMEWORK

3.1 Key Requirements

With the increasing distribution of computer technology through the firm, combined with increasing total resources invested in management support systems, there is a critical need for a strategic planning methodology that provides an integrated approach to the design of MIS, DSS, and ESS. We suggest two key requirements for this methodology. First, the methodology must provide for an appropriate context for the planning effort. Existing design methodologies, to varying degrees, address this need. For example, the BSP methodology uses the notion of generic business processes as the context for investigating specific information needs. The assumption-surfacing methodology by Mason and Mitroff (1981) provides a context for the planning process through evaluation of the positions and needs of key stakeholders. In essence, current MIS design theory recognizes Ackoff's (1967) proposition that users can not effectively respond to a noncontextual request for the definition of information needs. For a strategic process to address MIS, DSS, and ESS simultaneously, this context formulation step is critical.

Second, the methodology must delve deeply enough into the system design life-cycle process to support design at a technical level. Obviously there is a trade-off between maintaining a macro viewpoint consistent with strategic planning and generating the detail required for technical design. The need is to provide a pragmatic link from the conceptual design to the detailed design. Such a link must provide relevant insights from both the user, viewing the design from a strategic business perspective, and the technician, viewing the design from a technical requirements perspective.

The following section describes a methodology addressing both these needs. Section 3.2.1–3.2.3 clarifies how these needs are met by this methodology and discusses additional benefits derived from its use.

3.2 A CSF-Based Strategic Planning Approach

Building upon the Critical Success Factor (CSF) approach developed by Rockart (1979), the proposed method (Figure 1) creates a planning context using the CSF approach.[2] These CSFs provide the context for *definition* of three products: Critical Information Set (CIS), Critical Decision Set (CDS), and the Critical Assumption Set (CAS). The critical information set is the product of CSF analyses as they were first carried out. The extended method provides the means to analyze the critical assumptions underlying the CSFs and the decision processes that are critical to achieving these CSFs. Each of the set definitions becomes the basis for a functional analysis of the requirements for MIS, DSS, and ESS, respectively. Finally, these three sets of requirement definitions provide important insight into a strategic data model that identifies the necessary linkages to both the *internal* and *external* data sources.

3.2.1 Strategic MIS Planning

The difficulty of building information systems that effectively support management has long been acknowledged (Keen and Scott Morton, 1978). The history of information systems design, discussed earlier, is a broad commentary on the difficult trade-offs between the technical requirements of implementing organizational systems versus the needs of individual managers. As Rockart (1979) notes, the CSF methodology does provide a

FIGURE 1   A Strategic Planning Methodology

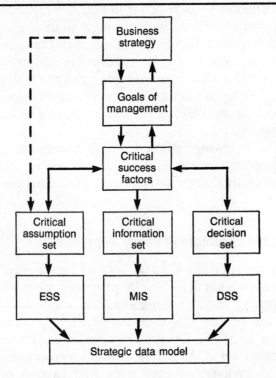

design focus on those few things that must go well to ensure success. However, the actual implementation of systems that provide these critical insights require extensive investment in the organizational information system infrastructure.

The original CSF process has helped direct this investment in technological infrastructure to achieve strategic goals. The methodology provides for direct assessment of goals and CSFs. The critical information set indicated by CSFs clarifies how the technological infrastructure can directly or indirectly support strategic goals.

The process of generating CSFs and eliciting the critical information set involves personal interviews with key management, but further steps are necessary to implement systems. As illustrated in Figure 1, this further analysis builds on the critical information set to define high-payoff MIS opportunities and to begin the development of a strategic data model. This function may be carried out in several ways but generally follows the top–down planning orientation of methodologies such as BSP. The strategic data model shows how sources of information, many of which currently exist, must be joined to provide the monitoring and analysis of a CSF. In practice, existing systems rarely are structured in a form directly capable of producing this critical information. Rather, elements of the necessary information reside in large transaction systems spread throughout the organization. Data external to the firm often must be integrated with this internal information. Finally, many information requirements are "soft" in nature, requiring subjective or expert opinion. Thus, the planning process must go beyond identifying the strategic requirements of the MIS. The process must indicate how the data supporting these strategic requirements will be derived from the existing systems or provided by investments in the new systems. The strategic data model attempts to identify the major sources of data classes and how these sources interrelate. In this way the data model provides one tangible link between the strategic direction provided by the CSF and the eventual technical and economic consequences of designing and implementing systems.

There is growing experience with strategic MIS planning approaches that utilize the CSF method as a strategic requirement definition. For example, Arthur Young (Arthur Young & Co., 1983) has used the CSF approach to provide the *strategic* direction for the information system plan in over 50 planning engagements. They combine the CSF approach with a modified version of the Business Systems Planning methodology to provide the basis for building a strategic data model. As a result, they not only provide a top–down strategic direction for MIS investment, but link this direction to a comprehensive data resource model of the firm.

3.2.2 Strategic DSS Planning

As discussed in Section 2, a key characteristic of DSS is its focus on specific critical decisions. Traditionally, the decision to design and build DSS has been made outside the framework provided by information systems planning. In fact, those involved in DSS design efforts often do not include representatives from the information services organization. This is not surprising. The decision focus creates a natural opportunity for end users or functional staff to work independently of the traditional MIS areas. However, Henderson and Treacy (1984) note that the end user trend can be viewed as DSS evolving from an isolated individual issue to an organizational issue. Both the level of resources consumed and the impact of DSS suggest a critical need to define a *strategic* direction for DSS. Rockart and Crescenzi (1984) illustrate how the identification of DSS can result from a CSF analysis. An organization must be selective in the allocation of resources for DSS development to ensure that those investments will contribute to improved decision making in *critical* areas. Thus, the need to identify a *Critical Decision Set* (CDS).

The Critical Decision Set serves the same function for DSS as the Critical Information Set does for MIS. It provides a strategic direction for development efforts in DSS. The CSFs provide a contextual frame for generating the Critical Decision Set. Most success factors will have one or more decision processes which are critical to the effective execution of activities associated with this factor. For example, the need to obtain and retain skilled personnel, a critical success factor, may suggest the hiring or merit pay increase decision may be critical. Each success factor will suggest one or more decision processes which are fundamental to success. It should also be noted that the DSS opportunities identified via the critical decision set will not constitute the entirety of the DSS activities within the firm. There will be significant DSS at an individual end user level. The intent of the strategic planning approach described herein is to ensure a significant portion of the DSS resources is directed toward strategic decisions.

As shown in Figure 1, the opportunities for DSS are developed through analysis of the critical decision set. Each DSS has information requirements that can be reflected in the strategic data model. As in the case with MIS, the strategic data model identifies sources of data, perhaps external to the firm, that are necessary for DSS. Often, the DSS analysis will identify or clarify MIS reporting data needs not recognized during the MIS analysis. For example, as will be discussed in Section 4, the importance of distinguishing specific property/1and tracts (the geographical data source) resulted from a decision analysis for project management. This clarification had a fundamental impact on the design requirements for MIS systems.

This clarification provides the means to integrate major activities in DSS with those in MIS. Thus, the priorities of the MIS action plan may be altered to provide necessary support for efforts related to implementing a given DSS. To the extent that the DSS may require data coming from the large transaction systems, this DSS linkage will provide a valuable basis for technical MIS design decisions.

3.2.3 Strategic ESS Planning

Rockart has noted the temporal nature of CSFs. Research on strategic planning has consistently highlighted the need to validate the planning context and adapt this context over time (Mason and Mitroff, 1981). The system designer or strategic planner must attempt to validate CSFs and consider when a particular set of success factors are no longer adequate. Mason and Mitroff (1981) argue a key to the validation problem, as well as to the dynamic character of information needs, lies in understanding the assumption set underlying the strategy. They argue that the assumptions held about the environment, competition, and particular businesses are key factors in the development and prioritization of management goals. In this light, there is a need to identify a *Critical Assumption Set* underlying the goals and CSFs for a strategic MIS plan.

The assumption-surfacing process may be similar to that suggested by Mason and Mitroff (1981). In their methodology, key stakeholder analysis provides the contextual frame for investigating the assumption set. They argue only individuals have goals; hence, any organizational strategy must be built upon the assumptions and goals of key stakeholders of that organization. This concept has proven effective in strategic business planning. We suggest CSFs provide an appropriate context for surfacing the critical assumptions of management in a strategic MIS planning effort.

The set of underlying assumptions provide the back drop for CSFs and the implied critical information set. Changes in these assumptions will be a primary cause of changes in CSFs. Analysis and monitoring of assumptions can, therefore, help to identify when CSFs and the subsequent MIS plans require change.

Obviously, an alternative source of change may be changing goals. However, changing goals are often due to changing assumptions; therefore, an assumption monitoring and analysis process will provide insight into both the CSF analysis and goal setting process. As shown in Figure 1, the Critical Assumption Set also is linked to the strategic business plans. Since changes in business strategy will impact goals and therefore CSFs, exploring the assumption set offers the added benefit of more closely linking the strategic information plan to the strategic business plan.

Given a critical assumption set, a further analysis can define the requirements of a system to monitor and analyze the status of these assumptions. We suggest that a major implicit reason for existing ESSs is to support executives in the analysis of critical assumptions. For example, an assumption underlying the establishment of acquiring skilled personnel as a critical success factor may relate to the ability of technology to replace or augment the activities of these individuals. With the growth in expert systems, this assumption may no longer be valid. An ESS data set could be developed to assist in the monitoring of the status of this assumption, and thus provide the means to identify when the CSFs should change.

Of course, the need for ESS creates yet another view of the strategic data model. The data model will, in turn, indicate where a linkage exists with DSS and MIS efforts and thereby provide the means to integrate investment and design efforts in these three areas.

In summary, the proposed planning methodology starts with a top level, business analysis to predict information requirements and to identify high payoff opportunities for management support systems of all types. Information needs of all types are integrated through a strategic data model. As shown in Figure 2, this strategic data model also depends upon the results of a more detailed information and technical analysis. The information analysis carries the functional requirements and the associated data resource needs to a technical level. This provides the opportunity to reflect the operational requirements of lower-level management and staff and to identify existing data resources.

The upper half of Figure 2, and the focus of this paper, provides a strategic perspective and, ultimately, a major basis for establishing priorities and implementation plans. Consistent with traditional bottom–up planning approaches, however, the lower half of Figure 2 is a planning process that yields specific hardware/software, major application systems, and data architecture recommendations. The strategic data model is a lens through which senior management can focus on the technical requirements of information system development. Similarly, it provides a mechanism for systems professionals to focus on how investments in the technological infrastructure will have an impact on both the specific needs of management support systems and the strategic issues of the firm.

FIGURE 2   An Integrated Framework for DSS, ESS, and MIS Planning

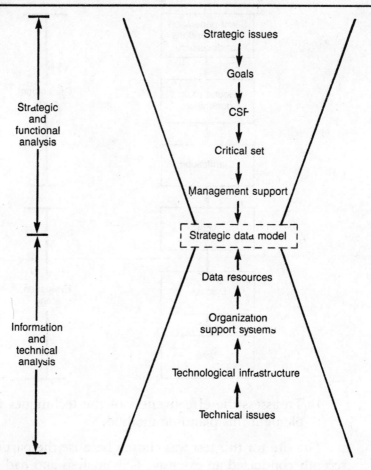

4.0 APPLICATION OF THE METHOD

4.1 A Case Study

A test of the extended CSF method was conducted with the CEO, President, and Vice President of Systems and Planning from a medium-sized energy-related firm. The objectives of this study were:

1. To identify opportunities for ESS and DSS development.
2. To assess the need to coordinate investments currently proposed in the MIS area.
3. To evaluate the quality of results generated by the method

FIGURE 3   The Planning Process

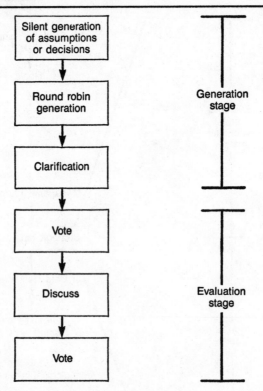

4. To assess the effectiveness of the techniques used to implement this planning method.

The site for this test was chosen because the participants had recently conducted an extensive CSF analysis and had linked their strategic business plan to the results of this analysis. Further, the organization had developed a comprehensive MIS investment plan based, in large part, on the information demands implied by the CSF analysis. Thus, the goals, CSFs, and Critical Information Set were well established.

The Nominal Group Process (Delbecq et al., 1975) was used to generate both the critical assumption and the critical decision sets (Figure 3). Two separate planning sessions were conducted, each lasting approximately two and a half hours.

The steps illustrated in Figure 3 were followed in both sessions. Tables 1A and 1B provide examples of the task statements generated for both the assumption set and decision set analysis. A round-robin generation and a clarification stage provided an opportunity to define issues, combine issues that were redun-

TABLE 1A   Critical Assumption Set*

1. Exploration programs will be funded by cash flow.
2. Improved ability to attract new capital from outside.
3. Stability of price, cost, demand.
4. Use cashflow to reduce debt.
5. Exploration can be managed.
6. All projects can be compared.
7. Stay in business, geographical and technical areas, where we have a competitive advantage.
8. We can grow without betting the company.
9. Technology will be disseminated so small companies can compete.
10. No restriction on approaches to adding reserves.
11. Cash flow is the most significant restriction to growth.
12. We maximize shareholders' wealth by operating company.
13. Quality people will make a difference.
14. Technology cannot replace high-skilled people.
15. Equity through stock market will not be available.
16. Increase shareholders' wealth as a means of attracting capital.
17. Can increase earnings within the defined risk posture.
18. Assume net income is relevant; e.g., net income is secondary to cash flow and reserves.
19. Continue cost-containment focus, but current organization size is appropriate.
20. Market for high-skilled people continues to be strong.
21. Bonus program will impact performance and increase retention of high-skilled people.
22. Strategic planning has an impact.
23. Investment in information technology will have an impact.
24. Total program will be funded by cash flow and asset sales.

*This set was generated in response to the direction, "For each CSF, list the primary assumptions (2 or 3) about your company, business environment, competitors, or industry that makes this a valid CSF."

dant, and ensure there was a common understanding of terms. An evaluation stage used a vote-discuss-vote technique to evaluate and prioritize the individual items. This technique provided a solid basis for debate, where the results of the first vote indicated areas of disagreement, and acted as a means to achieve group consensus (Delbecq et al., 1975). Finally, the results of the evaluation were used to identify primary and secondary opportunities for development of ESS and DSS. As will be discussed in the following sections, the criteria used during the evaluation were chosen to enable a meaningful discussion of needs and priorities for ESS and DSS.

The generation stage for the Critical Assumption Set re-

TABLE 1B   Critical Decision Set*

1. Allocation of expenditures, short and long-term.
2. Allocation between expenditures and debt retirement.
3. Exploration project selection.
4. Deciding which producing properties to sell, acquire, or retain.
5. Determine priority among exploration, development, acquisition.
6. Determine best organization structure and size to achieve item 5.
7. Whom to retain and how much to pay them.
8. Define the measures for success among different skills and disciplines.
9. Who has authority/responsibility and how much.
10. Balance of entrepreneurial/control and feedback.
11. Allocate rewards so as to impact each individual —reward success.
12. Match people and skills to project requirements.
13. Level of debt at a point in time.
14. Level of administration budget approval.
15. When to change production rates at a given well.
16. Determine areas of competitive advantage.
17. What is minimum economic parameter for project acceptability.
18. Acceptable level of investment for a project and acceptable level of risk.
19. Equity financing, debt/equity ratios for financial risk.
20. Should one objective be to have earnings parallel cash flow.
21. Determining what return on investment is acceptable to investors/owners and how to provide that return.

*This set was generated in response to the direction, "For each CSF, list the critical decisions that have the most impact on the successful execution of this CSF."

sulted in 34 assumptions. The clarification step eliminated 2 and combined 8, resulting in the 24 assumptions shown in Table 1A. The evaluation stage involved two steps. First, each participant was asked to select the 10 most important assumptions from the complete set of 24. The participants indicated the relative importance and the stability of these 10 assumptions. The definitions used in this evaluation are shown at the bottom of Figure 4.

The results of the vote were fed back in both a tabular and graphic format and used as a basis for discussion. Table 2 shows the voting pattern. This table facilitated discussion in two regards. First, high variance in the voting pattern indicated a need for discussion. For example, assumption 7 showed commonality on importance but high variance on stability. Subsequent discus-

FIGURE 4   Assumption Set Evaluation

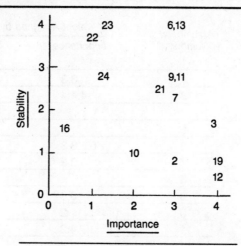

Stability: The extent to which an assumption is likely to remain constant or unchanged over the planning horizon.

Importance: The relative importance of any given assumption to the successful attainment of the CSFs.

sion indicated that one participant misinterpreted the meaning of stability in this context and changed his vote to be consistent with the other participants. In another instance, assumption 19 surfaced a fundamental disagreement about the appropriate asset base and size of the organization. One participant argued strongly that the existing organizational size was inappropriate to sustain growth. Another felt the size was adequate and management emphasis should be placed elsewhere. This disagreement was not resolved; rather, a need to monitor and continually analyze the need for further reduction in asset base and personnel was identified and given a high priority.

A second source of discussion centered around assumptions given very high importance by a single individual. This pattern reflects the unique demands and information needs of individual executives and underscores the importance of customized ESS.

Figure 4 is a graphical presentation of the voting results. The lower right corner is the primary opportunity set for ESS. The assumptions falling in this quadrant are critically important and yet unstable. Since many aspects of critical elements of the strategic business plan and current operations depend on these as-

TABLE 2   Voting Pattern for the Critical Assumption Set

Assumption Number*	Weight Assigned by Vote	
	Importance	Stability
1		
2	3,3	1,1
3	4,4,4	1,2,2
4		
5		
6	0.5,3,3	4,4,4
7	3,3,3	0,3,4
8		
9	3,3	2,4
10	2	1
11	4,2	3,3
12	4	0.5
13	4,2	4,4
14		
15		
16	2,0.5	1,2
17		
18		
19	4,4	1, 0.5
20		
21	2.5,3	2,3
22	1.75,2	3,4
23	1.25	4
24	1,2,3	1,5,4,1

*See Table 1A for assumption definitions.

sumptions remaining valid, there is a clear need to monitor and evaluate them continuously.

The assumptions in the upper right quadrant are also critically important but more stable. For example, the participants indicated a desire to monitor and evaluate a new bonus plan's impact on performance and retention of skilled employees. While they agreed that the need for such a bonus plan was a stable assumption, they felt the critical nature of the impact justified investment in an ESS so that senior management could carefully monitor the actual effect of the bonus program.

Finally, a brief examination of the information needs for a high-opportunity ESS was undertaken. Table 3 provides the set of information needs in relation to the assumption that the eco-

TABLE 3   ESS Information Set for Assumption 3

1. Spot price of crude (historical, current, projected).
2. Cost of oil field services and equipment.
3. Political unrest in Middle East.
4. Trend for demand in energy products.
5. Inter-fuel competition (oil or gas or coal).
6. Natural gas price negotiated last month.
7. Comparative finding and development cost.
8. Track tanker fleet movement.
9. Domestic political situation.
10. Crude oil/product inventories/natural gas storage user.
11. Track transactions competitors are using to raise funds.
12. General economic/monetary information.

nomics of the energy industry are positive and price and demand will be stable. Note the wide range of information sources implied by this list as well as the need for both quantitative and qualitative data. This list has clear implications for the linkage between the ESS and existing or planned MIS. For example, the need for comparative drilling and development information implies a requirement to access organizational information in a form compatible with industry or competitive data. Similarly, there are significant implications for consistent data definitions across organizational subunits implied by the macro financial and operational information that is required.

4.2 Critical Decision Set

The process shown in Figure 2 was also used to generate and evaluate the critical decision set. The initial generation resulted in 34 critical decisions. The clarification stage reduced this to 21 critical decisions (Table 1B). Two of the three participants selected the 10 most important decisions and evaluated them based on their relative importance and the need for enhanced analysis.[3] Figure 5 provides the definition of each criterion used to rate the decisions. The upper right quadrant of Figure 5 corresponds to these primary opportunities for DSS investment. That is, it corresponds to decisions that are very important and have high need for enhanced analysis. The firm may invest in a wide range of DSS via mechanisms such as end user computing. However, this planning process indicates those DSS which will have major strategic value.

FIGURE 5 Decision Set Evaluation*

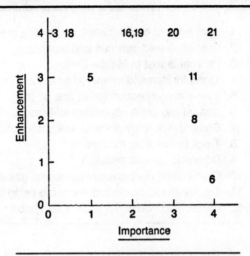

Enhancement: Potential for analytic aid or
enhancement in the deci-
sion process.
Importance: The relative importance of any
given assumption to the successful attainment of the CSFs.
*The "least important" have some exist-
ing support.

The need for integration between MIS and DSS is also apparent for this project. For example, the exploration project selection decision (Number 3, Table 1B) requires a comprehensive assessment of all projects, using a common methodology. The transaction systems that provide source data on operations and cost for these projects must be in place to provide common measures if such a project selection DSS is to be truly effective. Similarly, efforts to pursue competitive advantage (Number 16, Table 1B) could be supported with an ESS that monitors industry and competitive activity. Analysis of such interdependencies offers the opportunity to coordinate both investments and priorities among the various types of support systems.

4.3 A Strategic Data Model

The process of surfacing critical assumptions, information, and decisions and translating these issues into requirements for management support systems provides important input into the development of a strategic data model. Figure 6 shows a partial data model for this firm. A detailed data model results from a top–

FIGURE 6   Strategic Data Model

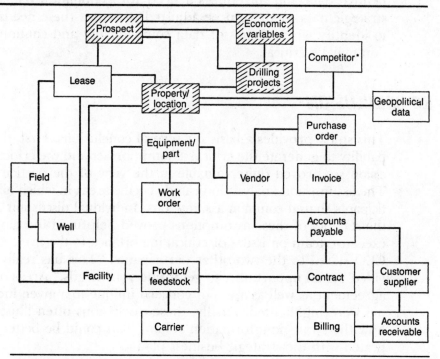

Notes: Shaded areas represent DSS opportunity. Asterisk (*) indicates opportunity for ESS.

down functional analysis of the ESS, DSS, and MIS opportunities. The model also reflects the need to address operational concerns via an information analysis (Figure 2). The model is presented as a modified entity/relation model that defines data classes and their relationships. Combinations of these data classes can portray subject area data bases. Each CSF will project on this data model differently. Further, DSS and ESS requirements will require joining different classes of data that may span across traditional subject area databases. Thus, the data model provides a means to examine and communicate strategic data requirements. For example, the need to monitor and manage drilling projects (a CSF) requires linking those data classes that are shaded in Figure 6. A DSS to support this area would include these classes plus additional specific types of competitive information. Further, the specific nature of the property/land data class changes significantly when viewed from a DSS perspective. Finally, an ESS designed to monitor and evaluate the assumption that drilling investments are being made in stable areas that maximize current competitive advantages extends the view of the required competitive data and introduces a need for geopolitical data. The strategic data model can be adjusted to reflect these needs and to identify where issues of data compatability and communication may be critical.

5.0 CONCLUSION

This study provides a basis for several conclusions. First, the capability to generate the critical assumption set and the critical decision set proved quite valuable in the view of the participants. The assumption analysis indicated specific areas in which all participants shared common assumptions. Individual discussion about the stability of these assumptions proved helpful in focusing the executive team on issues of critical importance to the firm. As the CEO stated to the two other participants, "This has really provided me an opportunity to get inside your heads." Areas of disagreement as well as areas of concern unique to a given individual were highlighted. Finally, these discussions often illustrated how the strategic information system plan could be better integrated with the strategic business plan.

Similar benefits resulted from the generation of the critical decision set. Yet it appeared that the level of enthusiasm waned as the discussion focused on the decision set. We suggest this relates to the responsibilities of those participating. The participants clearly understood the critical decision set. Yet this is an area in which they *can*, to varying degrees, delegate. The project selection decision, as critical as it is, is largely delegated by executive management via a well-structured capital budget process. The management of assumptions, on the other hand, can not be delegated. The assumption set is the domain of executive management and the responsibility for ensuring the validity of assumptions rests clearly with executive management. Thus, the discussion of the assumption set related more to the primary interests of the top executives. The authors believe this reduced interest in DSS opportunities is partly responsible for the lack of their evaluation by one of the participants. Nevertheless, the generation and prioritization of the critical decision set provided a direction for the MIS manager and offered the means to ensure that investments in the DSS area would have strategic impact.

A second conclusion is that the methodology does provide a means to integrate ESS, DSS, and MIS. In essence, the approach provides a comprehensive framework with which to build and refine a strategic data model for the firm. This data model illustrates the sources of data and indicates how they directly or indirectly affect a support system. By addressing the assumption, decision, and information sets simultaneously, a functional analysis draws from very broad views of the business. The strategic data model provides a means to represent these diverse needs in a form consistent with the insights gained through a more traditional information analysis. The strategic data model thus serves as a linking device between the strategic data needs of top management and the operational and technical needs of the IS organization.

Finally, the group process techniques used to generate and evaluate the CAS and CDS proved quite effective. These techniques were efficient and stimulated productive discussions. Of course, the original CSF analysis was conducted using individual interviews. These interviews between key managers and systems analysts are important in that they provide specific links to individual goals and, hence, organizational goals. The group techniques used to generate the CAS and CDS complement the traditional CSF approach by increasing communication between individuals. In this way, CSFs and goals are ultimately challenged and either verified or changed. Thus we see an implicit link from the assumption set back to organization goals and the overall business strategy.

The role of information technology in the competitive advantage of the firm is rapidly increasing. However, the opportunity for competitive advantages can not be fully exploited until management can coordinate its investments in professional and management support systems to ensure they will have an impact on the strategic issues of the firm. This study supports the notion that these investments can be coordinated in an efficient and effective manner.

Acknowledgement. The authors would like to acknowledge the many contributions and support of Mr. Douglas F. Aldrich, Mr. James R. Harrison, Mr. Dennis W. Loughridge, Mr. Clark R. Mandigo, and Mr. Richard W. Volk.

FOOTNOTES

1. The concept of management support systems is discussed in detail in Section 2.2.
2. See Bullen and Rockart (1981) for an excellent tutorial concerning the definition of CSF.
3. The lack of response was due both to time constraints and diminished interest. See discussion 5.0, Conclusion.

REFERENCES

Ackoff, R. L. "Management Misinformation Systems." *Management Science* 14, no. 4 (December 1967), pp. 147–56.

Arthur Young & Co. *Strategic Information Systems Planning*. New York: Arthur Young, 1983.

Boynton, Andrew C., and Robert W. Zmud, "Critical Success Factors: A Case-Based Assessment." *Sloan Management Review*, 25, no. 1 (Summer 1984).

Bullen, C. V., and J. F. Rockart. "A Primer on Critical Success Factors." *CISR Working Paper No. 69*, Center for Information Systems Research, Sloan School of Management, MIT, Cambridge, Mass., June 1981.

Cooper, R. B., and E. B. Swanson, "Management Information Requirements Assessment: The State of the Art." *Data Base Quarterly*, 11, no. 2 (Fall 1979), pp. 5–15.

Cresap, McCormick, and Paget, Management Consultants. *Information Systems Planning to Meet Business Objectives: A Survey of Practices*. Cresap, McCormick, and Paget, 1983.

Davis, G. B. "Comments on the Critical Success Factors Method for Obtaining Management Information Requirements in Article by John F. Rockart." *MIS Quarterly* 3, no. 3 (September 1979), pp. 57–58.

———. "Letter to the Editor." *MIS Quarterly* 4, no. 2 (June 1980), pp. 69–70.

Delbecq, A.; A. Van de Ven; and D. H. Gustafson. *Group Techniques for Program Planning*. Glenview, Ill.: Scott, Foresman, 1975.

Ferguson, C. R., and R. Dickinson. "Critical Success Factors for Directors in the Eighties." *Business Horizons*, May/June 1982, pp. 14–18.

Henderson, J. C., and D. A. Schilling. "Decision Support Systems in the Public Sector." *MIS Quarterly* 9, no. 2 (June 1985), pp. 157–69.

Keen, P. G. W., and M. S. Scott Morton. *Decision Support Systems: An Organizational Perspective.* Reading, Mass.: Addison-Wesley, 1978.

King, W. R., and R. W. Zmud. "Management Information Systems: Policy Planning and Operational Planning." *Proceedings, Second International Conference on Information Systems,* Cambridge, Mass., December 1982, pp. 299–308.

Martin, E. W. "Critical Success Factors of Chief MIS/DP Executives." *MIS Quarterly* 6, no. 2 (June 1982), pp. 1–9.

———. "Critical Success Factors of Chief MIS/DP Executives—An Addendum." *MIS Quarterly* 6, no. 4 (December 1982), pp. 79–81.

Mason, Richard O. "A Dialectical Approach to Strategic Planning." *Management Science* 18, (1969), pp. B403–14.

——— and Ian F. Mitroff. "Assumptions of Majestic Metals: Strategy through Dialects." *California Management Review,* Winter 1980.

———. *Challenging Strategic Planning Assumptions: Theory, Cases, and Techniques.* New York: Wiley, 1981.

Mitroff, Ian F., and James R. Emshoff, "On Strategic Assumption-Making: A Dialectical Approach to Policy and Planning." *The Academy of Management Review,* January 1979, pp. 1–12.

Munro, M. C., and B. R. Wheeler. "Planning Critical Success Factors, and Management's Information Requirements." *MIS Quarterly* 4, no. 4 (December 1980), pp. 27–38.

Parsons, Gregory L. "Information Technology: A New Competitive Weapon." *Sloan Management Review* 25, no. 1 (Fall 1983), pp. 3–14.

Quillard, Judith; J. F. Rockart; E. Wilde; M. Vernon; and G. Mock. "A Study of the Corporate Use of Personal Computers." *CISR Working Paper No. 109,* Center for Information Systems Research, Sloan School of Management, MIT, Cambridge, Mass., 1983.

Rockart, J. F. "Chief Executives Define Their Own Data Needs." *Harvard Business Review* 57, no. 2 (March/April 1979), pp. 81–93.

———. "The Changing Role of the Information Systems Executive: A Critical Success Factors Perspective," *Proceedings, Third International Conference on Information Systems,* Ann Arbor, Mich., December 1982, pp. 185–97 (reprinted from *Sloan Management Review,* Fall 1982).

——— and A. Crescenzi, "Engaging Top Management in Information Technology." *Sloan Management Review* 25, no. 4 (1984), pp. 3–16.

——— and M. S. Scott Morton, "Implications of Changes in Information Technology for Corporate Strategy." *Interfaces* 18, no. 1 (January/February 1983), pp. 84–95.

——— and M. E. Treacy. "The CEO Goes On-Line." *Harvard Business Review,* January/February 1982, pp. 82–88.

Scott Morton, M.S. "The State of the Art of Research in Management

Support," *CISR Working Paper No. 107,* Center for Information Systems Research, Sloan School of Management, MIT, Cambridge, Mass., 1983.

Sprague, R. H., Jr., and E. D. Carlson, *Building Effective Decision Support Systems.* Englewood Cliffs, N.J.: Prentice Hall 1982.

Zmud, R. W. *Information Systems in Organizations.* Glenview, Ill.: Scott, Foresman, 1983.

PART 4
THE END USER
EXPLOSION

As emphasized in the Introduction to this book, managerial support systems have evolved to the point of significantly influencing the very way we work. The term *end user computing* has been applied to describe the use of computer-based tools by anyone outside of the formal data processing or information systems area to support his or her work. This definition includes managers and professionals using personal computers, word processing done by secretaries, time sharing systems used by scientists, and electronic mail used by the CEO, to name a few examples. End user computing demands management attention since the magnitude of the movement to computer-based tools, despite occasional fallow periods, continues inexorably. For companies to plan successfully for, and manage, end user computing, they must comprehend its total extent.

The first type of end user computing in organizations was the use of time-sharing systems. These systems' users were the subjects of the CISR study, "The Management of End User Computing," which is the initial paper in this section. The authors examine the factors underlying the rapid growth in time-sharing use evident at that time. They propose a classification scheme for categorizing end users, and then look at various characteristics of time-sharing use and users. A major conclusion arising from this work is that the authors did not find strategic plans for end user computing, even in the organizations that had well-documented strategic plans for other information systems areas. In addition, the critical areas of end user education and support were being neglected. Finally, because the concept of end user computing crossed the boundary between information systems management and line management, very little management control existed.

The second paper in this section, "Looking at Micro Users," is a summary of research on the uses of personal computers. It first appeared in *Computerworld OA* in 1984. As part of documenting what was happening with personal computers in the workplace, this study highlighted the impact that personal computer use was having on the traditional information systems department.

Chapter Fourteen
The Management
of End User Computing

JOHN F. ROCKART
LAUREN S. FLANNERY

Today, interest in end user computing (EUC) is booming. While most information systems departments are still heavily involved in processing paperwork, there are a host of signs which suggest that this traditional focus will soon become a junior partner to user-developed and -operated computing. End-user oriented languages are increasingly plentiful and better than ever. Improved man–machine interfaces are being developed (15, 16); users are becoming more aggressive and more knowledgeable (3, 8). Formerly the sole province of scientists and engineers, end user computing is spreading throughout the entire organization. It is at the point where in some companies, EUC now utilizes 40–50 percent of the computing resource (11). This has led to increased attention to appropriate organizational forms to support this growing phenomenon (4, 7, 13).

Despite all this activity, end user computing is still poorly understood. There has been a mass of exhortative literature and occasional single case-based discussion of end user computing. But there has been a paucity of conscientious research into who the users are, what they are doing, what their needs are, and most significantly, how to manage this new phenomenon.

In order to shed more light on this, we interviewed 200 end users and 50 members of information systems staffs having the responsibility for supporting end user computing in seven major organizations. The companies involved were three Fortune 50 manufacturing companies, two major insurance companies, and two sizable Canadian companies. Users interviewed were all making use of time-sharing of one sort or another. We are just nearing the end of a parallel study of personal computer users in 10 major corporations. Preliminary data analysis suggests that although some details differ, managerial recommendations made at the end of this paper remain essentially the same.

1. METHOD

The interviews, which were confidential, began with an open-ended discussion of each participant's computing activities. The approach was aimed at surfacing key issues with regard to end user computing as perceived by the users themselves. The interview was guided by a structured questionnaire. Ultimately, after allowing the user to discuss all issues and aspects of EUC he or she believed to be important, each user was asked to comment on each of the questionnaire items upon which he had not touched. Quantitative data was not gathered in the early interviews, but as the issues became clear, such data was obtained from 140 of the users representing 271 different applications. Analysis of this data is noted.

In each company, interviewees were selected at random from a list of users designated by the company as "heavy and/or frequent users of time-sharing." It was felt that this procedure would provide a diverse, unbiased sample of the population of most interest—the major users: we believe it did. Our sample, however, is *not* representative in its proportions of the entire end user community. We will return to a discussion of the evident, and interesting, results of this method of user selection.

2. FINDINGS

We present both the *findings,* which were the facts observed during the study, and our *conclusions,* which are our interpretations of the findings. The findings of the research can be grouped into four major areas as follows: the significant growth evident in end user computing, the nature of the user population, attributes of the applications being performed, and the managerial processes being employed with regard to end user computing. Each of these are discussed in turn.

2.1 Growth

In each of the companies observed, end user computing was growing at a rate of approximately 50–90 percent per year. This was measured by either actual allocation of computer hardware power or external time-sharing budgets. The highest measured growth rate observed in the study companies was 89 percent. Later discussion, with a significantly larger sample of companies, strongly suggests that these figures generalize well. At the same time, traditional data processing oriented toward processing the paperwork of the company is growing at a far lesser rate. On the average, in both our sample companies and others, this growth rate appears to be only 5–15 percent. These widely divergent growth rates have led some observers such as Robert I. Benjamin at Xerox to predict that by 1990, end user computing will absorb 75 percent of the corporate computer resource (2).

Users were asked to note the factors underlying their growing utilization of end user computing. Four major clusters of reasons dominated their replies. The first of these is "a vastly increased awareness" of the potentials of EUC. A new generation of users has arrived which understands EUC and views it as a means of facilitating decision making and improving productivity. Most of these employees are recent graduates who have had experience with an end user language in college. At the same time, more senior personnel have been introduced to EUC by colleagues who have made use of EUC's capabilities. A second route to top management awareness is through managerial journals such as *Business Week* and *Fortune*, which have increasingly been informing their readers both of the potentials of EUC and of the software products available. Finally, users noted, hardware and software salesmen are making calls directly on them in their "end user" departments.

A second set of user-perceived reasons for the high growth rate of end user computing centered around recent improvements in "technical" capabilities which make end user computing increasingly more feasible and less costly. Vast improvements have been made in end user software (3, 7, 14). Today's languages, while not quite "user friendly," certainly are significantly easier to use than those even available three to four years ago. Decreasing hardware costs have made feasible the use of "cycle-eating" interpretative languages and relational databases. Users also refer to the increasing availability of both internally and externally purchasable databases, providing automated access to information previously unavailable, or which would have had to be painstakingly entered by hand.

The third set of reasons for the increase in EUC concerns the more difficult "business conditions" which prevail today. These conditions have intensified the need in all organizations for more effective analysis, planning, and control. High interest rates, inflation, and worldwide competitive pressures have made it increasingly important for both staff and line managers to have access to more, and often more detailed, information within a greatly decreased time frame.

Finally, and noted by almost all users, their needs cannot be satisfied through the traditional information systems organization. For a significant portion of their new applications, users find the tools, methods, and processes adhered to by the information systems organization as entirely inappropriate. Even for those applications where proven information systems (I/S) methods would be appropriate, however, users have turned to available end user languages, since the waiting period to get the application up and running through the I/S department—most often two to three years—is seen as intolerable.

2.2 The End Users

Clearly, if one is attempting to understand end user computing, it is important to know *who* the users are, *where* they are located, and *what* they do. We developed a classification of end users and their locations within the organizations we studied. The tasks that are being carried out by these users through EUC will then be noted in the next major section of this paper entitled "the applications."

2.2.1 Who are the users?   The literature provides three recent classifications on end users. The simplest available categorization is that provided by the Codasyl end user facilities committee (5).Their three-part breakdown includes "indirect" end users who use computers through other people (e.g., an airline passenger requesting a seat through his travel agent); "intermediate" end users who specify business information requirements for reports they ultimately receive (e.g., marketing personnel); and "direct" end users who actually use terminals. It is only the last category that is of interest to us here.

Two authors, Martin (7) and McLean (8), recently further broke down the "direct category." Their two classifications are almost exactly the same. McLean's classes are:

- DP professionals (who write code for others).
- DP amateurs (non-I/S personnel who write code for their own use).
- Non-DP trained users (who use code written by others in the course of their work, but know nothing about programming).

In the companies we studied, we observed a finer-grained and, we believe, more useful classification of end users. Six distinct classes of end users who differed significantly from each other in computer skills, method of computer use, application focus, education and training requirements, support needed, and other variables emerged. Although all utilized end user languages or the products of these languages, each user class is distinctly different from the others. They are:

- *Nonprogramming end users* whose only access to computer-stored data is through software provided by others. They neither program nor use report generators. Access to computerized data is through a limited, menu-driven environment or a strictly followed set of procedures.

- *Command level users* who have a need to access data on their own terms. They perform simple inquiries often with a few simple calculations, such as summation, and generate unique reports for their own purposes. They understand the available database(s) and are able to specify, access, and manipulate information most often utilizing report generators and/or a limited set of commands from languages such as FOCUS, RAMIS II, EXPRESS, SQL, or SAS. Their approach to the computer is similar to that of an engineer to a slide rule in days past. They are willing to learn just enough about the database and the software to assist the performance of their day-to-day jobs in functions such as personnel, accounting, or market research.

- *End user programmers* who utilize both command and procedural languages directly for their own personal information needs. They develop their own applications, some of which are used by other end users. This latter use is an incidental by-product of what is essentially analytic programming performed on a "personal basis" by quantitatively oriented actuaries, planners, financial analysts, and engineers.

- *Functional support personnel* who are sophisticated programmers supporting other end users within their particular functional areas. These are individuals who, by virtue of their prowess in end user languages, have become informal centers of systems design and programming expertise within their functional areas. They exist today as "small pockets of programmers" in each functional organization of the companies we studied. They provide the majority of the code for the users in their functions. In spite of the large percentage of time that these individuals spend coding (several estimated over 80 percent), they do not view themselves as programmers or data processing (DP) professionals. Rather, they are market researchers, financial analysts, and so forth, whose primary current task is providing tools and processes to get at and analyze data.

- *End user computing support personnel* who are most often located in a central support organization such as an "Information Center." Their exact roles differ from company to company. Most, however, are reasonably fluent in end user languages and, in addition to aiding end users, also develop either application or "support" software.

- *DP programmers* who are similar to the traditional Cobol shop programmers except that they program in end user languages. Some corporations have developed a central pool of these programmers to provide service to end user departments wishing to hire "contract programmers," to avoid high consultant/programmer fees, and to build a larger base of knowledge of end user language computing within the corporation.

The distribution of the end users whom we interviewed is shown in Table 1. This distribution is *not* representative of the entire user population in the companies we studied, but reflects the bias inherent in our selection of users who were the "major users of the computing resource." It is our belief, from discussion and observation in the companies studied, that with respect to the entire end user population, the first two classes of users

TABLE 1   Distribution of End Users Interviewed

User Class	Number	Percentage
Nonprogramming end user	13	9
Command-level end user	22	16
End user programmers	30	21
Functional support personnel	53	38
End user computing support personnel	7	5
Data processing programmers	15	11
Total	140	100

are seriously underrepresented in our sample, by perhaps an order of magnitude. (Upon reflection, however, we would not change our selection process. It led us to the most involved user population, and the one most capable of shedding light on the area.)

Four major "messages" come out of our user classification:

1. End users are a diverse set. There is no single, stereotyped "end user" with a single, defined set of characteristics. We have defined at least six major types—there may be more.

2. Diversity in the end-user population and what they do leads to a need for *multiple software tools* in the end user environment. Some sophisticated users need bit-level, procedural (e.g., BASIC, APL) languages to carry out their functions. For others, text processors, report generators, and simple command-level languages will suffice. Since no single end user language can meet the range of functions needed by these different users, a broad menu of end user tools must be supplied.

3. Diversity in the end user population also surfaces an evident need for strongly *differentiated education*, training, and support for the quite different classes of users. Nonprogramming users desire only well-written instruction sets. "Command-level" users want brief, limited training and education targetted to their specific interests. The more sophisticated "end user programmers" need in-depth understanding of the one or two software products more relevant to the particular function they perform. Finally, the functional support personnel members and professional DP

TABLE 2   User Functional Location

Staff	Number	Percentage	Cumulative Percentage
Corporate strategy, planning forecasting	16	11.4	11.4
Marketing—research	8	5.7	17.1
Marketing—planning	9	6.4	23.5
Finance—accounting	10	7.2	30.7
Finance—planning/analysis	7	5.0	35.7
Purchasing, scheduling, distribution	9	6.4	42.1
Human resources/personnel/ industrial relations	9	6.4	48.5
Actuarial	5	3.6	52.1
Operations research	5	3.6	55.7
Engineering	12	8.6	64.3
I/S—developer/support/user	20	14.3	78.6
Other—special projects, legal	3	2.1	80.7
Line:			
Management	3	2.1	82.8
Marketing/sales	9	6.4	89.2
Manufacturing	5	3.6	92.8
Claims/rating	6	4.3	97.1
Other	4	2.9	100.0
Total	140	100.0	

people desire and need more extensive training in a wider variety of software products. In all the companies studied, education, training, and support seem targetted at only a single segment of the end user population—usually the most sophisticated: this was a major source of user discontent.

4. Finally and most significantly, the classification highlights the *existence and importance of functional support personnel*. These people are not only the key utilizers of end user computing, but they are a source of significant opportunity and of potential problems for the I/S function.

2.2.2 User location.   Table 2 shows the location, function and role, of the users interviewed. The most significant point is that 81 percent of the users interviewed were in major definable staff groups in their corporations; this is natural. Staff personnel, almost by definition in most major organizations, are those respon-

TABLE 3 *Applications (by Primary Purpose)*

Purpose	Number	Percentage
1. Operational systems	24	9
2. Report generation	39	14
3. Inquiry/simple analysis	58	21
4. Complex analysis	135	50
5. Miscellaneous	15	6
Total	271	100

sible for the gathering, manipulation, analysis, and reporting of information.

It is clear that staff groups represent major "clumps" of end use computing activity. This is an important finding. It provides a positive response to the remarks of many interviewed I/S managers best expressed by one who, despairing of his ability to bring end user computing under control, noted that "end user computing is spread all over the company like grains of sand. I don't know how I can possibly plan for it, support it or manage it. I can't get my hands around it." Our data, which generalizes both through the seven companies studied and others with whom we have discussed this issue, suggests that with a limited number of fact-finding missions into the major staff groups in his organization, this manager could gain a significant insight into the bulk of the end user computing taking place in his organization. It appears that the 80/20 rule, once again, has validity.

2.3 The Applications

Of significant interest were the types of applications being performed by end users. Tables 3–6 record various aspects of these applications. Some 271 applications were discussed, on the average of about two per user, which was the design objective. Some users were involved with only one application. Up to four applications apiece were discussed with a few users.

Table 3 shows one classification of interest, the primary focus of the application. It shows a highly diverse range of systems, which ran the gamut from traditional "paperwork processing" to the provision of complex analytical assistance. As shown, about 10 percent of the systems were "operational" paperwork processing systems such as inventory systems or commission check pro-

TABLE 4   System Scope

Scope	Number	Percentage
Multidepartmental	45	17
Single departmental	141	52
Personal	85	31
Total	271	100

ducing systems which might alternatively have been coded in Cobol. Most were programmed in an end user language to "get them up quickly." Another 39 systems primarily served as "automated back ends" of Cobol-type systems. In most cases, these involved information databases taken from production systems (often with additional data keyed in) which turned out reports regularly or on demand. (We return to this class of system again during the discussion of Table 9.)

One fifth of the applications provided software to merely extract particular data items from a database or to do simple command-level manipulation of items in the database. Not surprisingly, however one half of the applications supported more complex analysis of data. Included in these systems were financial pro forma analysis, engineering calculations, operations research, optimization models, and simulations. Although the analytic techniques and software were complex (and usually developed by functional support personnel), many of these systems could be operated by a relatively naive user through the insertion of a few parameters—often in a menu-oriented way.

A second cut at understanding the applications used by end users is the "scope" of the system. Table 4 indicates that less than a third of the systems were "personal" in nature, being operated by a single person to carry out one of his or her tasks. More than half of the systems concern applications relevant to the operations of an entire department, with 17 percent of the systems being multidepartmental (most often multifunctional) in scope. In general, the scope of the data utilized followed quite precisely the functional scope of the system. The breadth of impact of these systems was surprising to us and to the management of the companies which we studied. We, and they, had expected a much larger proportion of single-person systems. On the contrary, we found in each company a large, and growing, number of very large information databases where moment-to-moment access was

TABLE 5 Primary Source of Data

Primary Source	Number	Percentage
Extract from production files	98	36
Keyed in from reports	92	34
Generated by user and keyed in	45	17
Process control	10	4
Extract from other end user systems	9	3
From purchased database	6	2
Other (time clock, log punch, etc.)	11	4
Total	271	100

absolutely necessary for the efficient functioning of major staff departments or combinations of departments. The users were adamant in stressing the importance of these systems and the information systems management implications of them.

Table 5 shows the *primary* source of the data used for each application. In about a fifth of the systems, data came from two or more of these sources, but Table 5 shows only the primary source. The importance of the paperwork-processing "production" systems as a data generator for end user analysis is clearly evident. As their primary input, 190 of the 271 applications rely on such data. Interestingly, and very significantly, this data is transmitted directly from the production files in only slightly more than half of these cases. For the other 92 systems, the data is laboriously keyed in from previously prepared reports. This emphatically indicates a "data extraction gap"—an area in which end users feel strongly that I/S is "dropping the ball." Unable to get the data directly, and needing it, users are resorting to keying it in themselves. The exhibit also illustrates the minimal interdependence from one end user system to another and a relatively limited use today of "externally purchased" data.

Table 6, which shows the six categories of end user on each dimension as users and developers (to whom outside consultants are added), illustrates patterns that are not at all suprising. Although the figures cannot be relied upon too precisely, it does appear both quantitatively (and qualitatively from user comments to us) that the bulk of the systems (approximately 48 percent) being used by end users are being developed for them by local "functional support" personnel. Behaviorally, it makes extreme sense that users would tend to rely on people within their own function who speak their own language and with whom

TABLE 6 Developers and Users of the Applications

Application Developers \ Application Users	Nonprogramming End Users	Command End Users	End User Programmers	Functional Support	Support Personnel	DP Programmers	Total (percent)
Nonprogramming end users	—	—	—	—	—	—	0 (0%)
Command level end users	—	34	—	—	—	—	34 (13%)
End user programmers	2	2	56	—	—	—	60 (22%)
Functional support personnel	112	6	1	12	—	—	131 (48%)
End user computer support personnel	6	—	—	1	2	—	9 (3%)
DP programmer	21	3	—	—	—	3	27 (10%)
Consultants	9	1	—	—	—	—	10 (4%)
Totals (Percentages)	150 (55%)	46 (17%)	57 (21%)	13 (5%)	2 (1%)	3 (1%)	271 (100%)

TABLE 7   Frequency of Use

Frequency	Number	Percentage
Daily	16	6
Weekly	34	12
Monthly	27	10
As needed	178	66
One-shot	16	6
Totals	271	100

communication of their system needs is relatively straightforward. Certainly, this was stressed to us by users at all levels. The overwhelming primary use of these systems by nonprogrammers (55 percent) is also not surprising. A significant number of departmental and multidepartmental databases (discussed above) exist today which can be accessed on a menu basis by accounting, marketing, financial, and other staff personnel.

Looking at the data in the cells of the matrix (Table 6) showing "who develops systems for whose use," an expected pattern emerges. In the lower right quadrant of the matrix, we see a few systems developed by functional support personnel and I/S professionals for their own use, but the bulk of the systems developed by them are for nonprogramming users. Almost all the systems developed by end user programmers are for their own use. (From further analysis of the available data, we learned that 75 percent of the applications developed by this developer class are complex analytic programs. The remainder are divided almost equally between simple inquiry systems and report-generating programs.) Command level "amateur" programmers, as expected, develop application programs only for themselves. Almost all of these are sets of commands to access the database through a QBE entry, an ADRS routine, or other report generation or simple inquiry routine.

One of the greatest advantages of creating and controlling a program for oneself is to be able to run it whenever it is useful rather than being bound by formal scheduled "run" procedures. Table 7 illustrates that end users take advantage of this. Fully two thirds of the applications are run only "as needed." Still, a significant portion of the applications are used on a regular weekly or monthly basis. As might be expected, these "regular" systems have a heavy population from the "operational" or "report generation" systems classified in Table 3.

Only 15 percent of all the systems, as seen in Table 8, utilize graphics. The most interesting finding, however, with regard to graphics is shown by the detail of this exhibit. Graphics systems use by the two least professional sections of the user population averages only 10 percent. On the other hand, systems developed for use by the four more professional segments show almost three times the frequency of graphics use. Since these systems, in almost all cases, are developed by each of these user classes for their own use, the perceived value of graphics by these user-developers is clear.

2.4 Management of End User Computing

A fourth level of facts we sought was data on the organizational structure and processes used to manage end user computing. Two different structures were apparent. These can be termed "traditional time-sharing management" and "centralized end user computing support."

Five of the seven organizations, including the three largest, were still primarily treating the surge in end user computing as just an extension of in-house time sharing. Management practices put in place a decade earlier to support and control a then limited amount of "time sharing" were still in effect. As a result, users were essentially given a hardware resource, one or few available software languages, and (sometimes) basic education classes on the most prominent software languages. In general, the information systems personnel managing these resources saw their major task as keeping the systems running and staying ahead, where possible, of the users and their demands for more capacity. A secondary task in several companies was the attempt to bring more expensive external time sharing onto the in-house facility. The three largest companies all had multiple time-sharing hardware in diverse geographic sites with little coordination evident to us or the users in their software offerings or data extraction procedures. In all cases, users felt there was "no one in charge" and felt significantly frustrated at their inability to locate data they knew was stored somewhere in the corporation's files or to get extracts of that data once located.

The two other organizations did provide support to end users desiring it, but in both cases, this came only from a centralized group at corporate headquarters. In one case, this was called an "Information Center"; in the other, it was designated a "Decision

TABLE 8 Graphics—User-by-User Category

Graphics \ User Class	Nonprogramming End Users	Command End Users	End User Programmers	Functional Support	Support Personnel	DP Programmers	Total
Yes	17 (11%)	4 (9%)	16 (28%)	4 (31%)	0 (0)	1 (33%)	42 (15%)
No	133	42	41	9	2	2	229
Totals	150	46	57	13	2	3	

Support Group." Both support groups were charged to find and bring up good software tools and to educate users in the use of these tools. In one of these companies, an "end user language programming group" had been set up in the traditional information systems organization to assist users wishing to contract out programming in end user languages.

In general, this latter, support-oriented approach to end user computing produced a more satisfied user population. Still, the centralized nature of the organization in both cases was troublesome to many end users. In both of these companies, we found users relying more heavily on the informal "functional support" personnel within their functions than on the central end user group. In both companies some users had rebelled against one or more of the corporation's "standard" software languages being supported by the centralized end user computing group. They had chosen instead to use similar, but different, software which their functional support people felt to be more appropriate. As user populations grow in size, solely centralized approaches of any form appear inadequate.

2.5 What We Did Not See

Perhaps more significant than the structures and processes we saw with regard to the end-user computing were those that we did *not* see. Among the most important missing processes were:

- *A strategy for end user computing.* Though all of these companies have well-documented, strategic, long-range plans for the "COBOL shop," there was, with one outstanding exception, little evidence of any strategic thinking with regard to end user computing and the resource mix, tools, processes, and structures which will be necessary for it over the next several years.

- *Development of end user computing priorities.* Most of the companies were very proactive with regard to developing priorities for paperwork-processing applications (through the use of Business Systems Planning (BSP) or similar planning devices), but end user computing was essentially in a "reactive" mode. No attempt had been made in any company to help users zero in on those end user systems which might most significantly affect the profitability or productivity of their organizations in the future.

- *Policy recommendations for top management.* There was an awareness in each organization that the information systems policies developed for the paperwork-processing eras of Information Systems would most probably not be appropriate in the end user era. However, only in one case had significant thought been given to recommending a new policy set for top management concurrence.

- *Control methods.* It was recognized in each company that the information systems department could *not* control the use of the end user computing resource. Most probably because of this attitude, control policies for end user computing were largely ignored. Those that existed were oriented around the decades-old, cost/benefit-oriented procedures which had been developed to manage and control an entirely different type of computer usage.

In short, the information systems management attitude toward end user computing in most of the companies was on the order of "this is the business of the users. We will give them the hardware, some software tools and perhaps some centralized support and let them do their thing. We really do not have the time to develop new procedures and policies. Even if we did, it's not clear that we are the appropriate people to do so."

3. RECOMMENDATIONS

It is impossible to talk to 250 people, both users and managers in the end user area, without coming away with some strong personal conclusions concerning the management of end user computing. Many of these are backed up by the data discussed in the previous section. Some, however, are based on a qualitative feel which is compounded through many hours of discussion. Our 14 conclusions group into three major areas: end user strategy, support of end users by the information systems organization, and control of end user computing.

3.1 Strategy

With regard to the end user computing arena, we reached six conclusions concerning strategy.

1. There should be an end user strategy. Little attention has been paid to the development of a strategy for end user computing either in the organizations we studied or in the perhaps two dozen organizations with which we have discussed these findings since the study. Most of these same organizations have extensive information systems strategic plans dealing with conventional paperwork-oriented data processing. Yet, when it comes to end user computing, they have, at best, put an information center or a "DSS group" in place with a relatively small budget and a cursory plan. If one believes: (1) that end user computing will reach 50–75 percent of the MIPS in almost every corporation in the next several years; (2) that end-user-oriented "information databases" have increasingly become an integral part of the working environment of major corporate staffs; and (3) that rapid change in the tools and techniques available in this area require guidance—then, the lack of a strategy and a clear long-range plan in this area is a serious mistake for the I/S function.

2. The marketplace for end user computing can be defined. As noted earlier, the usual statement one hears from an information systems manager when it is suggested that there should be a strategy in the end user computing area is "I can't develop a strategy in such a nebulous area. Conventional paperwork processing is centered in a few areas and a few systems and can be well defined. To the contrary, end user computing is 'everywhere'." Our data would suggest however, that by far, the bulk of the end user computing is generated by a few major staff groups (marketing, finance, quality assurance, personnel, etc.) in each organization. In defining the marketplace, it is clear that significant help can be gained by contacting a small and well-defined set of functional support personnel in each staff group.

3. There is a need to proactively help end users develop application priorities. To date, end user applications have been developed as the need has been perceived by each end user. On the contrary, for paperwork-processing systems, I/S has helped users through the utilization of planning processes, such as BSP, to zero in on those applications which are of high priority. Experience to date suggests that application planning processes, such as the Critical Success Factors method can be utilized in the same manner as BSP in the end user environment to direct attention to high-payoff end user applications (6,10). Much more effective use can be made of the financial and human resources currently expended on end user computing.

TABLE 9   The Three Environments

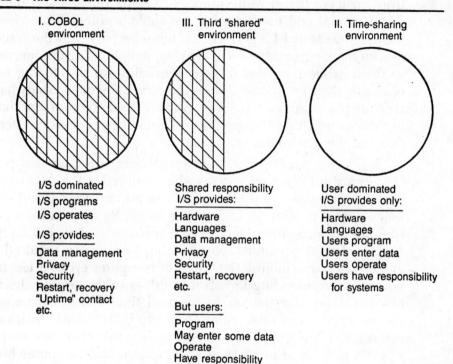

I. COBOL environment	III. Third "shared" environment	II. Time-sharing environment
I/S dominated	**Shared responsibility**	**User dominated**
I/S programs	I/S provides:	I/S provides only:
I/S operates		
	Hardware	Hardware
I/S provides:	Languages	Languages
	Data management	Users program
Data management	Privacy	Users enter data
Privacy	Security	Users operate
Security	Restart, recovery	Users have responsibility
Restart, recovery	etc.	for systems
"Uptime" contact		
etc.	**But users:**	
	Program	
	May enter some data	
	Operate	
	Have responsibility	
	for systems	

  4. *Emphasis should be placed on a strategy aimed at developing and managing the "third environment."* Two thirds of the applications we saw involved large departmental or multidepartmental information databases. This multiuser, shared database environment is a vast, growing, and clearly significant part of the data processing scene. By far, the majority of the purchasing, personnel, financial, and market research staff systems we saw are of this type. Increasingly, too, corporations are developing executive databases which involve multidepartmental bases (12).

  As Table 9 shows I/S in the past has supported two computing "environments," a *Cobol environment* and a time-sharing environment. These have supplied vastly different facilities. In the Cobol environment, I/S has taken total charge. It has provided a well-managed process in which it develops and programs the systems, operates them, and ensures that they are documented, well controlled, and secure. The traditional time-sharing environment, on the contrary, is only marginally served by I/S. I/S provides more hardware in one or more languages. The user does the rest.

A "third" or *shared* environment is now necessary to effectively manage the growing number of departmental and multi-departmental end user systems. As Table 9 notes, this environment demands that I/S perform its "housekeeping" functions, such as data management, privacy, security, maintainting uptime, and so forth, while the users take responsibility for developing and operating their programs. Two of the companies in our study have recently placed major attention on this shared environment, having discovered that the majority of their key end user systems demand this environment.

5. *There is a need for new corporate policies.* It is clear that policies toward information systems which worked in the days of paperwork-processing must be revised in an end user era. These policies must fit with the end user strategy. New justification policies are required for systems which enhance analysis but do not replace clerical personnel. New pricing policies are required in an era when distributing the "cost" of computer cycles is less important than providing signals to users as to the relative desirability of using internal versus external time-sharing, large machines versus personal computers, and "standard" software offerings versus user-unique systems. Several other new corporate I/S policies in areas such as education and computer budgeting are also needed in the end user area.

6. *The strategy should be promulgated.* End users today in many corporations are confused about the actions being taken by the information systems organization with regard to end user computing. They strongly (in many cases, vehemently) desire to know exactly what support and what future direction they can expect from information systems management. This knowledge is necessary so that they can make informed decisions on the increasing number of computing alternatives available to them.

3.2 Support

The second area with which information systems management must be concerned is that of *supporting* the end users. Although there are a multitude of areas which deserve attention in the support process, we believe through our data and our discussion with end users that four actions (below) are most necessary.

7. *The development of a "distributed" organization structure for support.* At the present time, most formal end user support struc-

tures are either located in a "time-sharing" office or an "information center." By their nature, these are primarily "centralized" organization structures located in offices, often near the hardware. Quite often the personnel are "product specialists," each knowing a different language or software package. Although the information center has proven very useful in a number of companies, in our view it is only the first stage of end user management. The second stage is "distributed" support. End users plead for two major things. The first of these is for a "focal point" person to whom they can go with all of their requests for assistance no matter which software language or product they are using. The second is that this "focal point" be as "local" as possible. In fact, for most major departments, the "functional support" personnel are serving exactly this function. Yet they are unrecognized by the formal I/S organization structure. If recognized as a resource and worked into the formal I/S end user support structure, probably through the lightest of matrix operations, the functional support personnel could be of significant assistance to the I/S organization in carrying out its strategic approach in end user computing. They would also become of increased use to end users through improved, routine contacts with new systems, languages, and procedures being introduced by the information systems function. In short, a "distributed" end user support organization could be developed to make more optimal use of both the technical expertise of the central I/S people and the functional area knowledge of the functional support personnel. Allen's research (1), which shows the importance of localness, is very relevant here.

8. *The provision of a wide spectrum of products.* Today, there is no "all-singing, all-dancing" software product which an end user can use to effectively perform calculations, develop spreadsheets, do text processing, and so forth, within the structure of a single software language or architecture. Each of these (despite recent efforts to combine them in some packages) is still essentially a specialized task. As a result, the end user computing establishment should offer a spectrum of at least a half dozen different types of available software. Otherwise, as was quite clearly occurring in many of the organizations we studied, users will stretch the available end user software products to do jobs in a manner far less efficient than could be done with the appropriate software.

9. The development of a substantial education program. This is a critical area today. Different types of education are necessary for the end user era. The first is the need to educate information systems personnel as to the capabilities and uses of end user software. At the present time, according to an informal survey we made, less than 10 percent of the more than 500 information systems people responding feel that they have an adequate knowledge of even one end user language. This leaves these information systems analysts in a very weak position when it comes to comprehending the end user world. At the simplest level, they are unable to recommend to user managers which methodologies (Cobol-based or end user language-based) they should be following for any particular system need.

Second, there is also a need for in-depth education in end user languages and capabilities for the more "professional" end user programmers (our Types 3 to 6). Third, there is a need for brief, "how-to," example-based education for the nonprogramming and command-level end users who desire to know only as much of an end user language or user system as they need to perform a few tasks of importance to them. Fourth, there is a need to educate line management and key staff managers at all levels in the basics of end user computing so that they can more effectively judge which systems they would like to have their people develop at what probable cost. As we will note below, information systems management *cannot* control all end user computing. The most effective control is to have functional management knowledgeable in the basics of end user computing. Finally, there is a need to educate top-line management—or at the very least the steering committee members—as to the tools, techniques, and potential impacts of the end user computing era, so that the need for effective policies (discussed in Point 6 above) can be understood.

This education load, it is true, is overwhelming. Certainly, the education of top management is the first priority. After that, each company must decide on the most effective allocation of a hopefully expanded education budget.

10. The developement of effective "data migration" procedures. A major complaint of many of the end users we interviewed was their inability to either locate where data was stored in the corporation, or, once located, have the data extracted and forwarded to them. As noted in our findings above, many of the end users solved this problem by rekeying data which they obtained in the form of hard copy reports from production systems. Obviously, this is a waste of corporate resources. Not only is there the time and energy involved in rekeying, but there is also significant potential for data errors in manual processes. It is very evident that, despite a few available packages such as IBM's *XPRS*, existing approaches to extracting and migrating data for end users have not been given enough attention, either by computing vendors or, in most cases, by information systems management.

3.3 Control

In addition to the need for a *strategy* for end user computing and significant steps to *support* end user computing, there is also an evident need for well-defined *control* processes for each organization in the end user area. Line and I/S managements are concerned that end user costs are rising too fast and are "out-of-control." They are concerned that little attention is being given to justification of these systems, that amateurish development processes are not well managed, and that they are approaching Nolan's third stage in the end user area (9). We saw several aspects of this. A control policy adapted to the special circumstances of the end user area is needed. The most important of the steps to be taken with regard to control are:

11. The need to flag "critical" applications. As noted earlier, 29 of the applications which we studied were *operational* in nature. Some of these feed other operational paperwork-processing systems in the Cobol domain. The failure of any of these systems to run would, therefore, significantly impair the ability of each of the corporations to function efficiently on a day-to-day basis. In almost all cases, the necessary documentation and/or controls usually developed by I/S professionals for operational systems were lacking in the end user developed systems. In each organization there should be a "control" process which identifies and highlights these systems for consideration of careful documentation, the incorporation of necessary edit and control features, and inspection by the corporation's auditors.

12. A need to exercise control primarily through line management— not information systems personnel. It is impossible for information systems personnel to be totally in touch with all of end user computing. Futher, the valuation process for these systems is highly subjective. Only functional managers can perform this valuation. It is therefore necessary for line management to implement and monitor justification and control procedures for those systems being developed and used by their subordinates. (See Point 9 above.)

13. A need for I/S expert involvement in the control process. Line management, however, cannot do it all. For large systems, at least, we believe there is a necessary procedure to ensure that professional information systems personnel assist line management in deciding whether the systems should be developed in an end user mode, *which software should be used,* whether the system is essentially a time-sharing environment or "third environment" system, and so forth. There is a clear role for a professional information systems consulting group to aid line management in this process.

14. The provision of I/S "environmental control" through incentives. One area in which the information systems organization can exert some "control" is in the development of the "environment" for end user computing. Standards for end user hardware and software should be developed and incentives (in terms of price and support processes should be offered) to motivate end users to adopt the organization standard relational database, word processing software, and so forth. The advantages of an I/S-managed environment are in allowing I/S professionals to better understand the software that is developed, to support users in questions they may have concerning the use of a limited set of software, and to keep critical systems running when the user or developer leaves the company. In one of the companies studied, several such incentives were being offered by I/S. For example, standard user software packages were being made available to end users at no cost. A predominantly standards-oriented environment was being created.

4. CONCLUSION

Developing the appropriate strategy, support processes, and control processes for end user computing is a staggeringly large job. The trends toward end user computing, however, are irreversible. There is little doubt in our minds that end user computing will be the dominant segment of information systems in most large companies by the end of this decade. It requires significant managerial attention.

REFERENCES

1. Allen, T. J. *Managing the Flow of Technology.* Cambridge. Mass.: MIT Press, 1977.

2. Benjamin, R. I. "Information Technology in the 1990's: A Long-Range Planning Scenario." *MIS Quarterly* 6, no. 2 (June 1982), pp. 11–31.

3. Canning, R. G. " 'Programming' by End Users." *EDP Analyzer* 19, no. 5 (May 1981).

4. ———— "Supporting End-User Programming." *EDP Analyzer* 19, no. 6 (June 1981).

5. Codasyl End-User Facilities Committee Status Report. North Holland Publishing Company, Information and Management Two (1979) pp. 137–163.

6. Davis, G. B. "Strategies for Information Requirements Determination." *IBM Systems Journal* 21, no. 1 (1982), pp. 4–30.

7. Martin, J. *Application Development without Programmers.* Englewood Cliffs. N.J.: Prentice-Hall, 1982, pp. 102–6.

8. McLean, E. R. "End Users as Application Developers." In *Application Development Symposium,* October 1974.

9. Nolan, R., and C. F. Gibson. "Managing the Four Stages of EDP Growth." *Harvard Business Review,* (January/February 1974), pp. 76–88.

10. Rockart, J. F. "Chief Executives Define Their Own Data Needs." *Harvard Business Review,* (March/April 1979, pp. 81–93.

11. Rockart, J. F., and L. S. Flannery. "The Management of End-User Computing." *Proceedings of Second International Conference on Information Systems,* Cambridge, Mass.: (December 1981), pp. 351–64.

12. Rockart, J. F., and M. E. Treacy. "The CEO Goes On-Line." *Harvard Business Review* (January/February 1982), pp. 82–88.

13. Rosenberger, R. B. "The Productivity Impact of an Information Center on Application Development." In *Guide 53 Proceedings,* Dallas, Tex., November 1981.

14. Sisson, R. L. "Solution Systems and MIS." *Proceedings of Twelfth Annual SMIS Conference,* Philadelphia, Pa., September 1980.

15. Sondheimer, N. K., and N. Relles. "Human Factors and User Assistance in Interactive Computing Systems: An Introduction." *IEEE Transactions on Systems, Man, and Cybernetics SMC-12.2*, March–April 1982, pp. 102–7.

16. Yavelberg, I. S. "Human Performance Engineering Considerations for Very Large Computer-Based Systems: The End User." *The Bell System Technical Journal 61*, no. 5, May/June 1982, pp. 765–97.

Chapter Fifteen
Looking
at Micro Users

JUDITH A. QUILLARD
JOHN F. ROCKART

In the corporate environment, the personal computer has become an integral part of—if not the major impetus behind—the phenomenon of end user computing. This article summarizes results from a research project conducted at MIT's Center for Information Systems Research (CISR). Our intent was to understand the way personal computers should be managed. We interviewed information systems managers and managers and professionals who use personal computers.

Of the 83 users interviewed, 68 held staff positions; the greatest concentrations were in finance (15) and corporate strategy/planning (11). Other staff groups represented were distribution, purchasing, research and development, management information systems (MIS), marketing, engineering, and personnel. The remaining 15 users held line positions.

Previous experience with computers ranged from 30 percent who had little if any prior experience to 13 percent who had been computer professionals at some point in their careers. Another 18 percent had had significant programming experience. The remainder of those interviewed had had some experience with traditional programming languages, fourth generation tools, or specialized applications such as word processing.

Multiple responses were allowed to a question of how people

initially learned to use their personal computers. Seventy-three of the 83 users said they taught themselves, primarily with the manual. Learning through formal classes, peers, and other options were mentioned only 21 times in total. It is clear that users of all backgrounds and experiences are turning to manuals and teaching themselves through trial and error.

This general picture of the users indicates people are formulating their own opinions of the usefulness of personal computers. They are able to learn about personal computers on their own time, using resources they feel comfortable with, rather than relying on information systems to provide them with information.

This picture of relative self-sufficiency may not always hold true, however. From the perspective of research on the diffusion of innovations, the users we interviewed are most likely the "innovators," "early adopters," and, perhaps, some "early majority" types. Innovation research has established that the different categories of adopters have different personality traits, socioeconomic characteristics, and communications behavior. The nature of the user population is likely to change as the use of personal computers spreads and, because of the obvious implications for education training and ongoing support, organizations should be aware of these differences.

A previous CISR study (of time-sharing users) defined several distinct types of end users. The categories were based on observations of "the computer skills, methods of computer use, application focus, education and training requirements, support needed, and other variables" of 200 time-sharing users.

This categorization is also useful in the personal computer study. The user types follow:

- *Nonprogramming end users* use software provided by others to access computerized data through a limited, menu-driven environment or a strictly followed set of procedures.
- *Command-level users* perform inquires and simple calculations and generate unique reports for their own purposes. They understand the available databases and are able to specify, access, and manipulate information.
- *End user programmers* utilize both command and procedural languages directly for their own personal information needs. They develop their own applications, some of which may be used by others.
- *Functional support personnel* support other end users within

FIGURE 1 *Classification of Personal Computer Users*

Nonprogramming end users	1
Command-level users	29
End-user programmers	30
Functional support personnel	17
End-user computing support personnel	6
Total	83

their particular functional areas. By virtue of their skill in end user languages, they have become information centers of systems design and programming expertise. In spite of the large percentage of time they spend supporting other end users, these individuals do not view themselves as programmers or DP professionals.

- *End user computing support personnel* are usually located in a central support organization, such as an information center. Their exact roles differ from company to company. Most are reasonably fluent in end user languages and, in addition to aiding end users, they sometimes develop either support or application software.

Figure 1 shows the classification of the 83 personal computer users. The most common types, as expected, were command-level users and end user programmers. It should be noted that, for the most part, these end user programmers were not utilizing traditional programming languages such as Basic and Fortran. Many were using software tools like Visicorp's Visicalc and DSS/F to develop complex models. Often they were familiar with several software packages.

An obvious question is whether a person's computing background could tell us the user category into which that person would fall. Although some patterns do emerge, previous computer experience cannot definitely predict the level of personal computer use. A safe generalization is that most user programmers and functional support types have had at least some prior programming experience. Also, at this point in time, most personal computer users with little previous computer experience are at the command level.

- *Applications:* During the interviews with personal computer users, a total of 187 applications were identified. For each person's most important applications (and, occasionally, for

FIGURE 2   Purpose of Application

	All 187	The 101
Analysis		
Financial	77	40
Marketing	8	6
Corporate planning	8	7
Statistical	8	4
Engineering/scientific	5	5
Production planning/scheduling	3	2
Other analysis	4	2
Report generation	19	12
Word processing	19	5
Monitoring	16	9
Operational	8	4
Communications	7	1
Data collection	5	4

the two or three most important), we completed an "application questionnaire" with detailed data on 101 "important" applications. For the others, only limited data was obtained.

The two columns in Figure 2 show the purpose of all 187 applications and of the 101 key applications. The significant majority of applications are analysis—primarily financial analysis, which covers a broad range of applications, from budgeting to product pricing to financial statement work.

Report generation, which includes presentation graphics, was rated second in importance. These applications perform minimal calculations such as column totaling: about 60 percent of them produce graphics, charts, or plots.

Although word processing (WP) is a popular use for the personal computer, only five of the total 19 WP applications were included in our sample of 101, and most people said other applications were more important. Our assessment of this finding is that, although WP is not the application for which people initially acquire personal computers, many managers and professionals find WP software to be a very useful tool and would now hate to be without it.

Monitoring applications, which captured forth place, consist of such things as project scheduling, maintenance of approved customer lists and tracking monthly environmental data from plant sites. Relatively few (only eight) of the 187 systems could be classified as operationally involved with the day-to-day transactions of the firm. These are traditional paperwork-processing systems, such as inventory control and product accounting.

Seven people mentioned that a significant use of their personal computer was communications with other systems. These applications included accessing external databases (such as Dow Jones) and using electronic mail. Finally, the data collection applications are those where the personal computer is interfaced to lab equipment in order to sample experimental data and perform scientific calculations.

As a rule, forth generation packages were used to develop these applications. More than 50 percent of the applications were developed using one or another of the available spreadsheet packages as a software tool.

Only 19 of the 101 applications were developed using traditional programming languages, and the most popular language was Basic. (The people who used these languages had prior programming experience.)

For the most part, the tools fit the applications. We did note a number of cases where users were overworking their software, especially Visicalc. They filled the spreadsheets to the maximum and noted poor performance and slow calculation and response time.

This data on applications contained no major surprises. In their use of the initial wave of personal computers, people are primarily utilizing them as stand-alone machines to perform analysis with spreadsheet packages.

The dominance of financial spreadsheet applications is easy to explain. First, high-quality software is available. Personal computer spreadsheets are easier to learn and easier to use than spreadsheet software currently available for mainframe time-sharing use (at least, that is the opinion of the users we studied).

Second, the design of financial spreadsheets is a conceptually straightforward process for personal computer users. The first logical step in applications development is to write a model of the application on paper. Many managers and professionals have long had well-conceptualized spreadsheets on paper. In addition, financial applications usually work with amounts of data that are not too large to be practical for current personal computers. The personal computers are operating as stand-alone machines, and this favors applications that handle smaller amounts of data. In

FIGURE 3   Why A Personal Computer?

Reason	Times Cited as Primary	Total Times Mentioned
Software only on PC	13	46
Cost	10	41
Feeling of control/independence	15	32
Assured access to computer	3	21
Response time	1	18
PC readily available	11	37
Fast/easy development	4	25
Frustration with I/S development	3	20
Told to by supervisor	4	15
Security	2	8
Other	7	29

66 percent of the applications, the data used was manually keyed in.

The third and final reason financial spreadsheets were dominant is that financial analysis involves applications that are probably low on the priority list of information systems development projects. A production planning application is probably a good mainframe candidate, given its scope, significance, and number of users. But a financial anaylsis application tracking the production department's budget and expenses probably is not.

Figure 3 presents the reasons why users chose a personal computer over other alternatives (such as the traditional information systems development process or time-sharing) for these applications. First on the list and most often mentioned is the statement that the software was available only on a personal computer, not on time-sharing. In other words, the evident, widely publicized availability of spreadsheet packages caused people to choose personal computers.

Cost was the next most frequently mentioned reason. Users said buying a personal computer with packaged software and then developing the application themselves was cheaper than other computing alternatives. A few people interviewed noted that they could justify the cost of a personal computer based on the reduction in their time-sharing expenditures.

The next three reasons on the list were often mentioned together. Underlying these statements is the fact that using a personal computer makes users independent of any other group for

---

FIGURE 4 Sources of Personal Computer Support

	Times Mentioned	Percent
Self-sufficient	22	28
Formal group in user department	5	6
People in department informally	17	21
Formal PC group within I/S	13	16
I/S department	13	16
Computer stores/other	10	13
	80	100%

Note: Data from 70 users; multiple responses allowed.

---

access to their application. Slow response times on time-sharing systems or difficulties with communications lines were factors for some people. Being in control of the tool was very important; it was even cited as the primary reason slightly more often than "software only on personal computer."

There is another important grouping of two interrelated reasons: "The personal computer is readily available; I have access to it and already know how to use it," and "It is relatively fast and easy to develop an application on the personal computer." People were implying that using a personal computer is easier than using time-sharing. After successfully implementing one application, a user was not at all reluctant to develop another. Our impression was that some of these applications were developed only because a personal computer was available.

Twenty people mentioned "frustration with information systems development" as one of the reasons for selecting a personal computer for their application. Out of 101 applications, 20 is not an overwhelming number. However, the reasons "fast/easy development" and "feeling of control/independence" are in some respects positive ways of stating dissatisfaction with information systems services.

A small number of people said their manager had decided a personal computer was the appropriate vehicle for the application. An even smaller number of users said security was a reason the personal computer was chosen.

Support: Although most of the 10 firms had established formal personal computer support groups, a significant number (28 percent) of users feel self-sufficient, as shown in Figure 4. Also, many users (21 percent) turn to someone within their depart-

THE MIS VIEW

The long-term strategies for end user computing were similar in all 10 companies and centered around the concept of the work station. It was generally agreed that each work station would be to some extent custom tailored to its particular user. Most companies viewed the personal computer as the forerunner of the multifunction work station.

In the short run, the 10 companies saw several important roles for the personal computer. Most often mentioned was the personal computer's ability to increase the level of computer literacy at these firms. Some companies mentioned the ability to reduce applications backlog faced by their information systems groups. Several companies were using the micro to bring computing to places where it would otherwise be impractical.

Current purchases of the majority of personal computers, however, are not part of a well-considered long-term strategy. They are being acquired because individual users want them.

Who has responsibility for formulating personal computer strategy? In seven companies, information systems management develops directives concerning personal computers. The other three had committees composed of user and information systems managers.

The "Big Eight" accounting firm was one of these three, apparently because of the potential impact of the personal computer on the way the firm will conduct future business. The committee is a user committee with information systems representation.

In two of the three firms, the major reason for a steering committee was to allow the active participation of user management.

ment for ongoing support, often on an informal basis. According to these statistics, many current personal computer users believe they know enough to solve most of their own problems; this belief may have resulted from their learning by reading the manuals and by trial and error.

Apparently, for several key reasons, users are turning to others in their departments for support. The first reason is physical proximity: it is simply easier to go to someone whose office is down the hall. Closely related is the fact that people are often less hesitant to ask for help from someone they already know, especially if they are unsure whether theirs is a "dumb question."

In addition, users often prefer to get computing advice from someone who knows the functional area and therefore can un-

Contrary to what users would prefer, strategy formulation for personal computers in most firms is rather isolated from strategy formulation for other end user computing (time-sharing) and office automation. This is true mainly because responsibility for these areas has been assigned to different groups within the information systems organizations. The notable exception was one company in which a committee sets policy in all areas.

All but one of the firms had issued a written policy statement specifically addressing the use of personal computers. These policies varied considerably in terms of formality, scope, and detail. Most organizations had developed policies and standards, or were considering doing so, in the key areas of justification, hardware, software, acquisition and servicing, data, copyright laws, and applications guidelines.

Organizational approaches to providing support to personal computer users varied among the 10 companies. Four firms had established separate and distinct "corporate personal computer groups," and two firms had given personal computer responsibility to existing information centers.

Four firms had given responsibility for support to divisions either through existing systems managers or by establishing new groups.

The personal computer group staff tended to number two to five persons.

The group manager was usually from the information systems organization, but very frequently had had significant experience interacting with users.

derstand the context of their problem much more completely Finally, many users do have a great deal of experience with various personal computer software packages. In some instances, their knowledge exceeds that of the information systems support group.

The importance of the functional support people we found in various user departments should not be underestimated. Functional support in all instances was outside the information systems organization. As noted earlier, the people providing functional support are personal computer users assisting others in their department. In three companies, we found cases where the role was a clearly acknowledged part of the person's job. The other functional support people were informal sources of support.

Although the number of users turning to other users for ongoing support is about equal to the number turning to information systems, this fact should not be misunderstood. Users do not think information systems support services are unimportant. We asked users (and information systems managers) about the provision and importance of various personal computer related services.

To summarize briefly, personal computer users believe many important services can be provided by a formal support group run by information systems. In some cases, users noted that although they personally might not need a given service, they could see its value for less experienced users. We found two especially important service areas, one relatively unimportant area, and one problem area.

The first of the two key areas in which personal computer users believed formal support was most important was consulting on appropriate solutions for a given application problem. Users would like to go to one designated person, not to separate personal computer, time-sharing, and office automation (OA) groups, for this advice.

The second area in which formal support was considered important was that of services that help personal computer users to get started. Following consulting, the specific services rated most important included access to software packages (to allow users to try them before buying them), central purchasing, and training. Users want knowledge of product evaluations and applications developed by others.

To a large extent, these areas were being actively supported by information systems. The most common services, offered by 9 of the 10 firms, were central purchasing, hardware evaluation, and consulting about whether a personal computer is an appropriate solution.

Software development services were rated relatively unimportant. Both users and information systems managers gave systems and applications software development the least important ratings of all services. These relatively low scores indicate users believe they can rely on themselves and the marketplace for most of their software needs. This is a logical extension of the findings that showed most applications use fourth generation tools such as spreadsheet packages.

The major problem area regarding support services involves data. Access to corporate data is an increasingly important service, and it will have to be provided by a central group in the information systems organization. According to the personal computer users we interviewed, information on the data available and help in obtaining extracts from corporate databases are important services, although not significantly more important than many other services we mentioned. In their view, data availability will become more critical over time as more and more users want to download data from the mainframe.

However, a reason for concern arises when we note that few information systems departments were providing data-related services. Users cannot go elsewhere for database extracts, as they can for some other services. Except in two companies that had policies forbidding personal computer users direct access to mainframe databases, information systems managers recognized the importance of the data issue. To be fair, the technical obstacles in trying to link personal computers and mainframes should be noted. In the early 1983 timeframe of these interviews, good, reliable hardware/software for personal computer–mainframe linkage did not widely exist—and is still far from what might be desired. This problem area continues to exist.

Implications and Recommendations. Personal computers must be managed in the context of end user computing. From a management perspective, the key implications of our study revolve around the need to clarify the roles and responsibilities of information systems management and user management with regard to end user computing strategy, control, and support.

Perhaps the most critical message is that organizations need a strategy for the use of personal computers. Even more important is the need for an overall strategy for end user computing. Eventually, this strategy must integrate time-sharing, personal computers, graphics systems, and OA and fit these tools into the overall information systems strategy.

This end user computing strategy must be reflected in plans and policies. Most information systems departments have four-inch-thick documents describing their plans for traditional information systems and only four-page memos for end user computing. A strategy is needed so that growth in end user computing is perceived as fitting into corporate long-range plans. This requires the involvement of key staff and line management in planning.

Users must be active in establishing personal computer strategy, plans, and policies. We advocate a committee composed of information systems management and user management—a very effective mechanism for making strategy and policy decisions. In our study, one company had such a committee responsible for OA, personal computers, and time-sharing; that company was doing a very effective job of managing end user computing.

User departments need to take additional computing management responsibility. End user computing means applications development is done by users. The user departments must control justifications and must manage use. Information systems cannot have primary responsibility for this process. The managers responsible for control and management should have a voice in strategy and policy. Clearly, to make information business judgments, user management will have to be educated about the potential benefits and drawbacks of personal computers (and other end user computing tools).

Information systems expertise is needed to help set policies and guidelines. The information systems department's role is to manage information technology for the firm. In order to ensure coherence with the overall information infrastructure of the firm, information systems must be active in the setting of strategy and standards. This implies that information systems must fully understand personal computers and other end user computing technologies.

In addition, the recognition of a joint effort between information systems management and user management should also extend into the area of providing support. As our study shows, users are getting support not only from information systems, but also from other users. The important role of these functional support people should not be overlooked. This strongly suggests that information systems should establish links with functional support people. And, since we know users often turn to other users because they are local, information systems support should not be totally centralized. End user computing support groups under the information systems umbrella should also be located at the divisional or even departmental levels.

In short, we need to redefine the roles of information systems management and user management in the new computing environment. Managing end user computing must now be a partnership effort.

PART 5
THE
FUTURE

It is appropriate that the author of the first paper in this final section is Michael Scott Morton, the co-author of the first paper in the book. Here the author centers on two issues—the nature of the field of management support in mid-1984 and the current state of research in the field. To do this, Scott Morton presents a review of some 300 articles published in the field from 1981 to 1984. He defines management support systems (MSS) broadly as "the use of information technologies to support management." As expected, he emphasizes the word *support*, because in his words it "differentiates MSS from many other applications of information technology."

Scott Morton reaches several interesting conclusions about research in the field. There is a disproportionately large amount of work in development of methodologies and frameworks. This coincides with a lack of empirical testing of these methods and concepts, and, in Scott Morton's opinion, far too little work on the impacts of MSS. In many other areas little or no work is being done, or at least reported, leaving MSS—and especially executive support and data support—badly in need of research.

The next paper switches the reader's attention toward what is to come. In "Expert Systems and Expert Support Systems," the authors briefly define and describe the concept of expert systems and demonstrate how this concept helps to clarify the categories of DSS. Where a DSS attempted to aid decision making by relieving the human of the more structured portion of the decision, the promise of expert systems is that they will help capture the knowledge and the reasoning process itself of the "best experts" in any field and make that information accessible to others. When and if this comes about, it will herald a new age in decision support systems.

The final paper, by Rockart, presents a brief summary, targeted at senior executives, of the differences between the paperwork-process eras and the "information and communication" era of computer use. Major implications of the emergence of this new era of computer use are highlighted. Of these, perhaps the most important is the need for senior line management to be actively involved in shaping the use of the technology in their companies. The new technology is of strategic importance.

Chapter Sixteen
The State of the Art of Research in Management Support Systems

MICHAEL S. SCOTT MORTON

BACKGROUND

This is a time of broad technological change; unprecedented "information power," in the form of the ubiquitous personal computer as well as the more traditional time-sharing system, is becoming available to users. Organizations are trying to cope quickly with a proliferation of varied computers by networking them internally and linking their systems to others outside. And the information systems field itself is undergoing rapid change. Systems professionals, in either the corporation or the university, are now clearly in the minority as innovators and implementors of information technology. They are surrounded and outnumbered by "end users," all of whom are increasingly armed with computer capacity and powerful software tools that they can apply directly.

The spread of information power to users is transforming management support systems (MSS) from an interesting but somewhat isolated use by a small core of creative individuals to a central management tool. One increasingly finds MSS woven into the very fabric of management. This evaluation has just begun; the magnitude of its impact has not yet been felt.

The goal of this paper is to identify some patterns in the on-

From F. Warren McFarlan, ed., *The Information Systems Research Challenge: Proceedings*. Boston: Harvard Business School Press. Copyright © 1984 by the President and Fellows of Harvard College. Reprinted by permission.

going research on MSS. The patterns have been drawn from a search through some 300 articles published over the last three years in the journals in the reference list. We selected 80 articles as representative of the best research work in the field. The final articles we chose focus most on the MSS dimension and are probably representative of the kind of work going on at this time. These publications are primarily American, but we did attempt to scan the relevant European journals.

DEFINITION

The term *management support systems* is open to a great many interpretations. For the purposes of this paper we define it as "the use of *information technologies* to support management." Rapid changes in technology make it necessary to include in MSS several forms of information technology that go beyond and are quite different from the computer used in traditional data processing—for example, teleconferencing, electronic databases, and graphics work stations. And our understanding of systems continues to evolve as new information technologies redefine the frontier of possibilities. This is why our definition of MSS is not restricted to *computer technologies*. However, the term *support* provides the foundation for our definition and differentiates MSS from many other applications of information technology. We have emphasized support in our review of the literature and excluded research whose primary goal is to replace rather than support managers.

Many writers in the past two years have begun to redefine our concept of *management systems* to delineate more clearly the importance of information and related technologies. The information era will require new and sophisticated forms of management (see Rockart and Scott Morton, 1983). Naisbitt, in his book *Megatrends* (1982), is perhaps the most visible author to highlight the shift to an information era. In his first chapter, on the transition from an industrial society to an information society, he provides some provocative illustrations of how far America has moved in this direction. He further outlines the implications of this evolution for organizations and their managers in his chapter on networking, where he quotes Intel's vice chairman, Robert Noyce: "What we've tried to do is to put people together in ways so that they make contributions to a wider range of decisions and do things that would be thwarted by a structured, line organization." Elsewhere Naisbitt gives examples of information technology providing the tools to do this.

TECHNOLOGIES

Technologies related to management support systems can be divided into four major categories: hardware, software, communications, and methodological tools.

Hardware

There is no reason to suppose that one form of computer hardware and related components is more relevant to management than any other. Therefore, MSS hardware includes the full spectrum of computers (micros to mainframes) and the full spectrum of ways they are made available to management (remote access from a central location or fully distributed access in one's local site or office).

Software

Software for management support takes many forms, including tailor-made special-purpose applications, general-purpose modeling packages, and information bases. At the core of each is a language that defines the software's capabilities.

Communications

Management support systems can now use communications via both narrow-band and broad-band paths that extend both inside and outside the organization. This allows applications, such as videoconferencing, that have not traditionally been considered part of the computer-based MSS domain. However, these uses are part of *information* support for management.

Methodological Tools

The continuing progress in behavioral science, management science, and the study of management decision making has made it apparent that a class of methodological tools exists which should be classified as "technologies." These include many of the techniques in decision analysis that have been exercised by the operations research community. Other methodological tools are oriented toward helping the MSS builder. These include techniques for determining information requirements and planning implementation strategies.

TYPES OF MSS

We will discuss three broad categories of MSS: data support, decision support, and executive support systems.

Data Support Systems

The traditional data processing use of technology is assumed to be largely confined to transaction processing and low-level (clerical) operational use—both outside the domain of this paper. However, to the extent that these systems produce information as a by-product, they fall in the purview of MSS. Thus, the databases that traditional data processing generates are a potential element of management support. Indeed, the whole area of building, maintaining, and providing access to information is directly relevant to MSS.

Research in this segment of the field has resulted in database management systems that can be and are being used as part of MSS. We will call these *data support systems*. These systems provide information regardless of use or user; examples are the Disclosure TM Service, The Source (belonging to *Readers' Digest*), the numerous information bases of the *New York Times*, and the databases of firms such as Data Resource Inc. The literature does not discuss data support system use, but faculty in the field are aware of dozens of applications.

Decision Support Systems

The second class of MSS are *decision support systems* (DSS). For the purposes of this paper DSS are considered a subset of management support systems focused on a specific decision or class of decisions. As many authors have pointed out, a general broadening (and consequent debasing) of the term *DSS* has caused it to lose most of its specific meaning. In particular, there has been

FIGURE 1   Classes of Decisions and Their Incidence

	Decision Made by Individual	Decision Made by Group
Ad Hoc Decision	SOME	VERY FEW
Institutionalized System (Ongoing Decision)	MANY	VERY FEW

a lack of differentiation between the system (of human decision maker and related computer-based support) and the tools with which the computer in the system is created. Thus, for example, Interactive Financial Planning System (IFPS) is a language—and by all reports an effective one—but for the purposes of this paper it is not a DSS. It is a tool for building a DSS.

One of the best broad discussions of the evolution of the concept of DSS is in Sprague and Carlson's *Building Effective Decision Support Systems* (1982). Their focus is on what DSS are and how to build them, not on their organizational impacts and implications. If those who used the term *DSS* would first read this book, we could better focus on a common definition. For our purpose, a system must apply to a particular class of decision to be considered a DSS. From examples in the literature it is possible to identify four distinct classes of decisions and estimate their incidence (see Figure 1).

The DSS reported in the literature are not necessarily representative of all that have been built. However, those covered in the reference list of this paper fall into the cells in Figure 1. It is instructive to compare four excellent papers by Bonczek, Holsapple, and Whinston (1979a, 1979b, 1980a, and 1980b) with Sprague and Carlson's book. Taken together, these sources highlight the inevitable conflict between our desire for generality and the demands imposed by specific problems. Bonczek, Holsapple, and Whinston are more optimistic about moving toward the general, although many of their ideas await confirmation in practice.

Bonczek, Holsapple, and Whinston (1980b) and Luconi and Scott Morton (1983) define the next generation of DSS, namely, *intelligent support systems*. Intelligent support systems are a form of

DSS in which the human decision maker combines heuristics and a knowledge base to produce answers for a certain class of unstructured problem. They are not presented in this paper as separate from DSS because they merely use different tools and therefore support a different class of decisions. They remain focused on a specific problem or class of problems. The intelligent support systems that are beginning to surface are outgrowths of the work in artificial intelligence and expert systems. It is interesting to note here that much of the work in expert systems is primarily aimed at *replacing* managers, not *supporting* them.

Three articles in our literature search in the general area of artificial intelligence apply to MSS. The most specific is by Ben-Bassat (1981), who looked at a military application that has useful implications for business. A more generic discussion is given in Bonczek, Holsapple, and Whinston (1980b). They provide some succinct descriptions of work in the expert systems field. None of their examples can really be described as MSS, but they do offer good samples of the current state of the art in artificial intelligence. Luconi and Scott Morton (1983) provide a framework that tries to position intelligent support systems as a logical outgrowth of DSS. Drawing on experience in building a prototype and testing it in use, they identify the opportunities and pitfalls that can be expected as intelligent support systems applications evolve. In this paper we have classified as support systems the one or two expert systems and related applications that have begun to be developed for supporting managers.

Executive Support Systems

Executive support systems (ESS) are focused on a manager's or group of managers' information needs across a range of areas. Rather than being limited to a single recurring type of decision, ESS incorporate in one system the data and analytic tools to provide information support for many managerial processes and problems. Thus, ESS encompass a broader concept than DSS. Executive support systems also differ in another important respect from DSS. The majority of ESS are data retrieval oriented, whereas most DSS are modeling oriented (see Figure 2).

Decision support systems tend to have as their foundation a model of some aspect of a particular type of problem. The model provides a structure for the relationships among relevant data and allows the decision maker to perform complex analysis with rel-

FIGURE 2

	Decision Support Systems (DSS)	Executive Support Systems (ESS)
Data Retrieval Oriented	FEW	MANY
Modeling Oriented	MANY	FEW

ative ease. In contrast, the broader focus of ESS cannot usually be accommodated by a model or series of models.

METHODS AND TOOLS

In looking at the literature on MSS it also proved useful to examine the tools and methods being applied. The literature shows six categories of tools, which we will identify on a continuum that roughly represents their portability—that is, the ease with which someone other than the original inventor or designer can use them. Starting with the least portable—methodologies and frameworks—the spectrum progresses to the most portable—hardware, including the physical computer, the network, and the color graphics terminal.

Methodologies

The methodologies proposed in the literature are predominantly concerned with how to build a DSS. As such, they would perhaps be better described as prescriptive processes, the results of which will yield a "good" system. Alter (1982) is of this type. The author sets out to identify the conditions under which a DSS can or should be developed and used without professional help. However, the methodologies described in such articles are difficult for others to adopt because they lack specific implementation directions. This is true even of some extensive methodological developments, such as the one Sprague and Carlson describe in Chapter 4 of their book (1982).

If these methodologies were capable of adoption, it would be possible to move to a level of research as yet largely unexplored and compare and contrast methodologies. The lone example of a comparison that surfaced in our literature search was Alavi and Henderson (1981). They make specific recommendations after comparing two different methodologies.

It is a measure of Herbert Simon's enormous contribution that all methodologies in the DSS arena, to the extent that they are grounded in theory at all, use his basic view of decision making. None of the material we found was based on anything more fundamental or recent than Simon's work—an impressive testimony to his insights.

In the emerging area of ESS, the most visible methodology is Rockart's critical success factors, based on work by Robert Anthony and Ronald Daniels. This methodology has been used successfully by others and thus can be said to meet the test of portability. However, it seems to be the only one that has been widely used, so if we are to take the absence of instances in the literature as a guide, methodologies are not easily transferable.

Database Technologies

Database technologies are a classic area of computer science that are very useful for MSS. However, the absence in the literature of illustrations of database technology application and use for MSS suggests that these technologies are still in the early phase of their life cycle. The popular literature offers evidence that they are being applied to the office; for example, *Fortune* magazine has run an extensive series of advertisements by International Data Corporation that focus on commercial applications. Experience in office support might lead to progress in applying database technology to real MSS.

An excellent overview of database technologies is given by Manola (1980). On the basis of Blanning's 1979 discussion of DSS functions, Manola identifies the software- and data-oriented requirements of a DSS and describes how database technology might contribute to satisfying them. In particular, he identifies six areas of database technologies:

1. Data models and database system architecture.
2. Data transmission and mapping.
3. Database access languages.
4. Active database management systems.
5. Distributed database systems.
6. Database hardware.

This list provides a sense of the enormous power that builders of MSS can draw on once tools are available. Manola illustrates the considerable progress in areas 1 and 2, where commercial products have recently been released. In area 3 he points out that database access work has shifted to providing powerful query-based capability for the casual user. This has involved considerably sophisticated system architecture to prevent the hardware requirements from becoming excessive. Progress, as Manola points out in his references, has been considerable. Areas 4, 5, and 6 are the focuses of intensive research and are beginning to yield results that are usable as parts of MSS, both decision and executive support systems.

Manola's article, and some of the references he mentions, implies that a crucial piece of technology is becoming available to those who wish to build and install MSS. The large body of literature coming from basic technology research by computer vendors and universities indicates that increasingly powerful database tools applicable to MSS will continue to become available.

Languages and Packages

Management support systems are fundamentally dependent on the power of the tools available for their development. The literature has a number of surveys of such languages; some of the more interesting are included in the reference list. One of the best is a survey of 237 firms by Brightman, Harris, and Thompson (1981). As they point out, there are two basic forms of language—general-purpose languages, such as FORTRAN and APL, and commercial modeling languages, such as IFPS, SIMPLAN, and CUFFS. There are well over 50 commercial modeling languages available. The study focuses on financial modeling languages, which are particularly useful for model building, one component of certain kinds of MSS. The results show that 53 percent of the firms surveyed used financial modeling systems. Of these, 44 percent were using a general language and 56 percent had a commercial language.

The survey was designed to investigate the impact of commercial modeling languages on the adoption and design of financial modeling systems. The authors establish that these languages do indeed simplify the model-building process and make it possible for decision makers or related staff to build their own systems without the aid of a "data processing" system person. They go on to document the advantages users found in support systems of this type. As one would hope in the use of an MSS, advantages include the ability to do more analysis and ask "what if" questions. However, other advantages include perceptible improvements in the decision process and better decisions. This study stands out as one of very few that actually takes the trouble to sample users and assess the state of current practice and user reactions. The authors also identify further issues on which to follow up, including the question of industry differences in patterns of use.

One very suggestive issue Brightman, Harris, and Thompson raise is barriers to use, in an organization, of financial modeling systems and, by analogy, of MSS in general. They find that the lack of a person to champion a model and the cost of the system are the biggest barriers. This suggests that we are still in an evolutionary stage of MSS (or at least DSS, which constitute all their examples) that might be described as "technology first." A "champion" is necessary for a model primarily if the *model* is being sold, rather than a *solution to a business problem*. The literature on languages spends almost no time on a "business need first" perspective. As tools become more user friendly, the use of DSS comes to be a more readily accepted way of doing business. Languages become just one more tool to build a DSS for supporting the solution of a business problem. Fortunately, the costs of building DSS with these languages and using them on the job are going down rapidly, so we can expect these two barriers to fall.

Models

Models are one of the tools often used as a basis for MSS. As represented by operations research, they are one of the oldest disciplines available to those interested in MSS. It is interesting that much of the literature on models in MSS, certainly in the journals we surveyed, deals with sophisticated, often optimization, models. However, no recent literature of which I am aware suggests when such models are appropriate.

The concept of simple models that provide insight to the manager was not represented in any of the literature in this survey. Nor does there seem to have been any published work on types of models since Alter's 1976 analysis of 56 case studies of DSS. In this study Alter identifies four categories of models used as part of DSS:

1. Accounting relationships—used for estimating the consequences of a decision.
2. Representational models, normally simulation models.
3. Optimization models.
4. Suggestion models.

Judging from the literature, the vast preponderance of model use is in the financial area and is of the accounting relationship form. There are some interesting exploratory efforts to develop a language, using predicate calculus, to formalize "stating modeling knowledge" (see Bonczek, Holsapple, and Whinston, 1981). If this project is successful, application-specific modeling knowledge will not need to be embedded in the computer program. However, this whole area requires extensive further research before implementation will be possible.

It is interesting to contrast the decision sciences view of models and their development in the context of MSS with views from a different discipline. For example, John Morecroft, of the Systems Dynamics Group at MIT, describes working with a group of senior marketing executives in a major U.S. manufacturing firm (1982). He discusses the concept of "support" and then particularizes this to "strategy support" and concludes that for highly unstructured strategy questions this means providing insight into the consequences of pursuing strategic initiatives once they have been formulated. Modeling is fit into a framework where mental models and formal computer models (in this case systems dynamics models) result in debate and discussion followed by reformulation and, finally, consensus on a strategy. Morecroft argues from his experience that a formal model in this context must

- Be a vehicle for extending argument and debate.
- Be a generator of opinions, not answers.
- Deal in concepts with which management is familiar.

Morecroft finds that the key for effective model-based strategic support is to use the model in a dialectical fashion, to challenge prevailing management opinion. He shows a very different view of the role of models—as vehicles for debate rather than providers of answers. Morecroft's paper is the only one in the current literature that follows a model through its use in practice.

Interface Technologies

One set of technologies that can significantly affect the growth and acceptability of MSS are those that address the interface between the human and the system. They include new hardware, such as joysticks and mice, and the software necessary to provide color graphics, windows, and other features.

Closer to the more obvious MSS needs is the work necessary to translate Bonczek, Holsapple, and Whinston's "language system" (1980b) into a general-purpose reality. This language system is defined as "the sum total of all linguistic facilities made available to the decision maker by the DSS." The authors point out that the system is characterized by the syntax that it furnishes to the decision maker and by "the statement commands or expressions that it allows the user to make." Thus, to them the language system is one of three components of DSS, the other two being the knowledge system and the problem processing system. This most useful generic description of a DSS allows the authors to make some interesting points about the role of artificial intelligence in the DSS of the future. They do not, however, expand on their view of the likely evolution of the language system.

Researchers do not appear to regard the interface question for MSS as worthy of much work; no serious articles on the subject surfaced in the recent journals. Occasionally, though, a theoretical piece raises some interesting ideas. One example is Studer's 1983 article on an adaptable user interface for DSS. The heart of his approach is twofold: first, system users should be provided with an "application model" through three types of graph structures:

- The application structure graph.
- The operator structure graph.
- The operator data graph.

Second, a dialogue should be provided that allows end users to select components and execute the existing model using facilities to "navigate" through the graph structures. Studer's description is extensive, but he gives no hint of experience with use, either in a labortory or an organization.

In short, there is a real dearth of practical experimentation in user interface work, and new ideas seem to move unusually slowly into testing. To the extent that the interface technologies are important, it appears that the widespread use of MSS will be held back by the absence of developmental work in this area.

Hardware and Networks

Much of the impetus in MSS appears to come from the relentless drop in cost of hardware and to be augmented by the changes in communications technology. An excellent article by Benjamin (1982) makes the point that in the future we can expect continued drop in cost and increase in functionality. This is represented by the migration of some MSS tools, such as languages, over to micros. Thus, a number of language vendors, such as IFPS, are making their languages, or subsets, available on personal computers. Downloading of central files from the mainframe to the personal computer also appears to be occurring. However, these and other hardware and communications changes are happening so rapidly that no research on them has yet appeared. One can merely pick up anecdotal illustrations from *Business Week* or *Fortune*. This suggests that much more research will be needed just to capture the implications of recent hardware developments.

One of the few articles published in this area is Keen (1983). He develops persuasive arguments for and against microcomputer-based DSS. The key points of his resulting policy statement are:

1. The role of the organization is to encourage use, not to control use.
2. Full authority is to be given to end users.
3. A coordinator role should exist to provide education, user support, and recommendations on software, hardware, and other issues

However, Keen does not go on to elaborate on the implications of these technological developments for computing in the organization. It seems obvious that MSS in an organization with such a sensible policy will become all-pervasive. Hardware changes will begin to blur the lines between what we see as a distinctive category, existing MSS, and the rest of the things managers do. In short, MSS will become part of the fabric of the management job.

RESEARCH TYPOLOGY

There are possibly as many ways of laying out a typology of research categories in MSS as there are professors active in the field. The criteria for judging a typology are vague, but surely one is that it be found useful. However, all researchers who develop their own typologies are likely to find them useful! With considerable trepidation, therefore, we submit the following nine categories as one possible typology: build a prototype, construct a methodology, develop a theory, formulate a concept, perform empirical tests (both laboratory and real world), conduct a survey, describe a case, and declare a "truth."

Each of these categories will be described briefly and an example of MSS research for each will be given. Of course, many research efforts fall in more than one category, for example, a prototype DSS that is tested in a laboratory setting.

Prototype

The prototype is basically an engineering concept of research, which, fortunately, has its proponents in the MSS field. An example, found in Moscowitz's "DSS/F" (1982), is a PASCAL-based DSS for financial applications with a number of innovative uses of virtual memory that permit an unusually interesting collection of features.

Methodology

A methodology is constructed whenever researchers take the trouble to base their procedure on theory or on the deductive process gained by trial and error over time in the field. An example would be Sprague and Carlson's (1982) work with ROMC (representations, operations, memory aids, and control mechanisms), their methodology for building a DSS.

Theory

To develop a theory is possibly the toughest research task of all. It requires not only extraordinary insight, but also extensive work with existing theories. We have found no new theories relevant to the MSS field in the recent literature. Of course, Simon's work on decision making remains as powerful as ever, as do many behavior theories, such as the Lewin-Schein model (see Schein, 1969).

Concept

The term *concept* here is meant to suggest a framework that is found useful in organizing ideas and suggesting actions. Concepts can in time lead to a theory. A recent example of a concept would be Rockart's work on critical success factors. This concept has gained credibility and usefulness through its testing by many people in actual empirical situations.

Empirical Laboratory Test

Empirical lab-testing attempts to simulate real-world behavior in an artificial setting using students or managers. The literature search for this paper uncovered only a few experiments; one of the most interesting was Alavi and Henderson (1981). They tested two alternative strategies—one traditional and one evolutionary. The process-oriented evolutionary strategy proved more effective. Such controlled lab experiments can be most valuable; their infrequent use is hard to understand.

Empirical Real-World Test

Empirical real-world tests should eventually be used to evaluate the effectiveness of any new concept, methodology, or system. Such tests can be of two types—focused or general. Rockart (1979) used the focused type to assess his critical success factors methodology. The general test is exemplified by Fuerst and Cheney (1982). They tested the factors affecting DSS usage of eight systems and 64 subjects. Their hypotheses were derived from prior studies, and the outcome of their study verifies the importance of the DSS's relevance and the quality of user training. The few real-world tests found in the literature indicate that they are performed, or at least reported, infrequently.

Survey

This category of research represents projects that survey a particular population (users, builders, or others) in organizations to determine the existence or absence of something. Surveys may be used to establish whether a particular class of language is used, or whether a user is satisfied with the quality of service received. Surveys differ from general empirical tests in that surveys do not attempt to establish causal relationships based on theory or deductive work from prior studies. The work by Rockart and Treacy (1982) represents a fine example of this genre; they found five common characteristics among 16 users of ESS.

Case

Describing a case often provides a rich sense of the context and nuances of an application. This seems to be particularly true in MSS work, which has so many dimensions and facets. One example would be Ben-Bassat's fascinating artificial intelligence-based DSS (1981).

"Truth"

Periodically workers in the field of MSS are moved to declare a "truth." Ideally, a declaration is made by a wise person whose experience has led to a genuine insight. When this occurs, the idea immediately strikes one as "right," even without the corroboration of theory, implementation, or use. The difficulty is that what strikes one reader as insightful may strike another as foolish. Only time can reveal the truth. Keen's "Policy Statement for Managing Microcomputers" (1983) is an example of this research style.

SUMMARY OF RESEARCH STATUS

We can use a three-dimensional matrix to look at the state of the art research in MSS (see Figure 3). We have suggested that three types of management support are adequate for our purposes: data support, decision support, and executive support. It should be no surprise to discover that, by far, the largest number of articles culled from the literature are in the decision support category. This testifies to the life cycle stage of the concept, if nothing else. However, if we now take each slice in turn to produce a two-dimensional grid, the patterns in Figures 4 through 7 emerge.

FIGURE 3 Categories of Research

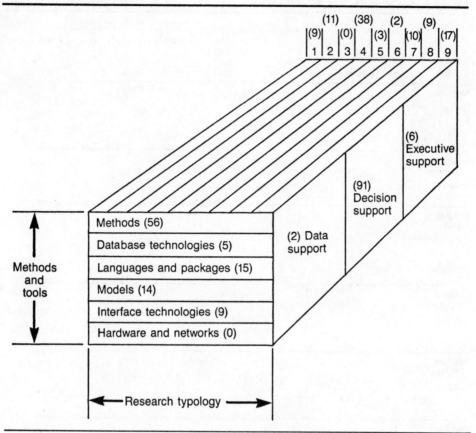

Note: Numbers in parentheses represent pieces of research, in each category, found in the literature search.

CONCLUSIONS

The patterns of research work, or lack of it, revealed in Figures 3 through 7 bring us to four specific conclusions and an overall observation.

1. We still appear to be in the very early phases of research in MSS. So far almost all the work has been with DSS; only around early 1982 did we begin to see published results on data and executive support systems. It will be interesting to see if the development of these "product" types will be accompanied by appropriate empirical testing and observation.

2. There appears to be a disproportionally large amount of

FIGURE 4 *Research on Data Support Systems*

Methods and Tools	1 Proto-type	2 Method	3 Theory	4 Concept	5 Empirical Tests Lab	6 Real	7 Survey	8 Case	9 "Truth"
Methods				X					
Database Technologies									
Languages and Packages									
Models				X					
Interface Technologies									
Hardware and Networks									

← ———————————————— Research Typology ———————————————— →

work in methodologies and frameworks. This is not in itself bad, but it is unfortunate that almost no work falls into the area of empirical testing of the methodologies or frameworks. Insights gained from testing, or at least reporting on use, could greatly improve the methodologies. A similar assessment can be made of the research on languages. The lack of testing or surveying experience in the field removes a major source of insights that could lead to important changes in a new generation of languages and in the practice of management.

3. The surprising failure to find published research on hardware and communications networks may well be the result of a

FIGURE 5 Research on Decision Support Systems

Methods and Tools	Proto-type	Method	Theory	Concept	Empirical Tests Lab	Real	Survey	Case	"Truth"
Methods	XX	XXXX XXXX		XXX XXXX XXXX XXXX XXX	XX X	X	XXXX	XXXX X	XXXX XXXX XXXX
Database Technologies	X			XX				X	
Languages and Packages	XX			XXXX			XXX		XXXX
Models	XX	XXX		XXX XXXX				X	
Interface Technologies	X			XXXX		X		XX	X
Hardware and Networks									

(Header spanning "Research Typology" over Prototype through "Truth")

faulty search process. It does not seem reasonable that hardware, at least, is not currently a primary research focus in MSS. However, our search, which included the Association for Computing Machinery publication *Computing Reviews,* did not produce any articles. It may also be that the business schools have, thus far, done most of the research and publishing in the MSS field. This community may not be drawn to focus on hardware. However, the increasing availability of low-cost MSS hardware tools may lead to more research in this area.

4. There is another surprising vacuum—the lack of work on the "impacts of MSS." Much work has been done on the impacts of traditional management information systems, but virtually nothing on the impacts of MSS. If this lack is real, and not sim-

FIGURE 6   Research on Executive Support Systems

Methods and Tools	Proto-type	Method	Theory	Concept	Empirical Tests Lab	Real	Survey	Case	"Truth"
Methods				X			XX		
Database Technologies	X								
Languages and Packages	X						X		
Models									
Interface Technologies									
Hardware and Networks									

(column heading: ←———————— Research Typology ————————→)

ply an error of our literature search, it is a sad commentary on the state of the field. A careful examination of the impacts of MSS is needed if we are to improve the effectiveness of their use. This literature survey indicates that those in the field make declarative statements and build interesting new tools which are never tested by practical use, comparative evaluation, or user opinion.

Overall, we have to conclude that there is an unfortunately large number of unexplored areas. A further dimension of this fact was revealed by the bibliographies of the 93 items referenced here. We counted the sources referenced in these bibli-

FIGURE 7   Research on Management Support Systems

Methods and Tools	1 Proto-type	2 Method	3 Theory	4 Concept	5 Empirical Tests Lab	6 Real	7 Survey	8 Case	9 "Truth"	
Methods	XX	XXXX XXX		XXXX XXXX XXXX XXXX XXXX	XX X	X	XXXX XX	XXXX X	XXXX XXXX XXXX	56
Database Technol-ogies	X	X		XX				X		5
Languages and Packages	XXX			XXXX			XXXX		XXXX	15
Models	XX	XXX		XXXX XXXX				X		14
Interface Technol-ogies	X					X		XX	X	5
Hardware and Networks										0
	9	11	0	34	3	2	10	9	17	

(Top of table: ← Research Typology →)

ographies and how many times each was cited (see Table 1). In the vast majority of cases a source was cited by only one author. In short, those in the MSS field do not build on collective experience; research efforts appear to be individualistic and fragmented.

Our four conclusions on the state of research in MSS are reflected in the many issues raised at the 1981 Conference on Decision Support Systems held by the American Institute for Decision Sciences. The discussions at this conference are summarized in Dickson (1980), Hackathorn (1980), Methlie (1980), and Wagner (1980). A major concern was the lack of research on the sup-

TABLE 1   Count of Sources Cited in Bibliographies of Ninety-Three Selected MSS Articles

Sources	Times Cited
259	1
40	2
27	3
10	4
1	5
3	6
0	7
1	8
2	9
2	10+

The heavily cited sources were:

	Times Cited
Keen and Scott Morton (1978)	20
Sprague (1980)	10
Alter (1980)	9
Bonczek, Holsapple, and Whinston (1980)	9
Gorry and Scott Morton (1971)	8

port needs of groups and committees. Participants in the conference felt that organizational MSS may represent many problems not found in single-user or single-decision MSS. Research into these issues may address our concern about a lack of research on executive and data support systems.

Other issues were raised at that conference regarding the tools of MSS: software languages and design, implementation, and evaluation methods. Particular concern was expressed about the lack of substantive results addressing the evaluation and justification of MSS. The discussants' concerns mirror our concern for more research on the impact of support systems on the organization. *The value of an MSS is in its impacts.* If we can study these in greater depth, understand and catalog them, then we move a step closer to understanding where best to apply MSS to improve the effectiveness with which organizations operate.

If the research we found is a measure of the maturity of the MSS field, then it has much growing to do. We hope that future research will begin to fill in the many blank areas in Figures 4–7.

One prospective area of study that may fill in some of these gaps is artificial intelligence. This topic has been worked on by some of the best researchers in the country for over 20 years. Its recent leap into the limelight (see Alexander, 1982, and "Artificial Intelligence," 1982) is partly the result of the availability of inexpensive and powerful programming tools for "heuristic" work. This is important because of the insatiable hardware appetite of any realistic application. There are years of work ahead (see Bonczek, Holsapple, and Whinston, 1980b). Research is needed in all the following areas: natural language; knowledge engineering (the ability to extract and encode the knowledge in a human's mind); tools and techniques to build domain-specific knowledge; and tools, techniques, and models to construct the general-purpose "inference engines" that will work on domain-specific knowledge.

In the meantime, for those interested in MSS there is the attraction of addressing a whole new class of management problems (see Luconi and Scott Morton, 1983). Their support will be particularly useful where precise rules cannot be made explicit in a computable form, but where heuristics can genuinely be helpful. Intelligent support systems may be one of the most fruitful areas of MSS research in the decade ahead.

This look at the future from a detail level can be instructive. However, it is also useful to look at the driving forces in the field from a macro perspective. This can be done in terms of both supply push and demand pull.

On the supply side we have, as always, the hardware vendors. However, with software becoming a major part of their sales, they are likely to keep flooding the market with tools that can be built into MSS. The resources of the hardware vendors are being mightily leveraged by the host of software firms and users who are launching new products.

The other supply push is the information coming from the 20 years of building internal transaction processing and other data processing systems, which in many firms are supplying the information. When we add to this information what is coming from external database purveyors, it is clear that there is an abundance of information, which causes an inevitable supply-side push in MSS.

The same pattern can be seen on the demand-pull side, where a multitude of forces converge on management. In response, a general MSS, such as we have defined in this paper, can be of real use. The widespread needs caused by the global economy, the necessity to increase productivity, and other forces all suggest that management at all levels must think "smarter." This has always been necessary, but it will be more so in the 1980s and 1990s. The ability to harness the burgeoning supply of new technology to meet business demands will prove invaluable. If MSS can reach their potential to help achieve this, they will become an integral part of business. Like the telephone, we will take them for granted.

Our literature survey suggests that we are far from being at such a point. But the trend is in the right direction. Certainly the new technologies are driving us ever forward.

Acknowledgement.   This paper could not have been written without the able help of my assistant, Andrea Hatch, and the work of John Poole and Marc Gordon, who did a great deal of the early literature search. Diane Gherson provided some much-needed assistance, particularly in the development of the positioning framework. I have benefitted from the input of all my colleagues and am particularly grateful for the substantive help given by Michael Treacy.

REFERENCES

Akoka, Jacob. "A Framework for Decision Support Systems Evaluation." *Information and Management* (Netherlands), July 1981.

Alavi, Maryam. "An Assessment of DSS as Viewed by Senior Executives." *MIS Quarterly*, December 1982.

Alavi, Maryam, and John C. Henderson. "An Evolutionary Strategy for Implementing a Decision Support System." *Management Science*, November 1981.

Alexander, Tom. "Thinking Machines." Series of two articles, *Fortune*, May 17, 1982, and June 14, 1982.

Alter, Steven L. "Computer-Aided Decision Making in Organizations: A DSS Typology." CISR Working Paper No. 11, Sloan School of Management Science, MIT, Cambridge, Mass., May 1976.

————. *Decision Support Systems: Current Practice and Continuing Challenges*. Reading, Mass.: Addison-Wesley, 1980.

————. "What Do You Need to Know to Develop Your Own DSS?" *DSS-82 Transactions*, June 1982.

"Artificial Intelligence: The Second Computer Age Begins." *Business Week*, March 8, 1982.

Bariff, Martin, and Michael Ginzberg. "MIS and the Behavioral Sciences: Research Patterns and Prescriptions." In *Proceedings of the Third International Conference on Information Systems,* Ann Arbor, Mich., 1982.

Ben-Bassat, Moshe. "Research into an Intelligent DSS for Military Situation Assessment." *DSS-81 Transactions,* June 1981.

Bendifallah, S. "Knowledge-Based Decision Support Systems: Social Significance." In *Proceedings of the Twenty-Sixth Annual Meeting of the Society for General Systems Research of the American Association for the Advancement of Science* 1, (1982), Washington, D.C.

Benjamin, Robert I. "Information Technology in the 1990s: A Long-Range Planning Scenario." *MIS Quarterly* 6, no. 2 (June 1982).

Blanning, Robert W. "A Relational Framework for Model Management in DSS." *DSS-82 Transactions,* June 1982.

Bonczek, Robert H.; Clyde W. Holsapple; and Andrew B. Whinston. "Computer-Based Support of Organizational Decision Making." *Decision Sciences,* April 1979a.

—————. "The Integration of Data Base Management and Problem Resolution." *Information Systems* 4, no. 2 (1979b).

—————. "The Evolving Roles of Models in DSS." *Decision Sciences* 11 (1980a).

—————. "Future Directions for Developing DSS." *Decision Sciences* 11 (1980b).

—————. "Generalized DSS Using Predicate Calculus and Network Data Base Management." *Operations Research* 29, no. 2 (March–April 1981).

Brightman, Harvey J.; Sydney C. Harris; and William J. Thompson. "Empirical Study of Computer-Based Financial Modeling Systems: Implications for Decision Support Systems." *DSS-81 Transactions,* June 1981.

Briggs, Warren G. "An Evaluation of DSS Packages." *Computerworld,* March 1982.

Chung, Chen-Hua. "Implementation Issues in Problem Processing of DSS." In *Proceedings of the Sixteenth Annual Hawaii International Conference on System Sciences,* June 1983.

De, Prabudda, and Arun Sen. "Logical Data Base Design in DSS." *Journal of Systems Management* 32, no. 5 (May 1981).

DeSanctis, Gerardine. "An Examination of an Expectancy Theory Model of DSS Use." In *Proceedings of the Third International Conference on Information Systems,* Ann Arbor, Mich., 1982.

Dhar, Vasant, and Ronald Daniels. "A Process Model of Information Requirements Analysis for Strategic Decision Support." In *American Institute for Decision Sciences, Thirteenth Proceedings,* 1981.

Dickson, Gary. "Issues for the Future in DSS." (Report of Discussion Group 1). In *DDS: Issues and Challenges.* Proceedings of the International Institute for Applied Systems Analysis (IIASA), June 1980.

Disclosure Online News, November 1981 (5161 River Road, Bethesda, Md., 20816).

Findler, Nicholas V. "An Expert Subsystem Based on Generalized Production Rules." In *Proceedings of the Sixteenth Annual Hawaii International Conference on System Sciences,* June 1983.

Fuerst, William, and Paul Cheney. "Factors Affecting the Perceived Utilization of Computer-based DSS in the Oil Industry." *Decision Sciences* 13, no. 4 (1982).

Ginzberg, Michael J. "DSS Success: Measurement and Facilitation." Center for Research on Information Systems Working Paper No. 20. New York University, 1981.

Gorry, Andrew, and Michael S. Scott Morton. "A Framework for Management Information Systems." *Sloan Management Review* 13, no. 1 (Fall 1971).

Gulden, Gary. "A Framework for Decisions." *Computerworld,* December 1982.

Gulden, Gary, and E. S. Arkush. "Developing a Strategy Profile for DSS." *DSS-82 Transactions,* June 1982.

Hackathorn, Richard D. "Issues for the Future in DSS." (Report of Discussion Group 4). In *DSS: Issues and Challenges.* Proceedings of the IIASA, June 1980.

Hackathorn, Richard D., and Peter G. W. Keen. "Organizational Strategies for Personal Computing in Decision Support Systems." *MIS Quarterly,* September 1981.

Hamilton, Scott; Blake Ives; and Gordon B. Davis. "MIS Doctoral Dissertations: 1973–1980." *MIS Quarterly,* September 1981.

Huber, George. "Organizational Science Contributions to the Design of DSS." In *DSS: Issues and Challenges.* Proceedings of the IIASA, June 1980.

—————. "The Design of Group DSS." In *Proceedings of the Sixteenth Annual Hawaii International Conference on System Sciences,* June 1983.

Ives, Blake. "Graphical User Interfaces for Business Information Systems." *MIS Quarterly,* Special Issue 1982.

Jacob, J. P., and Ralph H. Sprague, Jr. "Graphical Problem Solving in DSS." In *Proceedings of the Thirteenth Annual Hawaii International Conference on System Sciences, Database* (USA) 12, no. 1–2 (Fall 1980).

Keen, Peter G. W. "DSS and Managerial Productivity Analysis," CISR Working Paper No. 60, Sloan School of Management, MIT, Cambridge, Mass., October 1980a.

————. "DSS: Translating Analytic Technology into Useful Tools." *Sloan Management Review* 21, no. 3 (Spring 1980b).

————. "DSS: Lessons for the 80s." CISR Working Paper No. 70, Sloan School of Management, MIT, Cambridge, Mass., June 1981a.

————. "Value Analysis: Justifying DSS." *MIS Quarterly* 5, no. 1 (1981b).

————. "Adaptive Design for DSS." *Database* 12, no. 1–2 (Fall 1982).

————. "A Policy Statement of Managing Microcomputers." *Computerworld*, May 16, 1983.

Keen, Peter G. W., and Michael S. Scott Morton. *Decision Support Systems: An Organizational Perspective*. Reading, Mass.: Addison-Wesley, 1978.

Kingston, Paul. "Generic DSS." *Managerial Planning* 29, no. 5 (March 1981).

Larreche, Jean Claude, and Paul Srinivasan. "Strataport: A DSS for Strategic Planning." *Journal of Marketing* 45 (Fall 1981).

Lindgren, Richard. "Justifying a Decision Support System." *Data Management* 19 (May 1981).

Lucas, Henry C., Jr. "An Experimental Investigation of the Use of Computer-Based Graphics in Decision Making." *Management Science* 27, no. 7 (July 1981).

Luconi, Fred, and Michael S. Scott Morton. "Artificial Intelligence: The Next Challenge for Management." CISR draft working paper, Sloan School of Management, MIT, Cambridge, Mass., October 1983.

Manola, Frank. "Database Technology in DSS: An Overview." In *DSS: Issues and Challenges*. Proceedings of the IIASA, June 1980.

Martin, Merle P. "Determining Information Requirements for DSS." *Journal of Systems Management* 33, no. 12 (December 1982).

Methlie, Leif. "Issues for the Future of DSS." (Report of Discussion Group 2). In *DSS: Issues and Challenges*. Proceedings of the IIASA, June 1980.

Monypenny, Richard. "Person/Role Conflict in the DSS-Corporate Interface." *DSS-82 Transactions*, June 1982.

Moore, J. H., and M. G. Chang. "Design of DSS." In *Proceedings of the Thirteenth Annual Hawaii International Conference on Systems Sciences, Database* (USA) 12, no. 1–2 (Fall 1980).

Morecroft, John. "Strategy Support Models." Draft article, Massachusetts Institute of Technology, July 1982.

Moscowitz, Robert. "DSS/F: Paving the Way for Sophisticated Software." *Interface Age*, June 1982.

Naisbitt, John. *Megatrends*. New York: Warner Books, 1982.

Neumann, Seev, and Michael Hadass. "DSS and Strategic Decisions." *California Management Review.* 22, no. 2 (Spring 1980).

Paul, Louis. "DSS: An Idea in Search of an Identity." *Computerworld* 16, no. 44 (November 1982).

Pitt, Joel. "DSS/F: A Financial-Modeling and Reporting Package." *Info World,* May 17, 1982.

Rockart, John F. "Chief Executives Define Their Own Data Needs." *Harvard Business Review,* March–April 1979.

Rockart, John F., and Michael S. Scott Morton. "Implications of Changes in Information Technology for Corporate Strategy." CISR Working Paper No. 98, Sloan School of Management, MIT, Cambridge, Mass., January 1983.

Rockart, John F., and Michael Treacy. "The CEO Goes On-Line." *Harvard Business Review,* January–February 1982.

Sagalowicz, Daniel. "Using Personal Data Bases for Decision Support." In *DSS: Issues and Challenges.* Proceedings of the IIASA, June 1980.

Sage, A. P., and A. Lagomasino. "Knowledge Representation and Interpretation in Decision Support Systems." In the *Proceedings of the 1982 IEEE International Conference on Cybernetics and Society.* New York: Institute of Electrical and Electronics Engineers, 1982.

Sanders, G. Larry. "A DSS for Identifying Critical Success Factors." In the *American Institute for Decision Sciences. Thirteenth Proceedings,* 1981.

Schein, Edgar. *Process Consultation: Its Role in Organization Development.* Reading, Mass.: Addison-Wesley, 1969.

Scher, James M. "Distributed DSS for Management and Organizations." *DSS-81 Transactions,* June 1981.

Seils, Harold L. "Do DSS Really Support?" *Computerworld* 16, no. 26 (June 1982).

Sheinin, Roman L. "The Structure of Decision Support Systems." In *DSS: Issues and Challenges.* Proceedings of the IIASA, June 1980.

Shrivastava, P. "DSS for Strategic Ill-Structured Problems." *Proceedings of the Third International Conference on Information Systems,* Ann Arbor, Mich., 1982.

Sprague, Ralph H., Jr. "A Framework for Research on DSS." In. *Decision Support Systems: Issues and Challenges,* ed. Ralph H. Sprague, Jr., and Goran Fick. Elmsford, N.Y.: Pergamon Press, 1980a.

———. "A Framework for the Development of a DSS." *MIS Quarterly* 4, no. 4, December 1980b.

———. "DSS: A Tutorial." *DSS-81 Transactions,* June 1981.

Sprague, Ralph H., Jr., and Eric Carlson. *Building Effective Decision Support Systems.* Englewood Cliffs, N.J.: Prentice-Hall, 1982.

Sprague, Ralph H., Jr., and Raymond Panko. "Criteria for a DSS Generator." In *American Institute for Decision Sciences, Thirteenth Proceedings,* 1981.

Studer, R. "An Adaptable User Interface for DSS." In *Proceedings of the Sixteenth Annual Hawaii International Conference on System Sciences,* June 1983.

Suyderhoud, Jack P. "The Role of Risk Assessment in the DSS Evaluation Process." In *Proceedings of the Sixteenth Annual Hawaii International Conference on System Sciences,* June 1983.

Thierauf, Robert. *DSS for Effective Planning and Control: A Case Study Approach.* Englewood Cliffs, N.J.: Prentice-Hall, 1982.

Treacy, Michael. "Where DSS Technology Is Going." From a discussion, April 1983.

Tucker, J. H. "Implementation of Decision Support Systems." In *Proceedings of the 1981 IEEE International Conference on Cybernetics and Society,* New York: Institute of Electrical and Electronic Engineers, 1981.

Vierck, J. "DSS: An MIS Manager's Perspective." *DSS-81 Transactions,* June 1981.

Wagner, G. R. "Issues for the Future in DSS." (Report of Discussion Group 3). In *DSS: Issues and Challenges.* Proceedings of the IIASA, June 1980.

———. "Beyond Theory Z with DSS." *DSS-81 Transactions,* June 1981a.

———. "Computerized Mind Support for Executive Problems," *Managerial Planning* 30, no. 2 (October 1981b).

———. "DSS: The Real Substance," *Interfaces* 11, no. 2 (1981c).

———. "DSS: Dealing with Executive Assumptions in the Office of the Future," *Managerial Planning* 30, no. 5 (March–April 1982).

Wang, Michael S. Y. "Bridging the Gap between Modeling and Data Handling in a DSS Generator." In *American Institute for Decision Sciences, Thirteenth Proceedings,* 1981.

Wang, Michael S. Y., and Keh-Chiang Yu. "A Hierarchical View of Decision Support Software." In *Proceedings of the Sixteenth Annual Hawaii International Conference on System Sciences,* June 1983.

Watkins, Paul R. "Perceived Information Structure: Implications for Decision Support Design." *Decision Sciences* 13 (1982).

Welsch, Gemma. "Successful Implementation of DSS: The Role of the Information Transfer Specialist." In the *American Institute for Decision Sciences, Thirteenth Proceedings,* 1981.

Chapter Seventeen
Expert Systems and Expert Support Systems: The Next Challenge for Management

FRED L. LUCONI
THOMAS W. MALONE
MICHAEL S. SCOTT MORTON

INTRODUCTION

In this age of the "microchip revolution," effective managers are finding ways to learn and profitably use the myriad applications of the silicon chip. These applications include personal computers, office automation, robotics, computer graphics, and the various forms of broad-band and narrow-band communication. One of the most intriguing of these new applications to emerge from the research labs and move into the practical world of business is Expert Systems (ES). Most literature about Expert Systems describes the technical concepts upon which they are based and the small number of systems already in use.

In this article we shift this focus and discuss how these systems can be used in a broad range of business applications. We will argue that in many business applications, the knowledge that can be feasibly encoded in an Expert System is not sufficient to make satisfactory decisions by itself. Instead, we believe that our focus should increasingly be on designing Expert *Support* Systems (ESS) that will aid, rather than replace, human decision makers.

After briefly defining a few Expert Systems concepts, we offer an expansion of a classical framework for understanding managerial problem solving. We then use this framework to identify the limits of current Expert Systems and decision support systems technology and show how Expert Support Systems can be seen as the next logical step in both fields.

BASIC CONCEPTS

Broadly defined, Artificial Intelligence (AI) is the area which involves the design and construction of computer systems that can perform at the level of intelligent human behavior. The prospect of machines that *reason intelligently* has fueled the current publicity of AI in the popular press (3, 6). There is no doubt that AI has been grossly oversold, particularly with respect to the claims about natural language understanding, and progress in machine vision. Despite this business journal "hype" and the inevitable backlash that is just beginning, it is an indisputable fact that there are an increasing number of practical business applications of Expert Systems in use today.

When one stops to look at reality it turns out that AI technology has been used to develop two types of systems of particular interest to management: Expert Systems and a variation of Expert Systems that we will call Expert Support Systems.

Expert Systems

Expert Systems can be used to increase a human's ability to exploit available knowledge that is in limited supply. They do this by building on the captured and encoded relevant experience of an expert in the field. This experience is then available as a resource to the less expert. For example, the Schlumberger Corporation uses its "Dipmeter Advisor" to access the interpretive abilities of a handful of their most productive geological experts and make it available to their field geologists all over the world (16). The program takes oil well log data about the geological characteristics of a well and makes inferences about the probable location of oil in that region.

Another example of an early system in practical use is known as XCON. Developed at Digital Equipment Corporation in a joint effort with Carnegie-Mellon University, XCON uses some 3300 rules and 5500 product descriptions to configure the specific detailed components of VAX and other computer systems in response to the customers' overall orders. The system first determines what, if any, substitutions and additions have to be made to the order so that it is complete and consistent. Then this system produces a number of diagrams showing the electrical connections and room layout for the 50 to 150 components in a typical system (4).

This application was attempted unsuccessfully several times using traditional programming techniques before the AI effort was initiated. The system has been in daily use now for over four years and the savings have been substantial, not only in terms of the technical editor's scarce time, but also in ensuring that no component is missing at installation time, an occurrence that delays the customer's acceptance of the system (12)

Expert Support Systems

ESS (Expert Support Systems) take ES techniques and apply them to a much wider class of problems than is possible with pure Expert Systems. They do this by pairing the human with the Expert System, thus creating a joint decision process in which the human is the dominant partner, providing overall problem-solving direction as well as specific knowledge not incorporated in the system. Some of this knowledge can be thought of beforehand and made explicit, thus becoming embedded in the expert system. However, much of the knowledge may be imprecise and will remain below the level of consciousness, to be recalled to the conscious level of the decision maker only when triggered by the evolving problem context. Such systems represent the next generation of Decision Support Systems (DSS). (See Reference 11 for a discussion of Decision Support Systems).

Expert Systems are also called *knowledge-based systems*. They incorporate not only data but the expert knowledge that represents how that data is to be interpreted and used. Recent progress in the field of Expert Systems has been greatly aided by two factors. One has been the enormous increase in the computer power available per dollar. The so-called LISP machines are on the market at low prices and are well suited for dealing with heuristics which involve much probing and reprobing of the relevant knowledge base as the system weaves together an alternative worthy of suggestion (1).

A second factor making AI applications such as Expert Systems feasible today is the development of programming tools for nonspecialists that are capable of supporting symbol manipulation and incremental development. These facilities permit one to prototype, experiment, and modify as required, and have resulted in "Power Tools for Programmers" (14)—environments of significantly greater potential than those usually provided by traditional data processing resources.

Definitions

With these examples in mind we can now define Expert Systems as follows:

> Expert Systems—computer programs that use specialized symbolic reasoning to solve difficult problems well.

In other words, Expert Systems: (1) use specialized knowledge about a particular problem area (such as geological analysis or computer configuration) rather than just general-purpose knowledge that would apply to all problems, (2) use symbolic (and often qualitative) reasoning rather than just numerical calculations, and (3) perform at a level of competence that is better than that of nonexpert humans.

Expert Support Systems use all these same techniques but focus on helping people solve the problems:

> Expert Support Systems—computer programs that use specialized symbolic reasoning to *help people solve* difficult problems well.

Heuristic Reasoning

One of the most important ways in which Expert Systems differ from traditional computer applications is in their use of heuristic reasoning. Traditional applications are completely understood and therefore can employ algorithms, that is, precise rules that, when followed, lead to the correct conclusion. For example, the amount of a payroll check for an employee is calculated according to a precise set of rules. Expert Systems use heuristic techniques. A heuristic system involves judgmental reasoning, trial and error, and therefore is appropriate for more complex problems. The

FIGURE 1   *Expert Systems Architecture*

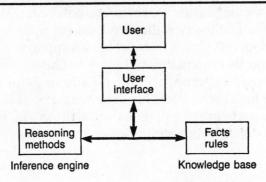

heuristic decision rules or inference procedures generally provide a good—but not necessarily optimum—answer.

Problems appropriate for AI techniques are those that cannot be solved algorithmically, that is, by precise rules. The problems are either too large, such as the possibilities encountered in the game of chess, or too imprecise, such as the diagnosis of a particular person's medical condition.

Components of Expert Systems

To begin to see how Expert Systems (and Expert Support Systems) are different from traditional computer applications, it is important to understand what the components of a typical expert system are (see Figure 1). In addition to the *user interface* for communicating with a human user, a typical expert system also has (1) a *knowledge base* of facts and rules related to the problem and (2) an *inference engine,* or reasoning methods, for using the information in the knowledge base to solve problems. Separating these two components makes it much easier to change the system as the problem changes or becomes better understood. For example, new rules can be added to the knowledge base, one by one, in such a way that all the old facts and reasoning methods can still be used.

Knowledge Base

In order to flexibly use specialized knowledge about many different kinds of problems, AI researchers have developed a number of new "knowledge representation" techniques. Using these techniques to provide structure for a body of knowledge is still very much an art, and is practiced by an emerging group of professionals known as "knowledge engineers." Knowledge engineers in this field are akin to the systems analysts of Data Processing (DP) applications. They work with the "experts" and draw out the relevant expertise in a form that can be encoded in a computer program. Three of the most important techniques for encoding this knowledge are: (1) production rules, (2) semantic nets, and (3) frames.

Production Rules. Production rules are particularly useful in building systems based on heuristic methods (17). These are simple "if-then" rules that are often used to represent the empirical consequences of a given condition, or the action that should be taken in a given situation. For example, a medical diagnosis system might have a rule like:

> If (1) The patient has fever, and
> (2) The patient has a runny nose,
> Then: It is very likely (.9) that the patient has a cold.

A computer configuration system might have a rule like:

> If (1) There is an unassigned single port disk drive, and
> (2) There is a free controller,
> Then: Assign the disk drive to the controller port.

Semantic Nets. Another formalism that is often more convenient than production rules for representing certain kinds of relational knowledge is called semantic networks or semantic nets. For example, in order to apply the rule about assigning disk drives that was shown above, a system would need to know what part numbers corresponded to single port disk drives, controllers, and so forth. Figure 2 shows how this knowledge might be represented in a network of "nodes" connected by "links" that signify which classes of components are subsets of other classes.

Frames. In many cases, it is convenient to gather into one place a number of different kinds of information about an object. For example, Figure 3 shows how several dimensions (such as length, width, and power requirements) that describe electrical components might be represented as different "slots" in a "frame" about electrical components. Unlike traditional records in a database, frames often contain additional features such as "default values" and "attached procedures." For example, if the default value for voltage requirement of an electrical component

---

FIGURE 2   Semantic Networks

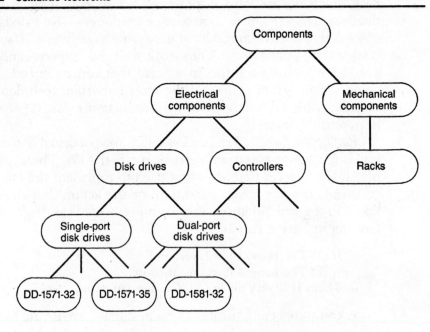

is 110 volts then the system would infer that a new electrical component required 110 volts unless explicit information to the contrary was provided. An attached procedure might automatically update the "volume" slot, whenever "length," "height," or "width" are changed.

These three knowledge representation techniques—production rules, semantic nets, and frames—have considerable power, as they permit us to capture knowledge in a way that can be ex-

---

FIGURE 3   Frames

Electrical component	
Part No.	
Length	
Width	
Height	
Volume	
Voltage	

FIGURE 4 Production Rules

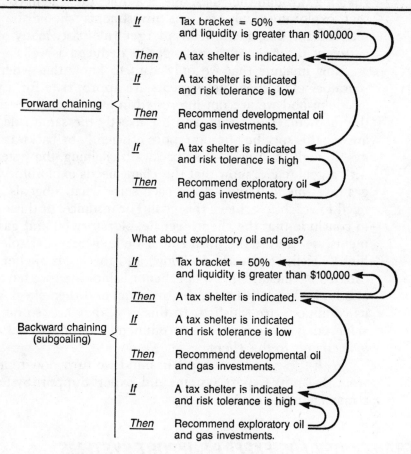

ploited by the "inference engine" to produce good, workable answers to the questions at hand.

Inference Engine

The inference engine contains the reasoning methods that might be used by human problem solvers when attacking problems. As these are separate from the knowledge base it permits either to be changed relatively independent of the other. Two reasoning methods often employed with production rules are *forward chaining* and *backward chaining*. Imagine, for instance, that we have a set of production rules like those shown in Figure 4 for a personal financial planning expert system. Imagine also that we know the current client's tax bracket is 50 percent, his liquidity is greater than $100,000, and he has a high tolerance for risk. By forward chaining through the rules, one at a time, the system could infer that exploratory oil and gas investments should be recommended for this client. With a larger rule base, many other investment recommendations might be deduced as well.

Now imagine that we only want to know that whether exploratory oil and gas investments are appropriate for a particular client and we are not interested in any other investments at the moment. The system can use exactly the same rule base to answer this specific question more efficiently by backward chaining through the rules. When backward chaining, the system starts with a goal (e.g., "show that this client needs exploratory oil and gas investments") and asks at each stage what subgoals it would need to reach to achieve this goal. For instance, in this example, to conclude that the client needs exploratory oil and gas investments, we can use the third rule if we know that risk tolerance is high (which we already do know) and that a tax shelter is indicated. To conclude that a tax shelter is indicated we have to find another rule (in this case, the first one) and then check whether its conditions are satisfied. In this case, they are, so our goal is achieved: we know we can recommend exploratory oil and gas investments to this client.

With these basic concepts in mind we turn now to a framework that puts Expert Systems and Expert Support Systems into a management context.

FRAMEWORK FOR EXPERT SUPPORT SYSTEMS

The framework developed in this section begins to allow us to identify those classes of business problems that are appropriate for Data Processing (DP), Decision Support Systems (DSS), Expert Systems (ES), and Expert Support Systems (ESS). We can, in addition, clarify the relative contributions of humans and computers in the various classes of applications.

This framework extends the earlier work of Gorry and Scott Morton, "A Framework for Management Information Systems" (8), in which they relate Herbert Simon's seminal work on structured versus unstructured decision making (15) to Robert Anthony's strategic planning, management control, and operational control (2). Figure 5 presents this original framework. Gorry and Scott Morton argued that to improve the quality of decisions, the

FIGURE 5

	Strategic Planning	Management Control	Operational Control
	←		→
Structured ↑			
Semistructured			
Unstructured ↓			

manager must seek not only to match the type and quality of information and its presentation to the category of decision, but also to choose a system that reflects the degree of the problem's structure.

With the benefit of experience in building and using decision support systems, and in light of the insights garnered from the field of artificial intelligence, it is useful to expand and rethink the structured/unstructured dimension of the original framework. Simon had broken down decision making into three phases: intelligence, design, and choice (I,D,C). It was argued in the original article that a structured decision was one where all three phases (I,D,C) were fully understood and "computable" by the human decision maker. As a result they could be programmed. In unstructured decisions, one or more of these three phases was not fully understood.

We can extend this distinction by replacing Simon's, "intelligence, design and choice" with Alan Newell's insightful categorization of problem solving (13), as consisting of the following components:

- Goals
- Constraints
- State space
- Search control knowledge
- Operators

In a business context, it seems helpful to relabel these problem characteristics and group them into four categories:

1. *Data*—the dimensions and values necessary to represent the state of the world that is relevant to the problem (i.e., the "state space").
2. *Procedures*—the sequences of steps (or "operators") used in solving the problem.
3. *Goals and constraints*—the desired results of problem solv-

FIGURE 6 Problem Types

	I DP	II DSS	III ES	IV ESS
Data				
Procedures				
Goals and constraints				
Flexible strategies				

▦ Done by computer

▤ Done by people

ing and the constraints on what can and cannot be done.

4. *Strategies*—the flexible strategies used in deciding which procedures to apply to achieve goals (i.e., the "search control knowledge").

Thus we argue that the structured–unstructured continuum of the original framework can be thought of using these four elements. A problem is fully structured when all four elements are well understood and fully unstructured when the four remain vague. Such a categorization helps us to match classes of systems with types of problems, as illustrated in Figure 6.

For some problems we can apply a standard procedure (i.e., an algorithm or formula) and proceed directly to a conclusion with no need for flexible problem-solving strategies. For example, we can use standard procedures to compute withholding taxes and prepare employee paychecks and we can use the classical economic order quantity formula to solve straightforward inventory control problems. In other cases a solution can be found only by identifying alternative approaches, and thinking through (in some cases via simulation) the effects of these alternative courses of action. One then chooses the approach that appears to create the best result. For example, to determine which of three sales strategies to use for a new product, a manager might want to explore the consequences of each for advertising expenses, sales force utilization, revenue, and so forth. In the remainder of this section we will discuss the range of these different types of problems and the appropriate kinds of systems for each.

Type I Problems—Data Processing

A fully structured problem is one in which all of the elements of the problem are structured. That is, we have well-stated goals, and we can specify the input data needed, and there are standard procedures by which a solution may be calculated. No complex strategies for generating and evaluating alternatives are needed. Fully structured problems are computable and one can decide if such computation is justifiable, given the amounts of time and computing resource involved.

These problems are well suited to the use of conventional programming techniques. In conventional programming, virtually everything about the problem is well defined. In effect, the expert (i.e., the analyst/programmer) has already solved the problem. He or she must only sequence the data through the particular program. Figure 6 represents pictorially the class of decision problems that can be solved economically using conventional programming techniques. We will refer to this class as Type I problems, problems historically thought of as ones suited for data processing.

It is interesting to note that the economics of conventional programming are being fundamentally altered with the provision of new tools such as an "analyst's workbench" (14). These are professional work stations used by the systems analyst to develop flowchart representations of the problem and then move automatically to testable, running code. The more advanced of these stations happen to use AI techniques, thus turning these new techniques into tools to make our old approaches more effective in classical DP application areas.

Type II Problems—Decision Support Systems

As we leave problems which are fully structured we begin to deal with many of the problems organizations have to grapple with each day. These are cases where standard procedures are helpful but not sufficient by themselves, where the data may be incompletely represented, and where the goals and constraints are only partially understood. Traditional data processing systems cannot solve these problems. Fortunately, we have the possibility in these cases, of letting the computer perform the well-understood parts of the problem solving, while relying on humans to use their goals, intuition, and general knowledge to formulate problems, modify and control the problem solving, and interpret the results. As Figure 6 shows, the human users may provide or modify data, procedures or goals, and they may use their knowledge of all these factors to decide on problem-solving strategies.

In many of the best-known decision support systems (11) for example, the computer applies standard procedures to certain highly structured data but relies on the human users to decide which procedures are appropriate in a given situation and whether a given result is satisfactory or not. For example, the investment managers who used the portfolio management system (11) did not rely on the computer for either making final decisions about portfolio composition or for deciding on which procedures to use analysis. They used the computer to execute the procedures they felt were appropriate, for example calculating portfolio diversity and expected returns, but the managers themselves proposed alternative portfolios and decided whether a given diversification or return was acceptable. Many people who use spreadsheet programs today for "what if" analyses follow a similar flexible strategy of proposing an action, letting the computer predict its consequences and then deciding what action to propose next.

Type III—Expert Systems

Using AI programming techniques like production rules and frames, expert systems are able to encode some of the same kinds of goals, heuristics, and strategies that people use in solving problems but that have previously been very difficult to use in computer programs. These techniques make it possible to design systems that don't just follow standard procedures, but instead use flexible problem-solving strategies to explore a number of possible alternatives before picking a solution.

For some cases, like the XCON system, these techniques can capture almost all the relevant knowledge about the problem. As of 1983, fewer than one out of every 1,000 orders configured by XCON was misconfigured because of missing or incorrect rules. Only about 10 percent of the orders had to be corrected for any reason at all and almost all of these errors were due to missing descriptions of rarely used parts (4).

We call the problems where essentially all the relevant knowledge for flexible problem solving can be encoded Type III problems. The systems that solve them are Expert Systems.

It is instructive to note, however, that even with XCON, which is probably the most extensively tested system in commercial use today, new knowledge is continually being added and humans still check every order the system configures. As the developers of XCON remark:

> There is no more reason to believe now than there was [in 1979] that [XCON] has all the knowledge relevant to its configuration task. This, coupled with the fact that [XCON] deals with an ever changing domain implies its development will never be finished. (4, p. 27)

If XCON, which operates in the fairly restricted domain of computer order configuration, never contains all the knowledge relevant to its problem, it appears much less likely that we will ever be able to codify all the knowledge needed for less clearly bounded problems such as financial analysis, strategic planning, and project management. Even in what might appear to be the fairly simple case of job shop scheduling, there are often very many continually changing and possibly implicit constraints on what people, machines, and parts are needed and available for different steps in a manufacturing process (7).

What this suggests is that for very many of the problems of practical importance in business we should focus our attention on designing systems that *support* expert users rather than replace them.

Type IV—Expert Support Systems

Even in situations where important kinds of problem-solving knowledge, in all four areas of the problem cannot feasibly be encoded, it is still possible to use Expert Systems techniques. This dramatically extends the capabilities of computers beyond previous technologies such as DP and DSS.

What is important, in these cases, is to design Expert Support Systems (see Figure 6) with very good and deeply embedded "user interfaces" that enable their human users to easily inspect and control the problem-solving process. In other words, a good Expert Support System should be both *accessible* and *malleable*. Many Expert Support Systems make their problem-solving process accessible to users by providing explanation capabilities. For example, the MYCIN medical diagnosis program can explain to a doctor at any time why it is asking for a given piece of information or what rules it used to arrive at a given conclusion. For a system to be malleable, users should be able to easily change data, procedures, goals, or strategies at any important point in the problem-solving process. Systems with this capability are still rare, but an early version of the Dipmeter Advisor suggests how it might be provided (5). In this version there was no satisfactory way to automatically detect certain kinds of geological patterns, so human experts used a graphical display of the data to mark and annotate these patterns. The system then continued its analysis using this information.

An even more vivid example of how a system can be made accessible and malleable is provided by the Steamer Program (10) for teaching people to reason about operating a steam plant. This system has colorful graphic displays of the schematic flows in the simulated plant, the status of different valves and gauges, and the pressures in different places. Users of the system can manipulate these displays (using a "mouse" pointing device) to control the valves, temperatures, and so forth. The system continually updates its simulation results and expert diagnostics based on these user actions.

Summary of Framework

This framework helps clarify a number of issues. First, it highlights, as did the original Gorry and Scott Morton framework, the importance of matching system type to problem type. In the original 1971 article, however, the primary practical points to be made were that traditional DP technologies should not be used for semistructured and unstructured problems where new DSS technologies were more appropriate; secondly, that interactive human/computer use opened up an extended class of problems where computers could be usefully exploited. The most important practical point to be made today is again twofold: first, that "pure" Expert Systems should not be used for partially understood problems where Expert Support Systems are more appropriate, and second, that Expert Systems techniques can be used to dramatically extend the capabilities of traditional decision support systems.

Figure 7 shows, in an admittedly simplified way, how we can view expert support systems as the next logical step in each of

FIGURE 7   Progressions in Computer System Development

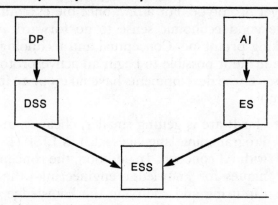

two somewhat separate progressions. On the left side of the figure, we see that DSS developed out of a practical recognition of the limits of DP for helping real human beings solve complex problems in actual organizations. The right side of the figure reflects a largely independent evolution that took place in computer science research laboratories and that developed from a recognition of the limits of traditional computer science techniques for solving the kinds of complex problems that people are able to solve. We are now at the point where these two separate progressions can be united to help solve a broad range of important practical problems.

THE IMPORTANCE OF EXPERT SUPPORT SYSTEMS FOR MANAGEMENT

The real importance of ESS lies in the ability of these systems to harness and make full use of our scarcest resource: the talent and experience of key members of the organization. There can be considerable benefits in capturing the expert's experience and making it available to those in an organization that are less expert in the subject in question.

As organizations and their problems become more complex, management can benefit from initiating prototype ES and ESSs. The question now facing managers is when to start, and in which areas.

The "when" to start is relatively easy to answer. It is 'now' for exploratory work. For some organizations this will be a program of education and active monitoring of the field. For others the initial investment may take the form of an experimental low-budget prototype. For a few, once the exploration is over, it will make good economic sense to go forward with a full-fledged working prototype. Conceptual and technological developments have made it possible to begin an active prototype development phase. These developments have taken place in several areas, for example:

- Hardware is getting smaller, cheaper, and more powerful. Programming languages such as LISP (18) enable us to deal with AI concepts. In addition, the concepts, tools, and techniques for knowledge engineering—the work involved in capturing and codifying the knowledge of an expert—are beginning to be understood. AI research has always been characterized by its need for large amounts of computing resources. As the cost of hardware becomes irrelevant to the economics of problem solution, the techniques of AI are becoming more economically viable.
- As companies begin to install global communications networks of either the broad or narrow band varieties, possibilities abound for the collection and interpretation of data. In some organizations, this development will provide the potential for enhanced decision making and the opportunity for effective use of AI techniques.
- The recent proliferation of firms offering specialized AI services has resulted in the creation of new software and an increasingly large group of knowledge engineers. Some have started companies and are hiring and training people who are focusing on business applications (3).

The second question facing managers is the one of where to start. One possible area for initial experimentation is the productive use of an organization's assets. In what looks to be a decade of low growth, it will be essential to acquire and use assets astutely. Digital Equipment Corporation's use of an Expert System for "equipment configuration control" is one example. A second sensible place in which to begin using AI is in those areas in which the organization stands to gain a distinct competitive advantage. Schlumberger would seem to feel that their ES used as a drilling advisor is one such example.

It is interesting that of the more than 20 organizations personally known to the authors to be investing in work in ES and

ESS almost none would allow themselves to be quoted. The reasons given basically boiled down to the fact that they were experimenting with prototypes that they were expecting to give them a competitive advantage in making or delivering their product or service. Examples of this where we can quote without attribution are cases such as an ESS for supporting the cross selling of financial services products, such as an insurance salesman selling a tax shelter. In another case it is the desire of a financial services organization to evaluate the credit worthiness of a loan applicant.

It is clear that there are a great many problem areas where even our somewhat primitive ability to deal with ES can permit the building of useful first generation systems. With ESS the situation is even brighter, as any help we can provide the beleaguered "expert" will provide leverage for the organization.

The Problems, Risks, and Issues

It would be irresponsible to conclude this article without commenting on the fact that Expert Systems and Expert Support Systems are in their infancy, and researchers and users alike must be realistic about the capabilities of these new systems. One risk, already apparent, is that the expert systems will be poorly defined and oversold, and the resulting backlash will hinder progress. It can be argued that the Western economies lost the most recent round on the economic battlefield to Japan, due in part to their failure to manage productivity and quality, as well as their inability to select the markets in which they wished to excel. We face a similar risk with Expert Systems and their applications, and if we are careless we will lose out in exploiting this particular potential of the information era.

There is a danger of proceeding too quickly, too recklessly, without paying careful attention to what we are doing. One example is that we may well embed our knowledge (necessarily incomplete at any moment in time) into a system that is effective when used by the person who created it. When this same system is used by others, however, there is a risk of misapplication; holes in another user's knowledge could represent a pivotal element in the logic leading to a solution. While these holes are implicitly recognized by the creator of the knowledge base, they may be quite invisible to a new user of the knowledge base.

The challenge of proceeding at an appropriate pace can be met if managers treat the subject of Artificial Intelligence, Expert Systems, Expert Support Systems, and Decision Support Systems as a serious topic which will require management attention if it is to be exploited properly. Managers must recognize the differences between Type I and II problems, for which the older techniques are appropriate, and the new methods available for Types III and IV.

CONCLUSIONS

There are, then, some basic risks and constraints which will be with us for some time. However, the potential of AI techniques are obvious, and if we proceed cautiously, acknowledging the problems, we can begin to achieve worthwhile results.

The illustrations used here are merely two of some 15 or 20 that have been described in some detail (see References) and have been built in a relatively brief period of time with primitive tools. This is a start-up phase for Expert Systems and Expert Support Systems: Phase Zero. Business has attempted to develop expert systems applications since 1980 and, despite the magnitude of some of the problems, has succeeded in developing a number of simple and powerful prototypes.

The state of the art is such that everyone building an expert system must endure this primitive start-up phase in order to learn what is involved in this fascinating new field. We expect that it will take until about 1990 for ES and ESS to be fully recognized as having achieved worthwhile business results.

However, Expert Systems and Expert Support Systems are with us now, albeit in a primitive form. The challenge for management is to harness these tools to increase the effectiveness of the organization and thus add value for its stakeholders. The pioneering firms are leading the way; once a section of territory has been staked out, the experience gained by these leaders will be hard to equal. The time to examine the options carefully is now.

REFERENCES

1. Alexander, T. "The Next Revolution in Computer Programming." *Fortune*, October 29, 1984, pp. 81–86.
2. Anthony, R. N. "Planning and Control Systems: A Framework for

Analysis." Boston: Harvard University Graduate School of Business Administration, 1965.

3. *Business Week.* "Artificial Intelligence: The Second Computer Age Begins." March 3, 1982.

4. Bachant, J., and J. McDermott. "R1 Revisited: Four Years in the Trenches." *AI Magazine,* Fall 1984. pp. 21–32.

5. Davis, R.; H. Austin; I. Carlborn; B. Frawley; P. Pruchnik; R. Sneiderman; and J. A. Gilreath. "The Dipmeter Advisor: Interpretation of Geological Signals." In *Proceedings of the Seventh International Joint Conference on Artificial Intelligence,* Vancouver, Canada: 1981, pp. 846–49.

6. *Fortune,* "Teaching Computers the Art of Reason." May 17, 1982, and "Computers on the Road to Self-Improvement," June 14, 1982.

7. Fox, M. S., "Constraint-Directed Search: A Case Study of Job-Shop Scheduling." Technical Report No. CMU-RI-TR-83-22, Carnegie-Mellon University Robotics Institute, Pittsburgh, Pa., 1983.

8. Gorry, Anthony, and Michael S. Scott Morton. "A Framework for Management Information Systems." *Sloan Management Review* 13, no. 1 (Fall 1971).

9. Hayes-Roth, Frederick; Donald A. Waterman; and Douglas B. Lenat, eds., *Building Expert Systems.* Reading, Mass.: Addison-Wesley, 1983.

10. Hollan, J. D.; E. L. Hutchins; and L. Weitzman. "Steamer: An Interactive, Inspectable Simulation-Based Training System." *AI Magazine,* Summer 1984, pp. 15–28.

11. Keen, Peter, and Michael S. Scott Morton. *Decision Support Systems: An Organizational Perspective.* Reading, Mass.: Addison-Wesley, 1978.

12. McDermott, John. "R1: A Rule-Based Configurer of Computer Systems." *Artificial Intelligence* 19, no. 1 (1982).

13. Newell, A. "Reasoning: Problem Solving and Decision Processes: The Problem Space As a Fundamental Category." In *Attention and Performance VIII,* ed. R. Nickerson. Hillsdale, N.J.: Erlbaum, 1980.

14. B. Sheil. "Power Tools for Programmers." *Datamation,* February 1983, pp. 131–44.

15. Simon, Herbert A. *The New Science of Management Decision.* New York: Harper & Row, 1960.

16. Winston, Patrick Henry. *Artificial Intelligence,* 2d ed. Reading, Mass.: Addison-Wesley, 1984, 1977.

17. ———. p. 88, 132–34.

18. Hayes-Roth. Chaps. 5, 6, 9.

Chapter Eighteen
The Role of the
Executive
in the New Computer Era

JOHN F. ROCKART

We are now in the early stages of "the third era" of computer utilization. This new era is not a mild evolution from its predecessors. Rather it is an abrupt revolution in the ways that computers can be utilized in the corporation. Most important, the third era's capabilities are putting significant demands on corporate executive leadership.

Corporate management has in almost all cases in the past, in effect said, "Let Harry do it." Responsibility for use and management of the computer resource was delegated to the "Harrys" of this world—the Information Systems Managers. Today, for a number of reasons, this position is no longer tenable. In my opinion, executive management must now be involved. There are a number of reasons for this. The computer and communication resource has now become integral to many companies' strategies. There is an excessive demand for computer resources on the part of all in the organization. Information systems people are, in general, poorly equipped to meet the new technological challenges, and, finally, the new era demands many new corporate policies which must be set at the highest level.

There are six key trends which, to my mind, are basic in understanding what has brought about this new era. A description of these trends and of the era will be followed by a discussion of

This paper is the text of a presentation delivered at the Symposium for Senior Executives, MIT Industrial Liaison Program, June 1983. Center for Information Systems Research Working Paper No. 105, Sloan School of Management, MIT, Cambridge, Mass., June 1983.

three major management implications. These are (1) a need to manage the end user computing environment, (2) a need to rethink the changing role of corporate I/S management, and (3) the need for executive involvement and leadership with regard to the computer/communications resource.

SIX KEY TRENDS

For the executive concerned with the computer resource there are six major trends which are of most significance. These are:

1. Decreasing hardware unit costs. The costs of computer hardware have decreased by 20–30 percent per year over the past two decades and will continue to do so for the foreseeable future. Thus, raw computer power, as demonstrated most recently by the personal computer, is rapidly coming within the cost–beneficial reach of almost everyone in the corporation.

2. Inflation. This needs no discussion. The cost of "labor" of all types in the corporation has increased vastly over the past two decades and will, it appears, continue to do so although perhaps at a somewhat reduced rate. This clearly encourages the use of computer-based systems to replace, or assist, people wherever possible.

3. Cost of communications. Communication costs have decreased somewhat, over the last several years, but not nearly at the same rate as the reduction in hardware unit costs. This ratio, together with the far better response-time characteristics of "local" machines as opposed to remote centralized systems, has enhanced the trend toward increasingly "local" systems and a move away from the centralized computing credo of yesterday.

4. Software development costs. The unit costs of producing software, affected both by increasing labor costs and ever better programming tools, has stayed approximately stable. The greatest hope in this area is the development of increasingly better tools for use by end users to "program" their access to data, thus eliminating the need for involvement with a professional I/S group wherever possible.

5. New technology. New computer technology—hardware and software alike—is being delivered to the market today at an ever increasing rate. This is enabling the development of a significant number of applications previously not feasible.

6. User demand. Given all the conditions above, the demand to make use of the computer/communications resource by managers and others at all levels in the corporation has skyrocketed. Dealing today with inflation, quality questions, and a need for increased productivity, managers increasingly perceive an absolute imperative to make use of the computer in all aspects of the value-added chain in the corporation.

THE THIRD ERA

The above trends have jointly led to a new era in computing. We have, in fact, progressed through three different eras of computing usage (see Figure 1). The first two were essentially concerned with automating the *paperwork-processing* functions of the firm. In the first era, computer systems were installed primarily to automate accounting functions. Payroll systems, accounts payable, and general ledger systems were instituted on increasingly powerful computer systems throughout the world. Because computer hardware was expensive, systems and the personnel to operate them were centralized to obtain higher productivity. A set of tools such as project management tools were developed. COBOL was determined as the key computer language. The data processing managers were "line" managers with all their people reporting directly to them.

In the second era the emphasis changed from systems serving the accountant to those designed to assist first-line operations personnel. Applications in this era included manufacturing control systems and on-line order-entry systems. As with the first, most of the second wave of systems merely enabled companies to do what they had previously done with regard to paperwork processing in a faster more accurate manner. However, the on-line nature of these applications, and the need to access—in most cases—only *local* databases, tended to move the computer systems closer to their users. We moved from an era in which "centralized" computing was paramount to one in which "distributed" computing, utilizing both central and local machines, became the norm. Moreover, in the second era, as the applications changed, the process of information systems management also changed. In this second era, as computers were distributed throughout the company, so were information systems personnel. The Director of Information Systems thus had to become a *matrix* manager with a "dotted-line" relationship to distributed information system personnel and all the problems inherent in

FIGURE 1   The Three Eras of Computing

Era	Applications	Hardware	I/S Tools	I/S Management
(1) Accounting	Payroll Accounts payable General ledger	Centralized Maxis Batch	Project management Capacity management COBOL	Line
(2) Operations	Order-entry Manufac-turing control	Decentralized Minis On-line	Project management Capacity management COBOL	Matrix
(3) Information	DSS XSS ?	Centralized/decentral-ized On-line	Evolutionary design Budget RAMIS, FOCUS, et al.	Matrix Staff Support Everyone a user

such an organization structure. The process of I/S management thus became much more complex.

During the past several years, however, a "third wave" of computer applications has begun in earnest. Following the "accounting" and "operational" systems eras, this new era of applications can be termed *the information-communication application era.* As opposed to paperwork processing, these applications are concerned with both access to and use of *information* and *communication* within an organization. The previous application era served the lower levels of corporations. Today, third era applications serve middle management, key staff personnel, and even the executive suite. The applications, which include decision support systems, executive support systems, end user computing of all types, electronic mail, and computer conferencing are unique and significant in several ways. These are:

- The procedures (for decision making and other uses) exist primarily in the minds of the managers and staff personnel who utilize them.
- It is impossible to justify these applications in traditional cost/benefit ways.
- Traditional means of systems development—through well-

defined project management techniques—are no longer applicable.

- The software languages being utilized are an entirely new breed—often not understood by the majority of information systems personnel.
- Significantly higher quality information systems personnel are necessary to work with these applications than were required in the past.
- Demand for access to data and the ability to communicate with those in the corporation is coming from all quarters of the corporation, as opposed to being centered in one or more paperwork-processing clerical groups.

In short, we are in a vastly new era whose tools, techniques, and managerial demands on the corporation are significantly different. Demands for this sort of computing are growing at 50 to 100 percent a year in most organizations today, approximately 5 to 10 times faster than the more traditional applications. What is more, there are a significant number of trends which are accelerating this demand. These trends, noted in Figure 2, can be summarized into: technical factors, more computer-savvy managers, and business conditions which are leading to the increased use of information and an increased need for communication.

INFORMATION DATABASES

One major result of the "third wave" of applications is the development of a "third environment" for computing. In the past, the information systems organization has supported two strikingly different environments. One is the "COBOL" environment in which the data processing shop has had full command. It designs the applications, programs them, schedules them, and runs them. In addition it has full responsibility for database maintenance and all other aspects of these systems. In the second, or time-sharing environment, to the contrary, the information systems group merely provides available hardware and software languages. The user does everything else—his own programming, running, database maintenance, etc.

The growth of significant end user computing has necessitated a third environment. In this environment, users and informations systems jointly share the responsibility for the develop-

---

**FIGURE 2   Factors Accelerating the Demand for Third Era End User
Computing and Communication**

Technical Factors

Vastly improved end user software
Microcomputers
Electronic mail, office systems
Hardware cost
User frustration with Cobol-based systems
Availability external databases
Availability internal databases
"Programmer" availability

More Computer-Savvy Managers

New generation of users
Salesman direct calls
Managerial journals
Demonstration effect

Business Conditions

Interest rates
Inflation
International competition
Need for improved planning and control

---

ment and operation of systems. In general, these systems are large departmental or corporate-wide databases, supporting users in such areas as market research, personnel, or the executive suite. For these systems, the information systems organization maintains the database, provides a continuously available operating environment, and assures that network communication is available. The users, however, do all the rest. They develop their own programs and run the systems when they so desire. Many of the "programs" are simple accesses to the database, although some are used for deeper analysis.

This third, or "shared," environment is becoming a more and more significant part of the information systems scene. It relies on several new tools, most particularly, end user languages and relational or pseudo-relational databases. It demands cooperation between users and the information systems organization to a degree previously unknown in the first two environments. Finally, it requires new policy guidelines.

Major examples of these third environment systems can be found both in staff areas and at the executive level. One example is IBM's market research system, a system now including in excess of nine billion characters of data concerning customers, industries, and economic conditions worldwide. The system is accessed by more than a thousand people concerned with marketing throughout IBM who utilize two end user tools, APL/DI and APL. A second example, a superb example of an executive database, used by the entire corporate office, is found at Northwest Industries (Rockart and Treacy, 1982). There, Ben Heineman, the Chief Executive Officer, other top line personnel, and the key corporate staffs all access a large database, including both internal data on Northwest Industries and its subsidiaries and external data on Northwest's competitors, industries, and the economy as a whole.

MANAGERIAL IMPLICATIONS

The third era is a revolution in computing. It has created a new computing environment, it utilizes totally new tools and techniques, and—most important—has provided users, for the first time, with direct access to computing power. For top executives there are three significant implications of this era. These are (a) the need to develop new rules, processes, and organizational structures to manage end user computing, (b) the need to rethink the role of corporate information systems management; and (c) the need for executive leadership and involvement.

For the information systems department the *management of end user computing* is an entirely new ball game. To spread the use of information systems from a few major "customers" (such as the people responsible for payroll, accounts payable, etc.) to the entire organization requires a new information systems organization structure, a new strategy, and new methods for support of users—in an era in which practically everyone in the organization will have a terminal on his or her desk. This task for the information systems department is akin only to a company moving from the industrial sales market (with a few major customers) to retail sales. An entirely new organization must be developed, with new marketing channels and entirely new methods of field support. Some major organizations have faced this new challenge directly. Most, however, have not.

In like manner, the role of the Chief Corporate Information Systems Executive has changed significantly in the new era. Often, he is no longer a *line* head of a computing organization but a *staff* person in the corporation. With ever more widespread computing, he must give up his role as the direct czar of computer resources. Rather, he must move into a role of providing staff expertise, guidelines, and policies so that almost totally decentralized computing organizations will be able to carry out their tasks and support their end users in appropriate ways. Most important, corporate strategies are now becoming increasingly dependent upon effective use of computer and communication potentials. As a result, a major segment of the role of the new corporate Chief Information Officer is concerned with providing expert advice to the top executive group as to the potential opportunities available through the technology to improve, redirect, or substantially change existing corporate strategies.

In this new era, corporate executives can no longer afford to "let Harry do it." One major reason for involvement is to ensure that the most appropriate use is being made of the new computer and communication technology in the development of corporate strategy. Another reason is to ensure that the corporation is not bogged down in first and second era use of computing without paying enough attention to less easily justified but extremely critical third era computing. Furthermore, there is a need for new corporate policies as a result of the increasingly widespread access to data engendered by the third era. New privacy and security policies must be originated. And, corporate policy with regard to new justification methods and levels of investment in computer-based technology must be ascertained.

A final major reason for executive involvement in computing today is the opportunity for top executives to define, for the first time, their own information needs. Techniques we have developed at the Sloan School (Rockart, 1979; Bullen and Rockart, 1981) have been found to be very useful in doing so. For the first time, there is an opportunity for senior executives to be able to get to the data they need when they need it. To gain this facility, top management must invest both time and energy to capitalize on this opportunity. A growing number of senior executives are doing so at this time.

REFERENCES

1. Rockart, John F., and Michael E. Treacy. "CEO Goes On-Line." *Harvard Business Review,* January–February 1982.

2. Rockart, John F. "Chief Executives Define Their Own Needs." *Harvard Business Review,* March–April 1979.

3. Bullen Christine V., and John F. Rockart. "A Primer on Critical Success Factors." CISR Working Paper No. 69, Sloan School of Management, MIT, Cambridge, Mass., June 1981.

APPENDIX

A Primer on Critical Success Factors

CHRISTINE V. BULLEN
JOHN F. ROCKART

I. INTRODUCTION

Faced with an increasingly complex world, managers today are deciding that they need access to the information which is pertinent to their particular roles and responsibilities. One method of determining precisely what information is most needed is the "critical success factors" (CSF) method. Introduced in a *Harvard Business Review* article entitled "Chief Executives Define Their Own Data Needs" (1), the CSF method is now being utilized in a growing number of organizations. This paper is written to provide additional background on the method. Most particularly, it is written as a primer for those who would like to carry out CSF interviews.

Critical success factors are the few key areas of activity in which favorable results are absolutely necessary for a particular manager to reach his goals. Because these areas of activity are critical, the manager should have the appropriate information to allow him to determine whether events are proceeding sufficiently well in each area. The CSF interview method is designed to provide a structured technique which can be used by an interviewer to assist managers to zero in on their critical success factors—and to determine the resulting information needs.

In order to gain a complete understanding of the CSF technique and its application, the reader should be thoroughly familiar with the original *Harvard Business Review* article. This primer

Center for Information Systems Research Working Paper No. 69, Sloan School of Management, MIT, Cambridge, Mass., June 1981.

assumes such a familiarity. Where appropriate, the material presented here references that article rather than repeating ideas.

This document contains three substantive parts following this introduction. First there are definitions and general background information on the critical success factor concept. The next section details the interview procedure. It emphasizes appropriate techniques for the interviewer to use in helping interviewees to think about and identify their CSFs. The final section concerns methods of analyzing the data.

The interview procedure section (III) contains those techniques which we have found, in three years of using the method, to be most successful in drawing out CSFs. The two most important ingredients in successful CSF interviews, however, are the *preparation* and *skills* which the interviewer brings to the interview itself. The interviewer must be thoroughly prepared. He must have as deep as possible an understanding of the industry, the specific company, and the job being performed by the manager being interviewed. In addition, the interviewer should (through training or experience) have a command of basic interviewing skills.

The CSF interview involves a lively exchange of ideas. The interviewer must be comfortable in her preparation and energetic in her participation. In sum, the interviewer must have all the attributes and preparation of a good consultant. The more consulting skills that one brings to the task, the better the interview will be. Given this requisite preparation, the interviewer will find the CSF method to be readily acceptable, interesting, thought-provoking, and enjoyable.

One of the important strengths of the CSF method is that it provides the interviewer with a logical way of relating to, and understanding, the managers who are interviewed. Managers think in the terms used in the CSF interview. As a result, the CSF method allows the interviewer to comfortably extract the manager's view of the world. Most important, it enables the manager to easily identify those few matters which demand continuing scrutiny by him. The process, therefore, ultimately provides the interviewer with an understanding of what information will *really* be perceived as useful (and actually used) by each manager.

The CSF method is also of direct and immediate use to the interviewed manager. It assists her to explicitly focus attention on what is really important. All good managers have *implicit* CSFs which they have been using, most often subconsciously, to help them to manage throughout their careers. The interview method helps make these critical factors *explicit*. Once the CSFs are explicit, managerial priorities can be set more knowledgeably and improved allocation of the manager's resources, especially time, can be made. This result from a CSF interview is useful and can be accomplished far before the requisite information systems can be built.

The words *critical success factors* are beginning to take their place with other basic terms concerned with the management of an organization. Like goals and objectives, CSFs appear at various levels in the management hierarchy. The next section therefore is aimed at placing the CSFs in their managerial context. Since this is written *as a primer,* we have tried to err on the side of oversimplicity. Some readers may wish to hurry through the next section where the material is very basic. CSFs and other managerial terms such as *strategy, goals,* and *objectives,* will be defined, compared, and contrasted. The CSF concept will be explored from many viewpoints. Finally, the hierarchical nature of CSFs will be illustrated through a set of examples.

II. DEFINITIONS AND CONCEPTS

The first part of this section defines critical success factors and places them within the perspective of basic terms concerned with the management of the organization. We then go on, in Part B, to provide additional conceptual background concerning critical success factors.

A. Definitions

1. *Critical Success Factors* (CSFs).   CSFs are the limited number of areas in which satisfactory results will ensure successful competitive performance for the individual, department, or organization. CSFs are the few key areas where "things must go right" for the business to flourish and for the manager's goals to be attained.

2. *Strategy.*   Strategy is the pattern of missions, objectives, policies, and significant resource utilization plans stated in such a way as to define what business the company is in (or is to be in) and the kind of company it is or is to be. A complete statement of strategy will define the product line, the markets and market segments for which products are to be designed, the channels through which these markets

will be reached, the means by which the operation is to be financed, the profit objectives, the size of the organizaiton, and the "image" which it will project to employees, suppliers, and customers.

3. *Objectives.* Objectives are general statements about the directions in which a firm intends to go, without stating specific targets to be reached at particular points in time.

4. *Goals.* Goals are specific targets which are intended to be reached at a given point in time. A goal is thus an operational transformation of one or more objectives.

5. *Measures.* Measures are specific standards which allow the calibration of performance for each critical success factor, goal, or objective. Measures can be either "soft"—that is, subjective and qualitative—or "hard"—that is, objective and quantitative.

6. *Problems.* Problems are specific tasks rising to importance as a result of unsatisfactory performance or environmental changes. Problems can affect the achievement of goals or performance in a CSF area.

Figure 1 summarizes the above definitions and uses an airline company example to illustrate the relationship among the six terms. Figure 2 notes, although in an overly simplistic way, the hierarchy of relationships of each of these terms from the viewpoint of an individual line manager. (The interlinking of strategy and objectives at the corporate level is shown by including them in the same box. The remainder of the concepts fall hierarchically.)

B. General Background on CSFs

This section is aimed at providing a fuller understanding for the reader of what CSFs are and their role in the management process. Building on the definitions provided in the preceding section, this section will explore:

1. The nature of CSFs.
2. The uses of the CSF concept with special attention to its key purpose—information systems planning.

1. The Nature of CSFs

Terms such as *goals* and *strategy* have a long and honored tradition in management literature. Their definitions are relatively

FIGURE 1   Comparison of Basic Terms in Airline Company Context

Term	Brief Definition	Brief Examples
Strategy	Basic decision of "What business are we in?"	Regional airline transportion
Objectives	General directional statements	Develop profitable route structure
		Change over to more fuel-efficient fleet
Goals	Specific targets for a period of time	Eliminate all routes with less than "N" percent average seat usage
		By year-end replace all "X" planes with "Y" planes
		Provide stockholders with 10 percent return on investment in 1981
CSFs	Key areas where things must go right in order to successfully achieve objectives and goals	Obtain certification for higher-density routes
		Develop bank financing for new equipment
Measures	Calibrations of performance	Average percent seat capacity used
		Percent of cash requirements under written, equipment loan agreements with banks
Problems	Tasks resulting from unsatisfactory performance or the environment	Increasing price of fuel
		Future competition from video-conferencing

precise today and the concepts are well understood. The same is not true of CSFs. What is or is not a critical success factor for any particular manager is a subjective judgment arrived at only after some thought. There is no clear algorithm which will aid an interviewer to assist a manager to find his CSFs.

Yet managers can, and do, determine their critical success factors. For those who have some difficulty in isolating their CSFs, a well-prepared, knowledgeable interviewer can assist greatly in the CSF-determination process. This section is designed to provide as much background as possible for potential CSF interviewers as to the "nature of the beast" with which they are dealing. Its aim is to supplement the material concerning the nature of CSFs found in the original *Harvard Business Review* article. We include material concerning:

FIGURE 2   Hierarchy of Management Concepts and Terms

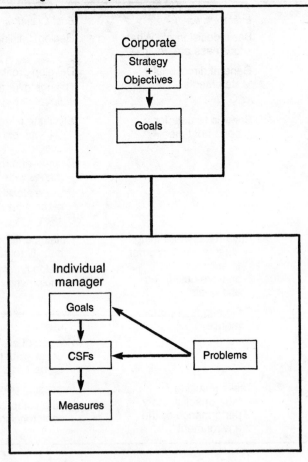

- The importance of CSFs.
- The need to "tailor" CSFs and information requirements to each individual manager's uniquely different situation.
- The sources of CSFs.
- A useful classification of CSFs.
- The hierarchical nature of CSFs.
- Examples of CSFs.

Let us look at each of these in turn.

a. The Importance of CSFs.   Critical success factors are the relatively small number of truly important matters on which a manager should focus her attention. For this reason, the term "critical success factors" is aptly chosen. They represent the few "factors" which are "critical" to the "success" of the manager concerned. There are, in every manager's life, an incredible number of things to which her attention can be diverted. The key to success for most managers is to focus their most limited resource (their time) on those things which really make the difference between success and failure.

In general, there are, for any manager, only a very limited number of critical success factors. Examples are given in the original article. Additional examples will be found in the final part of this section of this paper. For most managers this limited set of important factors is far from a mystery. Most managers spend considerable time and energy both on the job *and* in their leisure hours thinking about these few areas of activity which are "close to the bone." Much time is spent considering ways to improve performance in each of these areas. The value of the CSF process is to make these areas *explicit*, not merely implicit. They then can be used (as will be discussed more fully later) to aid in the company's planning process, to enhance communication among the firm's management, and to aid information systems development.

It is important for a manager to determine his goals—which are the targets he will shoot for. That is common managerial lore. It is equally important, however, to determine, in a conscious explicit manner, what the basic structural variables are which will most affect his success or failure in the pursuit of these goals. These are the critical success factors.

Critical success factors are of sufficient importance that these key areas of activities should receive constant and careful attention from management. The current status of performance in each area should be continually measured and status information should be made accessible for management's use.

b. Different Managers—Different CSFs—Different Information. CSFs are related to the specifics of a particular manager's situation. This means they must be tailored to the industry, the company, and the individual being interviewed. CSFs will certainly differ from manager to manager according to the individual's place in the organization's hierarchy. In addition, they often will change as the industry's environment changes, as the company's position within an industry changes, or as particular problems or opportunities arise for a particular manager.

In this light, it is important to understand what CSFs are not. They are *not* a standard set of measures, sometimes called "key indicators," which can be applied to all divisions of a company. They are *not* limited to factors which can be reported on by solely historical, aggregated, accounting information. On the contrary, the critical success factor method looks at the world from a manager's current operating viewpoint. CSFs are the particular areas of major importance to a *particular* manager, in a *particular* division, at a *particular* point in time. They therefore demand specific and diverse situational measures, many of which must be evaluated through soft, subjective information not currently gathered in an explicit formal way by the manager's organization. No standard set of organization-wide "key indicators" can provide the necessary operating information.

   c. Five Prime Sources of CSFs. CSFs arise from five major sources which should be researched by a potential CSF interviewer during the preparation for a series of interviews. The sources of CSFs are:

1. *The industry.* Each industry has a set of critical success factors that are determined by the characteristics of the industry itself. Each company in the industry must pay attention to these factors. For example, from the *Harvard Business Review* article, there are four CSFs for the supermarket industry. The manager of each and every supermarket firm must be concerned about these four. They are product mix, inventory, sales promotion, price. The rationale behind this industry set can be found in the referenced article.

2. *Competitive strategy and industry position.* Each company within an industry is in an individual situation determined by its history and current competitive strategy. The company's resulting position in the industry dictates some CSFs. For example, a small company in an industry must almost always be concerned about protecting its particular industry niche. Similarly, in an industry dominated by a single major firm, a CSF for all the others is understanding the leader's strategies and their probable impacts. In like manner, the geographic positioning of the company can also generate CSFs. For example, retail firms in rural areas may have transportation management as a CSF while for more urban companies this is less critical.

3. *Environmental factors.* Environmental factors are those areas over which an organization has little control. The organi-

zation must accomplish its mission while riding the tides of environmental change. Two obvious environmental sources of CSFs are the fluctuations of the economy and national politics. Some companies are sensitive to additional factors such as population trends, regulatory trends, and energy sources.

4. *Temporal factors.* These are areas of activity within an organization which become critical for a particular period of time because something out of the ordinary has taken place. Normally these areas would not generate CSFs. For example, a crisis such as the loss of a large number of executives in an airplane crash would generate the short-term CSF of "rebuilding the executive group." Similarly, while inventory control would not normally appear on the list of CSFs for a CEO, it could become a CSF for him under extreme circumstances of over- or understocking.

5. *Managerial position.* Each functional managerial position has a generic set of CSFs associated with it. For example, almost all manufacturing managers are concerned with product quality, inventory control, and cash control.

d. A Useful Classification of CSFs. One useful way of looking at CSFs is illustrated in Figure 3. Each CSF can be classified along three major dimensions. These are (1) internal versus external, (2) monitoring versus building-adapting, and (3) all the five sources discussed just above. All three dimensions are ways of categorizing CSFs. The pattern of CSFs which emerge provides a good insight into a manager's world view. But the resulting pattern can also serve an interviewer as a source of questions. The two dimensions not yet discussed are:

1. *Internal versus external*—Every manager will have *internal* CSFs relating to the department and people she manages. These can run a very wide gamut, including such diverse things as human resource development and inventory control. The primary characteristic of internal CSFs is that they deal with issues and situations within the manager's sphere of influence and control. *External* CSFs, however, pertain to situations generally less under the manager's control. For example, the availability or price of a particular critical raw material is an external CSF.

2. *Monitoring versus building/adapting*—Managers who are oriented toward emphasizing near-term operating results in-

vest considerable effort in tracking and guiding their organization's performance. *Monitoring* CSFs involves the continued scrutiny of existing situations. Almost all managers have some monitoring CSFs. Often these include financially oriented CSFs such as actual performance versus budget or the current status of product cost. Another monitoring-oriented CSF might be personnel turnover rates.

Managers who are either in reasonable control of day-to-day operations, or who are insulated from fire-fighting concerns, spend more time in *building* (or *adapting*) mode. These people are future-oriented planners whose primary purpose is to implement major change programs aimed at adapting the organization to a perceived new environment. Typical CSFs in this area include the successful implementation of major hiring and training efforts or new-product development programs.

In general, managers will have a mix of both monitoring and building/adapting CSFs. However, there is usually a strong tendency toward one of these quite different types of CSFs.

This three-dimensional classification can be used to visualize the clustering of a particular manager's CSFs by combining the characteristics as shown in the illustration in Figure 3. For example, "Company acquisitions" is an external, building CSF whose source is competitive strategy. "New skills acquisition" is an internal, building CSF arising from competitive strategy. "Employee morale" is an internal monitoring CSF, probably temporal, coming out of a current problem area. "Interest rate levels" is an external, monitoring CSF, generated by the environment.

We will note later (in section III, "The CSF Interview") that an interviewer can use this classification process with good effect in evaluating the results obtained from a CSF interview.

e. The Hierarchical Nature of CSFs.   From an individual manager's viewpoint, there is a set of his own CSFs on which the manager must primarily focus. From a company viewpoint, however, one can discern four different hierarchical levels of critical success factors, each of which must be considered. These are:

- Industry CSFs.
- Corporate CSFs.
- Sub-organization CSFs.
- Individual CSFs.

FIGURE 3   Major Dimensions of Critical Success Factors

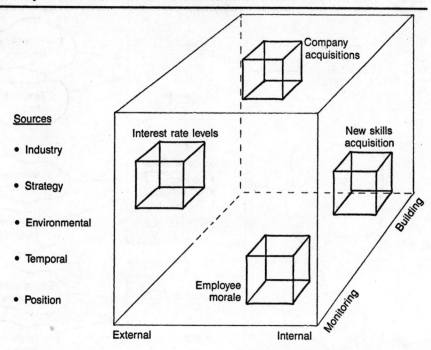

As Figure 4 suggests, *industry CSFs* affect each organization in an industry in the development of its strategy, objectives, and goals. No organization can afford to develop a strategy which does not provide adequate attention to the principal factors which underlie success in the industry.

In turn, the strategy, objectives, and goals developed by a company lead to the development of a particular set of critical success factors for the corporation (*corporate CSFs*). Given its strategy and objectives, as well as the other factors in its specific environment (see the automotive and computer industry and company examples in the following section), each corporation will develop a set of CSFs unique to its own circumstances.

In turn, corporate CSFs become an input into a similar CSF determination process for each sub-organization in the corporation. The analysis of sub-industry CSFs (where appropriate), corporate strategy, objectives, goals, and CSFs, and its own strategy, objectives, and goals, as well as environmental and temporal factors lead to a set of *sub-organizational CSFs* for each sub-organization in the company. The process can be continued for

FIGURE 4   From a Corporate Viewpoint

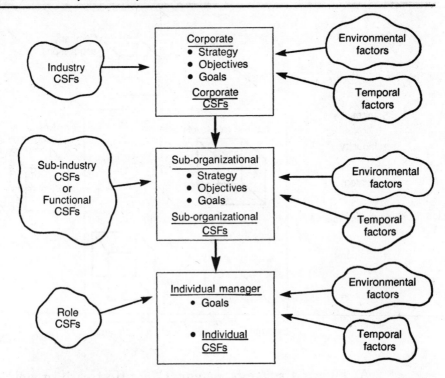

as many levels of organizational hierarchy as exist. Note that each sub-organization, whether a division or a function, will be affected in its development of strategy, objectives, goals, and CSFs by its *own* particular environmental and temporal factors as well as by the strategy, etc. of the next higher organizational level. Divisions will be affected by their sub-industry CSFs, functions by their functional role CSFs.

Managers at each of the organizational levels will have an *individual* set of CSFs which depend heavily upon their particular *roles* and on *temporal* factors, and less heavily upon the industry and the environment. (See examples in the next section.) Each of these individual sets of CSFs must be determined in the light of all the higher level managerial developments concerning strategy, objectives, goals, and/or CSFs.

From the viewpoint of CSFs alone, the hierarchy can be shown as illustrated in Figure 5. Conceptually, industry CSFs (at the top) heavily influence each company's CSFs. In turn, the company CSFs will play a significant role in determining the CSFs of the CEO

FIGURE 5   The CSF Hierarchy

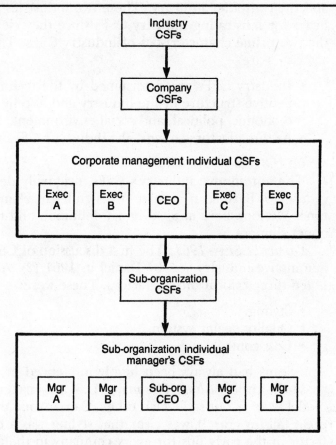

and all other executives at the corporate level. Each executive, however, will have individual CSFs, depending on his particular role and responsibilities. This top-down influence pattern is then repeated at each sub-organizational level.

In theory, the *development* of CSFs should be from the top down. However, where corporate or sub-organization CSFs have not been explicitly developed, they can be inferred upward from a careful analysis of each individual manager's stated CSFs. (We will return to this in section III.)

f. Examples of CSFs. Several examples of critical success factors are provided in the original article. This section is aimed at providing further structured examples to develop a fuller understanding of industry CSFs, organizational CSFs, and individual CSFs.

(1) Industry CSFs:

In this section we will discuss the U.S. automotive industry and the computer industry. These two industries are useful vehicles for illustrating industry CSFs since they clearly point out the two prime characteristics of industry CSFs. These two characteristics are:

- Industry CSFs are determined by the technical and competitive structure of the industry and also by the industry's economic, political, and social environment.
- As these factors change, the industry's CSFs will change.

(a) U.S. automotive industry

The automotive industry's CSFs, originally defined two decades ago, have seen at least two significant changes since that time. We look here at an original definition and the two subsequent changes.

Original CSFs—1961. The first discussion of CSFs in the U.S. automotive industry was by Daniel in 1961 (2). At that time he noted three critical success factors. These were:

- Styling.
- Quality dealer system.
- Cost control.

Americans had always been highly influenced in their car purchase choices by *styling*. The major U.S. automakers battled each model year to out-style each other. Can anyone ever forget the great tail-fin era? It was clear that styling was a critical success factor in the early 60s for every company in the automobile industry.

A second CSF noted in 1961 was the *quality of the dealer system*. The automakers' direct representative with the consumer is the car dealer. Not only do initial sales depend heavily on the dealer's quality, but follow-up contact through servicing is a constant reinforcement of the relationship. Good reinforcement leads to future new car purchases.

Cost control was the third industry CSF noted by Daniel, because profit per automobile (and therefore total earnings for each company) is heavily influenced by cost control. Since pricing is dictated primarily by competition, the more efficient the production and assembly line, the greater the profit.

A change in industry CSFs—1976–77. When we initially updated this discussion of CSFs in the U.S. auto industry in 1977, we included these three CSFs, but added a fourth—meeting energy standards. At that time, energy standards had become a CSF in the industry due to government-imposed pollution control standards. This was, then, an example of an environmentally generated CSF. Increasingly today this CSF has gained additional status as car buyers have added a new dimension to it. When fuel supplies were "limitless" and inexpensive, fuel economy was not an issue. Consumers today demand fuel economy, however, in the same way that they demanded styling 20 years ago. Thus, meeting energy standards is today doubly critical. In 1977, then, the industry CSFs were seen to be:

- Styling.
- Quality dealer system.
- Cost control.
- Meeting energy standards.

Yet another change—1978. Throughout 1977, disturbed only by the initial oil crisis in 1973–74, Americans continued to demand large cars. When in 1976 General Motors introduced the most fuel-efficient car on sale in the country, the Chevette, that car did so poorly in the market that it was being called "the Edsel of the 70s." In 1976 and 1977, the Big Three automakers had to close small-car plants while their big-car plants were on double shifts trying to keep up with the demand.

The second oil price surge in 1978, however, finally made a difference with the North American consumer. His image of the automobile as a stylish projection of his own personality changed, for most people, to a view of the car as a means of efficient transportation. (For the few who can afford it, however, one suspects the old image still lingers on. But the new view predominates.)

Thus, the industry CSFs have changed once more. It makes sense to remove "styling" from the list, and replace it with "image" where the image must be essentially one of quality and fuel efficiency. The U.S. automakers appear to have finally caught on to these new CSFs. They are attempting to lure buyers through improving on an image formerly attributed to foreign automakers. Foreign car dealers have succeeded in the past decade by creating an image of efficiency and reliability tinged with romance. U.S. automakers are now attempting to "one-up" this consumer perception by projecting a new image for the 80s combining efficiency, reliability, ease of maintenance, comfort, and patriotism.

Thus in 1980, we have a different set of industry CSFs. They are now:

- Image
- Quality dealer system
- Cost control
- Meeting energy standards

This evolution in automobile industry CSFs illustrates well the point that industry CSFs will change, sometimes in major ways, with shifts in the environment in which the industry exists. As economic, political, social, or competitive conditions change, the industry CSFs will change. To understand the current set of CSFs for an industry, one must closely analyze all these factors, with particular attention to the changes that are taking place.

(b) Computer Industry

In this dynamic, growth industry there are five industry CSFs at the present time:

- Choice of market niche
- Technological leadership
- Orderly product development
- Service and stability
- Attraction and retention of quality personnel

As a result of its youth and growth, this industry is extremely complex. In years to come it may devolve into several different industries. However, at this point, with the industry considered as a whole, it is imperative for a company to have a basic strategy, which answers the question, "What business are we in?" For many years, the sheer growth of the industry allowed almost any company to prosper. However, recently, as competition has become increasingly severe, companies are beginning to fail because they have not clearly defined the *market niche* appropriate to their particular skills, size, etc. Without a clear definition of the business, an organization cannot create well-defined strategies, objectives, and goals, and therefore most probably cannot succeed in the 80s.

Most successful new entrants into the computer industry concentrate on a new technology or a particularly creative adaptation of existing technology. This *technological leadership* (within its niche) makes it possible for a new company to get off the ground. Maintaining technological leadership will help to ensure success.

Once the strategic decision has been made with respect to the basic business niche, the *orderly development of products* for that market sector must be planned. As the industry's available technology improves, each company must upgrade its offerings. In turn, the company's customer base must be led smoothly through successive transitions to each new technology. Orderly product development thus must be based on such things as technological advances, growth in existing customer sophistication, changes in customer needs, and the need for the company to expand its markets. Coordinating the availability of new products with financing and market demand is a key issue in this CSF. Another is managing the growth of the business.

A major CSF for all companies in the industry, because of the past history of growth and instability, is the ability to provide ongoing high quality *service*. Data processing is increasingly intertwined with the most vital operations of a firm. Networks for major companies extend worldwide and into some very remote locations. Customers are concerned about the vendor's stability and whether their investment will be supported with service. There is yet another factor which has generated this "quality of service" CSF. The industry leader, IBM, has always maintained an excellent reputation for service, worldwide. It has therefore set a high standard in this area for companies in the industry.

The final industry CSF is *attraction and retention of quality personnel.* Competition for good people among the companies in the industry is fierce. Traditionally, there has been a shortage of qualified people. This has lead to high mobility, a short average tenure of position, and escalating salaries. Quality personnel are the foundation of an industry based on technology. Therefore the ability to attract and retain the skills needed to create, market, and service the products is an important CSF.

(2) Organizational CSFs:

As Figure 4 suggests, industry CSFs are one input—and a very large one—into the CSFs for particular organizations. However, each corporation has other *environmental, strategic,* and *temporal* conditions which also drive its CSFs. Working externally from the company, one can only estimate the effect of all these factors on the company's CSFs. This, however, is what this section attempts, given our knowledge of four companies in the automotive industry and one in the computer industry. This last computer-industry company is analyzed in some depth to provide the reader with an extensive description of "organization" CSFs at the corporate level.

FIGURE 6   Industry and Company CSFs

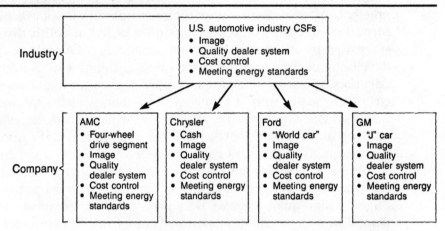

We deal primarily with the corporate level in this section. CSFs for sub-organizations (with their own sub-industry, environmental, strategic, and temporal conditions) could be described in exactly the same manner. The analytical process is the same.

(a) Automotive industry

As Figure 6 shows, each of the four companies noted must include the industry CSFs as part of their CSF list. Each, however, has an additional CSF which arises from its particular approach to, or position in, the industry.

Within the industry, individual automakers have differing CSFs—based on market niche, temporal problems, and competition. AMC, through its Jeep division, has the largest share in the four-wheel-drive market. This market provides a heavy share of AMC's profits. Maintaining the lead in this market niche is therefore one of AMC's CSFs.

Chrysler has a serious cash flow problem. They have an immediate, temporal (they hope!) CSF of obtaining enough cash to keep the production lines rolling. Ford and GM have chosen to meet the foreign competition head on, and are currently coming out with new product lines of small, economical, front-wheel-drive cars. Their common additional CSF is to successfully compete in this small-car market.

Any critical success factors list for any company will show the industry CSFs reflected in the individual company CSFs list. It will also show, however, that each company will have some individual CSFs which exist apart from the industry-wide ones.

(b) Computer industry

Recently we were asked to put ourselves in the shoes of the president of a major computer company (which we will call "The Computer Company" and to describe the CSFs we would see for that company. Since the philosophy of CSFs requires that they are based on the current strategy being followed by the company, the major objectives being pursued, and the personal world view of the top corporate officers, the following can only represent an outsider's view of all of these. Therefore, the CSFs noted are, at best, an outsider's evaluation of what that company's top officers might list as CSFs for the company at the current time. But they do provide an extensive illustration of one company's "organizational CSFs."

CSF 1: Market Understanding. The company deals in a rather complex marketplace and one which is shifting significantly. The emphasis is clearly changing from the processing of accounting transactions on large central machines to an increased emphasis on on-line transaction processing for operations, *and* to what we term *decision support* (or *information support*) for line managers, staff professionals, and even clerks. Office processing and message processing are becoming increasingly important. Software development is changing from an emphasis on "build your own" to "buy" and the use of multiple-use software in its several forms. Perhaps most important, the need is clear in the 1980s for computer companies to provide good networking capability (both hardware and software) in a marketplace which will be increasingly communication oriented.

Given the above complexity and change, an *understanding* of the real needs of the marketplace by the company is most critical. Available, but limited, resources must be spent to produce the products which are most needed. Resources are limited even for this large company. Although it has attempted in the past to span much of the market with at least some presence, it must have market understanding to select the major key market segments appropriate to it.

CSF 2: Insightful/Competitive Analysis. One way to understand the market is through the analysis of competitors. This analysis provides some input into the market segment selection process discussed in CSF #1. More critical, however, is analysis of competitive threats. The major new one obviously is Japan— which has significant muscle (through both private resources and government assistance) and appears to be a growing threat to the company and the other major companies in the industry in the next decade. Proper understanding of Japanese intentions and the development of counter-strategies are necessary—for the computer industry is perhaps the major Japanese target over the next decade.

CSF 3: Technological "Leadership."   Market understanding without the development of the appropriate technology is less than useful. Moreover as computers increasingly become a "commodity," the maintenance of a technological edge (or at the very least, parity) with the competition becomes increasingly necessary. It is also important for purposes of CSF #4.

CSF 4: Developing an Image.   The company has never had a clear image in the computer industry. At times it has provided product leadership. At yet other times it has focused on particular industries. At other times it has been seen as an "alternative source" to the industry leader, IBM. In the marketplace this changing purpose has lead to a less than robust image in the past. Internally, it has provided the potential, at least, for low morale. A decision on its market segment (CSF #2), and therefore its image (this CSF), appears critical at this increasingly competitive time in the industry.

CSF 5: Developing a More Effective Corporate Marketing Staff.   The company appears to have decided to be a major factor in the marketplace. Yet it has operated in a "lean and thin" manner. To gain better market and competitive understanding, it is very important to establish and develop a significantly larger and upgraded corporate marketing staff.

CSF 6: Quality People.   This is the driving force in every successful company. The Computer Company has done well in the marketplace by attracting and keeping high-quality employees. The need for increasing productivity in the industry makes this even more important today.

CSF 7: Service and Stability.   This is an industry CSF which is an industry "must." As explained in the industry discussion above, it is increasingly critical today.

Figure 7 shows how each company-specific Computer Company CSF relates to the computer industry CSFs previously discussed. CSFs 1, 2, 3, 6, and 7 tie directly to industry CSFs. CSF #4, "developing an image," is a temporal CSF specific to the company and therefore does not appear on the industry list. CSF #5, "developing a more effective corporate marketing staff," is another company-specific CSF whose source is corporate strategy.

FIGURE 7 **Company CSFs and Industry CSFs**

The Computer Company CSFs	Industry CSFs or Sources
1. Market understanding and creation	Market niche
2. Insightful competitive analysis	Market niche
3. Technological leadership	Technological leadership
4. Developing an image	Temporal CSF
5. Developing a more effective corporate marketing staff	Temporal CSF from company strategy
6. Quality people	Attraction and retention of quality people
7. Service and stability	Service

It should be clear from this example how one can fit some individual company critical success factors into the context of industry-wide CSFs. In addition, some CSFs are generated from the sources discussed previously.

(3) Individual manager CSFs:

Just as there exist individual company CSFs, there are CSFs for each sub-organization within a company, that is, each division, department, group, etc. And at every level of the organization there are a set of people, each of whom have individual CSFs. As Figure 4 noted, "individual manager" CSFs are affected by several factors. Heavy influences on an individual's CSFs include role-related and temporal factors.

Role-oriented CSFs cut across all industries. They are an integral part of the job itself and therefore persist regardless of pressures produced by other factors. For example, manufacturing managers invariably list quality control and cost control as CSFs. Presidents always have "corporate performance" in one form or another as a CSF. In performing a CSF study, it is important, therefore, to closely examine each individual's role.

Temporal factors for each manager are usually related to the current problems and opportunities which the manager is facing. This area is therefore an important source for CSFs. For example, the president of a large commercial bank would not normally review all loans to developing countries. However, the dynamic political environments today in many such countries may cause the portfolio of these loans to become a problem and, therefore, generate a CSF for the president. In performing the CSF study, the interviewer should look at the problems and opportunities facing a manager, and how she is dealing with them.

Other factors which generate CSFs for individual managers include strategy, objectives, goals, and CSFs from organizations and individuals above them in the corporate hierarchy. If, for example, a VP Marketing has set a goal of increasing overall sales by 25 percent in the coming year, the marketing managers for each product line will have both goals and CSFs related to achieving that goal.

Individuals are also affected by the organization's environment and industry, but to a lesser degree. For example, whereas the overall corporate CSFs can be enormously influenced by new competition conditions in the industry, more of a particular product-line manager's CSFs will be generated by the resulting corporate strategy, than by the competition itself.

To return to the computer industry, we can look at the example of the financial vice presidents of three dynamic, growing companies, such as DEC, Prime, and Apple. The managers all have at least one CSF in common—financing for growth and expansion. All three are managing in organizations which have grown rapidly during their lifetimes, and are doing so in a tight-money economy. This CSF is role oriented, arises from corporate strategy, and is temporal because of the current economy. How each vice president solves his particular problem will no doubt be different. (Apple, for example, went public in December 1980 to increase its cash available for growth.)

Figure 8 completes the hierarchy of CSFs for one company from the auto industry example—Chrysler—by reproducing the industry CSFs and organizational CSFs and then adding three sets of individual CSFs. The emphasis on role and temporal CSFs below the level of President (where CSFs are about identical with those of the corporation) should be noted.

2. Uses of the CSF Concept

Having discussed the CSF concept and placed it in relationship to other managerial concepts, we now turn to a discussion of the three major *uses* of the concept. These are:

- To help an individual manager determine his information needs.
- To aid an organization in its *general planning* process—for strategic, long-range, and annual planning purposes.

FIGURE 8   The Relationship of Company and Individual CSFs

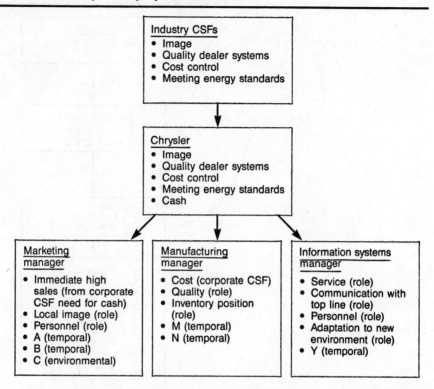

- To aid an organization in its *information systems planning* process.

Attention will be concentrated in this paper on the last of these uses. The first is discussed in depth in the original *Harvard Business Review* article. The reader who is specifically interested in it should review that article after reading the next section. The second use (as an aid in general corporate planning) is not the focus of this primer which is targeted toward the information systems field. Thus the "general" planning use of CSFs will also be treated relatively lightly. We will concentrate on the third use—information systems planning—which is today the primary use of the CSF concept from our perspective.

a. Determining an Individual Manager's Information Needs. As Figure 9 suggests, an individual manager lives within the context of a corporation and her own sub-organization. Where strategies, objectives, and goals exist at higher levels (and in most major organizations they do today), the individual manager must pay

FIGURE 9   The CSF Process Used in Determining Individual Managerial Information Needs

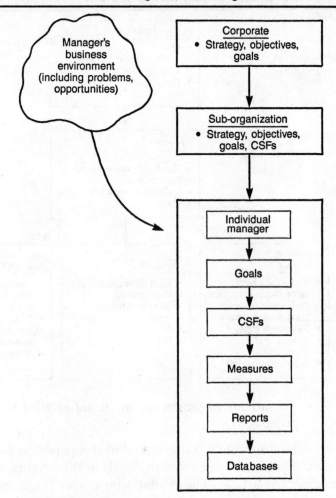

attention to these in determining her own goals. These goals, in turn, are the backdrop for the determination of the factors which are critical in obtaining these goals. Measures which will allow the determination of the status of each CSF must then be determined and the reports which will display the latest value of each measure must be designed. Finally, the databases from which the reports can be drawn are developed.

This is a rather straightforward, *top-down* process. The manager starts by thinking about his business environment, while paying requisite attention to the strategies, objectives, and goals of upper levels of his organization. (The higher the manager is in the organization, the less he is bounded by the strategies, objectives, and goals of others.) He then, by proceeding through the steps noted in Figure 9, moves from a *business* focus to an *information systems* focus in a series of clear steps which end up in the definition of data elements needed.

During the past two years we have found this to be a useful *conceptual* path. It has helped many top managers to clearly visualize their information needs. However, it takes time, dollars, and energy to build the requisite databases. By the time these are built, some of the appropriate measures and reports will have changed. Therefore, from a pragmatic viewpoint, the CSF concept is today being used for the most part as an aid in information systems planning in the manner described in Section *c* below. It is on this that we will concentrate this discussion.

b. CSFs As An Aid in General Corporate Planning.   Figures 4 and 5 in Section II*e* noted four different levels of CSFs: industry, corporate, sub-organization, and individual. There is every reason to make use of these various levels of CSFs in the *corporate planning* process, and this is being done by several organizations. Since CSFs designate the areas in which good results must be obtained to ensure success at any level of the organization, it makes sense for an organization or individual to consciously determine the pertinent CSFs so that resources can be allocated in the planning process to ensure successful efforts in each CSF area.

There are multiple possible uses of CSFs in planning. For example, industry CSFs can be utilized in determining corporate strategy. Similarly, corporate and sub-organization CSFs should be significant inputs to the short-term planning process, and individual CSFs should be used by each manager in developing her action plans for a particular year. The following paragraphs briefly discuss the first and last of these uses.

Industry CSFs, as noted in Figure 5, are a logical and necessary input into the corporate strategic planning process. Corporate strategy should be heavily based upon an in-depth understanding of industry CSFs. In fact, there is a significant literature concerning the use of CSFs in the development of corporate strategy. Many consulting firms who specialize in strategic planning use either the CSF concept directly or a concept similar to it. They tend to preach that for an organization to be successful, its strategy must be developed to allow it to excel in those areas where high performance is critical—or the organization must move into an industry niche in which, in effect, different CSFs exist.

FIGURE 10   Sequence of CSFs Used in Individual Planning

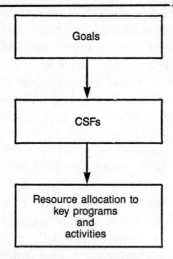

At the individual manager's level, CSFs are also useful in planning. After the manager's goals have been determined, the determination of the relevant CSFs will lead to improved insight into the "best" resource allocation to key programs and activities to ensure that critical areas are emphasized. Figure 10 illustrates this individual planning sequence.

c. The Use of CSFs in Information Systems Planning.   Currently the CSF method is being used primarily as a technique to aid in information systems planning. It is another tool, like IBM's BSP or Gibson and Nolan's "Stages," which can be used as a planning method. In this section, we will discuss (1) the CSF procedure as it is used for I/S planning purposes, (2) the concept of "information databases," which are the primary output of using the CSF process in this manner, and (3) the reasons underlying the growing use of the CSF process in this manner.

(1) Procedure:

Figure 11 diagrams the CSF procedure as it is used for I/S planning. The steps are as follows:

(*a*) In the chosen organization, most often a corporation or a major sub-organization such as a division, the top 10–20 managers are interviewed using the CSF interview process discussed in the next section (III) of this paper. Each manager's CSFs are determined. (Where time allows, the measures used for each CSF are also determined, but this is not a necessary part of this routine.)

FIGURE 11   CSF Procedure for I/S Planning

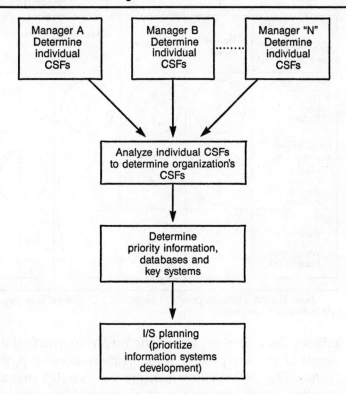

(*b*) Analysis of the results of the individual CSF interviews is performed. The individual manager's CSFs are charted, as shown in Figure 12, to determine the CSFs which have been identified by multiple managers and which, therefore, provide a good approximation of the organization's CSFs. Although each top manager's job is different—and his CSFs are therefore different in some ways from those of his colleagues—we have found that the intersection of all top managers' CSFs is the set of CSFs for that organization. These resulting CSFs are then checked with the organization's management.

(*c*) The organization's CSFs, as charted in step *b* above, in every case will indicate one or more key "information databases" or "data processing systems" which should receive priority in the information systems development process. For example, the CSFs shown in Figure 12 indicate the need for a Human Resources information database and a corporate strategy information database. Priority should be given to the development of these da-

FIGURE 12   Insurance Company Executives—Charts Individual CSFs

CSFs / Corporate executives	Human resources	Strategy	Efficiency of operation	Quality of service	Pricing strategy
Holding co. Harris Connors Wolsky	1 5 2	2 1 3	3 2 1	4	5 4
Property and casualty Pollack Contreras Jordan Holloway	3 1 2 5	1 4	5 1	2 3 1 2	2
Life Wensley Firenze Washington Rubenstein	3 3 4	1 4 1 1	2	1 3	4 2 2 2

Note: Numbers indicate priority (1 being high). Circles indicate concurrence on CSFs within an executive group.

tabases since they represent the means to satisfy the information needs of the key people in the organization—top management.

(*d*) The information concerning the top management perspective on information systems needs (developed in steps *a*, *b*, and *c* above) is then fed into the regular information systems planning process. Priorities are developed for information systems development.

(2) Information databases—the primary output:

As step *c* in the procedure above indicates, there are two major types of systems needs which are developed through this CSF procedure. The first is the need for particular data processing systems—such as an on-line order entry system. This type of system needs no further explanation. In fact, an indicated need for these operational data processing systems is not often a direct output of a CSF process, since top management is not usually interested in the information contained solely in a single operational transaction-processing system.

Most often the key systems needs indicated by the CSF procedure are the development of one or more "information databases." Top managers most often need information spanning various areas of the business. In general, the required informa-

FIGURE 13   A Comparison of Traditional and Information Support Databases

	Traditional Transaction Database	Information Support Database
Purpose and use	Support transaction processing systems	Data repository
Data attributes	Up-to-date Accurate Consistent Complete	Timeliness not critical "Hard" and "soft" data consistent Completeness not always possible
Storage method	Optimized for efficiency of computer resources	Tables of data designed for easy access and change
Ability to change the database	Difficult Only after much consideration of "downstream" effects	Easy to accomplish Database designed for change and evolution

tion cannot be supplied by a single operational system's database. Rather, an information database must be built.

Many examples of information databases are given in the "Executive Information Support Systems" paper (3). For a full discussion of information databases and relevant examples, the reader is referred to that paper.

Briefly, however, information databases are quite unlike the traditional transaction-processing databases such as those developed for accounts receivable, manufacturing control, etc. Those more traditional operational databases store files of data which are used to process the paperwork which is the mainstay of the day-to-day life of an organization. These databases must be up-to-date, accurate, and complete. They must have well-designed sequences of data storage, optimized as far as possible to facilitate *efficient* processing of the thousands of daily transactions which occur in major organizations.

Information support databases, on the other hand, are very different in purpose and the type of data they use (see Figure 13). They have no role in day-to-day operational paperwork. They are built primarily as *data repositories* to make information available for recall and analysis. They are fed in part, but only in part, by data from the operational databases. Moreover, much significant "soft" data from customer surveys, market sampling, and internal planning processes are often also included in the information support databases. "Externally purchased" data from any of the approximately 3,000 machine-processable databases also can be bought from information vendors today.

In technical structure, information support databases are also different from the conventional databases used primarily for transaction processing. Most information support databases are designed with very inefficient, yet simple and easily understood file structures. Primarily they exist as a "set of tables." This makes them inefficient with regard to computing-machine usage, but they are easy for a user to understand, simple to access, and very responsive to change and evolution.

(3) Reasons for the use of the CSF method as an aid to information systems planning:

The use of the CSF method for information systems planning is occurring because of several factors concerning both the data processing environment of the 1980s and the CSF method itself. These are:

(*a*) In 1980 a growing number of information systems executives are well aware of their operational paperwork-processing systems needs. They have been creating and working with these systems for the past 20–25 years. What they understand far less well, and therefore need to place emphasis on in the planning process, are the information needs of top management and the information databases which must be built to support these needs. The CSF method provides a technique to do this.

(*b*) The CSF method to aid information systems planning is a "rifle-shot" technique aimed at understanding top management's information needs. It attempts to do only this. Therefore, it takes only 1–3 hours of each manager's time. It can be completed in approximately a person-month of effort. It is, therefore, inexpensive as a planning tool.

(*c*) In addition to its yield for information systems planning, the CSF method provides an additional, perhaps equally important, benefit for the interviewer. This benefit is a relatively deep understanding of the way in which each senior manager interviewed views the world. In effect, the interviewed managers spend the interview time discussing their jobs as they see them, and the areas which they believe are most critical to them. Interviewers who have used the CSF process (in many cases the top person in information systems) have almost unanimously reported that this "insight into top management and its view of the business" has been, by itself, of significant value to the I/S department.

(*d*) Perhaps equally important, the CSF procedure provides top management with a vehicle for thinking about their information needs. In far too many organizations, top management has given little time to pondering their own information needs. Rather, they have been concerned with the traditional areas of marketing, manufacturing, finance, etc. In many organizations, top management has not yet made the shift to the realization that, with today's technology, it is not only feasible, but desirable (and some would say even necessary) for them to spend time thinking through their information requirements. The CSF method is a *business-based*, *logical*, and *time-sparing* entrée into this new endeavor for line management.

(*e*) Finally, the CSF method, used as an aid for information systems planning, focuses on the definition of those information databases which are necessary to support the information needs of *all* (or at least a significant number) of top managers. It is expensive to build an information database for only a single executive (even if he is the president). However, where it can be shown, as in this use of the method, that an information database will serve the information needs of many of the organization's top executives, the justification of the development of such a system is more straightforward.

III. INTERVIEW PROCEDURE AND TECHNIQUES

This section is written for the person who is about to undertake his first CSF interview. Here, we attempt to communicate all those things which appear to be important as we look back on three years of CSF interviewing. In addition, this section reflects the knowledge gained from our discussions with others who have used the CSF method. Three major areas of interview procedure and technique follow. They are:

- Objectives of the interview.
- Pre-interview preparation.
- Interview procedure.

A. Objectives of the Interview

A CSF interviewer has a unique opportunity. Given the managerial time and attention which has been made available, he should capitalize on it fully. Just coming out with the manager's CSFs is not enough. Rather, the interviewer should seek to accomplish all of the following four objectives:

1. To understand the interviewee's organization and the mission and role (the "world view") of the interviewee within the context of her organization as the interviewee perceives them.
2. To understand the goals and objectives of the interviewee.
3. To elicit CSFs and measures from the interviewee.
4. To assist the manager in better comprehending her own information needs. This may be the first time that the manager has confronted these information needs in a structured way. The CSF interview often presents the initial occasion to interact with the manager on the types of information support that might be useful to her. In the haste to "collect data" on CSFs and information needs, the reverse educational opportunity should not be overlooked.

B. Pre-Interview Preparation

As noted earlier in this guide, pre-interview preparation is important. It provides one not only with knowledge, but also with the confidence that knowledge brings. The following steps represent the major pre-interview actions we have found to be most useful to people desiring to conduct CSF interviews:

1. Read and be throughly familiar with the articles, "Chief Executives Define Their Own Data Needs" (1), "Executive Information Support Systems" (3), and earlier sections of this guide. All provide, in addition to the conceptual aspects and procedures of the CSF method, some useful examples which can be used when needed to explain the rationale for CSFs to an interviewee.
2. Be thoroughly familiar with the *industry*. Understand the industry competitive forces, trends, and environment. Know the current problems, issues, and news makers. This is important during the interview both in eliciting CSFs and in fully understanding the importance of each CSF.
3. Study the *company* or companies to be interviewed. Use publicly available sources such as annual reports, internally available company histories, and organization charts.

External sources such as articles in *The Wall Street Journal, Business Week, Forbes,* and *Fortune,* are often highly useful and are available in greater volume than is commonly thought. Most important, one should spend time with the people in the company who are sponsoring the study. Their insights into the company, its strategy, environment, current problems, and opportunities are invaluable. Internal company political issues should be probed, where possible, with these company contacts, since these are important. All of this background is highly useful for conducting each interview smoothly and intelligently.

4. Initiate the transmission of a letter from the top management of the company to all interviewees prior to the interview. The letter should explain the purpose of the undertaking and explicitly show top management support for it. This letter should also include background material to prepare the interviewee for the session. It is desirable to include a copy of "Chief Executives Define Their Own Data Needs" with a request that it be read prior to the interview. In addition, a brief outline of the interview process should be enclosed.

5. Plan to start interviews at the lowest level of management to be interviewed and work up. This provides the ability to review, in preparation for interviews with higher-level managers, the knowledge gained from the CSF interviews of managers at lower levels. In this way the interviewer can become increasingly more comfortable in discussing the company and industry issues before being confronted with the top two or three managers in the organization.

6. Plan to have, and enlist, a key manager from the company to accompany the interviewer on the interviews. There are pros and cons to this method. On the plus side, one has the benefit of an insider's insight in discussing the interview afterward. There is someone available who can help clarify company-related obscure points during the interview. In addition, the person from the company has a stronger stake in implementation if he has been part of the process. However, on the minus side, the interviewee may not be as honest and frank during the interview because an insider is present.

There is no available *objective* evidence as to whether the pros outweigh the cons on this issue. Suffice it to say that for all three positive reasons noted above, we generally want to have a key manager with us during the interviews.

7. Prior to the interview, assume the role of the interviewee and list, from all acquired knowledge, her probable objectives, goals, CSFs, and measures. This can be an enormous aid during the interview in eliciting a complete set of CSFs and measures quickly and easily. This technique is an aid in getting the interviewer's thinking on the right track. The danger in doing this is that the interviewer may try to force his own CSFs on the interviewee. Care must be taken to guard against this.

8. Brush up on interviewing skills. There are approaches and techniques for conducting interviews in an interpersonal setting which, used well, can enhance the success of a CSF interview.

C. Interview Procedure

With the necessary preparation out of the way, the day of the first interview arrives. This section provides a step-by-step outline of the several parts of a CSF interview. These are (1) opening the interview, (2) interviewee's description of mission and role, (3) discussion of interviewee's goals, (4) developing CSFs, (5) setting priorities for CSFs, and (6) determining measures.

1. Open the Interview. Give a brief introductory statement of how the CSF method is used to determine managerial information needs. Although the interviewee has had preparatory material, a few remarks to refresh his memory are never out of place. The response to these remarks will also help to determine his degree of understanding of the CSF concept. If it becomes apparent that the interviewee has not read the material provided, it is necessary for the interviewer to provide a more in-depth introduction to the CSF concept and the purpose of the interview.

a. Example of brief introductory statement: "As you know from the material you have received, we are using a new method for assisting managers in looking at the way they manage and, as a second step, for determining their information needs. This technique focuses on identifying those factors in a manager's environment which must go right in order for the manager to achieve his goals and objectives. These are called critical success factors or CSFs."

b. Example of lengthy introductory statement: "In the past, analysts have attempted, with only occasional success, to define the information needs of managers. For the most part this failure has been due to the lack of a common vocabulary, a poor understanding of the business on the part of the analyst, and an inability of the manager to relate his information needs to the demands of his day-to-day operations. As a result, many so-called "management information systems" were designed and built which in no way served management. We are currently using an interview method which appears to have overcome many of the shortcomings of previous methods. This new technique focuses on identifying those factors in a manager's environment which are the most important and for which good results must be obtained in order for the manager to achieve his goals and objectives. These are called critical success factors or CSFs. In the past, information systems have been designed primarily to report on levels of achievement toward managerial goals. Using the CSF method we can design information systems which report on the results in areas underlying eventual success or failure in the achieving of goals. CSFs answer the basic question of 'Where should you place managerial attention?' Once that question has been answered an information system can be designed to report on the current status of areas which require most attention.

"In this interview we are going to start by describing your mission and role, move on to your objectives and goals, and then discuss the critical success factors that support these."

If the interviewee needs examples to clarify her understanding of the concept, use examples from the *Harvard Business Review* article or this guide. Choose examples which are appropriate to the interviewee, the company, and the industry.

2. Ask the Interviewee to Describe His Mission and Role. This initial question serves two major purposes. First, it is an easy way to get the interviewee into the process and to start him talking. He is asked to discuss that which he knows best, his company and his job. Second, as the manager discusses his job he almost always provides clues as to how he "views the world." Is he strategically oriented? Does he view his job as one which is set up to introduce change into the organization, or is he a "caretaker" put in the job to carry out the routines which have been developed by past managers? Many of the things which are important to him come to light during this exposition, including, often, a few critical success factors. The interviewer should take careful notes during this section of the interview. It should provide a cross-check on what is said later, since the manager's CSFs should consistently relate to his role as it is perceived.

3. Discuss the Manager's Goals.   Some definitions are often necessary in this part of the interview. Managers will often ask "Do you mean goals or objectives? Short-term or long-term?" We zero in on *goals* (see definition in Section II), because objectives, as defined in this guide, are not very meaningful with regard to CSFs. As to the time horizon for goals, the manager should be asked to respond with the time horizon (short or long) that is most meaningful for him. Most managers pick a one-year horizon; some provide both long- and short-term goals. The choice of the time span and nature of the goals selected is meaningful in itself since it provides further insight into the way the manager views his job.

A fair number of managers, given this question, will reach into a drawer and pull out the set of goals, often determined by an MBO process, on which they are being measured during the current year. Seeing this list, our response—in addition to writing them down—most often is to ask, "All right, this is the set of goals on which you are to be measured, but managers often have other less formally stated goals. Some of these informal goals are often as important, if not more important, than the agreed-upon goals. Do you have any goals which fit this category?" Here managers sometimes expose significant, unspoken goals. For example, a manager in one company had, as a primary goal, the elevation of his sub-organization higher in the company to give it (and him) more power. Since a good part of some managers' critical success factors relate to these unstated—yet very important—informal goals, it is highly useful where possible to bring these goals to the surface.

4. Develop the Manager's CSFs.   The process of determining the manager's CSFs can be quite simple or rather difficult. If the manager has done the prerequisite reading and has given some thought to his CSFs he may even have a written list to present to the interviewer together with an appropriate explanation of each

CSF. Alternatively, a manager who has not thought much about his job and its responsibilities may prove to be a poor subject. Fortunately, the latter case is not often found at the top of reasonably sized organizations. (We note ways of working with "difficult" interviewees later in this section.)

(*a*) Some questions that are helpful in eliciting CSFs:

No matter how smoothly the interview goes, it is useful to triangulate in on the manager's CSFs through a series of questions. The first, and obvious, question is.

> Will you please tell me, in whatever order they come to mind, those things that you see as critical success factors in your job at this time?

As the manager proceeds, the interviewer should not hesitate to ask for clarification of a CSF where it is unclear. At the end of the list, however, we find it useful to get the manager to think about her CSFs from two other perspectives which can elicit additional CSFs or, at the very least, assist in prioritizing CSFs. The two additional questions are:

> Let me ask the same question concerning critical success factors in another way. In what one, two, or three areas would failure to perform well hurt you the most? In short, where would you most hate to see something go wrong?

and

> Assume you are placed in a dark room with no access to the outside world, except for food and water, today. What would you most want to know *about the business* when you came out two weeks later?

As simple as these questions seem, they have turned out to be highly effective in assisting managers to zero in on the few most critical areas of their responsibility. One must, of course, use a manager with at least a *slight* sense of humor to react well to it. In general, each CSF interviewer tends to develop his own set of "CSF-checking" questions. These are the ones we use, however, and they can serve as a starting point.

(*b*) Things to do while the manager is telling you her CSFs:

The skillful CSF interviewer is always in "multiprocessing" mode during the interview. The following are among the things that are helpful to do while the manager is talking and you are writing down her CSFs (or even in a few "dead" moments toward the end of the interview if necessary).

(1) Using the CSF classifications summarized in Figure 5, mentally check the list of CSFs to ensure that the interviewee has not focused on only one type of CSF. For example, some managers tend to think only of their internal issues and overlook the roles they play externally. The interviewer should be aided in uncovering this oversight by the initial mission and role description given by the interviewee. In addition, the background research which was performed should also help the interviewer to ask about relevant areas that the interviewee has not mentioned, particularly in the area of external and environmental CSFs. For example, especially at the presidential level, consider CSFs that might arise out of issues involving environmental factors such as competition, new technology, and regulatory issues.

(2) "Aggregate" CSFs to ensure that one CSF is not being discussed in multiple ways. Some interviewees get stuck discussing one area that is of particular concern at the moment. They will often echo the same CSFs in different ways and think they are talking about new CSFs. The interviewer should be aware of this possibility and be ready to suggest that several CSFs are really one. Then using techniques described earlier, try to draw out others. Of course, it *is* possible for a manager to have only one or two CSFs; therefore the interviewer should not try to persuade her into more CSFs if it is not appropriate.

(3) Check to ensure that all CSFs are being elicited, not only those that can be measured with hard data. Even though the CSF method avoids talking about computer-based information systems, some interviewees limit their thinking to what they believe to be appropriate CSFs for "computerization." Be sure to stress that the method is designed to elicit all information needs—soft as well as hard. Use examples of soft CSFs like "relationship with the boss," "supportive spouse and family" to illustrate this point.

In sum, doing the interviews, the interviewer should check to be sure his involvement is "helpful," not directive. He should be careful when asking questions about areas not covered directly by the manager to not indicate a judgment on his part. His job is not to *convince* the interviewee of her CSFs but to draw them out. Most managers will not be unduly influenced by the interviewer but one should be sensitive to the possibility.

On the other hand, as suggested by the three points above, the interviewer should be sure that he has "stretched" the manager as far as possible in her thinking during the interview. The majority of interviewees have no difficulty in responding with their CSFs. Some, however, do not understand the concept and need a great deal of prompting. (Where possible, the interviewer should be ready with examples and anecdotes from past interviews to assist in such a situation.) This is a situation in which one must be extremely sensitive to the problem of "leading the witness." The interviewer must walk the narrow line of eliciting information without creating the answers.

5. Setting Priorities for CSFs. Some further insight into the manager is often gained by having the interviewee put CSFs in priority order. Absolute priorities are not essential: general indications of what the interviewee views as most important will suffice. In fact, many managers will not set priorities, and it is not necessary to do so. They are, after all, a small high-priority set of things—all of which are critical. Quite often no one is more critical than the others.

6. Determine Measures. Where time permits, it is useful to determine measures for CSFs and to identify the sources of these measures. After the CSFs have been determined and ordered, the interviews should proceed to discuss possible ways of measuring each. This is an area for great creativity. The interviewee may come up with measurements which are meaningful to her but which appear unusual. The interviewee is indicating the ways in which she measures the status of each factor *now*. The interviewer may wish to make suggestions based on his initial preparation or subsequently acquired knowledge. There is no danger of "leading" here. The interviewer may suggest a way of measuring that the interviewee did not think of but likes and will use.

In general, this final step, determining measures, does *not* need to be carried out during the initial CSF interview. It is certainly useful if one has extra time at the end of the initial interview. However, it can wait until after the entire initial CSF exercise described in this primer has been completed. Then, when the desired information databases have been decided upon, a more probing second-stage interview can be held. Here measures should be defined in great detail to zero in on the contents of the required information databases.

IV. ANALYSIS OF DATA

There are two major steps in the analysis process. They are described below:

A. Reviewing CSFs

Each interviewee's CSFs should be reviewed against the classification and dimensions noted in Section III to check whether the interviewee has covered all the major areas of his job (e.g., if the interviewee is a manufacturing manager, are "role" CSFs such as quality, costs, and inventory control noted?). In addition, one can check interviewees "against" each other to see if each fits a "pattern" of CSFs which appear due to a common managerial perception of problems, opportunities, industry structure, current competitive conditions, and so forth. The interviewer has the background of his research, the interview, and his own experience to assist him in this review. Primarily, however, the interviewer will have a good "feel" for the company after the start of the interviewing. If there are major gaps, this should be brought up in a subsequent review meeting with the particular interviewee.

It is highly desirable to prepare a written version of the CSFs to be reviewed and approved by the interviewee. In addition to ensuring that the facts are correct, this step may elicit additional information.

B. Aggregating CSFs from the Individual Manager Interviews

As noted earlier, interviewing several executives in one company is the initial step toward determining the CSFs for the company as a whole. By then aggregating the CSFs from the individual interviews the interviewer can discover exactly which information databases are most necessary to support the managers.

For example, in several instances, we have had interviewees list CSFs that deal with market analysis. In most of these cases some of the information needed to track progress with regard to these CSFs was internally generated, e.g., sales "hit/miss" reports. Other information was external in origin; for example, competitors' actions, customers' response patterns, and market share data. In sum, however, the CSFs pointed directly to the need for a marketing information database.

In another situation the president named a CSF of improving employee morale. Farther down the management chain, executives were concerned about professional development and training for their employees. One interviewee mentioned that employee turnover in his area was higher than desirable. Many other CSFs in this company hit the "personnel" theme. The need for a human resources database was easily identified.

A CSF chart, such as the one shown on Figure 12, can be very useful in this aggregating process. One can easily circle the CSFs which point to particular information databases.

At this point, the CSF data should be in convenient form to feed into the company's information systems planning process. The information databases required for top management should be given consideration for priority development. Not too surprisingly, top management is often willing to allocate additional resources for the development of these systems.

Once a decision is made to go ahead with a particular information database, a *second phase* of interviews begins. Here the emphasis switches from *identifying* the CSFs, to determining each manager's *measures* for his CSFs and the *data* needed for each measure. In this way, the necessary data structure for each information database can be established.

REFERENCES

1. Rockart, John F. "Chief Executives Define Their Own Data Needs." *Harvard Business Review,* March–April 1979, p. 81.

2. Daniel, D. Ronald. "Management Information Crisis." *Harvard Business Review,* September–October 1961, p. 111.

3. Rockart, John F. and Treacy, Michael E. "Executive Information Support Systems." CISR Working Paper No. 65, Sloan School of Management, MIT, Cambridge, Mass., November 1980 (Revised: April 1981).

Contributors

CHRISTINE V. BULLEN Assistant Director, CISR, and Research Associate, Sloan School of Management, MIT, is currently involved in studies of future office technologies and the impact of information systems on decision making. She is specifically interested in office system design, the use of computer conferencing, how new technologies affect the manager-secretary team relationship, and the physical design of future offices to enhance productivity. She has conducted research concerning career path issues for I/S professionals, the use of the critical success factors methodology, and the design and implementation of distributed processing.

ADAM D. CRESCENZI is Vice President of Index Systems in Cambridge, Massachusetts. He consults to senior executives on management issues of information technology and its use in the implementation of business strategies. Index Systems is one of CISR's 25 corporate sponsors.

DAVID W. DE LONG is Research Associate at CISR and has done extensive research on the implementation and impacts of executive support systems. He is a widely published writer whose work has appeared in such journals and magazines as *Harvard Business Review, Inc., Newsweek International, Data Training, Industrial Marketing,* and *Business Computer Systems.*

LAUREN S. FLANNERY is Vice President of Cornelius Architectural Products in Pittsburgh, Pennsylvania. Her past research interests have included time-sharing use and all aspects of end user computing. Ms. Flannery was formerly a research consultant to CISR.

G. ANTHONY GORRY is Vice President for institutional development at Baylor College of Medicine in Houston, Texas. His current research interests include the effect of information technology on organizational development and the applications of artificial intelligence in medical problem solving. Dr. Gorry was formerly a member of the faculty at the Sloan School of Management.

RICHARD D. HACKATHORN is Associate Professor at the College of Business Administration, University of Colorado, Denver. His current research interests include decision support systems, end user computing, and analysis of organizational information. Dr. Hackathorn received his Ph.D. from the University of California—Irvine.

JOHN C. HENDERSON is Associate Professor of Management Science at MIT's Sloan School of Management. He has taught and published extensively in the fields of decision support systems, MIS design and implementation, and the strategic impacts of information technology. Prior to joining the faculty of MIT, Dr. Henderson held faculty appointments at Wharton, Ohio State, and Florida State universities. He serves on the editorial boards of *Management Science, MIS Quarterly, Office: Technology* and *People, and Systems, Objectives and Solutions.*

PETER G. W. KEEN is President of Informational Technology Services, Inc., in Newton, Massachusetts, and is editor of the journal *Office: Technology and People.* His current research and consulting are in the areas of DSS, telecommunications and business policy, strategic computer education, and the management of change. Dr. Keen has held faculty positions at MIT, Stanford, Wharton, and Harvard. He is co-author of *Decision Support Systems: An Organizational Perspective* (with M. S. Scott Morton) and author of *Business without Bounds: Telecommunications and Business Policy.*

ELIOT LEVINSON is a consultant based in Newton, Massachusetts, working with firms on issues of technology and organizational change. His current research interest is the role of line managers in the design, introduction, and maintenance of information systems. Dr. Levinson is a former visiting scholar at MIT's Sloan School of Management and was a member of the management science department at the Rand Corporation. He received his Ph.D. from Stanford.

FRED L. LUCONI is President and CEO of Applied Expert Systems, Inc. in Cambridge, Massachusetts. A former executive vice president and co-founder of Index Systems, he currently consults in the strategy, organization, and overall management of the information systems function.

THOMAS W. MALONE is Associate Professor of Management Scie at MIT's Sloan School of Management. He focuses his research on user interface design, expert systems, and organizational design of both human and computer systems. Before joining the MIT faculty, Prof. Malone was a research scientist for four years at the Xerox Palo Alto Research Center (PARC), where he designed educational software and office information systems. He received his Ph.D. from Stanford.

JUDITH A. QUILLARD is Associate Director of CISR. She is currently conducting research on the management of the data resource and has been involved in CISR's case-based research on the management and support of end user computing. Prior to joining CISR, she worked as a technical project manager responsible for the design and implementation of commercial banking systems.

JOHN F. ROCKART is Director of CISR and a Senior Lecturer of Management Science at MIT's Sloan School of Management. He has taught and conducted research in areas of management planning and control and the use of computer-based information systems. His most recent research interests are the "critical success factors" concept, the use of information by top management, and the management of end user computing. Dr. Rockart serves on the boards of directors of three organizations and consults and lectures for several major companies.

DAVID A. SCHILLING is Associate Professor of Management Science at Ohio State Unive sity. His research interests include multicriteria decision making, model-based decision support systems, group decision making, and facility location analysis. He has published articles in *Management Science, Decision Sciences, European Journal of Operations Research,* and *Omega,* among others. He received his Ph.D. from Johns Hopkins University.

MICHAEL S. SCOTT MORTON is Professor of Management at MIT's Sloan School of Management. He has extensive research and consulting experience in the design and implementation of management support systems. Dr. Scott Morton is author of *Management Decision Systems, Decision Support Systems: An Organizational Perspective* (with P. G. W. Keen), *Management Decision Support Systems* (with A. McCosh), and *Computers and the Learning Process* (with J. F. Rockart). His current research addresses the impact of information technology on corporate strategy. Dr. Scott Morton is directing the Sloan School's "Management in the 1990s" research program.

JOHN G. SIFONIS is a partner in the national office of Arthur Young. He is the national director of information technology consulting services for the firm and is based in the company's Southwest regional office in Dallas, Texas.

MICHAEL E. TREACY is Assistant Professor of Management Science at MIT's Sloan School of Management. He focuses his teaching and research on decision support systems, the impact of information technology on corporate strategy, and the design of support systems for senior executives. He has a special interest in measuring and evaluating the impacts of information systems on performance and profitability. Dr. Treacy received his Ph.D. from MIT.

Index